Fodor's

BIG ISLAND OF HAWAI'I

2nd Edition

Fodor's Travel Publications   New York, Toronto, London, Sydney, Auckland
www.fodors.com

Be a Fodor's Correspondent

Your opinion matters. It matters to us. It matters to your fellow Fodor's travelers, too. And we'd like to hear it. In fact, we need to hear it.

When you share your experiences and opinions, you become an active member of the Fodor's community. That means we'll not only use your feedback to make our books better, but we'll publish your names and comments whenever possible. Throughout our guides, look for "Word of Mouth," excerpts of your unvarnished feedback.

Here's how you can help improve Fodor's for all of us.

Tell us when we're right. We rely on local writers to give you an insider's perspective. But our writers and staff editors—who are the best in the business—depend on you. Your positive feedback is a vote to renew our recommendations for the next edition.

Tell us when we're wrong. We're proud that we update most of our guides every year. But we're not perfect. Things change. Hotels cut services. Museums change hours. Charming cafés lose charm. If our writer didn't quite capture the essence of a place, tell us how you'd do it differently. If any of our descriptions are inaccurate or inadequate, we'll incorporate your changes in the next edition and will correct factual errors at fodors.com immediately.

Tell us what to include. You probably have had fantastic travel experiences that aren't yet in Fodor's. Why not share them with a community of like-minded travelers? Maybe you chanced upon a beach or bistro or B&B that you don't want to keep to yourself. Tell us why we should include it. And share your discoveries and experiences with everyone directly at fodors.com. Your input may lead us to add a new listing or highlight a place we cover with a "Highly Recommended" star or with our highest rating, "Fodor's Choice."

Give us your opinion instantly at our feedback center at www.fodors.com/feedback. You may also e-mail editors@fodors.com with the subject line "Big Island of Hawai'i Editor." Or send your nominations, comments, and complaints by mail to Big Island of Hawai'i Editor, Fodor's, 1745 Broadway, New York, NY 10019.

You and travelers like you are the heart of the Fodor's community. Make our community richer by sharing your experiences. Be a Fodor's correspondent.

Aloha!

Tim Jarrell

Tim Jarrell, Publisher

FODOR'S BIG ISLAND OF HAWAI'I
Editors: Joanna G. Cantor, lead project editor; Carissa Bluestone

Editorial Production: Evangelos Vasilakis
Editorial Contributors: Cathy Sharpe, Amy Westervelt
Maps & Illustrations: Henry Colomb and Monk Stroud, Moon Street Cartography; David Lindroth, Inc.; William Wu; Bob Blake and Rebecca Baer, *map editors*
Design: Fabrizio LaRocca, *creative director*; Guido Caroti, Siobhan O'Hare, *art directors*; Tina Malaney, Chie Ushio, Ann McBride, *designers*; Melanie Marin, *senior picture editor*; Moon Sun Kim, *cover designer*
Cover Photo (Lava from Kilauea volcano enters the Pacific): Roger Ressmeyer/Corbis
Production/Manufacturing: Steve Slawsky

2nd Edition

ISBN 978-1-4000-0724-0

ISSN 1934–5542

SPECIAL SALES
This book is available at special discounts for bulk purchases for sales promotions or premiums. Special editions, including personalized covers, excerpts of existing books, and corporate imprints, can be created in large quantities for special needs. For more information, write to Special Markets/Premium Sales, 1745 Broadway, MD 6-2, New York, New York 10019, or e-mail specialmarkets@randomhouse.com.

AN IMPORTANT TIP & AN INVITATION
Although all prices, opening times, and other details in this book are based on information supplied to us at press time, changes occur all the time in the travel world, and Fodor's cannot accept responsibility for facts that become outdated or for inadvertent errors or omissions. So **always confirm information when it matters,** especially if you're making a detour to visit a specific place. Your experiences—positive and negative—matter to us. If we have missed or misstated something, **please write to us.** We follow up on all suggestions. Contact the Big Island of Hawai'i editor at editors@fodors.com or c/o Fodor's at 1745 Broadway, New York, NY 10019.

PRINTED IN SINGAPORE
10 9 8 7 6 5 4 3 2 1

BIG ISLAND OF HAWAI'I

1 EXPERIENCE THE BIG ISLAND . . 9
Welcome to the Big Island 10
Big Island Planner 12
Top Big Island Experiences 14
When To Go 16
Great 1-Day Itineraries 18
Weddings & Honeymoons 20
Kids & Families 22
Cruising the Hawaiian Islands 24
A Snapshot of Hawai'i 26

**2 EXPLORING THE BIG
ISLAND 31**
The Kohala District 34
Waimea   40
Kailua-Kona 43
South Kona & Kealakekua Bay . . . 48
Ka'ū & Ka Lae (South Point) 53
Volcano 64
Puna 68
Hilo 74
Hāmākua Coast 80
Mauna Kea 87

3 BEACHES 91
Kohala Coast 92
Kailua-Kona 99
South Kona & Ka'ū 102
Hilo Side 105

**4 WATER ACTIVITIES &
TOURS 109**
Boogie Boarding & Bodysurfing . 112
Deep-Sea Fishing 113
Kayaking 115
Parasailing 119
Sailing 120
Scuba Diving 120

BIG ISLAND OF HAWAI'I IN FOCUS

HAWAI'I VOLCANOES NATIONAL
    PARK 58
BIRTH OF THE ISLANDS 69
SNORKELING IN HAWAI'I 125
HAWAI'I'S PLANTS 101 147
ALL ABOUT LEIS 161
MORE THAN A FOLK DANCE 182
LŪ'AU: A TASTE OF HAWAI'I 199

Snorkeling 123
Snuba 129
Submarine Tours 129
Surfing 129
Whale-Watching 130
Windsurfing 132

**5 GOLF, HIKING & OUTDOOR
ACTIVITIES 133**
Aerial Tours 134
ATV Tours 136
Biking 137
Golf 140
Hiking 145
Horseback Riding 151
Skiing 152
Tennis 154

6 SHOPS & SPAS 155
Shops 156
Spas 169

**7 ENTERTAINMENT &
NIGHTLIFE 177**
Entertainment 178
Nightlife 187

CONTENTS

8 WHERE TO EAT 189
Where to Eat Planner 190
Best Bets for Big Island Dining . . 191
Kohala Coast 193
Waimea 198
Kailua-Kona 205
South Kona 213
Volcano 215
Hilo & Puna 217

9 WHERE TO STAY 221
Where to Stay Planner 222
Best Bets for Big Island Lodging . . 223
Kohala Coast 225
Waimea 236
Kailua-Kona 238
South Kona & Ka'u 246
Volcano 248
Puna 251
Hilo 253
Hāmākua Coast 256

HAWAIIAN VOCABULARY . . 259
BIG ISLAND ESSENTIALS . . . 262
Getting Started 263
Booking Your Trip 266
Transportation 278
On The Ground 284
INDEX 288
ABOUT OUR WRITERS 296

CLOSEUPS

Graffiti 39
Green Hawai'i 46
Kona Coffee 54
If Trees Could Talk 77
Pele & the Night Marchers 85
Protecting the Humpback Whale . . 132

Ironman & Friends 138
In Search of Birdies, Eagles &
Whales 142
Hawaiian Cowboys? 152
Hawaiian Healing 171
Roasted Pigs, Poi & Hula: the Lū'au
Explained 180
Green Hawai'i: Farm Tours 206
The Plate Lunch Tradition 219

MAPS & CHARTS

The Big Island of Hawai'i 36
The Kohala District 38
Kailua-Kona 44
South Kona & Ka'u 51
Hawai'i Volcanoes National Park . . 60
Puna 72
Hilo Vicinity 76
Hāmākua Coast & Mauna Kea 84
Big Island Beaches 94
Kohala Coast Beaches 96
Kailua-Kona Beaches 100
South Kona and Ka'u Beaches . . 103
Hilo Side Beaches 107
The Big Island's Top Three Water
Activities 116
Where to Eat on the Kohala Coast
and Waimea 204
Where to Eat on the Kona
Coast 207
Where to Eat on Hilo Side &
Volcano 216
Where to Stay on the Kohala Coast
& Waimea 228
Where to Stay on the Kona
Coast 240
Where to Stay on Hilo Side &
Volcano 249

ABOUT THIS BOOK

Our Ratings

Sometimes you find terrific travel experiences and sometimes they just find you. But usually the burden is on you to select the right combination of experiences. That's where our ratings come in.

As travelers we've all discovered a place so wonderful that its worthiness is obvious. And sometimes that place is so experiential that superlatives don't do it justice: you just have to be there to know. These sights, properties, and experiences get our highest rating, **Fodor's Choice**, indicated by orange stars throughout this book.

Black stars highlight sights and properties we deem **Highly Recommended**, places that our writers, editors, and readers praise again and again for consistency and excellence.

By default, there's another category: any place we include in this book is by definition worth your time, unless we say otherwise. And we will.

Disagree with any of our choices? Care to nominate a place or suggest that we rate one more highly? Visit our feedback center at ⊕*www. fodors.com/feedback*.

Budget Well

Hotel and restaurant price categories from ¢ to $$$$ are defined in the Where to Eat and Where to Stay chapters. Real prices are listed at the end of each restaurant and hotel review. For attractions, we always give standard adult admission fees; reductions are usually available for children, students, and senior citizens. Want to pay with plastic? **AE, D, DC, MC, V** following restaurant and hotel listings indicate if American Express, Discover, Diners Club, MasterCard, and Visa are accepted.

Restaurants

Unless we state otherwise, restaurants are open for lunch and dinner daily. We mention dress only when there's a specific requirement and reservations only when they're essential or not accepted—it's always best to book ahead.

Hotels

Hotels have private bath, phone, and TV, unless we state otherwise. We always list facilities but not whether you'll be charged an extra fee to use them, so when pricing accommodations, find out what's included.

Many Listings

★	Fodor's Choice
★	Highly recommended
⊠	Physical address
↔	Directions
⌂	Mailing address
☎	Telephone
🖷	Fax
⊕	On the Web
✐	E-mail
☞	Admission fee
⊙	Open/closed times
Ⓜ	Metro stations
⊟	Credit cards

Hotels & Restaurants

🏨	Hotel
↵	Number of rooms
⌾	Facilities
⅋◎⅋	Meal plans
✕	Restaurant
⌾	Reservations
⌇	Smoking
𝄞	BYOB
✕🏨	Hotel with restaurant that warrants a visit

Outdoors

⚐	Golf
⚠	Camping

Other

ℭ	Family-friendly
⇨	See also
⊠	Branch address
☞	Take note

Experience the
Big Island

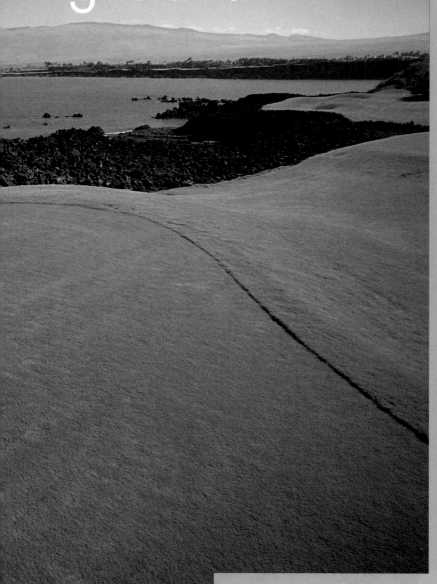

1

WELCOME TO THE BIG ISLAND

GETTING ORIENTED

You could fit all of the other Hawaiian Islands onto the Big Island and still have a little room left over—hence the clever name. Locals refer to the island by side: Kona side to the west and Hilo side to the east. Most of the resorts, condos, and restaurants are crammed into 30 mi of the sunny Kona side, while the rainy, tropical Hilo side is much more local and residential. Beautiful views make for pleasant drives, and the island's climate and vegetation change rapidly from one region to the next. Turn a corner from west to east on the north side of the island and you move quickly from hot, dry beaches to cool, lush valleys; the 40-mi drive to Waimea from Kailua-Kona affords awesome views of the coast below and the rolling pasture lands of the upcountry; and the drive east along the Hāmākua Coast from Waimea to Hilo (45 mi) is the stuff Hawaiian dreams are made of, with rainbows jumping over majestic cliffs and waterfalls, and green valleys hiding pristine swimming holes.

■ TIP→ Directions on the island are often given as mauka (toward the mountains) and makai (toward the ocean).

The sparkling turquoise **Kohala Coast** is where all those long Hawaiian white-sand beaches are found, and the expensive resorts that go with them.

Kailua-Kona is a seaside town bustling with tourists.

In **South Kona**, younger residents and transplants have turned defunct coffee farms into lively art communities overlooking beautiful Kealakekua Bay.

Ranches sprawl across the cool, upland meadows surrounding **Waimea** (Kamuela). This is *paniolo* (cowboy) country.

Waterfalls, dramatic cliffs, ancient hidden valleys, the greenest green you'll ever see, rain forests, and flowers you didn't know existed await on the **Hāmākua Coast.**

The rainy side of the island takes its name from the large fishing town of **Hilo,** nicknamed the City of Rainbows.

Puna, the part of the island most recently covered by lava, has brand-new, jet-black beaches punctuated with volcanically-heated hot springs.

Hawai'i Volcanoes National Park is growing, as active Kīlauea Volcano sends lava spilling into the ocean, creating new land. The nearest village is **Volcano.**

HĀMĀKUA COAST

Waipi'o Valley — 240 — Honoka'a
19 (Māmalahoa Hwy.)
Waimea (Kamuela)
Hawai'i Belt Rd.
Kamuela Airport
HĀMĀKUA
NORTH HILO
Mauna Kea 13,796 ft
19
Saddle Rd.
200
Hilo Bay
HILO
Hilo
Saddle Rd.
200
SOUTH HILO
11 **Hilo International Airport (General Lyman Field)**
Stainback Hwy.
Kūlani Honor Camp
Ola'a Rain Forest
130
Pāhoa
132
Mauna Loa 13,679 ft
Hawai'i Belt Rd.
Volcano Village
Kīlauea Crater
PUNA
Kīlauea 4,069 ft
130
11
Hawai'i Volcanoes National Park
KA'U
Hawai'i Belt Rd.
Punalu'u
Honu'apo Bay
Waikapuna Bay
Pu'u Nāhāhā Point
South Point (Ka Lae)

BIG ISLAND PLANNER

When You Arrive

The Big Island's two airports are directly across the island from each other. Kona International Airport on the west side is about a 10-minute drive from Kailua-Kona and 30 to 45 minutes from the Kohala Coast. On the east side, Hilo International Airport, 2 mi from downtown Hilo, is about 40 minutes from Volcanoes National Park. A 20-minute flight on Island Air or a 2½-hour drive connects Hilo and Kailua-Kona.

Renting a Car

You will need a car on the Big Island. Get a four-wheel-drive vehicle if you're at all interested in exploring. Some of the island's best sights (and most beautiful beaches) are at the end of rough or unpaved roads. ■TIP➜ **Talk to the agency in advance if you want to pick up a car at one airport and drop it off at the other. Though they allow this, most charge an additional fee of up to $50. If you arrange it ahead of time, they can often be talked into waiving the fee.**

Most agencies make you sign an agreement that you won't drive on the Saddle Road, the path to Mauna Kea and its observatories. Though smoothly paved, the Saddle Road is remote, winding, unlit, and bereft of gas stations. Harper's, a local rental company, is the sole exception.

Timing Is Everything

You can see humpback whales clearly off the western coast of the island from about January until May. The Ironman Triathlon takes place every October in Kailua-Kona. Shortly after the Ironman, the first 10 days of November are devoted to the Kona Coffee Cultural Festival—each day brings numerous caffeinated events including a cooking competition, a picking competition, a barista competition, and of course the cupping competition, which is all about the taste and quality of each coffee. Coffee connoisseurs from all over the world flock to Kona for the festival, and the whole west side of the island goes crazy for coffee.

Dining & Lodging on the Big Island

Hawai'i is a melting pot of cultures, and nowhere is this more apparent than in its cuisine. From luaus and "plate lunch" to sushi and steak, there's no shortage of interesting flavors and presentations. The same "buy local" trend that is spreading through the rest of the country is really taking hold on the Big Island. This is a giant shift from years past, in which everything but the pineapple was imported, and it's a happy trend for visitors, who get to taste juicy, flavorful Waimea tomatoes and creamy handmade Hāmākua goat cheese.

Whether you're looking for a quick snack or a multicourse meal, turn to chapter 8 to find the best eating experiences the island has to offer. Jump in, and enjoy!

Choosing vacation lodging is a tough decision, but fret not—our expert writers and editors have done most of the legwork.

Looking for a tropical forest retreat, a big resort, or a private vacation rental? Chapter 9 will give you all details you need to book a place that suits your style. Quick tips: Reserve your room far in advance. Be sure to ask about discounts and special packages (hotel Web sites often have Internet-only deals).

Island Hopping

There is enough on the Big Island to keep visitors active and entertained for weeks. However, if you're spending more than 10 days here, you might be interested in checking out one of the other islands and comparing notes. Maui is the Big Island's closest neighbor—on a sunny day you can see it clearly from the Kohala Coast—and the flight there is barely half an hour. For nightlife-deprived visitors, a weekend trip to check out the lively bars and restaurants on Maui might be the perfect solution. If you're visiting in October, consider hopping to Maui for its famous Halloween party. Go, Aloha, and Hawaiian all offer island-hopping flights, usually at very low prices.

Remember to book your island-hopping flights as soon as you decide to hop—the flights are small and can fill up fast, particularly during Halloween when many Big Islanders make their way to Maui, and during Christmas and Thanksgiving when locals hop to the neighbor islands to visit family.

If you're planning a longer trip and considering including a few islands, see Big Island Essentials for more information.

Island Driving Times

Due to the Big Island's size, it can take quite a bit of time to get from one region of the island to another. Added to that, the island's increasing traffic problems are making driving times even longer, particularly between Kona and the Kohala Coast, and Kona to Kealakekua Bay and Kau.

The state is working on widening Highway 19, which circles the island, and the hope is that the wider highway will cut down on traffic. In the meantime, the following are average driving times between some of the Big Island's most popular sights.

Kailua-Kona to Kealakekua Bay	15 minutes
Kailua-Kona to Kohala Coast	30 minutes
Kailua-Kona to Waimea	40 minutes
Kailua-Kona to Hāmākua Coast	1 hour
Kailua-Kona to Volcano	2 hours
Kailua-Kona to Hilo	2.5 hours
Kohala Coast to Waimea	20 minutes
Kohala Coast to Hāmākua Coast	40 minutes
Hilo to Volcano	30 minutes

Will I See Flowing Lava?

The best time to see lava is at night. However, you may or may not see flowing lava. Anyone who tries to tell you they can guarantee it or predict it is lying or trying to sell you something. Your best bet is to call the visitor center at the national park before you head out; even at that you could be pleasantly surprised or utterly disappointed. Keep in mind that the volcano is a pretty amazing sight even if it's not spewing fire.

The hike out to the closest viewing station to the flowing lava requires roughly three to four hours each way—the best way to handle it is to head out in the late afternoon, arrive at the viewing station by nightfall, and then start the trek back when you've had your fill of Pele's fireworks. ■TIP→ **Bring a flashlight and be prepared for some rough going over the lava fields at night.**

There are viewing stations along the way as well, so you don't necessarily have to make an eight-hour roundtrip journey. In fact, depending on how the lava is flowing, a viewing station farther from the lava could actually afford better views. *For more information about visiting Volcanoes National Park, see Chapter 2.*

TOP BIG ISLAND EXPERIENCES

The Lava Show
(A)Watch as fiery red lava pours, steaming, into the ocean; stare in awe at nighttime lava fireworks; and hike across the floor of a crater at Volcanoes National Park.

Green Sand Beach
(B)It's a hike, but this is the only place in the world to see green sand. And it happens to be surrounded by turquoise waters and dramatic cliffs.

Exploring Waipi'o Valley
(C)Whichever way you choose to get there—on horseback, in a 4WD, or on foot—you'll discover that the "Valley of the Kings" is full of sky-high waterfalls, lush green cliffs, and a mystical quality that can't quite be described or rivaled.

A Window on the Universe
(D)Teams of astronomers from all over the world come to Mauna Kea for the clearest skies and best conditions anywhere. Head up the mountain in the late afternoon for the prettiest sunset on this island and the best stargazing on this planet.

Play at a Perfect Beach
(E)Whether you follow the paved roads to Hāpuna, Kauna'oa (also known as Mauna Kea), or Kua Bay, or brave the rocky routes to Makalawena, you'll find that the Big Island is full of postcard-perfect beaches.

A Swim Through Coral Gardens
Diving or snorkeling in the crystal clear waters off the coast is like being let loose in your very own ocean-sized aquarium. Bright yellow, purple, and rose-colored

coral creates surreal kingdoms ruled by octopi, turtles, rays, dolphins, and fish in every color of the rainbow.

Stunning Waterfalls

(F) Watch rainbows forming in the mist then take a refreshing dip in the cold, deep pools fed by the powerful waterfalls spilling over the dramatic cliffs of the Hāmākua Coast.

Snooze with a Sea Turtle

(G) Hang out at Punaluʻu Beach, where sea turtles surf the waves and nap on the black sands.

A Healing Lomi Lomi Massage

(H) Beginning with a chant, the lomi lomi technique uses a combination of arms, elbows, hands, and breath to impart the overall sense of well-being associated with this ancient healing tradition.

A Kona Coffee Farm Tour

(I) Spend an hour discovering why it is that Kona coffee commands those high prices. Watch as "cherries" become beans, enjoy the smoky coffee smell of the roasting process, then indulge in the freshest cup of coffee you'll ever have. Did we mention that it's all free?

Whale the Day Away

(J) From December to May, you can sit on any beach on the west side of the island and watch the humpback whale migration. The sight of their backs, glistening as they move through the water, or the occasional perfect fluke cutting through the surface, is a matchless experience.

WHEN TO GO

Long days of sunshine and fairly mild year-round temperatures make Hawai'i an all-season destination. Most resort areas are at sea level, with average afternoon temperatures of 75°F–80°F during the coldest months of December and January; during the hottest months of August and September the temperature often reaches 90°F. Higher "Upcountry" elevations typically have cooler and often misty conditions. Only at mountain summits does it reach freezing.

Moist trade winds drop their precipitation on the north and east sides of the Islands, creating tropical climates, while the south and west sides remain hot and dry with desert-like conditions. Rainfall can be high in winter, particularly on those north and east shores.

Most travelers head to the Islands in winter, specifically from mid-December through mid-April. This high season means that fewer travel bargains are available; room rates average 10%–15% higher during this season than the rest of the year.

Climate

The following are average maximum and minimum temperatures for Honolulu; the temperatures throughout the Hawaiian Islands are similar.

Forecasts **Weather Channel Connection** (⊕ *www.weather.com*).

ONLY IN HAWAI'I HOLIDAYS

If you happen to be in the Islands on March 26 or June 11, you'll notice light traffic and busy beaches—these are state holidays not celebrated anywhere else. March 26 recognizes the birthday of Prince Jonah Kūhio Kalaniana'ole, a member of the royal line who served as a delegate to Congress and spearheaded the effort to set aside homelands for Hawaiian people. June 11 honors the first island-wide monarch, Kamehameha I; locals drape his statues with lei and stage elaborate parades. May 1 isn't an official holiday, but it's the day when schools and civic groups celebrate the quintessential Island gift, the flower lei, with lei-making contests and pageants. Statehood Day is celebrated on the third Friday in August (Admission Day was August 21, 1959). Most Japanese and Chinese holidays are widely observed. On Chinese New Year, homes and businesses sprout bright-red good-luck mottoes, lions dance in the streets, and everybody eats *gau* (steamed pudding) and *jai* (vegetarian stew). Good Friday is a state holiday in spring, a favorite for family picnics.

DID YOU KNOW

It's only a myth that the Big
Island lacks beaches. There
are plenty of perfect white
sandy beaches on the Big
Island; there's just also more
island, so getting to the
beaches can be slightly less
convenient.

GREAT 1-DAY ITINERARIES

Green Hawaii

Take full advantage of Hawai'i's living classroom. Visit one of the island's botanical gardens in the morning, then head to the Natural Energy Lab for a peek at its desalination plants, sustainable aqua farms, and various natural energy projects. Finish your day with a farm tour in the afternoon, followed by an evening spent enjoying the delicious products of the Big Island at one of Waimea's top restaurants, such as the island favorite Merriman's Café or its nearby neighbor Chef Daniel's Seafood Café.

Black and Green Sand

Check out some of the unusual beaches you'll only find on the Big Island. Start with a hike into Green Sand beach and plan to spend some time sitting on the beach, dipping into the bay's turquoise waters, and marveling at the surreal beauty of this spot. When you've had your fill, hop back in the car and head south about half an hour to Punalu'u, the island's best-known black-sand beach and favorite resting place of the Hawaiian sea turtle. Although the surf is often too rough to go swimming with the turtles, there are typically at least two or three napping on the beach at any given time of the day.

Sun & Stars

Spend the day lounging on a Kohala Coast beach (Hāpuna, Kauna'oa—also known as Mauna Kea—or Kua Bay), but throw jackets and boots in the car because you'll be catching the sunset from Mauna Kea's summit. Bundle up and stick around after darkness falls for some of the world's best stargazing. Book a tour or head straight for the visitor center, join their free tour of the summit at sunset, and return to the center to use their telescopes.

Hike Volcanoes

Devote a full day (at least) to Volcanoes National Park. Head out on the Kīlauea Iki trail—a 4-mi loop at the summit—by late morning. Grab a sandwich at the Volcano House when you've finished and take in their fantastic views of the craters. After lunch, head down Chain of Craters Road to the coast and the active lava flows. Bring water, snacks, and a flashlight if you intend to hike out to the end of the road where the lava flows into the ocean. Start your hike during the day (by 4 PM or earlier) to ensure that you're as close as you can safely be when night falls and to prepare yourself for a spectacular nighttime lava show.

Majestic Waterfalls & Kings' Valleys

Take a day to enjoy the splendors of the Hāmākua Coast—any gorge you see on the road is an indication of a waterfall waiting to be explored. For a sure bet, head to beautiful Waipi'o Valley. Book a horseback, hiking, or 4WD tour or walk on in yourself (just keep in mind that it's an arduous hike back up—25% grade for a little over a mile). Once in the valley, take your first right to get to the black sand beach. Take a moment to sit here—the ancient Hawaiians believed this was where souls crossed over to the afterlife. Whether you believe it or not, there's something unmistakably special about this place. Waterfalls abound in the valley, depending on the amount of recent rainfall. Your best bet is to follow the river from the beach to the back of the valley, where a waterfall and its lovely pool await.

Underwater Day

Explore the colorful reefs populated with tropical fish off the Big Island's coast for one day, and we defy you to stop thinking about the world beneath the waves when you're back on land. Our favorite spots include Two Step (near the Place of Refuge), Kealakekua Bay, and the Kapoho Tide Pools. Early morning is the best time to see the Hawaiian spinner dolphins that frolic off this coast, but you're likely to see turtles any time of day, along with yellow and white angelfish, spotted moray eels, trumpet fish, and a myriad of other brightly colored varieties.

Volcano Hot Springs & Boiling Pots

Most tourists skip Puna. Venture into this remote area for a morning, and you'll be rewarded with lava tube hikes (Kīlauea Caverns of Fire), volcanically heated pools (Ahalanui Beach Park), and tide pools brimming with colorful coral, fish, and the occasional turtle (Kapoho). Head to Hilo in the afternoon to catch a glimpse of the Boiling Pots waterfalls, Banyan Drive, and Queen Liliʻuokalani Gardens, before dining at one of Hilo's great restaurants.

Pololū & Paniolo Country

North Kohala is a world away from the resorts of the coast. Visit the quaint artists' community of Hāwī, then head to Pololū Valley for amazing views. A steepish ½-mi hike leads to a fantastic black-sand beach surrounded by beautiful sheer green cliffs. Back on the road, head up Highway 250 to Waimea and the pastures of paniolo country. Indulge in a memorable meal at one of the fantastic restaurants (we recommend Merriman's, Daniel Thiebaut, or Edelweiss).

Go Off-Road

Book an ATV tour or take your 4WD for a spin to check out some of the Big Island's isolated beaches. There are green beaches (in addition to "the" Green Sand

RAINY-DAY DRIVING TIPS

■ **From Kailua-Kona to Volcano:** Take the southern route, following Highway 11 through South Kona and Kaʻū around South Point to Volcano (125 mi, just under three hours).

■ **Betwen Kailua-Kona and Hilo:** Starting in Kailua-Kona, take Highway 190 east to Highway 19. Follow 19 through Waimea to Hilo (96 mi, two hours or less).

■ **From Kohala to Waimea:** Take Highway 11 to Waikoloa Road (9 mi south of Hāpuna Beach) and follow it 10 mi to Highway 190. Turn left on 190 and follow it another 11 mi to Waimea (30 mi, 40 minutes).

Beach) waiting in the Kaʻū region and ruggedly beautiful white beaches with perfect turquoise water along the Kohala Coast; deal with the tough, 4WD-only roads into these beaches and you're likely to be rewarded with a pristine tropical beach all to yourself.

WEDDINGS & HONEYMOONS

There's no question that Hawai'i is one of the country's foremost honeymoon destinations. Romance is in the air here, and the white, sandy beaches and turquoise water and swaying palm trees and balmy tropical breezes and perpetual summer sunshine put people in the mood for love. It's easy to understand why Hawai'i is fast becoming a popular wedding destination as well, especially as the cost of airfare has gone down, and new resorts and hotels entice visitors. A destination wedding is no longer exclusive to celebrities and the super rich. You can plan a traditional ceremony in a place of worship followed by a reception at an elegant resort, or you can go barefoot on the beach and celebrate at a lū'au. There are almost as many wedding planners in the islands as real-estate agents, which makes it oh-so-easy to wed in paradise, and then, once the knot is tied, stay and honeymoon as well.

The Big Day

Choosing the Perfect Place. When choosing a location, remember that you really have two choices to make: the ceremony location and where to have the reception, if you're having one. For the former, there are beaches, bluffs overlooking beaches, gardens, private residences, resort lawns, and, of course, places of worship. As for the reception, there are these same choices, as well as restaurants and even lū'au. If you decide to go outdoors, remember the seasons—yes, Hawai'i has seasons. If you're planning a winter wedding outdoors, be sure you have a backup plan (such as a tent), in case it rains. Also, if you're planning an outdoor wedding at sunset—which is very popular—be sure you match the time of your ceremony to the time the sun sets at that time of year.

If you choose indoors, ask for pictures of the environs when you're planning. You don't want to plan a pink wedding, say, and wind up in a room that's predominantly red. Or maybe you do. The point is, it should be your choice.

Finding a Wedding Planner. If you're planning to invite more than a minister and your loved one to your wedding ceremony, seriously consider an on-island wedding planner who can help select a location, help design the floral scheme and recommend a florist as well as a photographer, help plan the menu and choose a restaurant, caterer, or resort, and suggest any special Hawaiian traditions to incorporate into your ceremony. And more: Will you need tents? Of course, a cake. Music. Maybe transportation. Lodging. Many planners have relationships with vendors, providing packages—which mean savings.

If you're planning a resort wedding, most have on-site wedding coordinators; however, there are many independents around the island and even those who specialize in certain types of ceremonies—by locale, size, religious affiliation, and so on. A simple "Hawai'i weddings" Google search will reveal dozens. What's important is that you feel comfortable with your coordinator. Check references. Share your budget. Get a proposal in writing. Ask how long they've been in business, how much they charge, how often you'll meet with them, and how they select vendors. Request a detailed list of the exact services they'll provide. If your idea of your wedding doesn't match their services, try someone else. If you can afford it, you might want to consider meeting the planner in person.

Getting Your License. The good news about marrying in Hawai'i is that no waiting period, no residency or citizenship requirements, and no blood tests or shots are required. However, both the bride and groom must appear together in person before a marriage license agent to apply for a marriage license. You'll need proof of age—the legal age to marry is 18. (If you're 19 or older, a valid driver's license will suffice; if you're 18, a certified birth certificate is required.) Upon approval, a marriage license is immediately issued and costs $60, cash only. After the ceremony, your officiant will mail the marriage license to the state. Approximately 120 days later, you will receive a copy in the mail. (For $10 extra, you can expedite this process. Ask your marriage-license agent when you apply for your license.) For more detailed information, visit www.hawaii.gov or call 808/241–3498.

Also—this is important—the person performing your wedding must be licensed by the Hawai'i Department of Health, even if he or she is a licensed minister. Be sure to ask.

Wedding Attire. In Hawai'i, basically anything goes, from long, formal dresses with trains to white bikinis. Floral sundresses are fine, too. For the men, tuxedos are not the norm; a pair of solid-colored slacks with a nice aloha shirt is. In fact, tradition in Hawai'i for the groom is a plain white aloha shirt (they do exist) with slacks or long shorts and a colored sash around the waist. If you're planning a wedding on the beach, barefoot is the way to go.

If you decide to marry in a formal dress and tuxedo, you're better off making your selections on the mainland and hand-carrying them aboard the plane. Yes, it can be a pain, but ask your wedding-gown retailer to provide a special carrying bag. And when it comes to fittings, again, that's something you'll want to take care of before you arrive in Hawai'i.

Local customs. When it comes to traditional Hawaiian wedding customs, the most obvious is the lei exchange in which the bride and groom take turns placing a lei around the neck of the other—with a kiss. Bridal lei are usually floral, whereas the groom's is typically made of maile, a green leafy garland that drapes around the neck and is open at the ends. Brides often also wear a haku lei—a circular floral headpiece. Other Hawaiian customs include the blowing of the conch shell, hula, chanting, and Hawaiian music.

The Honeymoon

Do you want champagne and strawberries delivered to your room each morning? A maze of a swimming pool in which to float? A five-star restaurant in which to dine? Then a resort is the way to go. If, however, you prefer the comforts of a home, try a bed-and-breakfast. A B&B is also good if you're on a tight budget or don't plan to spend much time in your room. On the other hand, maybe you want your own private home in which to romp naked—or just laze around recovering from the wedding planning. Maybe you want your own kitchen in which to whip up a gourmet meal for your loved one. In that case, a private vacation-rental home is the answer. Or maybe a condominium resort. That's another beautiful thing about Hawai'i: the lodging accommodations are almost as plentiful as the beaches, and there's one to match your tastes and your budget.

KIDS & FAMILIES

With dozens of adventures, discoveries, and fun-filled beach days, Hawai'i is a blast with *keiki* (kids). The entire family (parents included) will enjoy surf lessons, discovering a waterfall in the rain forest, and snorkeling with sea turtles. And there are plenty of organized activities for kids that will free parents' time for a few romantic beach strolls.

Choosing a Place to Stay

Resorts: All of the big resorts make kids' programs a priority, and it shows. A handful go above and beyond kid friendly, with exotic animals, monorails, and the sort of pool slides that make kids squeal with delight. When you are booking your room, ask about "kids eat free" deals and the number of kids' pools. Also, check out the size of the groups in the children's programs and find out whether the cost of the programs includes lunch, equipment, or other activities.

The Hilton is every kid's fantasy vacation come true, with dozens of pool slides, one lagoon for snorkeling and one filled with dolphins, and even a choice between riding a monorail or taking a boat to your room. Not to be outdone, the Four Seasons Hualālai Resort has a fantastic program that will keep your little ones happy and occupied all day, as does the Kona Village Resort, which also offers a kids' dinner and a teens' dinner seating to give parents the option of a solo date night.

Condos: Condos and vacation rentals are a fantastic value for families. You can cook your own food, which is cheaper than eating out and sometimes easier (especially if you have a finicky eater in your group), and you'll get twice the space of a hotel room for about a quarter of the price. If you decide to go the condo route, be sure to ask about the size of the complex's pool (some try to pawn a tiny soaking tub off as a pool) and whether barbecues are available.

Condos in Kailua-Kona (on or near Ali'i Drive) are the best value on the Big Island. We like Kona Pacific for its pool, barbecues, size of the units, and proximity to town, and Casa de Emdeko for its oceanfront pool and on-site convenience store. On the Kohala Coast, the Vista Waikoloa complex provides extra-large condos and is walking distance to a beautiful, sandy beach (A-Bay). Affordable food is available at restaurants in Kona, if you are looking for a family night out or, even better, for date night.

Ocean Activities

On the Beach: Most people like being in the water, but toddlers and school-age kids tend to be especially enamored with it. The swimming pool at your condo or hotel is always an option, but don't be afraid to hit the beach with a little one in tow. There are several beaches that are nearly as safe as a pool—completely protected bays with pleasant white sand beaches. As always, use your good judgment and heed all posted signs and lifeguard warnings.

Calm beaches to try include Kamakahonu Beach and Kahalu'u in Kailua-Kona; Spencer Beach Park, Kauna'oa (aka Mauna Kea Beach), and Hāpuna Beach in Kohala; and Onekahakaha Beach Park in Hilo.

On the Waves: Surf lessons are a great idea for the older kids. Beginner lessons are always on safe and easy waves and tend to last anywhere from two to four hours.

For school-age and older kids, book a four-hour surfing lesson with Ocean Eco Tours and either join them out on the break or say aloha to a little parents-only time.

The Underwater World: If your kids are ready to try snorkeling, Hawai'i is a great place to introduce them to the underwater world. Even without the mask and snorkel, they'll be able to see colorful fish darting this way and that, and they may also spot turtles and dolphins at many of the island beaches.

Kahalu'u Beach in Kailua-Kona is a great introductory snorkel spot. You can see fish darting just below the surface even before you get into the water, and Hawaiian sea turtles often waddle up on to the rocks or swim around close to the shore.

On the southern tip of the island, Punalu'u provides opportunities to see the sea turtles up close—though the water can be rough, the sea turtles nest here and there are nearly always one or two napping on the black-sand beach. At nighttime, head to the Sheraton Keauhou or Huggo's on the Rocks in Kailua-Kona to view manta rays; each spot shines a bright spotlight on the water to attract the rays. Anyone, but especially kids, could sit and watch them fly through the ocean in graceful circles for hours. No snorkel required!

Another great option is to book a snorkel cruise or opt to stay dry inside the Atlantis Submarine. Kids love crawling down into a real-life submarine and viewing the ocean world through its little portholes.

Land Activities

In addition to beach experiences, Hawai'i has rain forests, botanical gardens, numerous aquariums, and even petting zoos and hands-on kids' museums that will keep your kids entertained and out of the sun for a day.

On the Big Island, Volcanoes National Park is a must on a family vacation. Even grumpy teenagers will acknowledge the coolness of lava tubes, steaming earth, and a fiery nighttime lava show.

On the Hilo side, the Pana'ewa Rainforest Zoo is small, but free, and lots of fun for the little ones, with a small petting zoo. Just a few miles north, on the Hāmākua Coast, the Hawai'i Tropical Botanical Garden is beautiful and fun to meander through, checking out huge lily pads and the noisy local frogs.

School-age and older kids will get a kick out of the ATV tours at Kahua Ranch or the Parker Ranch in Waimea, and horseback rides through Waipi'o Valley with Na'alapa Stables.

After Dark

At nighttime, younger kids get a kick out of lū'aus, and many of the shows incorporate young audience members, adding to the fun. The older kids might find it all a bit lame, but there are a handful of new shows in the islands that are more modern, incorporating acrobatics, lively music, and fire dancers. On the Big Island, teens and adults alike are sure to enjoy the music, lighting, acrobatics, fire eating, and overall theatrical quality of "Kamaha'o—The Wondrous Myths of Hawai'i" at the Sheraton Keauhou.

Stargazing from Mauna Kea is another treat. The visitor center has telescopes set up for all visitors to use. If you'd rather leave the planning to someone else, book a tour with Hawai'i Forest and Trail.

CRUISING THE HAWAIIAN ISLANDS

Cruising has become extremely popular in Hawai'i. For first-time visitors, it's an excellent way to get a taste of all the islands; and if you fall in love with one or even two islands, you know how to plan your next trip. It's also a comparatively inexpensive way to see Hawai'i. The limited amount of time in each port can be an argument against cruising—there's enough to do on any island to keep you busy for a week, so some folks feel short-changed by cruise itineraries.

Cruising to Hawai'i

Until 2001 it was illegal for any cruise ships to stop in Hawai'i unless they originated from a foreign port, or were including a foreign port in their itinerary. The law has changed, but most cruises still include a stop in the Fanning Islands, Ensenada, Mexico, or Vancouver, British Columbia–Canada. Gambling is legal on the open seas, and your winnings are tax-free; most cruise ships offer designated smoking areas and now enforce the U.S. legal drinking age (21) on Hawai'i itineraries.

Carnival Cruises. They call them "fun ships" for a reason—Carnival is all about keeping you busy and showing you a good time, both on board and on shore. Great for families, Carnival always plans plenty of kid-friendly activities, and their children's program rates high with the little critics. Carnival offers itineraries starting in Ensenada, Vancouver, and Honolulu. Their ships stop on Maui (Kahului and Lahaina), the Big Island (Kailua-Kona and Hilo), O'ahu, and Kaua'i. ☎888/227–6482 ⊕www.carnival.com.

Celebrity Cruises. Celebrity's focus is on service, and it shows. From their waitstaff to their activity directors to their fantastic Hawaiian cultural experts, every aspect of your trip has been well thought out. They cater more to adults than children, so this may not be the best line for families. Celebrity's Hawai'i cruises depart from Los Angeles and stop in Maui (Lahaina), O'ahu, the Big Island (Hilo and Kailua-Kona), and Kaua'i. ☎800/647–2251 ⊕www.celebrity.com.

Holland America. The grande dame of cruise lines, Holland America has a reputation for service and elegance. Holland America's Hawai'i cruises leave and return to San Diego, California, and Seattle, Washington, with either a brief stop at Ensenada or British Columbia. In Hawai'i, the ship ties up at port in Maui (Lahaina), the Big Island (Kailua-Kona and Hilo), O'ahu, and for half a day on Kaua'i. Holland America also offers longer itineraries (30-plus days) that include Hawai'i, Tahiti, and the Marquesas. ☎877/724–5425 ⊕www.hollandamerica.com.

Princess Cruises. Princess strives to offer affordable luxury. Their prices start out a little higher, but you get more bells and whistles (more affordable balcony rooms, nice decor, more restaurants to choose from, personalized service). They're not fantastic for kids, but they do a great job of keeping teenagers occupied. Princess's Hawaiian cruise is 15 days, round-trip from Los Angeles, with a service call in Ensenada. The *Island Princess* stops in Maui (Lahaina), the Big Island (Hilo and Kailua-Kona), O'ahu, and Kaua'i. For the cruise-goer looking for the epic voyage, Princess Cruises offers a Sydney, Australia, to Los Angeles route which includes stops in Hawai'i and Tahiti. ☎800/774–6237 ⊕www.princess.com.

Royal Caribbean. Royal Caribbean's cruises stop in Maui (Lahaina), Kaua'i, O'ahu and the Big Island (both Hilo and Kailua-Kona). In keeping with its reputation for being all things to all people, Royal Caribbean offers a huge variety of activities and services on board and more excursions on land than any other cruise line. ☎800/521–8611 ⊕www.royalcaribbean.com.

Cruising within Hawai'i

If you'd like to cruise from island to island, Norwegian is the only major cruise-line option. For a different experience, Hawai'i Nautical offers cruises on smaller boats.

Norwegian Cruise Lines. Norwegian is the only major operator to offer interisland cruises in Hawai'i. Several of their ships cruise the islands. The main one is *Pride of America* (Vintage Americana theme, very new, big family focus with lots of connecting staterooms and suites), which offers 7-day or longer itineraries within the Islands, stopping on Maui, O'ahu, the Big Island, and overnighting in Kaua'i. ☎800/327–7030 ⊕www.ncl.com.

Hawai'i Nautical. Offering a completely different sort of experience, Hawai'i Nautical provides private multiple-day interisland cruises on their catamarans, yachts, and sailboats. Prices are higher, but service is completely personal, right down to the itinerary. ☎808/234–7245 ⊕www.hawaiinautical.com.

CRUISING TIPS

■ On all but the *Pride of America* (operated by Norwegian Cruise Lines), you must bring a passport, as you will be entering foreign ports of call.

■ Think about booking your own excursions directly (except on Maui). You'll often pay less for greater value. For example, if you want to take a surfing lesson on O'ahu, visit one of the beachside shacks to find excellent instructors who offer better deals to individuals than they do to the cruise lines. The downside, though, is that whereas cruise-booked tours guarantee the ship will wait for you should your tour run late, if you make your own plans and miss the "all aboard," you'll have to find your own way to the ship at the next port.

■ Tendering in Maui can be a tedious process—if you want to avoid a little bit of the headache (and hours waiting in the sun), be sure to book an excursion there through the ship and you'll have smooth sailing.

■ Most mainland cell phones will work without a hitch on board between the Islands and at all Hawaiian ports of call.

A SNAPSHOT OF HAWAI'I

The Islands

O'ahu. The state's capital, Honolulu, is on O'ahu; this is the center of Hawai'i's economy and by far the most populated island in the chain—900,000 residents adds up to 71% of the state's population. At 597 square mi O'ahu is the third largest island in the chain; the majority of residents live in or around Honolulu, so the rest of the island still fits neatly into the tropical, untouched vision of Hawai'i. Situated southeast of Kaua'i and northwest of Maui, O'ahu is a central location for island hopping. Surfing contests on the legendary North Shore, Pearl Harbor, and iconic Waikīkī Beach are all here.

Maui. The second largest island in the chain, Maui's 729 square mi are home to only 119,000 people but host approximately 2.5 million tourists every year. Maui is northwest of the Big Island, and close enough to be visible from its beaches on a clear day. With its restaurants and lively nightlife, Maui is the only island that competes with O'ahu in terms of entertainment; its charm lies in the fact that although entertainment is available, Maui's towns still feel like island villages compared to the heaving modern city of Honolulu.

Hawai'i (The Big Island). The Big Island has the second largest population of the islands (167,000) but feels sparsely settled due to its size. It's 4,038 square mi and growing—all of the other islands could fit onto the Big Island and there would still be room left over. The southernmost island in the chain (slightly southeast of Maui), the Big Island is home to Kīlauea, the most active volcano on the planet. It percolates within Volcanoes National Park, which draws 2.5 million visitors every year.

Kaua'i. The northernmost island in the chain (northwest of O'ahu), Kaua'i is, at approximately 540 square mi, the fourth largest of all the islands and the least populated of the larger islands, with just under 63,000 residents. Known as the Garden Isle, Kaua'i claims the title "wettest spot on Earth" with an annual average rainfall of 460 inches. Kaua'i is a favorite with honeymooners and others wanting to get away from it all—lush and peaceful, it's the perfect escape from the modern world.

Moloka'i. North of Lāna'i and Maui, and east of O'ahu, Moloka'i is Hawai'i's fifth largest island, encompassing 260 square mi. On a clear night, the lights of Honolulu are visible from Moloka'i's western shore. Moloka'i is sparsely populated, with just under 7,400 residents, the majority of whom are native Hawaiians. Most of Moloka'i's 85,000 annual visitors travel from Maui or O'ahu to spend the day exploring its beaches, cliffs, and former leper colony on Kalaupapa Peninsula.

Lāna'i. Lying just off Maui's western coast, Lāna'i looks nothing like its sister islands, with pine trees and deserts in place of palm trees and beaches. Still, the tiny 140-square-mi island is home to nearly 3,000 residents and draws an average of 90,000 visitors each year to two resorts (one in the mountains and one at the shore), both operated by Four Seasons.

Geology

The Hawaiian Islands comprise more than just the islands inhabited and visited by humans. A total of 19 islands and atolls constitutes the State of Hawai'i, with a total landmass of 6,423.4 square mi. The Islands are actually exposed peaks of a submersed mountain range

DID YOU KNOW

On Banyan Drive, also known
as the Hilo Walk of Fame,
there are over 50 banyan
trees that have been planted
by visiting celebrities like
Babe Ruth and Amelia Ear-
hart. Take a walk under the
lovely canopy formed by the
trees.

A SNAPSHOT OF HAWAI'I

called the Hawaiian-Emperor seamount chain. The range was formed as the Pacific plate moved very slowly (around 32 mi every million years) over a "hot spot" in the Earth's mantle. Because the plate moved northwestwardly, the Islands in the northwest portion of the archipelago (chain) are older, which is also why they're smaller—they have been eroding longer.

The Big Island is the youngest, and thus the largest, island in the chain. It is built from seven different volcanoes, including Mauna Loa, which is the largest shield volcano on the planet. Mauna Loa and Kīlauea are the only Hawaiian volcanoes still erupting with any sort of frequency. Mauna Loa last erupted in 1984. Kīlauea has been continuously erupting since 1983. Mauna Kea (Big Island), Hualālai (Big Island), and Haleakalā (Maui) are all in what's called the Post Shield stage of volcanic development—eruptions decrease steadily for up to 250,000 years before ceasing entirely. Kohala (Big Island), Lāna'i (Lāna'i), and Wai'anae (O'ahu) are considered extinct volcanoes, in the erosional stage of development; Ko'olau (O'ahu) and West Maui (Maui) volcanoes are extinct volcanoes in the rejuvenation stage—after lying dormant for hundreds of thousands of years, they began erupting again, but only once every several thousand years.

There is currently an active undersea volcano called Lo'ihi that has been erupting regularly. If it continues its current pattern, it should breach the ocean's surface in tens of thousands of years.

Flora & Fauna

Though much of the plant life associated with Hawai'i today (pineapple, hibiscus, orchid, plumeria) was brought by Tahitian, Samoan, or European visitors, Hawai'i is also home to several endemic species, like the koa tree and the yellow hibiscus. Long-dormant volcanic craters are perfect hiding places for rare plants (like the silversword, a rare cousin of the sunflower, which grows on Hawai'i's three tallest peaks: Haleakalā, Mauna Kea, and Mauna Loa, and nowhere else on Earth). Many of these endemic species are now threatened by the encroachment of introduced plants and animals. Hawai'i is also home to a handful of plants that have evolved into uniquely Hawaiian versions of their original selves. Mint, for example, develops its unique taste to keep would-be predators from eating its leaves. As there were no such predators in Hawai'i for hundreds of years, a mintless mint evolved; similar stories exist for the Islands' nettle-less nettles, thorn-less briars.

Hawai'i's climate is well suited to growing several types of flowers, most of which are introduced species. Plumeria creeps over all of the Islands; orchids run rampant on the Big Island; bright orange 'ilima light up the mountains of O'ahu. These flowers give the Hawaiian lei their color and fragrance.

As with the plant life, the majority of the animals in Hawai'i today were brought here by visitors. Axis deer from India roam the mountains of Lāna'i. The Islands are home to dozens of rat species, all stowaways on long boat rides over from Tahiti, England, and Samoa; the mongoose was brought to keep the rats out of the sugar plantations—a failed effort as the mongoose hunts by day, the rat by night. Many of Hawai'i's birds, like the nēnē (Hawai'i's state bird) and the pu'eo (Hawaiian owl) are endemic; unfortunately, about 80% are also endangered.

The ocean surrounding the Islands teems with animal life. Once scarce manta rays have made their way back to the Big Island; spinner dolphins and sea turtles can be found off the coast of all the Islands; and every year from December to May, the humpback whales migrate past Hawai'i in droves.

History

Long before both Christopher Columbus and the Vikings, Polynesian seafarers set out to explore the vast stretches of open ocean in double-hulled canoes. Now regarded as some of the world's greatest navigators, the ancestors of the Hawaiian people sailed across the Pacific Ocean using the stars, birds, and sea life as their guides. From Western Polynesia they traveled back and forth between Samoa, Fiji, Tahiti, the Marquesas, and the Society Isles, settling the outer reaches of the Pacific, Hawai'i, and Easter Island, as early as AD 300. The golden era of Polynesian voyaging peaked around AD 1200, after which the distant Hawaiian Islands were left to develop their own unique cultural practices in relative isolation.

When the British explorer Captain James Cook arrived in 1778, he found a deeply religious, agrarian society governed by numerous ali'i, or chiefs. Revered as a god upon his arrival, Cook was later killed in a skirmish over a stolen boat. With guns and ammunition purchased from Cook, the Big Island chief, Kamehameha, gained a significant advantage over the other Hawaiian ali'i. He united Hawai'i into

one kingdom in 1810, bringing an end to the frequent interisland battles that had previously dominated Hawaiian life. Tragically, the new kingdom was beset with troubles. Their religion was abandoned. European explorers brought foreign diseases with them; within a few short years the Hawaiian population was cut in half. It was further weakened by the onset of the sandalwood trade in the mid-1800s. All able-bodied men were sent into the forest to harvest the fragrant tree, so that Kamehameha's successor, Liholiho could pay off debts incurred to American merchants. Onto this stage came rowdy foreign whalers, ambitious entrepreneurs, and well-intentioned but perhaps misguided missionaries. New laws regarding land ownership and religious practices eroded the cultural underpinnings of precontact Hawai'i. Each successor to the Hawaiian throne sacrificed more control over the island kingdom. Finally in 1893, the last Hawaiian monarch, Queen Lili'uokalani, was overthrown by a group of American and European businessmen and government officials, aided by an armed militia. This led to the creation of the Republic of Hawai'i, which quickly became a territory of the United States through resolutions passed by Congress (rather than through treaties). Hawai'i remained a territory for 60 years; Pearl Harbor was attacked as part of the United States in 1941 during World War II. It wasn't until 1959, however, that Hawai'i was officially admitted as the 50th State.

Legends & Mythology

Ancient deities play a huge role in Hawaiian life today—not just in daily rituals, but in the Hawaiians' reverence for their land. Gods and goddesses tend to be associated with particular parts of the land,

A SNAPSHOT OF HAWAI'I

and most of them are connected with many places thanks to the body of stories built up around each.

The goddess Pele lives in Kīlauea Volcano and rules over the Big Island. She is a feisty goddess known for turning enemies into trees or destroying the homes of adversaries with fire. She also has a penchant for gin, which is why you'll see gin bottles circling some of the craters at Volcanoes National Park. It's not the litter it appears to be, but rather an offering to placate the Volcano goddess. The Valley Isle's namesake, the demigod Maui, is a well-known Polynesian trickster. When his mother Hina complained that there were too few hours in the day, Maui promised to slow the sun. Upon hearing this, the god Moemoe teased Maui for boasting, but undeterred, the demigod wove a strong cord and lassoed the sun. Angry, the sun scorched the fields until an agreement was reached: during summer, the sun would travel more slowly. In winter, it would return to its quick pace. For ridiculing Maui, Moemoe was turned into a large rock that still juts from the water near Kahakualoa.

One of the most important ways the ancient Hawaiians showed respect for their gods and goddesses was through the hula. Various forms of the hula were performed as prayers to the gods and as praise to the chiefs. Performances were taken very seriously, as a mistake was thought to invalidate the prayer, or even to offend the god or chief in question. Hula is still performed both as entertainment and as prayer.

Hawai'i Today

After a long period of suppression, Hawaiian culture and traditions have experienced a renaissance over the last few decades. There is a real effort to revive traditions and to respect history as the Islands go through major changes and welcome more and more newcomers every day. New developments often have a Hawaiian cultural expert on staff to ensure cultural sensitivity and to educate newcomers.

Nonetheless, development remains a huge issue for all Islanders—land prices are skyrocketing, putting many areas out of reach for the native population. Traffic is becoming a problem on roads that were not designed to accommodate all the new drivers, and the Islands' limited natural resources are being seriously tapped. The government, though sluggish to respond at first, is trying to make development in Hawai'i as sustainable as possible. Rules for new developments protect natural as well as cultural resources, and local governments have set ambitious conservation goals (Honolulu's mayor is actively pursuing mass transit and light rail options for the city's commuters). Despite all efforts to ease its effect on the land and its people, large-scale, rapid development is not anyone's ideal, and Islanders are understandably less than thrilled with the prospect of a million more tourists visiting every year or buying up property that residents themselves can't afford.

That said, the aloha spirit is alive and well. Though you may encounter the occasional "haole hater" (haole—pronounced "howlie"—is a somewhat pejorative term for caucasians), the majority of Islanders are warm, a welcoming people who are eager to share their culture with those who respect it.

Exploring the Big Island

WORD OF MOUTH

"The Big Island has LOTS of things to do! We were there for 10 days and I still didn't get to do all of the things I wanted to do! I liked the Big Island because it was not so commercialized as the other islands."

—ChristieP

By Amy
Westervelt

Nicknamed "The Big Island," Hawai'i the island is a micro-cosm of Hawai'i the state. From long white-sand beaches and crystal clear bays to rain forests, waterfalls, lū'aus, exotic flowers, and birds, all things quintessentially Hawaiian are well represented here.

But an assortment of happy surprises also distinguish the Big Island from the rest of Hawai'i—an active volcano (Kīlauea) oozing red lava and creating new earth every day, the clearest place in the world to view stars in the night sky (Mauna Kea), and some seriously good coffee (Kona, of course).

GEOLOGY

Home to 11 climate zones (missing only tundra), this is the land of fire (thanks to active Kīlauea Volcano) and ice (compliments of not-so-active Mauna Kea, topped with snow and expensive telescopes). At just under a million years old, Hawai'i is the youngest of the Hawaiian Islands. The east rift zone on Kīlauea has been spewing lava intermittently since January 3, 1983; an eruption occurred at Kīlauea's summit in 2008 for the first time since 1982. Mauna Loa's explosions caused some changes back in 1984, and she's due to blow again any minute. Though these two are the only of the island's five volcanoes considered active, the others haven't been pronounced officially dead just yet.

FLORA & FAUNA

Sugar was the main agricultural and economic staple of all the Islands, but especially the Big Island. The drive along the Hāmākua Coast from Hilo illustrates recent agricultural developments on the island. Sugarcane stalks have been replaced by orchards of macadamia-nut trees, eucalyptus, and specialty crops (from lettuce to strawberries). Macadamia nuts on the Big Island supply 90% of the state's yield, and coffee continues to be big business, dominating the mountains above Kealakekua Bay. Orchids keep farmers from Honok'a to Pāhoa afloat, and small organic farms produce meat, fruits, vegetables, and even goat cheese for high-end resort restaurants.

HISTORY

Though no longer home to the capital, the state's history is nonetheless rooted in that of its namesake island, Hawai'i. Kamehameha, the greatest king in Hawaiian history and the man credited with uniting the Islands, was born here, raised in Waipi'o Valley, and died peacefully in Kailua-Kona. The other man who most affected the history of Hawai'i, Captain James Cook, spent the bulk of his time here, docked in Kealakekua Bay (he landed first in Kaua'i, but had little contact with the natives there). Thus it was here that Western influence was first felt, and from here that it spread to the rest of the Islands.

DID YOU KNOW

Most of the over 2,200 plant species found in the Hawaiian Islands are not native to Hawai'i. The red and green Lobster Claw is originally from South America.

The Big Island is in a period of great change. In the last few years, Wal-Mart, Kmart, and Costco opened, development went wild, and real estate prices skyrocketed. These sorts of things make locals unhappy. Work is underway to counteract some of the poorly planned development of the island. New developments are required by law to consult with a Hawaiian cultural expert, and most of the island's hotels have a Hawaiian historian on staff to teach visitors about the ancient customs and keep developers from breaking with Hawaiian traditions any more than is absolutely necessary.

THE KOHALA DISTRICT

If you had only a weekend to spend on the Big Island, this is probably where you'd want to go. Kohala is a mix of the island's best beaches and swankiest hotels just minutes from ancient valleys and temples, waterfalls, and funky artist enclaves.

North of Kona International Airport, along Highway 19, brightly colored bougainvillea stand out in relief against miles of black lava fields stretching from the mountain to the sea. Most of the lava flows are from the last eruptions of Mt. Hualālai, in 1800 and 1801. The black lava fields created by those flows are interrupted only by green oases of irrigated golf courses surrounding the glamorous luxury resorts of the Kona-Kohala Coast. The resorts lay claim to some of the island's finest restaurants and its only destination spas. But the real attractions here are the island's best beaches. On a clear day you can see Maui from the Kohala Coast, and during the winter months, glistening humpback whales cleave the waters just offshore.

Rounding the northern tip of the island, the arid coast suddenly gives way to the lush green valley of Pololū in North Kohala, and hot sunny days at the beach become cool misty evenings in the Kohala mountains. In the sugar-plantations-turned-artsy enclaves of Hāwī and Kapa'au, new galleries are interspersed with charming reminders of old Hawai'i—wooden boardwalks, quaint local stores, delicious neighborhood restaurants, friendly locals, and a delightfully slow pace. With beaches, waterfalls, resorts, and villages within a few short miles of each other, Kohala is one-stop shopping for all things Hawaiian.

LOGISTICS   Two days is sufficient time for experiencing each unique side of Kohala—one day for the resort perks: the beach, the spa, the golf, the restaurants; one day for hiking and admiring the waterfalls and valleys of North Kohala, coupled with a wander around Hāwī and Kapa'au. Diving and snorkeling are great along this coast, so bring or rent equipment. If you're staying at one of the resorts, they will usually have any equipment you could possibly want. If you're feeling adventurous, get your hands on a four-wheel-drive vehicle and head to one of the unmarked beaches along the Kohala Coast—you may end up with a beach to yourself. The best way to explore the valleys of north Kohala is with a hiking tour. Look for a tour that includes lunch and a dip in one of the area's waterfall pools. Lunch options in the north are limited, but Hāwī has a couple of great dinner spots.

MAIN ATTRACTIONS

Hāwī and Kapaʻau. These two neighboring villages thrived during plantation days. There were hotels, saloons, and theaters—even a railroad. They took a hit when "Big Sugar" left the island, but both towns are blossoming once again today, thanks to strong local communities and an influx of artists keen on honoring the towns' past. Old historic buildings have been restored and now hold shops, galleries, and eateries. In Kapaʻau, browse through the Hawaiian collection of **Kohala Book Shop** (⊠ *54-3885 Akoni Pule Hwy.* ☎ *808/889–6400* ⊕ *www.kohalabooks.com*), the second-largest bookstore in the state. ⊠ *Hwy. 270, North Kohala.*

NEED A BREAK? If you're looking for something sweet, Kohala Coffee Mill & Tropical Dreams (⊠ *Hāwī* ☎ *808/889–5577*) serves great local coffee plus locally made ice cream that is *da kine* (translation: awesome, amazing—pick any superlative).

★ **Moʻokini Heiau.** This National Historic Landmark, an isolated *heiau* (ancient place of worship), is so impressive in size it may give you goose bumps. Its foundations date to about AD 480, but the high priest Paʻao from Tahiti expanded it several centuries later to offer sacrifices to please his gods. You can still see the lava slab where hundreds of people were killed, which gives this place a truly haunted feel. A nearby sign marks the place where King Kamehameha was born in 1758. The area is now part of the Kohala Historical Sites State Monument. ✢ *Turn off Hwy. 270 at sign for ʻUpolu Airport, near Hāwī, and hike or drive in a four-wheel-drive vehicle 1½ mi southwest* ☎ *808/974–6200.*

Pololū Valley. A steep trail leads through this lush green valley and down to Pololū Beach, which edges a rugged coastline ribboned by silver waterfalls. Even if you're not in the mood for a hike down into the valley, Pololū is still worth a visit for the stunning views from the lookout. ⊠ *End of Hwy. 270.*

★ **Puʻukoholā Heiau National Historic Site.** In 1790 a prophet told King Kamehameha to build a *heiau* on top of Puʻukoholā (Hill of the Whale) and dedicate it to the war god Kūkāʻilimoku by sacrificing his principal rival, Keōua Kūahuʻula. By doing so the king would achieve his goal of conquering the Hawaiian Islands. The prophecy came true in 1810. A short walk over arid landscape leads from the visitor center to **Puʻukoholā Heiau** and to **Mailekini Heiau,** a navigational aid con-

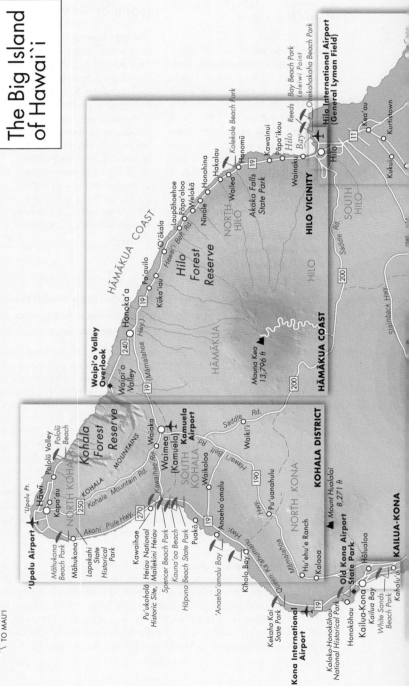

The Big Island of Hawai'i

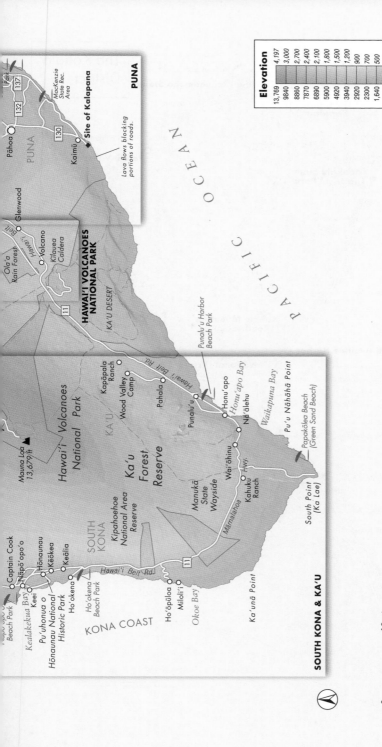

PUNA

Site of Kalapana

Lava flows blocking portions of roads.

HAWAI'I VOLCANOES NATIONAL PARK

Kīlauea Caldera

Volcano

Ola'a Rain Forest

Glenwood

Pāhoa

Kaimū

KA'U DESERT

PACIFIC OCEAN

Mauna Loa 13,679 ft

Hawai'i Volcanoes National Park

Kapāpala Ranch

Wood Valley Camp

Pāhala

Punalu'u

Punalu'u Harbor Beach Park

Honu'apo

Honu'apo Bay

Nā'ālehu

Waikapuna Bay

Pu'u Nāhāhā Point

KA'U

Ka'u Forest Reserve

Wai'ōhinu

Kahuku Ranch

Papakōlea Beach (Green Sand Beach)

South Point (Ka Lae)

Mānakea

Manukā State Wayside

Kipahoehoe National Area Reserve

SOUTH KONA

Captain Cook

Nāpō'opo'o

Hōnaunau

Kealakekua Bay

Keei

Kēōkea

Keōlia

Pu'uhonua o Hōnaunau National Historic Park

Hō'ōkena

Hō'ōkena Beach Park

KONA COAST

Hawai'i Belt Rd.

Hō'ōpūloa

Miloli'i

Okoe Bay

Ka'unā Point

Hawai'i Belt Rd.

SOUTH KONA & KA'U

137
132
130
Mackenzie State Rec. Area
PUNA

11
11

0   10 mi
0   10 km

The Kokala
District

'Upolu Point

Mo'okini Heiau
Kamehameha
Birthplace

Kēōkea Beach Park

King Kamehameha Statue

Kapa'a
Beach Park

Hāwī and
Kapa'au

Makapala

Mahūkona
Beach Park

NORTH KOHALA

Pololū Beach

Mahūkona

Pololū Valley

Lapakahi State
Historical Park

250

KOHALA MOUNTAINS

POLOLŪ VALLEY

Kohala Mountain Rd.

Akoni Pule Hwy.

270

WAIPI'O VALLEY

PACIFIC OCEAN

Kohua
Ranch

Kohala Mountain
Road Lookout

Parker Ranch
Visitor Center
& Museum

'Imiola
Congregational
Church

Kawaihae Harbor

Kawaihae

Pu'ukoholā Heiau
National Historic Site

Waiaka

Samuel M. Spencer Beach Park

Kawaihae Rd.

19

Kamuela
Museum

Waimea
(Kamuela)

Kauna'oa Beach
(aka Mauna Kea Beach)

Firehouse
Gallery

Hāpuna Beach State Park

SOUTH
KOHALA

Holoholokai Beach Park

Mamalahoa Hwy.

Puako

Waikoloa

19

Saddle Rd.

'Anaeho'omalu
Bay

'Anaeho'omalu

Waikoloa Rd.

200

Waiki'i

Ki'holo Bay

Ka'ahumanu Hwy.

Ki'holo

NORTH KONA

190

Queen Ka'ahumanu Hwy.

Puuanahulu

0   4 mi

0   4 km

Hawai'i Belt Rd.

CLOSE UP

Graffiti

You will no doubt notice that the black-lava fields lining Highway 19 from Kona International Airport into Kailua-Kona or out to the Kohala resorts are littered with white-coral graffiti. This has been going on for decades, and locals still get a kick out of it, as do tourists. The first thing everyone asks is "where do the white rocks come from?" and the answer is this: they're bits of coral and they come from the ocean. Now

that we've figured out that coral isn't totally expendable, no one starts from scratch anymore. If you want to write a message in the lava, you've got to use the coral that's already out there. This means that no one's message lasts for long, but that's all part of the fun. Some local couples even have a tradition of writing their names in the same spot on the lava fields every year on their anniversary.

structed about 1550. An even older temple, dedicated to the shark gods, lies submerged just offshore. The center organizes Hawaiian arts-and-crafts programs on a regular basis. Although the *heiau* was damaged by the 2006 earthquakes, the walkway is still intact, as is the majority of the structure. ⊠*Hwy. 270, Kawaihae* ☎*808/882–7218* ⊕*www.nps.gov* ⊠*Free* ☉*Daily 7:30–4.*

ALSO WORTH SEEING

Kawaihae Harbor. This commercial harbor, where in 1793 the first cattle landed in Hawai'i, is a hub of activity. It's especially busy on weekends, when paddlers and local fishing boats float on the waves. Second in size only to Hilo Harbor on the east coast, the harbor is often home to the *Makali'i*, one of three Hawaiian sailing canoes. King Kamehameha and his men launched their canoes from here when they set out to conquer the neighboring islands. ■TIP➜ **There are several restaurants with nice sunset views in Kawaihae should you be nearby at dinnertime.** ⊠*Kawaihae Harbor Rd. off Hwy. 270.*

King Kamehameha Statue. This is the original of the statue in front of the Judiciary Building on King Street in Honolulu. It was cast in Florence in 1880 but lost at sea when the German ship transporting it sank near the Falkland Islands. A replica was shipped to Honolulu. Two years later an American sea captain found the original in a Port Stanley (Falkland Islands) junkyard and brought it to the Big Island. The legislature voted to erect it near Kamehameha's birthplace. Every year, on King Kamehameha Day (June 11), a magnificent abundance of floral leis adorns the statue of Hawai'i's great king. It's in front of the old Kohala Courthouse next to the highway. ⊠*Hwy. 270, Kapa'au.*

NEED A BREAK?

Kohala Rainbow Cafe (☎*808/889–0099*), across from the King Kamehameha statue in Kapa'au, serves wraps, salads, smoothies, and sandwiches all day long. Try the Kamehameha wrap—filled with Hawaiian-style kālua pork, organic greens, tomatoes, onions, cheeses, and Maui onion dressing. Open Monday and Wednesday to Friday 10–6, weekends 11–5.

Mauna Kea's snowcapped summit towers ahead on a drive south from Waimea.

★ **Lapakahi State Historical Park.** A self-guided, 1-mi walking tour leads through the ruins of the once-prosperous fishing village Koaiʻe, which dates as far back as the 15th century. Displays illustrate early Hawaiian fishing and farming techniques, salt gathering, games, and legends. A park guide is often on-site to answer questions. Since the shoreline near the state park is an officially designated Marine Life Conservation District, and part of the site itself is considered sacred, swimming is discouraged. For some reason a distinction is made between swimming and snorkeling; the latter is allowed and superb. ⌂*Hwy. 270, between Kawaihae and Māhukona, North Kohala* ☎*808/974–6200 or 808/882–6207* ⌸*Free* ☉*Daily 8–4.*

WAIMEA

Just up the hill from Kohala, past Saddle Road (the route to Mauna Kea), Waimea offers a completely different experience from the rest of the island. Rolling green hills, large open pastures, cool evening breezes and morning mists, cattle everywhere, and regular rodeos are just a few of the surprises you'll stumble upon here in *paniolo* (Hawaiian for "cowboy") country. In addition to the horses and cattle, this is also where some of the island's top resort chefs are sent out to pasture, which makes Waimea an ideal place to find yourself stranded at dinnertime. In keeping with the recent Big Island restaurant trend toward locally farmed ingredients, a handful of Waimea farms and ranches supply most of the restaurants on the island, and many sell to the public as well. With its galleries, restaurants, and museum, as well as the Parker Ranch, Waimea is well worth a stop if you're heading to Hilo or Mauna Kea. ■TIP→ **And the short highway that connects Waimea to North Kohala (Hwy. 170) affords some of our favorite Big Island views.**

LOGISTICS You can see most of what Waimea has to offer in one day, but if you're heading up to Mauna Kea for stargazing (which you should), it could easily be stretched to two. If you stay in Waimea overnight (there are a few B&B options), or just get up really early, you could go for a morning horseback ride around the Parker Ranch, spend the afternoon browsing through town or touring some of the area's fantastic farms and ranches, then indulge in a gourmet dinner—all before heading up Saddle Road for world-renowned stargazing atop Mauna Kea. One word to the wise—there are no services or gas stations on Saddle Road, the only way to reach Mauna Kea. Fill up on gas and bring water and/or snacks with you (there are plenty of gas stations, cafés, and shops in Waimea).

> ### FUN THINGS TO DO: KONA SIDE
>
> ■ Hit the beach. Live out your Blue Hawai'i fantasy at Hāpuna or 'Anaeho'omalu (A-Bay).
>
> ■ Tour a coffee farm and taste the best Kona coffee.
>
> ■ Go for a morning swim with dolphins in Kealakekua Bay, then seek refuge with the sea turtles at the Place of Refuge.
>
> ■ See the artsy side of the Island in Hāwī, Hōlualoa, or Kainaliu.

MAIN ATTRACTIONS

Kohala Mountain Road Lookout. The lookout here provides a splendid view of the Kohala Coast and Kawaihae Harbor far below. On clear days, you can see well beyond the resorts. It's one of the most scenic spots on the island and great for a picnic. Often, thick mists drift in, casting an eerie feeling. ⊠*Kohala Mountain Rd. (Hwy. 250).*

Kekela Farm Tour. Gourmet Cooking Hawai'i recently launched this Big Island version of its popular Honolulu tours. Visitors tour the Kekela Farm in Waimea, helping famed local chef Daniel Thiebaut pick out produce, then return to Thiebaut's restaurant, Daniel's Seafood Café in Waimea, to cook a three-course meal, side-by-side with the chef. Participants get a true taste of what the island has to offer, and pick up some key regional Hawaiian cooking techniques in the process. ☎*808/735–7788* ⊕*www.gourmetcookinghawaii.com* ⊠*$150, including lunch* ☉*Daily 8:30–2:30.*

Merriman's Farm Visits and Dinner. Hawai'i Forest and Trail operates this half-day tour, which is one of the best ways to delve into the Big Island's burgeoning food scene. Chef Peter Merriman, the godfather of Hawai'i regional cuisine, put together the itinerary. It includes visits to Kahua Ranch where all of the top chefs buy their pork and beef and to Honopua Farms, a top organic produce farm. Honopua Farms is also home to lei maker and native Hawaiian Marie McDonald, who was named a "living treasure" by the Smithsonian Institution. After touring the farms, the group returns to Merriman's Restaurant in Waimea for a gourmet four-course meal comprised of various farm-fresh items. ☎800/464–1993 ⊕*www.hawaii-forest.com* ⬚*$155, including dinner* ⊙*Mon.–Thurs., from 2:30–7:30.*

Parker Ranch Visitor Center & Museum. The center chronicles the life of John Palmer Parker (and his descendants), who founded Parker Ranch in 1847. Parker married the grand-

daughter of King Kamehameha and bought two acres of land from the king for the sum of $10. Purchase your tickets here for the **Parker Ranch Historic Homes,** a couple of miles south of town. The original family residence, Mānā, is built entirely from native woods such as koa. Puʻōpelu, added to the estate in 1879, was the residence of Richard Smart, a sixth-generation Parker who expanded the house to make room for his European art collection. On Friday, Hawaiian crafts demonstrations take place at the homes. A wagon ride allows you a comfortable, albeit old-fashioned, visit to the pastures. Also available are horseback rides, ATV rides, and guided hunting or walking tours *(See Cowboys of Hawaiʻi ATV Rides in Chapter 5, Golf, Hiking & Outdoor Activities).* ✉*Parker Ranch Shopping Center, 67-1185 Māmalahoa Hwy., Waimea* ☎*808/885–7655, 808/885–5433, 800/262–7290 toll-free* ⊕*www.parkerranch.com* ⬚*Museum $7, homes $8.50, both $14* ⊙*Museum Mon.–Sat. 9–5, homes daily 10–5.*

ALSO WORTH SEEING

Firehouse Gallery. Walk across the Parker Ranch Shopping Center parking lot to a historic 77-year-old fire station, now a gallery, to glimpse what the artists in Hāmākua and Kohala are up to. The Waimea Arts Council sponsors free *kaha kiʻis* (one-person shows). ✉*Near main stoplight in Waimea, toward Kailua-Kona on Hwy. 190, Waimea* ☎*808/887–1052.*

ʻImiola Congregational Church. Stop here to admire the dark koa interior and the unusual wooden calabashes hanging from the ceiling. Be careful not to walk in while a service is in progress, as the front entry of this church, which was established in 1832 and rebuilt in 1857, is behind the pulpit. ✉*65-1084 Mamalahoa Hwy., on "Church Row," Waimea* ☎*808/885–4987.*

Kamuela Museum. This small private museum has a fascinating collection of artifacts from Hawaiʻi and around the world. The eclectic collection includes Hawaiian weapons and a satiny-smooth koa table that once graced ʻIolani Palace in Honolulu. There are also period furniture pieces, artwork, and military and war memorabilia. ✉*Hwys. 19 and 250, Waimea* ☎*808/885–4724* ⬚*$5* ⊙*Daily 8–5.*

NEED A BREAK?

Stop by **Waimea Coffee & Company** (✉*Parker Sq., 65-1279 Kawaihae Rd., Waimea* ☎*808/885–4472*) for a steaming latté and a warm pastry. Sit out on their veranda, staring at the manicured lawns and ranch-style building and try to believe you're in Hawai'i.

KAILUA-KONA

A fun and funky seaside village, Kailua-Kona has the souvenir shops and open-air restaurants you'd expect in a major tourist hub, with the added bonus of a surprising number of historic sites. Except for the rare deluge, the sun shines year-round. Mornings offer cooler weather, smaller crowds, and more birds singing in the banyan trees; you'll see dozens of tourists and locals out running on Ali'i Drive, the town's main drag, by about 5 AM every day. Afternoons sometimes bring clouds and drizzly rain, but evenings are great for cool drinks, brilliant sunsets, and lazy hours spent gazing out over the ocean. Though there are better beaches north of the town on the Kohala Coast, Kailua-Kona is home to a few gems, including a fantastic snorkeling beach (Kahalu'u) and a tranquil bay perfect for kids (Kamakahonu Beach, in front of the King Kamehameha Hotel).

Scattered amongst the shops, restaurants, and condo complexes of Ali'i Drive are King Kamehameha I's resting place (he died here in 1819), the last royal palace in the U.S. (Hulihe'e Palace), and a battleground dotted with the graves of ancient Hawaiians who fought for their land and lost. It was also here in Kailua-Kona that Kamehameha's successor, King Liholiho, broke and officially abolished the ancient *kapu* (roughly translating as "forbidden," it was the name for the strict code of conduct islanders were compelled to follow) system by publicly sitting and eating with women. The following year, on April 4, 1820, the first Christian missionaries came ashore here, changing the islands forever. If you want to know more about the village's fascinating past, arrange for a 75-minute guided walking tour with the **Kona Historical Society** (⊠ *81-6551 Māmalahoa Hwy.* ☎ *808/323–3222* ⊕ *www.konahistorical.org*).

LOGISTICS Half a day is plenty of time to explore Kailua-Kona; most of the town's sights are located in or near the downtown area. Still, if you add in a beach trip (Kahalu'u Beach has some of the best and easiest snorkeling on the island), it's easy to while away the bulk of a day. Another option for making a day of it is to tack on a short trip to the charming artists' village of Hōlualoa or to the coffee farms in the mountains just above Kealakekua Bay. There are a few great restaurants here that are far more affordable than those on the Kohala Coast and in Waimea. The town closest to the Kona International Airport (it's about 7 mi away), Kailua-Kona is a convenient home-base from which to explore the island.

MAIN ATTRACTIONS

Hōlualoa. Hugging the hillside above Kealakekua Bay, the tiny village of Hōlualoa is just up winding Hualālai Road from Kailua-Kona. A charming surprise, it's the kind of place where locals sit on their porches or in front of the stores and "talk story" (Hawaiian for shoot the breeze) all day long. It's comprised almost entirely of galleries in which all types of artists, from woodworkers to jewelry-makers and more traditional painters, work in their studios in back and sell the fin-

Hulihe'e
Palace **4**

Kailua Pier **3**

Kamakahonu **2**

King
Kamehameha's
Kona Beach
Hotel **1**

Kona Inn Shopping
Village **6**

Kuamo'o
Battlefield and
Lekeleke Burial
Grounds **9**

Moku'aikaua
Church **5**

St. Michael's
Church **7**

St. Peter's of
Kahalu'u **8**

ished product up front. Formerly the exclusive domain of coffee plantations, it still has quite a few coffee farms offering free tours and cups
of joe. Duck into the only café in town, the cleverly named **Hōluakoa
Cafe** (⊠ *76-5900 Mamalahoa Hwy.* ☎ *808/322–2233*)—it means Holy
Ground—and grab a cup to sip while you stroll through town.

❻ Kona Inn Shopping Village. Originally a hotel, the Kona Inn was built in
1928 to woo a new wave of wealthy travelers. As newer condos and
resorts opened along the Kona and Kohala coasts, it lost much of its
appeal, and was eventually transformed into a low-rise mall with dozens
of clothing boutiques, art galleries, gift shops, and island-style eateries.
Broad lawns with coconut trees on the ocean side are lovely for afternoon picnics and the open-air Kona Inn restaurant is a local favorite for
evening mai tais. Prior to the construction of the inn, the personal *heiau*
of King Liholiho stood on this shore. ⊠ *75-5744 Ali'i Dr.*

**NEED A
BREAK?**

Grab a tasty croissant sandwich and knock back some of Kona's best coffee
at Hula Bean (⊠ *75-5719 Ali'i Dr.* ☎ *808/329–6152*), directly across from the
Kona Village Shopping Center. If it's late afternoon, it's time to unwind with
one of those umbrella drinks. For cocktails head to the Kona Inn Restaurant
(⊠ *75-5744 Ali'i Dr.* ☎ *808/329–4455*), a local favorite.

Natural Energy Lab of Hawai'i. Driving south from the Kona International Airport towards Kailua-Kona you'll spot a large mysterious group of buildings with an equally large and mysterious photovoltaic (solar) panel installation just inside its gate. Although it looks like some sort of top-secret military station, this is the site of the Natural Energy Lab of Hawaii, NELHA for short, where scientists, researchers, and entrepreneurs are developing and marketing everything from new uses for solar power to energy-efficient air-conditioning systems and environmentally friendly aqua-culture techniques. Visitors are welcome at the lab, and there are 1½-hr tours for those interested in learning more about the experiments being conducted. ✉ 73-4460 Queen Ka'ahumanu Hwy., #101 📞 808/329–7341 ⊕ www.nelha.org 💰 Free, $8 tour ⊙ Weekdays 8–4; Tours Tues., Wed., Thurs. at 10.

> **WORD OF MOUTH**
>
> "You need to understand that the Big Island is very laid back. There are golf courses and a couple of movie theaters. The old town of Kona is pretty funky and simple. It's right on the water and has many open air restaurants. But nothing super fancy."
>
> —JPJH

ALSO WORTH SEEING

④ Hulihe'e Palace. A lovely rambling old stone home surrounded by jewel-green grass and sweeping ocean views and fronted by an elaborate wrought-iron gate, Hulihe'e Palace is one of only three royal palaces in America. The two-story residence was built by Governor John Adams Kuakini in 1838, a year after he completed Moku'aikaua Church. During the 1880s it served as King David Kalākaua's summer palace. It's constructed of local materials, including lava, coral, koa wood, and 'ōhi'a timber. The oversize doors and furniture bear witness to the size of some of the Hawaiian people. On weekday afternoons hula schools rehearse on the grounds. Though severely damaged by the 2006 earthquakes, Hulihe'e Palace reopened to the public in October 2007. The palace is still clearly damaged, but it is structurally sound and visitors can tour the central lobby and hallway, and peek into the damaged side parlors. The palace is operated by the Daughters of Hawai'i, a nonprofit focused on maintaining the heritage of the Islands, and its entrance fees, together with donations, are helping to repair the damage. ✉ 75-5718 Ali'i Dr. 📞 808/329–1877 ⊕ www.huliheepalace.org 💰 $5 ⊙ Weekdays 9–4, weekends 10–4.

③ Kailua Pier. Though most fishing boats use Honokōhau Harbor, this pier dating from 1918 is still a hub of ocean activity. Outrigger canoe teams practice, tour boats depart from these docks most days, and boats shuttle cruise ship passengers to and from Kailua-Kona. Along the seawall children and old-timers cast their lines daily, careful not to hook the pair of sea turtles nesting nearby. For youngsters, a bamboo pole and hook are easy to come by, and plenty of locals are willing to give pointers. Each October close to 1,500 international athletes swim 2.4 mi from the pier to begin the grueling Ironman Triathlon competition. ✉ Next to King Kamehameha's Kona Beach Hotel; seawall is

CLOSE UP

Green Hawai'i

With its isolated location, multiple climate zones, agriculture, and unique cultural and natural resources, the Big Island has long been considered a "living classroom" by geologists, biologists, anthropologists, and environmental scientists. In recent years, rapid development has also made the island a study in conservation—what works, what doesn't, and what can be reversed. The scarcity of natural resources is more striking on an island than in most other places, and on the Big Island this holds especially true. The last two decades of rapid growth have the island and its infrastructure bursting at the seams. Small island roads that have never known traffic are piled up bumper to bumper during rush hour, a concept that was foreign to this island until recently. Locals, priced out of the expensive new housing market, have been pushed farther and farther away from their jobs, creating longer commutes and more traffic. Even fresh water is at a premium.

Local residents, scientists, and the government have teamed together in the last several years to push for sustainable development on the Big Island and in Hawai'i in general. Affordable housing developments for locals are in the works; resorts and new developments must retain at least one staff member who is well-versed in Hawaiian history and culture to protect the island's traditions; and the Kohala Coast resorts have instituted organic landscaping techniques and marine protection programs to mitigate their environmental impact.

Scientists are also devising ways to maximize the island's resources. Researchers at the Natural Energy Lab of Hawai'i are particularly concerned with alternative energy sources, as the island has no natural sources of fossil fuels. In addition to solar power, lab scientists have pioneered uses for deep seawater. The super cold water pumped from the depths of the ocean keeps virtually energy-free air-conditioning units running at the labs and surrounding offices, a practice that will soon be adopted by the hotels and shops of downtown Honolulu.

But the green side of the Big Island is not solely of interest to scientists. Many visitors to the island are curious to learn about its natural resources and protection of them. Of particular interest are the **Natural Energy Lab of Hawai'i** *(see Kailua-Kona, above)*; the **'Imiloa Astronomy Center** *(see Hilo, below)* which informs visitors about Mauna Kea conservation efforts, the mountain's spiritual significance in Hawaiian tradition, and the impact that research there has on both the scientific community and the world at large; and several **Botanical Gardens** throughout the island. You might also try a nature hike with **Hawai'i Forest and Trail** (☎ *800/464-1993* ⊕ *www. hawaii-forest.com*), whose guides are full of information about endangered native plants and birds, as well as about protection efforts.

For more information on the island's ongoing conservation movement, pick up a copy of **Environment Hawai'i** magazine, or visit their Web site(⊕ *www.environment-hawaii.org*).

between Kailua Pier and Hulihe'e Palace on Ali'i Dr. ☑*$4.*

❷ **Kamakahonu.** King Kamehameha
★ spent his last years, from 1812 to 1819, near what is now King Kamehameha's Kona Beach Hotel. Part of what was once a 4-acre homestead complete with several houses and religious sites has been swallowed by Kailua Pier, but a replica of the temple, **Ahu'ena Heiau,** keeps history alive. Free tours start from King Kamehameha's Kona Beach Hotel. Small but pleasant King Kamehameha Beach is a great place to lie in the sun and take an easy swim after the tour. ☒*75-5660 Palani Rd.* ☎*808/329–2911* ☑*Free* ☺*Tours weekdays at 1:30.*

> ### WHERE DO I PARK?
>
> The easiest place to park your car is at King Kamehameha's Kona Beach Hotel ($3). Some free parking is also available: When you enter Kailua via Palani Road (Hwy. 190), turn left onto Kuakini Highway, drive for a half block, and turn right into the small marked parking lot. Walk *makai* (toward the ocean) on Likana Lane a half block to Ali'i Drive and you'll be in the heart of Kailua-Kona.

❶ **King Kamehameha's Kona Beach Hotel.** Stroll through the high-ceiling lobby of this Kailua-Kona fixture to view displays of Hawaiian artifacts and mounted marlin from Hawaiian International Billfish tournaments (from when Kailua Pier was still the weigh-in point). These "granders," marlin weighing 1,000 pounds or more, are the big attraction here. Classes in Hawaiian arts and crafts are given regularly. ☒*75-5660 Palani Rd.* ☎*808/923–4511 or 800/367–6060* ⊕*www.konabeachhotel.com.*

❾ **Kuamo'o Battlefield and Lekeleke Burial Grounds.** In 1819 an estimated 300 Hawaiians were killed on this vast, black-lava field, and you can still see their burial mounds there today. After the death of his father, King Kamehameha, King Liholiho was crowned king; shortly thereafter he ate at the table of women, thereby breaking the ancient *kapu* (taboo) system. Chief Kekuaokalani, who held radically different views about religious traditions, unsuccessfully challenged King Liholiho in battle here. ☒*South end of Ali'i Dr.*

❺ **Moku'aikaua Church.** A thatch hut, erected on this site by missionaries
★ in 1820, served as the first Christian church on the Islands. A more permanent structure was built in 1836 with black stone from an abandoned *heiau.* The stone was mortared with white coral and topped by an impressive steeple. Inside, behind a panel of gleaming koa wood, is a model of the brig *Thaddeus.* ☒*75-5713 Ali'i Dr.* ☎*808/329–0655.*

❼ **St. Michael's Church.** The site of Kona's first Catholic church, built in 1840, is marked by a small thatch structure to the left of the present church, which dates from 1850. In front of the church a coral grotto shrine holds 2,500 coral heads, harvested in 1940, when preservation was not yet an issue. ☒*75-5769 Ali'i Dr.* ☎*808/326–7771.*

NEED A BREAK?

The laid-back Island Lava Java (☒ *75-5799 Ali'i Dr.* ☎*808/327–2161*), in the Ali'i Sunset Plaza, has great coffee, breakfast sandwiches, bagels, and the best and biggest cinnamon rolls on the island. In the afternoon stop by for fresh fish or *kālua* pig tacos, sandwiches, fruit smoothies, and ice cream. The large outdoor seating area has a bird's-eye view of the ocean. Locals hang out here to read the paper, play board games, or just watch the surf.

❽ St. Peter's of Kahalu'u. The definition of "quaint" with its crisp white and blue trim, this tiny old-fashioned steeple church sits on the rocks overlooking the ocean near Kahalu'u Beach. It has appeared on many a Kailua-Kona postcard, and its charm and views bring hundreds of visitors every year. ⊠*Ali'i Dr., north of mile marker 5.*

SOUTH KONA & KEALAKEKUA BAY

South of Kailua-Kona, Highway 11 hugs splendid coastlines, leaving busy streets behind. A detour along the winding narrow roads in the mountains above takes you straight to the heart of coffee country where lush plantations and jaw-dropping views offer a taste of what Hawai'i was like before the resorts took over. Tour one of the coffee farms to find out what the big deal is about Kona coffee, and snag a free sample while you're at it. A half-hour back on the highway will lead you to magical Kealakekua Bay, where Captain James Cook arrived in 1778, changing the Islands forever. Hawaiian spinner dolphins frolic in the bay, now a marine preserve nestled alongside high green cliffs more reminiscent of popular images of Ireland than posters of Hawai'i. Snorkeling is superb here, as it is a protected marine reserve, so you may want to bring your gear and spend an hour or so exploring the coral reefs. This is also a nice kayaking spot; the bay is extremely calm. ■TIP→The 2006 earthquakes shook rocks and dirt from the cliffs surrounding the bay and sunk them straight into the water, causing the bay to close for a few months. It's open again, but orange buoys mark the area that officials still deem potentially dangerous, closest to the cliffs. One of our favorite ways to spend a morning is to throw some snorkel gear in a kayak, paddle across the bay, go for a swim and a snorkel, and paddle back, dodging dolphins along the way.

The winding road above Kealakekua Bay is home to a quaint little painted church, as well as several reasonably priced bed-and-breakfasts with great views. The communities surrounding the bay (Kainaliu and Captain Cook) are brimming with local and transplanted artists, making them great places to stop for a meal, some unique gifts, or an afternoon stroll.

LOGISTICS Between the coffee plantations, artsy towns, and Kealakekua Bay, South Kona has plenty of activities to keep you occupied for a day. Bring a swimsuit and snorkel gear, and hit Kealakekua Bay first thing in the morning. You'll have a better chance of a dolphin sighting, and you'll beat the large snorkel cruise groups. Follow the signs off Highway 11 to the bay, then park at Nāpō'opo'o Beach (not much of a beach, but it provides easy access into the water). You can rent kayaks at any of a number of stands along the highway, but there are no rental options once you start the 10-minute trek down to the bay. After a morning of swimming and kayaking, grab your morning coffee for free on a coffee farm tour, then head to one of the great cafés in nearby Kainaliu to

Kealakekua Bay is one of the most beautiful spots on the Big Island.

refuel (we like the Aloha Angel Cafe in the Aloha Theater for breakfast, and Cafe Nasturtium for lunch).

MAIN ATTRACTIONS

Captain Cook Monument. No one knows for sure what happened on February 14, 1779, when English explorer Captain James Cook was killed on this spot. He had chosen Kealakekua Bay as a landing place in November 1778. Cook, arriving during the celebration of Makahiki, the harvest season, was welcomed at first. Some Hawaiians saw him as an incarnation of the god Lono. Cook's party sailed away in February 1779, but a freak storm off the Kona Coast forced his damaged ship back to Kealakekua Bay. Realizing that no god could be thwarted by a mere rainstorm, the Hawaiians were not so welcoming this time, and various confrontations arose between them and Cook's sailors. The theft of a longboat brought Cook and an armed party ashore to reclaim it. One thing led to another: shots were fired, daggers and spears were thrown, and Captain Cook fell, mortally wounded. Strangely enough, this didn't deter other Westerners from visiting the Islands; Captain James Cook and his party had effectively introduced the Hawaiian Islands to the world. Soon after, Western influences arrived on Hawai'i's shores: whalers, sailors, traders, missionaries, and more, and they brought with them crime, debauchery, alcohol, disease, and a world unknown to the Hawaiians. A 27-foot-high obelisk marks the spot where Captain Cook died on the shore of Kealakekua Bay. Locals like to point out that the land the monument sits on is British territory (to clarify: the British government owns the land that the monument occupies, but it's still U.S. territory).

Kealakekua Bay. This is one of the most beautiful spots on the island. Dramatic cliffs surround crystal clear, turquoise water chock-full of stunning coral and tropical fish. Before the arrival of Captain Cook in the late 18th century, this now tranquil state marine park and sanctuary lay at the center of Hawaiian life. Historians consider Kealakekua Bay to be the birthplace of the post-contact era.

> ### HAWAIIAN CHERRIES
>
> Driving around the towns of South Kona—Hōnaunau, Captain Cook, Kainaliu, and Hōlualoa—you'll often see signs referring to "cherries," and either the buying or selling of them. Before you scratch your head too much, wondering when the Hawaiian cherry trade got so hot, we should tell you that these signs refer to coffee cherries. When coffee beans are first picked off of trees, they are encased in red husks that make them look like big bright cherries.

The term "beach" is used a bit liberally for **Nāpōʻopoʻo Beach,** on the south side of the bay. There's no real beach to speak of, but there are easy ways to enter the water. To the left of the parking lot is an old cement pier that serves as a great ladder for swimmers going into or coming out of the bay. This is a nice place to swim as it's well protected from weather or currents, so the water is almost always calm and clear. Excellent snorkel cruises can still be booked through Fair Wind Cruises (*see Chapter 4, Water Activities & Tours*), the only company allowed to dock in Kealakekua. ⊠ *Bottom of Nāpōʻopoʻo Rd.*

NEED A BREAK?

Before or after winding down Nāpōʻopoʻo Road, treat yourself to awesome views of Kealakekua Bay at the Coffee Shack (⊠ *83-5799 Māmalahoa Hwy.* ☎ *808/328-9555* ⊕ *www.coffeeshack.com*), a deli and pizza place with just nine tables on an open, breezy lānai. The bread is home-baked, the eggs Benedict is a local breakfast favorite, the sandwiches are generous, and the staff is friendly.

★ **Puʻuhonua O Hōnaunau** (*Place of Refuge*). This 180-acre National Historic Park was once a safe haven for women in times of war as well as for *kapu* breakers, criminals, and prisoners of war—anyone who could get inside the 1,000-foot-long wall, which was 10 feet high and 17 feet thick, could avoid punishment. **Hale-o-Keawe Heiau,** built in 1650 as the burial place of King Kamehameha's ancestor Keawe, has been restored. South of the park, tide pools offer another delight—most notably the crowd of sea turtles feeding there regularly. Demonstrations of poi pounding, canoe making, and local games are occasionally scheduled. ⊠ *Rte. 160, about 20 mi south of Kailua-Kona* ☎ *808/328–2288* ⊕ *www.nps.gov/puho* 🎫 *$3–$5* ⊙ *Park Mon.–Thurs. 6 AM–8 PM, Fri.–Sun. 6 AM–11 PM; visitor center daily 8 AM–4:30 PM.*

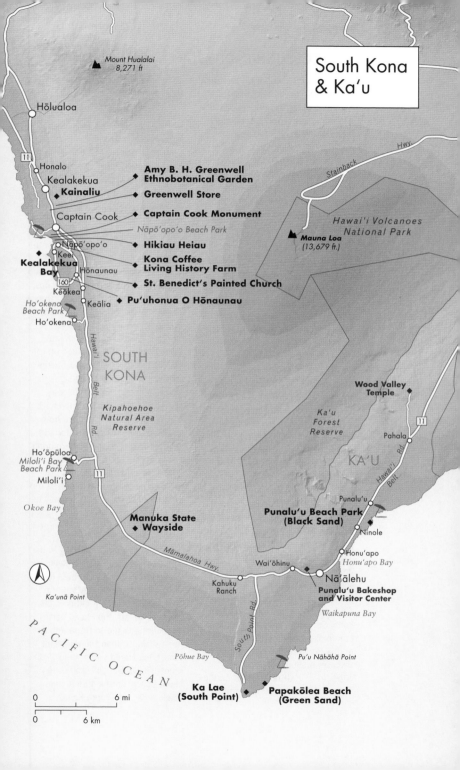

A CIRCLE ISLAND TOUR

Given the large amount of territory to cover, we recommend that those interested in circling the Big Island stay at different spots throughout. This also allows you to break up your time between hotels, vacation rentals, and B&Bs. Following are routes around the island originating in either Hilo or Kona. These are seven-day itineraries, but they can easily be shortened by leaving out stops and increasing the amount of driving per day.

STARTING IN HILO

Book a night at a B&B in 🔲 Hilo and get up early to explore the town. By late morning, head to 🔲 **Volcano.** It's less than an hour away, but if you stay the night you can take the nighttime lava walk and explore Volcanoes National Park. In the morning, head south on Highway 11 to Ka Lae (South Point), stopping on the way at Punalu'u Beach (30 mi/35 minutes from Volcano) for a quick swim with the sea turtles. Once at South Point (15 mi/20 minutes from Punalu'u), park and hike down to Papakōlea Beach (Green Sand Beach). Back on the road, drive north 45 mi/one hour on Highway 11 to 🔲 **Kealakekua Bay.** Stay the night, and get up early to spend the morning kayaking and snorkeling in Kealakekua Bay and exploring the ancient Place of Refuge. Drive back up the hill from these sites to spend some time in Kainaliu or take a coffee farm tour. A 10- to 15-minute drive north will get you to Kailua-Kona. Get out to wander around, then make a beeline to Huggo's on the Rocks or the Kona Inn for a sunset mai tai and pūpū. Stay either in 🔲 **Kailua-Kona** or on the 🔲 **Kohala Coast** (30 mi north of Kailua-Kona). Spend the next day at local favorite Hāpuna Beach.

In the morning of the following day, set out north on Highway 11 and veer left to continue north on Highway 270 deeper into the North Kohala region. You'll pass through the charming village of Kapa'au and dead-end at the Pololū Valley lookout. Head back through Kapa'au and turn onto Highway 250 to Hāwī. Next it's up the hill to Waimea. This road offers our favorite views on the island—it's only about 20 mi, but it will likely take you an hour, between the slow curves and the photo ops. Check into a B&B and spend the rest of the day exploring 🔲 **Waimea,** dining at one of the town's terrific restaurants. In the morning, drive south on Highway 19 to the Hāmākua Coast; follow the brown-and-white Heritage Coast signs to points of interest along the way, then turn off at Honoka'a to check out Waipi'o Valley. The drive from Waimea to Honoka'a is under 15 mi. Spend the rest of the day exploring the coastline and stay the night on the 🔲 **Hāmākua Coast.** It's just over 40 mi to the Hilo airport, a trip that should take you 50 minutes to an hour.

STARTING IN KONA

We recommend overnighting in the same towns if you start in Kailua-Kona, and just reversing the order. If you fly into Kona, stay your first and second nights in either Kailua-Kona or Kohala, then head north around the island to North Kohala, then Waimea, then the Hāmākua Coast, followed by Hilo, the Volcano, Punalu'u, South Point, and Green Sand Beach, finishing up in Kealakekua Bay and South Kona.

ALSO WORTH SEEING

Amy B. H. Greenwell Ethnobotanical Garden. Often overlooked, this garden fosters a wealth of Hawaiian cultural traditions. On 12 acres grow 250 types of plants that were typical in an early Hawaiian *ahupua'a*, pie-shaped land divisions that ran from the mountains to the sea. Call to find out about guided tours or drop in between 8:30 AM and 5 PM. ✉ *82-6188 Māalahoa Hwy., Captain Cook* ☎ *808/323–3318* ⊕ *www. bishopmuseum.org/greenwell.*

Greenwell Store. Established in 1850, the homestead of Henry N. Greenwell served as cattle ranch, sheep station, store, post office, and family home all in one. Now, all that remains is the 1875 stone structure, which is listed on the National Register of Historic Places. It houses a fascinating museum that has exhibits on ranching and coffee farming. It's also headquarters for the **Kona Historical Society,** which organizes walking tours of Kailua-Kona. ✉ *81-6551 Māmalahoa Hwy.* ☎ *808/323–3222* ⊕ *www.konahistorical.org* ✉ *Donations accepted* ⊙ *Weekdays 9–3.*

Hikiau Heiau. This stone platform was once an impressive temple dedicated to the god Lono. When Captain Cook arrived in 1778, ceremonies in his honor were held here. ✉ *Bottom of Nāpō'opo'o Rd.*

Kainaliu. Like many of the Big Island's old plantation towns, Kainaliu is experiencing a bit of a renaissance. In addition to a ribbon of funky old stores, many of them traditional Japanese family-operated shops, a handful of new galleries and shops have sprung up in the last few years. Browse around Oshima's, established in 1926, and Kimura's, established in 1927, to find authentic Japanese goods beyond tourist trinkets, then pop into one of the local cafés for a tasty vegetarian snack. Cross the street to peek into the 1932 Aloha Theatre, where community-theater actors might be practicing a Broadway revue. ✉ *Hwy. 11, mile markers 112–114.*

Kona Coffee Living History Farm. Known as the D. Uchida Farm, this site is on the National Register of Historic Places. Completely restored by the Kona Historical Society, it includes a 1913 farmhouse surrounded by coffee trees, a Japanese bathhouse, *kuriba* (coffee-processing mill), and *hoshidana* (traditional drying platform). Tours of the farm are available by reservation only and cost $20. ✉ *81-6551 Māmalahoa Hwy., Kealakekua* ☎ *808/323–3222* ⊕ *www.konahistorical.org.*

St. Benedict's Painted Church. The walls, columns, and ceiling of this Roman Catholic church depict colorful biblical scenes through the paintbrush of Belgian-born priest Father Velghe. Mass is still held every weekend. The view of Kealakekua Bay from the entrance is amazing. ✉ *Painted Church Rd. off Hwy. 160, Hōnaunau* ☎ *808/328–2227.*

KA'Ū & KA LAE (SOUTH POINT)

The most desolate region of the island, Ka'ū is nonetheless home to some spectacular sights. Mark Twain wrote some of his finest prose here, where macadamia-nut farms, green-sand beaches, and tiny vil-

Kona Coffee

Even if you're not a java fiend, it's easy to get into the history and culture surrounding Kona coffee. From the hundreds of cafés, stores, and restaurants selling Kona coffee to the farm tours to the annual Gevalia Kona Coffee Cupping Competition, coffee is a major part of life on the Big Island and represents one of only a few non-tourism-related industries in Hawai'i. Hawai'i is the only U.S. producer of commercially grown coffee, and, though it may seem like the Kona coffee craze is a relatively recent thing, coffee has been growing here since 1828, when Reverend Samuel Ruggles, an American missionary, brought a cutting over from the O'ahu farm of Chief Boki, O'ahu's governor. That initial coffee plant was a strain of Ethiopian coffee called Coffee Arabica, and it is the same coffee being produced on the Big Island today, although a Guatemalan strain of Arabica introduced in the late 1800s is produced in far higher quantities.

In the latter half of the 1800s, many coffee plantations closed to make room for more lucrative sugar plantations, and by the early 1900s, the era of the large Hawaiian coffee plantation had ended. Plantation owners subdivided their lots and began leasing smaller parcels to local tenant farmers, a practice that continues today. The majority of the tenant farmers were Japanese families who managed their farms as family businesses with no outside labor. At one point in the 1930s, local schools switched summer vacation to "coffee vacation" from August to November so that the kids could help with the coffee harvest, a practice that held until 1969.

Coffee is harvested as "cherries"—the beans are encased in a hard red shell. The cherries are shelled and the beans roasted to a dark brown. Despite family control of the harvest, the production process was controlled by just two firms until the late 1950s, when farmers and cooperatives began to buy and operate mills. Today most farms—owned and operated by Japanese-American families, west coast Mainland transplants, native Hawaiians, and descendants of Portuguese and Chinese immigrants—control production from harvest to cup.

COFFEE-FARM TOURS

Several coffee farms around the South Kona and Upcountry Kona coffee-belt area welcome visitors with tours that let you in on the whole coffee process, from harvesting green beans to packaging. Some tours are self-guided, and most are free, with the exception of the Kona Coffee Living History Farm. The brew, of course, is always ready.

Greenwell Farms. ✉ *81-6581 Māmalahoa Hwy., Kealakekua* ☎ *808/323–2862* ⊕ *www. greenwellfarms.com.*

Hōlualoa-Kona Coffee Company. ✉ *77-6261 Old Māmalahoa Hwy., Hwy. 180, Hōlualoa* ☎ *808/322–9937 or 800/334–0348* ⊕ *www.konalea.com.*

Kona Coffee Living History Farm (D. Uchida Farm). *See South Kona & Kealakekua Bay, above.*

Royal Kona Coffee Museum & Coffee Mill. ✉ *83-5427 Māmalahoa Hwy., next to tree house in Hōnaunau* ☎ *808/328–2511.*

DID YOU KNOW

Kealakekua Bay is generally considered the best snorkeling spot on the Big Island, with stunning coral reefs—especially around the Captain Cook Monument—calm waters, and spinner dolphins.

lages offer largely undiscovered beauty. The 50-mi drive from Kailua-Kona to windswept South Point, where the first Polynesians came ashore as early as AD 750, winds away from the ocean through a surreal moonscape of lava-covered forests. Past South Point, glimpses of the ocean return and hidden Green Sand Beach tempts hikers to stop awhile before the highway narrows and returns to the coast, passing verdant cattle pastures and sheer cliffs on the way to the black-sand beach of Punalu'u, the nesting place of the Hawaiian sea turtle.

LOGISTICS   Ka'ū and Ka Lae are destinations usually combined with a quick trip to the volcano from Kona. This is probably cramming too much into one day, however. The volcano fills up a day and then some, and the sights of this region are worth more than a cursory glance. Our recommendation? Make Green Sand Beach or Punalu'u your destination for a beach day at some point during your stay, and stop to see some of the other sights on the way there or back. Bring sturdy shoes if Green Sand Beach is your choice (reaching the beach requires a hike) and snorkeling gear if you're heading to Punalu'u. The drive from Kailua-Kona to Ka Lae is a long one (roughly 2½ hours). It's a good idea to fill up on gasoline and pack a lunch before you leave, as there are few amenities along the way. There are a few places to eat if you forget or can't be bothered, but what's better than a beach picnic? As with the rest of the island, a 4-wheel-drive vehicle will make it much easier to explore this area. Weather tends to be warm, dry, and windy.

MAIN ATTRACTIONS

★ **Ka Lae (South Point).** Windswept Ka Lae is the southernmost point of land in the United States. It's thought that the first Polynesians came ashore here. Check out the old canoe-mooring holes that are carved through the rocks, possibly by settlers from Tahiti as early as AD 750. Some artifacts, thought to have been left by early voyagers who never settled here, date to AD 300. Driving down to the point, you pass Kama'oa Wind Farm; although the rows of windmill turbines are still fueled by the nearly constant winds sweeping across this coastal plain, the equipment and facilities are falling into disrepair due to neglect. Indeed, some of the windmills no longer turn at all. Continue down the road (parts at the end are unpaved, but driveable), bear left when the road forks and park in the lot at the end; walk past the boat hoists toward the little lighthouse. South Point is just past the lighthouse at the southernmost cliff. ■ TIP➔ **Don't leave anything of value in your car, and know that you don't have to pay for parking. It's a free, public park, so anyone trying to charge you is likely running some sort of scam.** ⊠ *Turn right past mile marker 70 on Māmalahoa Hwy., then drive 12 mi down South Point Rd.*

Papakōlea Beach (Green Sand Beach). It takes awhile to get down and even longer to get back, but where else are you going to see a green-sand beach? Add to that the fact that the rock formations surrounding the beach are surreally beautiful, and this is a detour worth taking *(see Chapter 3, Beaches).* ⊠ *2½ mi northeast of South Point.*

Continued on page 64

HAWAI'I VOLCANOES NATIONAL PARK

Exploring the surface of the world's most active volcano—from the moonscape craters at the summit to the red-hot lava flows on the coast to the kīpuka, pockets of vegetation miraculously left untouched—is the ultimate ecotour and one of Hawai'i's must-dos.

The park sprawls over 520 square miles and encompasses Kīlauea and Mauna Loa, two of the five volcanoes that formed the Big Island nearly half a million years ago. Kīlauea, youngest and most rambunctious of the Hawaiian volcanoes, erupted at its summit from the 19th century through 1982. Since then, the top of the volcano had been more or less quiet, frequently shrouded in mist; an eruption in the Halema'uma'u Crater in 2008 ended this period of relative inactivity.

Kilauea's eastern side sprang to life on January 3, 1983, shooting molten lava four stories high. This eruption has been ongoing, and lava flows are generally steady and slow, appearing and disappearing from view. Over 500 acres have been added to Hawai'i's eastern coast since the activity began, and scientists say this eruptive phase is not likely to end anytime soon.

If you're lucky, you'll be able to catch creation at its most elemental—when molten lava meets the ocean, cools, and solidifies into brand-new stretches of coastline. Even if lava-viewing conditions aren't ideal, you can hike 150 miles of trails; camp amid wide expanses of *'a'ā* (rough) and *pahoehoe* (smooth) lava; or sip cocktails at Volcano House, a hotel perched on the rim of Kīlauea Caldera. There's nothing quite like it.

⌂ P.O. Box 52, Hawai'i Volcanoes National Park, HI 96718

☎ 808/985-6000

⊕ www.nps.gov/havo

💳 $10 per vehicle; $5 for pedestrians and bicyclists. Ask about passes. Admission is good for seven consecutive days.

🕑 The park is open daily, 24 hours. Kīlauea Visitor Center: 7:45 am–5 pm. Thomas A. Jaggar Museum: 8:30–5. Volcano Art Center Gallery: 9–5.

(top) Kīlauea Iki Trail
(left) Fuming rim of Pu'u' Ō'ō, source of the current eruption

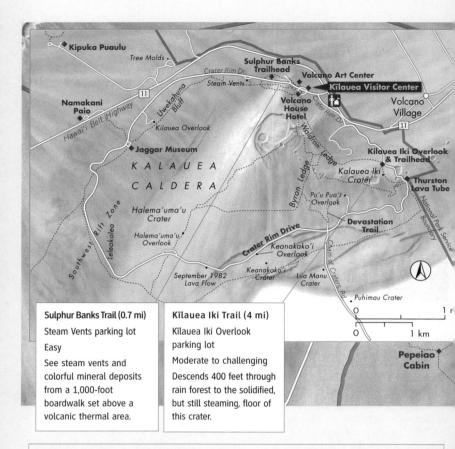

Sulphur Banks Trail (0.7 mi)

Steam Vents parking lot

Easy

See steam vents and colorful mineral deposits from a 1,000-foot boardwalk set above a volcanic thermal area.

Kīlauea Iki Trail (4 mi)

Kīlauea Iki Overlook parking lot

Moderate to challenging

Descends 400 feet through rain forest to the solidified, but still steaming, floor of this crater.

SEEING THE SUMMIT

The best way to explore the summit of Kīlauea is to cruise 11-mile Crater Rim Drive, which encircles the volcano's massive caldera. Volcano House's dining room offers front-row views of this eerie, awe-inspiring spot, which bears an uncanny resemblance to those old Apollo moon photos.

Depending on the number of stops you make, it'll take one to three hours to complete the circuit. Highlights include sulfur and steam vents, a walk-through lava tube, and the southwest rift zone—deep fissures, fractures, and gullies along Kīlauea's flanks.

There's also Halema'uma'u Crater, an awesome depression in Kīlauea Caldera measuring 3,000 feet across and nearly 300 feet deep. When skies are clear, this is a good place to see Mauna Loa and Mauna Kea.

The Thomas A. Jaggar Museum offers breathtaking looks at Halema'uma'u and Kīlauea Caldera, geologic displays, video presentations of volcanic eruptions, and exhibits of seismographs once used by volcanologists at the adjacent Hawaiian Volcano Observatory (not open to the public).

Kipuka Puaulu

SEE LEFT

11

Kīlauea Visitor Center

Volcano Village

Kīlauea Caldera

Crater Rim Dr.

Lua Mone Crater

EAST RIFT ZONE

Kupaianaha Lava Shield

Ko'oko'olau Crater

Puhimau Crater

Pu'u' Ō'ō (Source of Current Eruption)

Pu'u Huluhulu

Kane Nui o HamoLava Shield

Pauahi Crater

Napau Crater

Cone Crater

Mauna Ulu Lava Shield

Makaopuhi Crater

Twin Pit Craters

1983– Present Lava Flow

Chain of Craters Rd.

Hawai'i Volcanoes National Park

HILINA PALI

End of Road & Mobile Ranger Station

Hilina Pali Overlook

Pu'u Loa

Holei Sea Arch

Ka'ena Point

Pacific Ocean

Pu'u Huluhulu Trail (2.5 mi)

Mauna Ulu parking lot

Moderate

Great view of the ocean, Mauna Kea, Mauna Loa, Kīlauea, and Pu'u' Ō'ō cinder cone from atop this cinder cone formed 400 years ago.

Pu'u Loa Petroglyphs Trail (1.5 mi)

Pu'u Loa Petroglyphs parking lot

Easy to moderate

Spotlighted here: ancient petroglyphs the Hawaiians created on smooth lava flows to ensure the health and safety of their children.

SEEING LAVA

Before you head out to find flowing lava, pinpoint the safe viewing spots at the Visitor Center. One of the best places usually is at the end of 19-mile Chain of Craters Road. Magnificent plumes of steam rise where the rivers of liquid fire meet the sea.

There are three guarantees about lava flows in HVNP. First: They constantly change. Second: Because of that, you can't predict when and where you'll be able to see them. Third: New land formed when lava meets the sea is highly unstable and can collapse at any time. Never go into areas that have been closed.

■**TIP**➔**The view of brilliant red-orange lava flowing from Kīlauea's east rift zone is most dramatic at night.**

People watching lava flow at HVNP

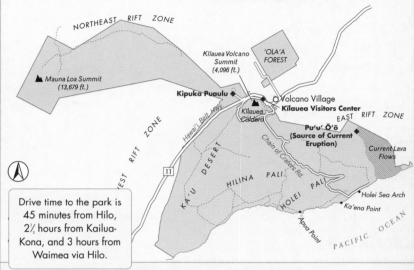

NORTHEAST RIFT ZONE

Kīlauea Volcano Summit (4,096 ft.)

'OLA'A FOREST

Mauna Loa Summit (13,679 ft.)

Kipuka Puaulu

Volcano Village

Kīlauea Visitors Center

Kīlauea Caldera

EAST RIFT ZONE

Pu'u' Ō'ō (Source of Current Eruption)

Current Lava Flows

Hawai'i Belt Hwy.

WEST RIFT ZONE

11

KAU DESERT

HILINA PALI

HOLEI PALI

Chain of Craters Rd.

Holei Sea Arch

Ka'ena Point

Apua Point

PACIFIC OCEAN

Drive time to the park is 45 minutes from Hilo, 2¼ hours from Kailua-Kona, and 3 hours from Waimea via Hilo.

Lava entering the ocean

WHERE TO START

Begin your visit at the Visitor Center, where you'll find maps, books, and DVDs; information on trails, ranger-led walks, and special events; and current weather, road, and lava-viewing conditions. Free volcano-related film showings, lectures, and other presentations are regularly scheduled.

WEATHER

Weather conditions fluctuate daily, sometimes hourly. It can be rainy and chilly even during the summer; the temperature usually is 14° cooler at the 4,000-foot-high summit of Kīlauea than at sea level.

Expect hot, dry, and windy coastal conditions at the end of Chain of Craters Road. Bring rain gear, and wear layered clothing, sturdy shoes, sunglasses, a hat, and sunscreen.

Photographer on lava table filming lava flow into ocean

FOOD
Volcano House has the only food concessions at HVNP; it's a good idea to bring your own favorite snacks and beverages. Stock up on provisions in Volcano Village, 1½ miles away.

PARK PROGRAMS
Rangers lead daily walks into different areas; check with the Visitor Center for details as times and destinations depend on weather conditions.

Over 60 companies hold permits to lead hikes at HVNP. Good choices are Hawai'i Forest & Trail (www. hawaii-forest.com), Hawaiian Walkways (www.hawaiianwalkways.com), and Native Guide Hawai'i (www. nativeguidehawaii.com).

CAUTION
"Vog" (volcanic smog) can cause headaches; breathing difficulties; lethargy; irritations of the skin, eyes, nose, and throat; and other health problems. Pregnant women, young children, and people with asthma and heart conditions are most susceptible, and should avoid areas such as Halema'uma'u Crater where fumes are thick.

Wear long pants and boots or closed-toe shoes with good tread for hikes on lava. Stay on marked trails and step carefully. Lava is composed of 50% silica (glass) and can cause serious injury if you fall.

Carry at least 2 quarts of water on hikes. Temperatures near lava flows can rise above 100°F, and dehydration, heat exhaustion, and sunstroke are common consequences of extended exposure to intense sunlight and high temperatures.

Remember that these are active volcanoes, and eruptions can cause parts of the park to close at any time. Check the park's Web site or call ahead for last-minute updates before your visit.

Volcanologists inspecting a vent in the East Rift Zone

Punalu'u Beach Park (Black Sand Beach). This easily accessed beach is well worth at least a short stop for two reasons: it's a beautiful black-sand beach, and it's where the Hawaiian sea turtles like to nest, so the water and beach are swarming with them. The turtles are used to people by now, and have no problem swimming right alongside you, or continuing their nap in the sand while you snap a photo *(see Chapter 3, Beaches)*. ⊠ *Turn right down driveway into beach off Hwy. 11 south. Beach is well marked off hwy.*

NEED A BREAK?

Punalu'u Bakeshop & Visitor Center (⊠ *Hwy. 11, Na'alehu* ☎ *808/366–3501* ⊙ *Daily 9–5*) is a bit of a tourist trap, but it's also a good spot to grab a snack before heading back out on the road. Try some Portuguese sweet bread or a homemade ice-cream sandwich paired with some local Ka'ū coffee (that's right, not Kona, but equally tasty).

ALSO WORTH SEEING

Manuka State Wayside. This dry, upland forest spreads across several lava flows. A rugged trail follows a 2-mi loop past a pit crater and winds around ancient trees such as *hau* and *kukui*. It's an okay spot to get out of the car and stretch your legs—you can wander through the well-maintained arboretum, snap a few photos of the eerie forest, and let the kids scramble around trees so large they can't get their arms around them. However, we don't recommend spending too much time here, especially if you're planning on driving all the way down to South Point. The pathways are not well maintained, but restrooms, picnic areas, and telephones are available. ⊠ *Hwy. 11, north of mile marker 81* ☎ *808/974–6200* ⌷ *Free* ⊙ *Daily 7–7.*

OFF THE BEATEN PATH

Pahala. About 16 mi east of Na'alehu, beyond Punalu'u Beach Park, Highway 11 flashes past this little town. You'll miss it if you blink. Pahala is a perfect example of a sugar-plantation town. Behind it, along a wide cane road, you enter Wood Valley, once a prosperous community, now just a road heavily scented by eucalyptus trees, coffee blossoms, and night-blooming jasmine. Here you'll find **Wood Valley Temple** (☎ *808/928–8539* ⊕ *www.nechung.org*), a serene and beautiful Tibetan Buddhist temple dedicated by the Dalai Lama during his 1980 visit. Today, you can explore the gardens and the temple, attend a service, or book lodging in the Temple's guesthouse for a complete Buddhist retreat.

VOLCANO

Few visitors realize that in addition to "the Volcano" there's also Volcano, the town. Conveniently located next to—you guessed it—Hawai'i Volcanoes National Park, Volcano Village is a charming little hamlet in the woods that offers a dozen or so inns and B&Bs, a decent Thai restaurant, some killer (although strangely expensive) pizza, and a handful of things to see and do that don't include the village's namesake. For years, writers, artists, and meditative types have been coming to the Volcano to seek inspiration, and many of them have settled in and around Volcano Village. Artist studios (open to the public by appoint-

You may see flowing lava at Kīlauea, the Big Island's youngest and most active volcano.

ment) are scattered throughout the hills, and writers' retreats are hidden in the tranquil rain forests surrounding the area. If you plan to do a nighttime lava hike at Volcanoes National Park, spending a night in Volcano Village is the ideal way to go about it.

LOGISTICS There are a handful of dining options, a couple of stores, and a gas station available in Volcano, so most of your needs should be covered. If you can't find what you're looking for, Hilo is only about a 30-minute drive away, and Pahoa is an even-closer 15-minute drive. Bring a fleece or a sweater if you plan to stay the night; temperatures drop at night and mornings are cool and misty. One of the main reasons people choose to stay the night in Volcano is to do the night hike to the lava flow in the park. If you're planning on making the trek, bring hiking shoes, a flashlight (check the batteries), and water. ■TIP➔ **Also, make sure you have enough gas to get down to the flow and back up.** The entrance to Volcanoes National Park is about one minute from Volcano Village, but the drive down is nearly 30 minutes. Remember that you'll be coming back from the hike at around midnight, long after the rangers have gone home.

EXTRA-VOLCANIC ACTIVITY

Kīlauea Caverns of Fire. Strap on a miners hat and gloves and get ready to explore the underbelly of the world's largest active volcano. Tours through these fascinating caves and lava tubes underneath the volcano must be arranged in advance, but are well worth a little extra planning. Located off Highway 11 between Hilo and Volcanoes National

Park, the Caverns are comprised of four main tubes, each 500–700 years old and full of stalactites, stalagmites, and a variety of different-colored flowstone. The largest lava tube in the world is here—40 mi long, it has 80-foot ceilings and is 80 feet wide. Tours can range from safe and easy (safe enough for children five years old and up) to long and adventurous. ⊠ *Off Hwy. 11, between Kurtistown and Mountain View* ☎ *808/217–2363* ⊕ *www.kilaueacavernsoffire.com* ✑ *$29 for walking tour* ⊗ *By appointment only.*

GREEN SAND?

Formed by the lava flows of Mauna Loa, Papakōlea (Green Sand Beach) gets its color from eroded olivine crystals. Wind and heavy surf have intensified the beach's color by stripping away lighter grains of sand (made from volcanic ash), leaving the denser olivine crystals behind. Though this is commonly thought to be the only green-sand beach on the Big Island, there are actually two others nearby, formed by the same lava flow.

Volcano Farmers Market. Local produce, flowers, and food products are on offer every Sunday morning at one of the better farmers' markets on the island. It's not swarmed with people the way the Hilo market can be, but it's best to get there early, as vendors tend to sell out of the best stuff quickly. The revolving schedule of additional events includes "meet public officials day" (2nd Sunday of the month) and "arts and crafts day" (4th Sunday). ■TIP➡ There are also more prepared-food vendors at the Volcano market than Hilo, with such temptations as a gourmet picnic lunch, fresh-baked croissants and pastries, or homemade Thai food. ⊠ *Cooper Center, Wright Rd.* ☎ *808/967–7800* ⊕ *www.volcanogallery.com/volcano_farmers.htm* ⊗ *Sun. 8–10* AM.

NEED A BREAK?

Lava Rock Cafe (⊠ *Old Volcano Hwy., Volcano* ☎ *808/967–8526*) **is not great for a sit-down meal (slow service), but their to-go "seismic sandwiches" are perfect to bring along for a day of hiking around the park or exploring the rest of the area.**

Volcano Garden Arts. Located on the former Hopper Estate, the Volcano Garden Arts complex includes a gallery, several acres of landscaped sculpture gardens, and dozens of art studios all housed in redwood buildings built in 1908. The grounds are immaculately maintained, and there are several trails leading up to and through the surrounding rain forest. A recently renovated one-bedroom "artist's cottage" is available for rent on the estate grounds as well. ⊠ *19-3438 Old Volcano Rd.* ☎ *808/985–8979* ⊕ *www.volcanogardenarts.com* ✑ *Free* ⊗ *Tues.–Sat. 10–4.*

Volcano Golf Course and Country Club. Don't let the "country club" bit fool you, this is nothing like the snooty courses on the Kohala coast. First off, the green fees are way lower; second, the course is well maintained but not overly manicured; and third, there are rarely crowds so play is continuous and moves quickly. The course itself is reasonably challenging—an 18-hole, par 72 course—but the real draws are the views and the location. It might be the only course in the world built on an active volcano (Kīlauea), with views of Mauna Kea and Mauna Loa, as well as frequent hawk, wild turkey, and nēnē sightings. The small golf course restaurant also serves a great (and cheap) breakfast or lunch. ⊠ *Pi'i Mauna Dr., across from the entrance to Volcanoes National Park* ☎ *808/967–7331* ⊕ *www.volcanogolfshop.com* ☱ *Green fee $63* ⊙ *Daily 7–5.*

Volcano Winery. Lava rock may not seem like ideal soil for the cultivation of grapes, but that hasn't stopped the Volcano Winery from producing award-winning wines

> ### SLOW DOWN, BRO
>
> Speed limits in this area are low for a reason. Paved roads can become unpaved within a few feet; heed the speed limits so that you don't go flying onto a bumpy dirt road at 70 mph. There are also tons of kids riding around on ATVs (and some of them might be going way faster than you're allowed to). It's best to be able to dodge them without landing in a palm tree.

combining their Volcano-grown grapes with various island ingredients. Their Macadamia Nut Honey Wine works well as an after-dinner drink, although it may be a touch too sweet for some. Their white Symphony wines have garnered the most praise from critics and visitors to the winery. The wines here are good, but not amazing. The primary reason to visit is the novelty of the winery itself—wine produced from an active volcano is undeniably interesting and appealing. And it makes for a great, unique (and fairly reasonable) gift to bring home. The winery is in a pleasant setting, looking out over the vineyard and nearby golf course; staff are friendly and helpful; and their gift store has a well-chosen selection of local crafts and goods. ⊠ *35 Pi'i Mauna Dr.* ☎ *808/967–7772* ⊕ *www.volcanowinery.com* ☱ *Free tasting* ⊙ *Daily 10–5:30.*

PUNA

The Puna District is a wild place in every sense of the word. The jagged black coastline is changing all the time; the trees are growing out of control, forming canopies over the few paved roads; the land is dirt-cheap and there are no building codes; and the people, well, there's something about living in an area that could be destroyed by lava at any moment (as Kalapana was in 1990) that makes the laws of modern society seem silly. So it is that Puna has its well-deserved reputation as the "outlaw" region of the Big Island. That said, it's a unique place that's well worth a detour, especially if you're in this part of the island anyway. There are volcanically heated springs, tide pools bursting with interesting sea life, and some mighty fine people-watching opportunities in Pāhoa, a funky little town that the outlaws call home. This is also farm country (yes, that kind of farm, but also the legal sort). Local farmers grow everything from orchids and anthuriums to papayas, bananas, and macadamia nuts. Several of the island's larger, rural residential subdivisions are between Kea'au and Pāhoa, including Hawaiian Paradise Park, Orchidland Estates, Hawaiian Acres, Hawaiian Beaches, and others. When night falls the air fills with the high-

Continued on page 72

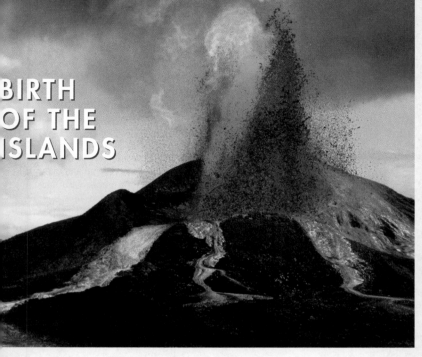

BIRTH OF THE ISLANDS

How did the volcanoes of the Hawaiian Islands evolve here, in the middle of the Pacific Ocean? The ancient Hawaiians believed that the volcano goddess Pele's hot temper was the key to the mystery; modern scientists contend that it's all about plate tectonics and one very hot spot.

Plate Tectonics & the Hawaiian Question: The theory of plate tectonics says that the Earth's surface is comprised of plates that float around slowly over the planet's molten interior. The vast majority of earthquakes and volcanic eruptions occur near plate boundaries—the San Francisco earthquakes in 1906 and 1989, for example, were the result of activity along the nearby San Andreas Fault, where the Pacific and North American plates meet. Hawai'i, more than 1,988 miles from the nearest plate boundary, is a giant exception. For years scientists struggled to explain the island chain's existence—if not a fault line, what caused the earthquakes and volcanic eruptions that formed these islands?

What's a hotspot? In 1963, J. Tuzo Wilson, a Canadian geophysicist, argued that the Hawaiian volcanoes must have been created by small concentrated areas of extreme heat beneath the plates. Wilson hypothesized that there is a hotspot beneath the present-day position of the Big Island. Its heat produced a persistent source of magma by partly melting the Pacific Plate above it. The magma, lighter than the surrounding solid rock, rose through the mantle and crust to erupt onto the sea floor, forming an active seamount. Each flow caused the seamount to grow until it finally emerged above sea level as an island volcano. Plausible so far, but why then, is there not one giant Hawaiian island?

AGE OF VOLCANIC ROCK	
Kaua'i	5.1 million yrs
O'ahu	3 million yrs
Moloka'i	1.8 million yrs
Lāna'i	1.5 million yrs
Maui	1.3 million yrs
Hawai'i	400,000 yrs
Lo'ihi	-100,000 yrs

PACIFIC OCEAN

PACIFIC PLATE

SOLID DENSE ROCK

FIXED HOTSPOT

KEY

▲ Volcano

← Direction of plate movement

Volcanoes on the Move: Wilson further suggested that the movement of the Pacific Plate itself eventually carries the island volcano beyond the hotspot. Cut off from its magma source, the island volcano becomes dormant. As the plate slowly moved, one island volcano would become extinct just as another would develop over the hotspot. After several million years, there is a long volcanic trail of islands and seamounts across the ocean floor. The oldest islands are those farthest from the hotspot. The exposed rocks of Kaua'i, for example, are about 5.1 million years old, but those on the Big Island are less than .5 million years old, with new volcanic rock still being formed.

An Island on the Way: Off the coast of the Big Island, the volcano known as Lo'ihi is still submerged but erupting. Scientists long believed it to be a retired seamount volcano, but in the 1970s they discovered both old and new lava on its flanks, and in 1996 it erupted with a vengeance. It is believed that several thousand years from now, Lo'ihi will be the newest addition to the Hawaiian Islands.

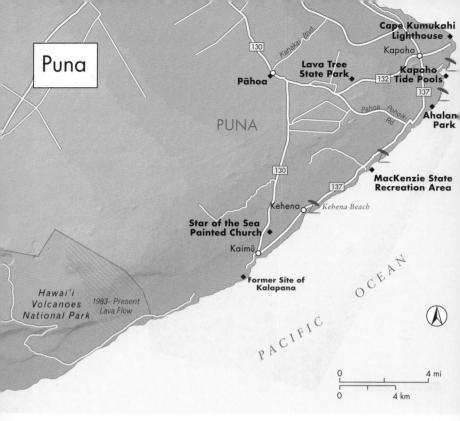

pitched symphony of hundreds of coqui frogs. Though they look cute on the signs and sound harmless, the coqui frogs are a pest both to local crops and to locals, tired of their loud, shrill all-night song.

LOGISTICS   Puna is close to both Hilo and Volcano, and, if you're staying in either place for the night, driving around Puna is a great way to spend a morning. The roads connecting Pāhoa to Kapoho and the Kalapana coast form a loop that's about 25 mi long; driving times are from two to three hours, depending on the number of stops you make and the length of time at each stop. There are restaurants, stores, and gas stations in Pāhoa, but services elsewhere in the region are spotty. There are long stretches of the road that may be completely isolated at any given point; this can be a little scary at night but beautiful and tranquil during the day. Compared to big city living, it's pretty tame, but there is a bit of a "locals only" vibe in parts of Puna, and a growing drug problem in Pāhoa, so don't go wandering around at night.

MAIN ATTRACTIONS

Cape Kumukahi Lighthouse. The lighthouse, 1½ mi east of the intersection of highways 132 and 137, was miraculously unharmed during the 1960 volcano eruption here that destroyed the town of Kapoho. The lava flowed directly up to the lighthouse's base but instead of pushing it over, actually flowed around it. According to Hawaiian legend, Pele, the volcano goddess, protected the Hawaiian fisherfolk by sparing the lighthouse. The lighthouse itself is a simple metal-frame structure with a light on top, similar to a tall electric-line transmission tower. Seeing the hardened lava flows skirting directly around the lighthouse is worth the visit. ⊠ *Past intersection of Hwys. 132 and 137, Kapoho.*

Kapoho Tide Pools. This network of tide pools at the end of Kapoho-Kai Road is great for a swim or a snorkel, or even just a beautiful view of new coastline. Some of the pools are volcanically heated, so if your back's a little sore from exploring the island, stop for a 10-minute soak and you'll feel better immediately. Take the road to the end, turn left, and park. Some of the pools are on private property, but those closest to the ocean, Waiʻōpae (ponds), are open to all. ⊠ *End of Kapoho-Kai Rd., off Hwy. 137.*

MacKenzie State Recreation Area. This is a coastal park located on rocky shoreline cliffs in a breezy, cool ironwood grove. There are picnic tables, restrooms, and a tent-camping area; bring your own drinking water. The park is significant for the restored section of the old "King's Highway" trail system, which circled the coast in the era before Hawaiʻi was discovered by the Western world. In those days, tribal kings and chiefs used these trails to connect the coastal villages, allowing them to collect taxes and maintain control over the people. Short hikes of an hour or less are possible along the existing sections of the rough rocky trail. There are views of rugged coast, rocky beach, and coastal dry forest. ⊠ *Hwy. 137, Puna District.*

Pāhoa. Sort of like a town from the Wild West, this little town is all wooden boardwalks and rickety buildings. The secondhand stores, tie-dye clothing boutiques, and art galleries in quaint old buildings are fun to wander through during the day. Pāhoa's main street boasts a handful of island eateries, the best of which is **Luquin's Mexican Restaurant.** ⊠ *Turn southeast onto Hwy. 130 at Keaʻau, drive 11 mi to right turn marked Pāhoa.*

ALSO WORTH SEEING

Ahalanui Park. This park was established with a federal grant in the mid-1990s to replace those lost to the lava flows at Kalapana. It's 2½ mi south of the intersection of highways 132 and 137 on the Kapoho Coast, southeast of Pāhoa town. There's a half-acre pond fed by thermal freshwater springs mixed with seawater, which makes for a relaxing soak. ■TIP→ **There have been occasional reports of bacterial contamination by the health department, which is typical with hot springs. Check with on-duty lifeguards and follow any posted advisory signs.** Facilities include portable restrooms, outdoor showers, and picnic tables; no drinking water is available. ⊠ *Hwy. 137, 2½ mi south of junction of Hwy. 132, Puna.*

Lava Tree State Park. Tree molds that rise like blackened smokestacks formed here in 1790 when a lava flow swept through the ʻōhiʻa forest. Some reach as high as 12 feet. The meandering trail provides close-up looks at some of Hawaiʻi's tropical plants and trees. There are restrooms and a couple of picnic pavilions and tables. ■TIP→ **Mosquitoes**

live here in abundance, so be sure to bring repellent. ⊠*Hwy. 132, Puna District* ☎*808/974–6200* ☜*Free* ☉*Daily 30 min. before sunrise–30 min. after sunset.*

Star of the Sea Painted Church. This historic church, now a community center, was moved to its present location in 1990 just ahead of the advancing lava flow that destroyed

the Kalapana area. The church, which dates from the 1930s, was built by a Belgian Catholic missionary priest, Father Evarest Gielen, who also did the detailed paintings on the church's interior. Though similar in style, the Star of the Sea and St. Benedict's were actually painted by two different Belgian Catholic missionary priests. Star of the Sea also has several lovely stained-glass windows. ⊠*Hwy. 130, 1 mi north of Kalapana.*

HILO

When compared to Kailua-Kona, Hilo is often described as "the real Hawai'i." With fewer tourists than residents, more historic buildings, and more Hawaiian cultural events, life does seem more Hawaiian on this side of the island. This quaint, traditional fishing village stretches from the banks of the Wailuku River to Hilo Bay, where a few hotels line stately Banyan Drive. The wonderful old buildings that make up Hilo's downtown have recently been spruced up as part of a revitalization effort. Nearby, the 30-acre Lili'uokalani Gardens, a formal Japanese garden with arched bridges and waterways, was created in the early 1900s to honor the area's Japanese sugar-plantation laborers. It also became a safety zone after a devastating tidal wave swept away businesses and homes on May 22, 1960, killing 60 people.

With a population of almost 50,000 in the entire district, Hilo is the fourth-largest city in the state and home to the University of Hawai'i at Hilo. Although it is the center of government and commerce for the island, Hilo is primarily a residential town. Mansions with yards of lush tropical foliage surround older wooden houses with rusty corrugated roofs. It's a friendly community, populated primarily by descendants of the contract laborers—Japanese, Chinese, Filipino, Puerto Rican, and Portuguese—brought in to work the sugarcane fields during the 1800s.

One of the main reasons visitors have tended to steer clear of the east side of the island is its weather. With an average rainfall of 130 inches per year, it's easy to see why Hilo's yards are so green, and its buildings so weather worn. Hilo is rain forests and waterfalls, very unlike the hot and dry white-sand beaches of the Kohala Coast. But when the sun does shine, the snow glistens on Mauna Kea, 25 mi in the distance, and the town sparkles. Most days the rain blows away by noon, leaving behind the colorful arches that earn Hilo its nickname: the City of Rainbows.

LOGISTICS Hilo is a great base for exploring the eastern and southern parts of the island—just be sure to bring an umbrella for sporadic showers. If you're just passing through town or making a day trip, make the first right turn into the town off Highway 19 (it comes up fast) and grab a parking spot in the lot on your left or on any of the surrounding streets. Downtown Hilo is best experienced on foot. The **Downtown Hilo Improvement Association** (✉ *329 Kamehameha Ave.* ☎ *808/935–8850* ⊕ *www.downtownhilo.com* ☉ *Mon.–Fri. 8:30–4:30*) provides an excellent and free self-guided walking tour to downtown Hilo. The tour includes historical information, a map, and directions to 18 historic sites. You can download it from their Web site or pick it up in person at their downtown Hilo office.

> ## FUN THINGS TO DO, HILO SIDE
>
> ■ Enjoy the best shower you've ever had beneath an ancient waterfall.
>
> ■ Watch the world's largest active volcano make the earth beneath your feet.
>
> ■ Take in a starry night on the tallest mountain in the world, Mauna Kea.
>
> ■ Swim with sea turtles at Punalu'u Black Sand Beach, then hike into Green (yes, green) Sand Beach.
>
> ■ Relax in nature's hot tub— the volcanically heated springs of Puna.

There are plenty of gas stations and restaurants in the area. Hilo is a good spot to load up on food and supplies—just south of downtown there are several large budget chains. The Merrie Monarch Hula Festival takes place in Hilo every year during the second week of April, and dancers and admirers flock to the city from all over the world. If you're planning a stay in Hilo during this time, be sure to book your room well in advance.

MAIN ATTRACTIONS

Hilo Farmers' Market. An abundant and colorful market draws farmers and shoppers from all over the island. Bright orchids, anthuriums, and birds-of-paradise create a feast for the eyes, while exotic vegetables, tropical fruits, and baked goods satisfy the stomach. Craft and jewelry makers and clothing vendors round out the market. Don't dawdle, as it closes in the early afternoon. ✉ *Mamo and Kamehameha Sts.* ☉ *Wed. and Sat. 6:30 AM–2:30 PM.*

'Imiloa Astronomy Center. Part Hawaiian cultural center, part astronomy museum, the 'Imiloa Astronomy Center provides an educational and cultural complement to the research being conducted atop Mauna Kea. Although visitors are welcome at Mauna Kea, its primary function is research center—not observatory, museum, or education center. Those roles have been taken on by 'Imiloa in a big way. With its exhibits, full-dome planetarium shows, and regularly scheduled talks and events, the center is a must-see for anyone interested in the stars, the planets, or Hawaiian culture and history. The center, five minutes from downtown Hilo, also provides an important link between the scientific research

Hilo Vicinity

Hilo International Airport

Hilo Bay

Wailoa State Park

SEE INSET 16—17

TO 'IMILOA ASTRONOMY CENTER

Banyan Drive	1	Kalākaua Park	10
Big Island Visitors Bureau	9	Keawe Street	8
Coconut Island	3	Lili'uokalani Gardens	2
Haili Church	11	Lyman Museum & Mission House	13
Hilo Coffee Mill	19	Mauna Loa Macadamia Factory	18
Hilo Farmers' Market	6		

Naha and Pinao stones	12	Pe'epe'e Falls	15
Nani Mau Gardens	16	Rainbow Falls	14
Pacific Tsunami Museum	7	S. Hata Building	5
Pana'ewa Rain Forest Zoo	17	Wailoa Center	4

If Trees Could Talk

CLOSE UP

The history of the trees lining Hilo's Banyan Drive is one of the Big Island's most interesting and least-known stories. Banyan Drive was named for these trees, which were planted by VIP visitors to Hilo. Altogether, some 50 or so banyans were planted between 1933 and 1972.

The majority are Chinese banyans, and each one is marked with a sign naming the VIP who planted it and the date on which it was planted. The first trees were planted on October 20, 1933, by a Hollywood group led by director Cecil B. DeMille, who was in Hilo making the film *Four Frightened People*. Soon after, on October 29, 1933, another banyan was planted by the one and only George Herman "Babe" Ruth, who was in town playing exhibition games.

President Franklin D. Roosevelt planted a tree on his visit to Hilo on July 25, 1934. And in 1935, famed aviatrix Amelia Earhart put a banyan in the ground just days before she became the first person to fly solo across the Pacific Ocean.

Trees continued to be planted along Banyan Drive until World War II. The tradition was then revived in 1952 when a young and aspiring U.S. senator, Richard Nixon of California, planted a banyan tree. Nixon's tree was later toppled by a storm and was replanted by his wife, Pat, during a Hilo visit in 1972. On a bright, sunny day, strolling down Banyan Drive is like going through a green, shady tunnel. The banyans form a regal protective canopy over Hilo's own "Walk of Fame."

---

being conducted at Mauna Kea and its history as a sacred mountain for the Hawaiian people. ⊠*600 'Imiloa Pl., at the UH Hilo Science & Technology Park, off Nowelo and Komohana* ☎*808/969–9700* ⊕*www.imiloahawaii.org* ⊞*$14.50* ☉*Tues.–Sun. 9–4.*

❷ **Lili'uokalani Gardens.** Designed to honor Hawai'i's first Japanese immi-
★ grants, the 30-acre park's fish-filled ponds, stone lanterns, half-moon bridges, elegant pagodas, and ceremonial teahouse make it a favorite Sunday destination. The surrounding area used to be a busy residential neighborhood until a tsunami in 1960 swept the buildings away, taking the lives of 60 people in the process. ⊠*Banyan Dr. at Lihiwai St.* ☎*808/961–8311.*

❶ **Pe'epe'e Falls** *(Boiling Pots).* Four separate streams fall into a series of circular pools, forming the Pe'epe'e Falls. The resulting turbulent action—best seen after a good rain—has earned this stretch of the Wailuku River the name Boiling Pots. ■TIP→ **There's no swimming allowed at Pe'epe'e Falls or anywhere in the Wailuku river, due to dangerous currents and undertows.** ⊠*3 mi northwest of Hilo on Waiānuenue Ave.; keep to right when road splits and look for a green sign for Boiling Pots.*

❶ **Rainbow Falls.** After a hard rain, these falls thunder into the Wailuku
★ River gorge. If the sun peeks out in the morning hours, rainbows form above the mist. ⊠*Take Waiānuenue Ave. west of town 1 mi; when road forks, stay on right of Waiānuenue Ave.; look for Hawaiian warrior sign.*

ALSO WORTH SEEING

1 ★ Banyan Drive. The more than 50 leafy banyan trees with aerial roots dangling from their limbs were planted some 60 to 70 years ago by visiting celebrities. You'll find such names as Amelia Earhart and Franklin Delano Roosevelt on plaques affixed to the trees. ⊠ *Begin at Hawai'i Naniloa Resort, 93 Banyan Dr.*

9 Big Island Visitors Bureau. Marked by a red-and-white Hawaiian warrior sign, the bureau is worth a visit for brochures, maps, and up-to-date, friendly insider advice. ⊠ *250 Keawe St., at Haili St.* ☎ *808/961–5797* ⊕ *www.bigisland.org* ⊙ *Weekdays 8–4:30.*

3 ★ Coconut Island. This small island, just offshore from Lili'uokalani Gardens, is accessible via a footbridge. It was considered a place of healing in ancient times. Today children play in the tide pools while fisherfolk try their luck. ⊠ *Lili'uokalani Gardens, Banyan Dr.*

11 Haili Church. This church was originally constructed in 1859 by New England missionaries, but the church steeple was rebuilt in 1979 following a fire. The Church is known for its choir, which sings hymns in Hawaiian during services. ⊠ *211 Haili St.* ☎ *808/935–4847.*

19 Hilo Coffee Mill. With all the buzz about Kona coffee, it's easy to forget that coffee is produced throughout the rest of the island as well. The Hilo Coffee Mill is a pleasant reminder of that fact. In addition to farming their own coffee on-site, the Mill has partnered with several local small coffee farmers in East Hawai'i in an effort to put the region on the world's coffee map. You can sample the efforts of all of the farmers, as well as touring the Mill and watching the roasters in action. The shop sells coffee and other locally produced goods. Even if you don't have time for the tour or shopping, the Mill's café is a great pit stop on the way to Volcanoes National Park from Hilo. ⊠ *17-995 Volcano Rd., between mile markers 12 and 13, Mountain View* ☎ *808/968–1333* ⊕ *www.hilocoffeemill.com* ⊡ *Free* ⊙ *Mon.–Fri. 8–4.*

10 Kalākaua Park. King Kalākaua, who revived the hula, was the inspiration for Hilo's Merrie Monarch Festival. A bronze statue, erected in 1988, depicts the king with a taro leaf in his left hand to signify the Hawaiian peoples' bond with the land. The park also has a huge spreading banyan tree and small fishponds, but no picnic or recreation facilities. In a local tradition, families that have had recent funerals often leave leftover floral displays and funeral wreaths along the fishpond walkway as a way of honoring and celebrating their loved ones. ⊠ *Kalākaua and Kino'ole Sts..*

NEED A BREAK?

For breads and sandwiches, soups, mouthwatering apple pies, croissants, and biscotti, O'Keefe & Sons Bread Bakers (⊠ *374 Kino'ole St.* ☎ *808/934– 9334*) is the place to go. The tiny retail shop is filled with specialties such as five-grain sourdough, banana bread, and cinnamon toast.

8 Keawe Street. Buildings here have been restored to their original 1920s and '30s plantation styles. Although most shopping is along Kamehameha Avenue, the ambience on Keawe Street offers a nostalgic sampling of Hilo as it might have been 80 years ago.

⑬ Lyman Museum & Mission House. Built in 1839 for David and Sarah Lyman, Congregationalist missionaries, the Lyman House is the oldest frame building on the island. In the adjacent museum, dedicated in 1973, there's a realistic magma chamber and exhibits on the islands' formation. There's also an interesting section on Hawaiian flora and fauna. The gift shop sells Hawaiian books, cards, gifts, and music. ✉*276 Haili St.* ☎*808/935–5021* ⊕*www.lymanmuseum.org* 🖃*$10* ⊙*Mon.–Sat. 9:30–4:30.*

⑱ Mauna Loa Macadamia Factory. Acres of macadamia trees lead to a processing plant with viewing windows. A videotape depicts the harvesting and preparation of the nuts, and there are free samples in the visitor center. Children can run off their energy on the nature trail. ✉*Macadamia Rd. off Hwy. 11, 5 mi south of Hilo* ☎*808/966–8618* ⊕*www. maunaloa.com* ⊙*Daily 8:30–5:30.*

⑫ Naha and Pinao stones. These two huge, oblong stones are legendary. The Pinao stone is purportedly an entrance pillar of an ancient temple built near the Wailuku River. King Kamehameha is said to have moved the 5,000-pound Naha stone when he was still in his teens. Legend decreed that he who did so would become king of all the islands. They're in front of the Hilo Public Library. ✉*300 Waiānuenue Ave.*

⑯ Nani Mau Gardens. The name means "forever beautiful" in Hawaiian,
★ and that's a good description of this 20-acre botanical garden filled with several varieties of fruit trees and hundreds of varieties of ginger, orchids, anthuriums, and other exotic plants. A botanical museum details the history of Hawaiian flora, and guided tours by tram are available. There's also a café with a lunch buffet. ✉*421 Makalika St., off Hwy. 11* ☎*808/959–3500* ⊕*www.nanimau.com* 🖃*$10, tram tour $15* ⊙*Daily 8–5.*

❼ Pacific Tsunami Museum. A memorial to all those who lost their lives in
☼ the tragedies that have struck this side of the island, this small museum offers a poignant history of tsunamis. In a 1931 C. W. Dickey–designed building—the former home of the First Hawaiian Bank—you'll find an interactive computer center, a science room, a theater, a replica of Old Hilo Town, a children's corner, and a knowledgeable, friendly staff. In the background, a striking quilt tells a silent story. ✉*130 Kamehameha Ave.* ☎*808/935–0926* ⊕*www.tsunami.org* 🖃*$7* ⊙*Mon.–Sat. 9–4.*

❼ Pana'ewa Rain Forest Zoo. Children enjoy the spider monkeys, the pygmy
☼ hippopotamus, and the white tiger (feedings are every day at 3:30) in this quiet zoo, the only rain-forest zoo in the United States. There is a variety of native Hawaiian species, such as the state bird, the *nēnē* (Hawaiian goose), as well as a small petting zoo every Saturday 1:30–2:30. ✉*Left on Mamaki off Hwy. 11, just past the "Kulani 19, Stainback Hwy" sign* ☎*808/959–7224* ⊕*www.hilozoo.com* 🖃*Free* ⊙*Daily 9–4.*

❺ S. Hata Building. Erected as a general store in 1912 by Sadanosuke Hata and his family, this historic structure now houses shops, restaurants, offices, and a museum called Mokupapapa: Discovery Center for Hawai'i's Remote Coral Reefs. During World War II the Hatas were interned and the building confiscated by the U.S. government. When the war was over, a daughter repurchased it for $100,000. A beautiful example of Renaissance-revival architecture, it won an award from the state for the authenticity of its restoration. ⊠*308 Kamehameha Ave., at Mamo St.*

❹ Wailoa Center. This circular exhibition center, adjacent to Wailoa State Park, has shows by local artists that change monthly. There's also a photographic exhibit of the 1946 and 1960 tsunamis. Just in front of the center is a 12-foot-high bronze statue of King Kamehameha I, made in Italy in the late 1980s. Check out his gold Roman sandals. ⊠*Pi'opi'o St. off Kamehameha Ave.* ☎*808/933–0416* ⊙*Mon., Tues., Thurs., and Fri. 8:30–4:30, Wed. noon–4:30, Sat. 9:30–3.*

HĀMĀKUA COAST

The spectacular waterfalls, mysterious jungles, emerald fields, and stunning ocean vistas along Highway 19 northwest of Hilo are collectively referred to as the Hilo–Hāmākua Heritage Coast. Brown signs featuring a sugarcane tassel reflect the area's history: thousands of acres of sugarcane are now idle, with no industry to support since "King Sugar" left the island in the early 1990s. The 45-mi drive winds through little plantation towns, Pāpa'ikou, Laupāhoehoe, and Pa'auilo among them. It's a great place to wander off the main road and see "real" Hawai'i— untouched valleys, overgrown banyan trees, tiny coastal villages. In particular, ■ TIP→ the "Heritage Drive," a 4-mi loop just off the main highway, is well worth the detour. Once back on Highway 19, you'll pass the road to Honoka'a, which leads to the end of the road bordering Waipi'o Valley, ancient home to Hawaiian royalty. The isolated valley floor has maintained the ways of old Hawai'i, with taro patches, wild horses, and a handful of houses.

LOGISTICS Any turn off along this coast could lead to an incredible view, so take your time and go exploring. Where there's a gorge there's usually a waterfall, and many of them fall into lovely swimming holes, so you might want to bring both hiking shoes and a swimsuit. Gas stations, stores, and restaurants are hard to come by on the coast, so it's a good idea to fuel up your car and your tummy before hitting the road. ■ TIP→ If you're driving from Kailua-Kona, rather than driving around the northern tip of the island, cut across on the Mamalahoa Highway (190) to Waimea and then catch the 19 to the coast.

If you've stopped to explore the quiet little villages with wooden boardwalks and dogs dozing in backyards, or if you've spent several hours in Waipi'o Valley, night will undoubtedly be falling by the time you've had your fill of the Hāmākua Coast. Don't worry: the return to Hilo via Highway 19 only takes about an hour, or you can continue on the same road to stop for dinner in Waimea (30 minutes) before heading back to

DID YOU KNOW

The dramatic 'Akaka Falls
is only one of hundreds of
waterfalls on the Hāmākua
Coast. Many falls tumble into
pristine swimming holes, so
bring your swimsuit when
you explore this area.

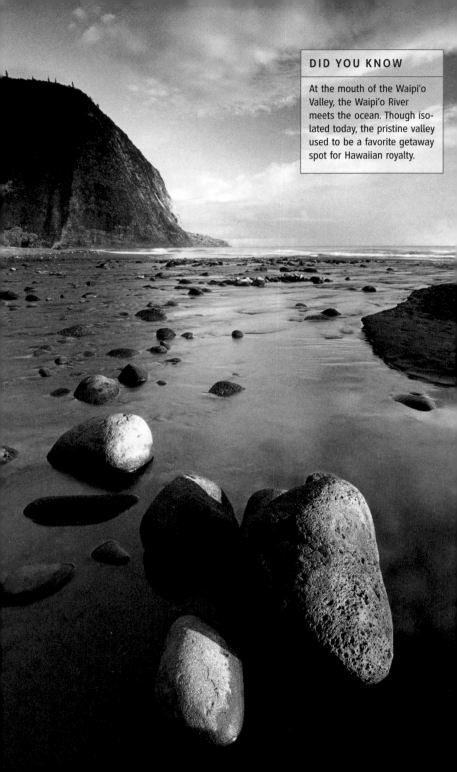

DID YOU KNOW

At the mouth of the Waipi'o Valley, the Waipi'o River meets the ocean. Though isolated today, the pristine valley used to be a favorite getaway spot for Hawaiian royalty.

the Kohala Coast resorts (another 25 to 45 minutes). Although you shouldn't have any trouble exploring the Hāmākua coast in a day, a handful of romantic B&Bs are available along the coast if you want to spend more time.

MAIN ATTRACTIONS

★ **'Akaka Falls State Park.** A meandering 10-minute loop trail takes you to the best spots to see the two cascades, **'Akaka** and **Kahuna.** The 400-foot Kahuna Falls is on the lower end of the trail. The majestic upper 'Akaka Falls drops more than 442 feet, tumbling far below into a pool drained by Kolekole Stream amid a profusion of fragrant white, yellow, and red torch ginger. ✉ *4 mi inland off Hwy. 19, near Honomū* ☎ *808/974–6200* ✉ *Free* ⊙ *Daily 7–7.*

Fodor's Choice
★ **Waipi'o Valley.** Bounded by 2,000-foot cliffs, the Valley of the Kings

WAIPI'O

If the steep [...] Valley is n[...] pect, cons[...] range fro[...] depending on the [...] the transport mode.

Na'alapa Stables (☎ *808/775–0419* ⊕ *www.naalapastables.com*) Horseback riding trips.

Waipi'o Ridge Stables and Waipi'o Rim Backroad Adventures (☎ *808/775–7291 for stables, 808/775–1122 for backroad adventures* ⊕ *www.waipioridgestables.com*) Horseback riding, 4x4, or ATV trips.

Waipi'o Valley Shuttle (☎ *808/775–7121*) Four-wheel-drive tours.

was once a favorite retreat of Hawaiian royalty. Waterfalls drop 1,200 feet from the Kohala Mountains to the valley floor, and the sheer cliff faces make access difficult. Though completely off the grid today, Waipi'o was once the center of Hawaiian life; somewhere between 4,000 and 20,000 people made it their home between the 13th and 17th centuries. In 1780 Kamehameha I was singled out here as a future ruler by reigning chiefs. In 1791 he fought Kahekili in his first naval battle at the mouth of the valley. In 1823 the first white visitors found 1,500 people living in this Eden-like environment amid fruit trees, banana groves, taro fields, and fishponds. The 1946 tidal wave drove most residents to higher ground.

Now, as then, waterfalls frame the landscape, but the valley has become one of the most isolated places in the state. To preserve this pristine part of the island, commercial transportation permits are limited—only four outfits offer organized valley trips—and Sunday the valley rests. A four-wheel-drive road leads down from the **Waipi'o Valley Overlook** (✉ *Follow Hwy. 240 8 mi northwest of Honoka'a*), but only four-wheel-drive vehicles should attempt the steep road. The walk down into the valley is less than a mile from here—but keep in mind, the climb back up is strenuous in the hot sun. A crescent of black sand makes it a popular spot for surfers. ■ TIP→ **Continued overuse of the beach area and lack of sanitary facilities have caused serious unhealthy conditions to persist since 2003. Until it's cleaned up we don't recommend getting into the water.**

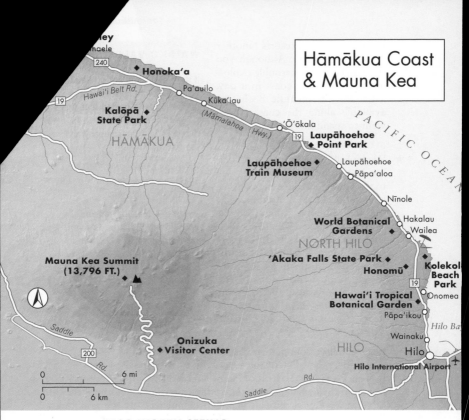

ALSO WORTH SEEING

★ **Hawai'i Tropical Botanical Garden.** Eight miles north of Hilo, stunning coastline views appear around each curve of the 4-mi scenic jungle drive that accesses the privately owned nature preserve beside Onomea Bay. Paved pathways in the 17-acre botanical garden lead past ponds, waterfalls, and more than 2,000 species of plants and flowers, including palms, bromeliads, ginger, heleconia, orchids, and ornamentals. ⊠*27-717 Old Māmalahoa Hwy., Pāpa'ikou* ☎*808/964–5233* ⊕*www.hawaiigarden.com* ⊠*$15* ☉*Daily 9–4.*

Honoka'a. In 1881 Australian William Purvis planted the first macadamia-nut trees in Hawai'i near what is now this funky little town. But Honoka'a's true heyday came when sugar was king in the early part of the 20th century. During World War II, this was the place for soldiers stationed around Waimea to cut loose. Today, little eateries and stores crammed with knickknacks, secondhand goods, and antiques occupy its historic buildings. ⊠*Mamane St., Hwy. 240.*

NEED A BREAK?

A quick stop at Tex Drive-In (⊠*45-690 Pakalana St. and Hwy. 19* ☎*808/775–0598*) will give you a chance to taste the snack that made it famous: *malasada,* a puffy, doughy Portuguese doughnut without a hole. These deep-fried

CLOSE UP

Pele & the Night Marchers

The best-known deity in Hawaiian lore is Pele, the beautiful volcano goddess. Although visitors are warned not to remove lava rocks from Pele's domain without her permission, some do and find themselves dogged by bad luck until they return the stolen items. The Hawai'i Volcanoes National Park Service often receives packages containing chunks of lava along with letters describing years of misfortune.

Tales of Pele's fiery temper are legendary. She battled Poli'ahu, ruler of snowcapped Mauna Kea on the Big Island, in a fit of jealousy over the snow goddess's extraordinary beauty. She picked fights with her peace-loving sister, Hi'iaka, turning the younger goddess's friends into pillars of stone. And her recurring lava-flinging spats with suitor Kamapua'a, a demigod who could change his appearance at will, finally drove him into the sea, where he turned into a fish to escape her wrath. In addition to battling the elements and each other, gods were thought to have intervened in the daily lives of early Hawaiians. Storms that destroyed homes and crops, a fisherman's poor catch, or a loss in battle were blamed on the wrath of angry gods.

According to legend, an industrious race of diminutive people called *menehune* built aqueducts, fishponds, and other constructs requiring advanced engineering knowledge unavailable to early Hawaiians. Living in remote hills and valleys, these secretive workers toiled only in darkness and completed complex projects in a single night. Their handiwork can still be seen on all the Islands.

Also at night, during certain lunar periods, a traveler might inadvertently come across the Night Marchers—armies of dead warriors, chiefs, and ancestral spirits whose feet never touch the ground. They float along the ancient highways, chanting and beating their drums, pausing only to claim the spirits of their brethren who died that night. It was believed that such an encounter would bring certain death unless a relative among the marchers pleaded for the victim's life.

beauties are best eaten hot. They also come in cream-filled versions, including vanilla, chocolate, and coconut.

Honomū. A plantation past is reflected in the wooden boardwalks and tin-roof buildings of this small, struggling town. It's fun to poke through old dusty shops such as Glass from the Past, where you'll find an assortment of old bottles. The Woodshop Gallery/Café showcases local artists. ⊠ *2 mi inland from Hwy. 19 en route to 'Akaka Falls State Park.*

☼ ★ **Kalōpā State Park.** Past the old plantation town of Pa'auilo, at a cool elevation of 2,000 feet, lies this 100-acre state park. There's a lush forested area with picnic tables and restrooms, and an easy ¾-mi loop trail with additional paths in the adjacent forest reserve. Small signs identify some of the plants. ⊠ *12 mi north of Laupāhoehoe and 3 mi inland off Hwy. 19* ☎ *808/775–8852* ☜ *Free* ☉ *Daily 7–7 or by permit.*

Kolekole Beach Park. This rocky beach on the Kolekole River offers an idyllic setting for a barbecue or picnic. A large banyan tree leans over

The world's largest optical and infrared telescopes are located at the Keck Observatory on Mauna Kea's summit.

the river, and its rope swing is a hit with local kids during lazy summer days. An old train bridge crosses the river where it empties into the ocean. The surf can be rough, so only experienced swimmers should venture past the river's mouth. Back on the road, a scenic drive takes you from the top of the park through the old town of Wailea back to Highway 19. ⊠ *Off Hwy. 19* ☎ *808/961–8311* 🎟 *Free* ⊗ *Daily 7 AM–sunset.*

Laupāhoehoe Point Park. Come here to watch the surf pound the jagged black rocks at the base of the stunning point. This is not a safe place for swimming, however. Still vivid in the minds of longtime area residents is the 1946 tragedy in which 21 schoolchildren and three teachers were swept to sea by a tidal wave. ⊠ *On northeast coastline, Hwy. 19, makai side, north of Laupāhoehoe* ☎ *808/961–8311* 🎟 *Free* ⊗ *Daily 7 AM–sunset.*

Laupāhoehoe Train Museum. Behind the stone-loading platform of the once-famous Hilo Railroad, constructed around the turn of the 20th century, the former manager's house is a poignant reminder of the era when sugar was the local cash crop. The railroad, used to transport sugar from the plantations to the port, was one of the most expensive built in its time. It was washed away by the 1946 tsunami. Today one of the old engines is running again on a short Y-track at the museum. ⊠ *Hwy. 19, Laupāhoehoe* ☎ *808/962–6300* 🎟 *$3* ⊗ *Weekdays 9– 4:30, weekends 10–2.*

🕒 **World Botanical Gardens.** About 300 acres of former sugarcane land are slowly giving way to a botanical center, which includes native Hawaiian plants such as orchids, palms, gingers, hibiscus, and heliconias. In the 10-acre arboretum children love to wind their way through a maze made of shrubs. From within the gardens you have access to splendid views of one of the prettiest waterfalls on the isle, triple-tiered **Umauma Falls.** You may feel a little bit cheated, since it's $8 per person to essentially drive in, park, get out, and view the falls from a distance, but unfortunately this is the only place to view Umauma without some pretty rigorous hiking and scrambling. ⊠*Hwy. 19, from Hilo just past mile marker 16* ☎*808/963–5427* ⊕*www.wbgi.com* ☑*$8* ⊗*Mon.–Sat. 9–5:30.*

MAUNA KEA

You can go snowboarding in Hawai'i. Seriously. You do have to be in pretty good shape and a close-to-expert boarder to get up the mountain and down again with no lifts, but lack of snow is definitely not a problem. Mauna Kea is the antithesis of the typical island experience. Freezing temperatures and arctic conditions are common at the summit, and snowstorms can occur year-round. From its base below the ocean's surface to its summit, Mauna Kea is the tallest island mountain on the planet. It's also home to Lake Waiau, one of the highest lakes in the world.

In addition to being a unique spot in all the ways mentioned above, Mauna Kea's summit—at 13,796 feet—is reputedly the clearest place in the world for viewing the night sky. For this reason, the summit is home to the world's largest astronomical observatory. Research teams from eleven different countries operate 13 telescopes on Mauna Kea, several of which are record-holders: the world's largest optical/infrared telescopes (the Keck telescopes), the world's largest dedicated infrared telescope (UKIRT), and the largest submillimeter telescope (the JCMT).

Mauna Kea is tall, but there are taller mountains in the world, so what makes this spot so great for astronomy? It has more to do with atmosphere than with height. A tropical inversion cloud layer below the summit keeps moisture from the ocean and other atmospheric pollutants down at lower elevations. As a result, the air around the Mauna Kea summit is extremely dry, which helps in the measurement of infrared and submillimeter radiation from stars, planets, and the like. There are also no clouds; the annual number of clear nights here blows every other place out of the water. And, because the mountain is far away from any interfering lights (not a total coincidence—in addition to the fact that the nearest town is nearly 30 mi away, there is an official ordinance limiting light on the island) skies are dark for the astronomers' research. To quote the staff at the observatory, astronomers here are able to "observe the faintest galaxies that lie at the very edge of the observable Universe."

Teams from various universities have used the telescopes on Mauna Kea to make major astronomical discoveries, including new satellites

BIG ISLAND SIGHTSEEING TOURS

Guided tours on the island are great for specific things: seeing Mauna Kea, exploring Waipi'o Valley, maybe even touring Volcanoes National Park (especially if your time is short). Sticking to a guided tour the whole time, though, would not be a great idea. Half the fun of the island is in exploring it on your own. Plus, if you stick to a guided tour, you'll only see the major tourist attractions, none of the Big Island's many hidden treasures.

Local tour-bus operators conduct volcano tours and circle-island tours, with pickup at the major resorts. Costs range from $38 to $160, depending on pickup location and length of tour. The circle-island tour is a full 12-hour day, but Jack's and Polynesian Adventure Tours also offer half-day tours to the volcano, Mauna Kea observatory, and around Kailua-Kona. Hawai'i Forest & Trail offers a volcano tour, Mauna Kea tour, several other specific sights tours, and the option of customizing a private tour.

Jack's Tours. ☎ 808/329–2555 in Kona, 808/961–6666 in Hilo, 800/442–5557 ⊕ www. jackstours.com.

Polynesian Adventure Tours. ☎ 808/329–8008 in Kona, 800/622–3011 ⊕ www.polyad.com.

Roberts Hawai'i. ☎ 808/329–1688 in Kona, 808/966–5483 in Hilo, 800/831–5541 ⊕ www.roberts hawaii.com.

Hawai'i Forest & Trail. ☎ 808/464–1993 ⊕ www.hawaii-forest.com.

around Jupiter and Saturn, new "Trojans" (asteroids that orbit, similar to moons) around Neptune, new moons and rings around Uranus, and new moons around Pluto. Their studies of galaxies are changing the way scientists think about time and evolution.

What does all this mean for you? In addition to the best sunrises and sunsets—we're gonna go ahead and say it—in the world, a visit to Mauna Kea is a chance to see more stars than you've likely ever seen before and an opportunity to learn more about mind-boggling scientific discoveries in the very spot where these discoveries are being made. A trip to Mauna Kea may just be the highlight of your trip.

If you have a budding interest in astronomy, be sure to visit the 'Imiola Astronomy Center in Hilo *(See Hilo, above)*. The Center has presentations and planetarium films about the mountain and the science being conducted there.

LOGISTICS Mauna Kea is only 34 mi from Hilo and 18 from Waimea, but the drive takes an hour to an hour and a half from Hilo and half an hour to an hour from Waimea thanks to some rough driving. Between the ride there, sunset on the summit, and stargazing, we recommend allotting at least four hours for your Mauna Kea visit.

There are a few potential obstacles to enjoying Mauna Kea, but nothing you can't avoid with a little planning. The first hurdle is getting there. To reach the summit, you must drive on Saddle Road. Saddle Road, which is a shortcut across the island, is a steep and winding

2

road with no services, and parts of it are unpaved and rough. The road to the Visitor Center at Mauna Kea is fine, but the road from there to the summit is a bit more precarious, unpaved, and very steep. Thanks to recent improvements on Saddle Road, visitors no longer have to worry about rental cars making it up the mountain. Although the road from the Visitor Center to the summit is still unpaved, most cars can make it up slowly, and 4-wheel-drive vehicles won't have any trouble at all. If you're worried about your rental making the drive, you can still head for the summit with one of a handful of tour operators who will take care of everything. If you plan to drive yourself, fill up on gas and bring water and snacks with you, as there is nowhere along the way to stock up.

The second thing, which is extremely important to remember, is the altitude. ■TIP→ **Whether you're hiking or driving to the summit, take the change in altitude seriously—stop at the Visitor Center for at least half an hour, and don't overexert yourself, especially at the top.** Scuba divers must wait at least 24 hours before attempting a trip to the summit to avoid getting the bends. The observatory recommends that children under 16, pregnant women, and those with heart, respiratory, or weight problems not go higher than the Visitor Center.

The last potential obstacle: it's cold. The military personnel stationed in Hawai'i do their cold-weather training atop Mauna Kea. It is cold, and the snow never completely melts. It's difficult to find cold weather clothing in Hawai'i, so, if you plan to visit Mauna Kea, pack your favorite warm things from home.

ONIZUKA VISITOR CENTER

★ **Onizuka Center for International Astronomy Visitor Information Station.** At a 9,300-foot elevation, this is the best amateur observation site on the planet, with a handful of telescopes and a knowledgeable staff. It hosts nightly stargazing sessions from 6 to 10. This is also where you should stop to acclimate to the altitude if you're heading for the summit. On weekends the Onizuka Center offers escorted summit tours, heading up the mountain in a caravan. Reservations are not required for the free tours, which depart at 1 PM. To get here from Hilo, which is about 34 mi away, take Highway 200 (Saddle Rd.), and turn right at mile marker 28 onto the John A. Burns Way, which is the access road to the summit. ☎808/961–2180 ⊕www.ifa.hawaii.edu/info/vis ☉Daily 9 AM–10 PM.

THE SUMMIT

Head to the summit either just before sunset or, if you don't mind driving the steep road in the dark, after night has fallen. Only the astronomers are allowed to use the telescopes and equipment up here, but the scenery can be enjoyed by anyone. So, watch the sun sink into the horizon and then head down to the Visitor Center to warm up and stargaze. Or do your stargazing first and then head up here to get a different perspective—if you were blown away by the number of stars crowding the sky over the Visitor Center, this vantage point will really make you speechless. Just take it easy if you're driving back down in the dark—slow and cautious is the name of the game on this steep road.

If you haven't rented a four-wheel-drive vehicle, don't want to deal with driving to the summit, or don't want to wait in line to use the handful of telescopes at the Visitor Center, consider booking a tour. Operators provide transportation to and from the summit, and expert guides; some also provide parkas, gloves, telescopes, dinner, hot beverages, and snacks. Excursion fees range from $90 to $185.

Arnott's Lodge & Hiking Adventures. A bit cheaper than the others at $90 per person, Arnott's tours leave from Hilo; their tour does not include dinner, and they do not bring warm clothing for guests or their own telescope. Focusing more on the experience of the mountain than astronomy, Arnott's brings binoculars for each guest and provides an informative lesson on major celestial objects and Polynesian navigational stars. ☎ *808/969–7097* ⊕ *www.arnottslodge.com.*

Hawai'i Forest & Trail. This outfitter stops for dinner along the way at a historic ranch, and brings parkas, gloves, and their own telescope along. Cookies and hot chocolate make cold stargazing more pleasant. The price is $165 per person. ☎ *808/331–8505 or 800/464–1993* ⊕ *www.hawaii-forest.com.*

Jack's Tours. Jack's follows the same itinerary as the other tours—sunset on the summit, followed by stargazing from the Visitor Center. They take larger groups than the other outfitters, and their guides speak English and Japanese. Boxed dinner, hot tea, bottled water, light snack, telescopes, and use of jackets and gloves are included. The price is $165 per person. ☎ *800/442–5557* ⊕ *www.jackstours.com.*

Mauna Kea Summit Adventures. As the first company to specialize in tours to the mountain and the only company to offer only Mauna Kea tours, Mauna Kea Summit Adventures has a bit more cred than the rest of the pack. They use cushy new van coaches for their tours, bring along parkas and gloves, and serve dinner at the Visitor Center before heading up to sunset on the summit. They also bring along their own powerful telescope. The price is $185 per person. ☎ *808/322–2366* ⊕ *www. maunakea.com.*

Onizuka Visitor Center Tours. If you want to charge the summit with a group but don't fancy paying for one of the tours above, consider joining one of the Visitor Center's free summit tours, which depart from 1 PM to 5 PM every Saturday and Sunday. Reservations are not required, but a 4-wheel-drive vehicle is—visitors follow the center's staff up the summit in their own cars. ☎ *808/961–2180* ⊕ *www.ifa. hawaii.edu/info/vis.*

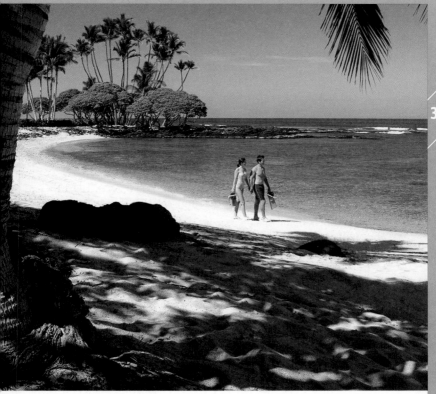

Beaches

WORD OF MOUTH

"The Hāpuna beach is great, free of anything but soft sand. If you want a beach, the Hāpuna beach and the Mauna Kea beach are the best swimming beaches in the [Kohala] area."

—sandinmytoes

Updated
by Amy
Westervelt

Don't believe anyone who tells you that the Big Island lacks beaches. It's just one of the myths about Hawai'i's largest island that has no basis in fact.

It's not so much that the Big Island has fewer beaches than the other islands, just that there's more island, so getting to the beaches can be slightly less convenient. That said, there are plenty of those perfect white-sand stretches you think of when you hear "Hawai'i," and the added bonus of black- and green-sand beaches, thanks to the age of the island and its active volcanoes. New beaches appear and disappear regularly, created and destroyed by volcanic activity. In 1989 a black-sand beach, Kamoamoa, formed when molten lava shattered as it hit cold ocean waters; it was closed by new lava flows in 1992. It's part of the ongoing process of the volcano's creation and change dynamic.

The bulk of the island's beaches are on the northwest part of the island, along the Kohala Coast. Black-sand beaches and green-sand beaches are in the southern region, along the coast nearest the volcano. On the eastern side of the island, beaches tend to be of the rocky-coast–surging-surf variety, but there are still a few worth visiting, and this is where the Hawaiian shoreline is at its most picturesque.

KOHALA COAST

Most of the white sandy beaches are found on the Kohala Coast, which is, understandably, home to the majority of the island's first-class resorts. Hawai'i's beaches are public property. The resorts are required to provide public access to the beach, so don't be frightened off by a guard shack and a fancy sign. There is some limited public parking as well. The resort beaches aside, there are some real hidden gems on the Kohala Coast accessible only by boat, four-wheel drive, or a 15- to 20-minute hike. It's well worth the effort to get to at least one of these. ■TIP➡ **The west side of the island tends to be calmer, but still the surf gets rough in winter.** The beaches here are listed in order from north (farthest from Kailua-Kona) to south.

Pololū Valley Beach. On the North Kohala peninsula is one of the Big Island's most scenic black-sand beaches. About 8 mi past Hāwī town, Highway 270 terminates at the overlook of remote Pololū Valley. Beach access is gained by a 15-minute hike down (twice as long back up) a generally steep and rocky trail that can be muddy and slippery. Caution is advised. The beach itself is a nice wide expanse of fine black sand surrounded by sheer green cliffs and backed by high dunes dotted with pine trees. A gurgling stream leads from the beach to the back of the valley. ■TIP➡ **This is not a particularly safe swimming beach even though locals do swim, bodyboard, and surf here. Dangerous rip currents and usually rough surf pose a real hazard.** And because this is a remote, isolated area far from emergency help, extreme caution is advised. The valley leading back from the beach was once farmed with taro patches but is

DID YOU KNOW

Most locals rate Hāpuna Beach, with its long expanse of white sand, the best beach on the island. Its turquoise water is calm during summer but rougher in winter.

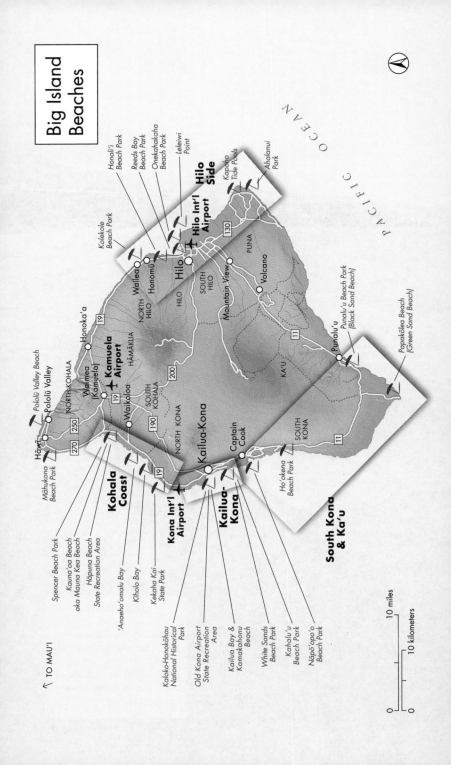

Big Island
Beaches

PACIFIC OCEAN

↖ TO MAU'I

Kohala Coast

Māhukona Beach Park
Spencer Beach Park
Kauna'oa Beach aka Mauna Kea Beach
Hāpuna Beach State Recreation Area
'Anaeho'omalu Bay
Kīholo Bay
Kekaha Kai State Park

Kailua-Kona

Kaloko-Honokōhau National Historical Park
Old Kona Airport State Recreation Area
Kailua Bay & Kamakahonu Beach
White Sands Beach Park
Kahalu'u Beach Park
Nāpō'opo'o Beach Park

South Kona & Ka'u

Ho'okena Beach Park

Kona Int'l Airport

Pololū Valley Beach

Hāwī
Pololū Valley

270
250
NORTH KOHALA

Honoka'a

Waimea (Kamuela)
Kamuela Airport

19
Waikoloa
SOUTH KOHALA
HĀMĀKUA

19
190
200

NORTH KONA

Kailua-Kona

Captain Cook
SOUTH KONA

11

NORTH HILO
SOUTH HILO
HILO

Kolekole Beach Park
Honoli'i Beach Park
Reeds Bay Beach Park
Onekahakaha Beach Park
Leleiwi Point

Wailea
Honomū
Hilo

Hilo Int'l Airport

Hilo Side

130

Mountain View
PUNA

Volcano

Kapoho Tide Pools

Ahalanui Park

Punalu'u Beach Park (Black Sand Beach)
Papakōlea Beach (Green Sand Beach)

Punalu'u
KA'U
11

0   10 miles
0   10 kilometers

no longer being used. There is very limited parking at the turnaround and along the roadside here. ⊠*End of Hwy. 270* ☞*No facilities.*

Māhukona Beach Park. Snorkelers and divers will find excitement in the clear waters of this small beach park. Long ago, when sugar was the economic staple of Kohala, this harbor was busy with boats waiting for overseas shipments. Now it's a great swimming hole and an underwater museum of sorts. Remnants of shipping machinery, train wheels and other parts, and what looks like an old boat are easily visible in the clear water. There's no sandy beach here, but a ladder off the old dock makes getting in the water easy. It's best to venture out only on tranquil days, when the water is calm. A camping area is available. ⊠*Off Hwy. 270, between mile markers 14 and 15, Māhukona* ☎*808/961–8311* ☞*Toilets, showers, picnic tables, grills, parking lot.*

> ### TOP BEACHES
>
> ▪ Kauna'oa Beach (also known as Mauna Kea Beach) is a beautiful palm-lined golden crescent.
>
> ▪ Hāpuna Beach is a wide expanse of fine sandy playground and aquamarine water.
>
> ▪ 'Anaeho'omalu Beach's lovely curving crescent provides lots of water sports options.
>
> ▪ Makalawena has fine sand, turquoise water, and is generally uncrowded.
>
> ▪ Punalu'u Beach Park has black sand *and* guaranteed turtle-watching.

☺ **Spencer Beach Park.** This smaller beach, gently sloping with white sand and a few pebbles, is popular with local families because of its reef-protected waters. ▪ TIP➔ **It's probably the safest beach in west Hawai'i for young children.** It's also safe for swimming year-round, which makes it an excellent spot for a lazy day at the beach. Unfortunately, it does tend to get crowded on weekends, and the beach is often dotted with litter, but the water is crystal clear, although there aren't loads of fish here. The beach park lies just below Pu'ukoholā Heiau National Historic Park, site of the historic temple built by King Kamehameha the Great in 1795. ⊠*Off Hwy. 270, uphill from Kawaihae Harbor* ☎*808/961–8311* ☞*Lifeguard, toilets, showers, picnic tables, grills, parking lot.*

Fodor'sChoice ★ **Kauna'oa Beach** (Mauna Kea Beach). Hands-down one of the most beautiful beaches on the island, Kauna'oa is a long white crescent of sand. The beach, which fronts the Mauna Kea Beach Hotel, slopes very gradually. It's a great place for snorkeling. When conditions permit, there is good body- and board surfing also. Currents can be strong, and powerful winter waves can be dangerous, so be careful. At this writing, the Mauna Kea Beach Hotel was closed for repairs to damages sustained in the 2006 earthquake, but the hotel's outdoor Hau Tree gazebo bar and restrooms are still open to beachgoers. ▪ TIP➔ **While the hotel undergoes renovation, there are more public parking spots than usual, but when it reopens public spots will again be limited to only 30, in which case it's best to arrive before 10 AM. If the lot is full, head to nearby Hāpuna Beach, where a huge parking lot is never full, and try this spot** again a different morning. ⊠ *Off Hwy. 19; entry through gate to Mauna Kea Beach Resort* ☞ *Lifeguard, toilets, showers, parking lot.*

Fodor'sChoice
★

Hāpuna Beach State Recreation Area. By any measurement, this is one fine beach. Guidebooks usually say it's a toss-up between Hāpuna and Kauna'oa for "best beach" on the island, but most locals give the prize to Hāpuna. There is ample parking so you don't have to get here at dawn, although the lot can fill up by midday. And while the north end of the beach fronts the Hāpuna Beach Prince Hotel, rest assured that this is a public beach. The beach itself is a long (½-mi), white, perfect crescent, one of the Big Island's largest. The turquoise water is very calm in summer, with just enough rolling waves to make bodysurfing or boogie boarding fun. There's some excellent snorkeling around the jagged rocks that border the beach on either side, but a strong current means it's only for experienced swimmers. In winter, surf can be very rough. Hāpuna tends to get a little windy in the late afternoon; even that can have a benefit, as everyone else leaves just in time to give you a private, perfect sunset. ■TIP➔ **There are a couple of small protected coves at the north end of the beach with shallow, sandy-bottomed pools ideal for youngsters.** ⊠ *Hwy. 19, near mile marker 69, at Hāpuna Beach Prince Hotel* ☎ *808/974–6200* ☞ *Lifeguard, toilets, showers, food concession, picnic tables, grills/fire pits, parking lot.*

★ **'Anaeho'omalu Beach (A-Bay).** This expansive beach of golden sand mixed with black lava grains fronts the Waikoloa Beach Marriott and is perfect for swimming, windsurfing, snorkeling, and diving. It's along a well-protected bay, so even when surf is rough on the rest of the island, it's fairly calm here. Snorkel gear, kayaks, and boogie boards are available for rent at the north end. Graceful coconut palms line the beach and behind it are two old Hawaiian fishponds, Ku'uali'i and Kahapapa, that served the Hawaiian royalty in the old days. A walking trail follows the coastline to the Hilton Waikoloa Village next door, passing by tide pools and ponds. Footwear is recommended for the trail. ⊠ *Follow Waikoloa Beach Dr. to Kings' Shops, then turn left; parking lot and beach right-of-way south of Waikoloa Beach Marriott* ☞ *Toilets, showers, food concession, picnic tables, parking lot.*

Kīholo Bay. The brilliant turquoise waters of this bay are a cooling invitation on a warm Kohala day, and a new gravel road to the shoreline makes it an absolute must-see (previously you'd have to hike over lava for 20 minutes). Thanks to Mauna Loa, what was once the site of King Kamehameha's gigantic fishpond is now several freshwater ponds

Kua Bay is protected from wind by the rocky shores that surround it.

encircling a beautiful little bay. The water's a bit cold and hazy because of the mix of fresh and salty water, but there are tons of green sea turtles in residence year-round here, and the snorkeling is great. If you follow the shoreline southwest toward Kona, just past the big yellow house is another public beach where you'll find some naturally occurring freshwater pools inside a lava tube. This area, called Queen's Bath, is as cool as it sounds. ⊠*Hwy. 19, gravel road between mile markers 82 and 83* ☞*No facilities.*

Kua Bay. Remoteness does have its merits at this lovely beach, the northernmost beach in the stretch of coast that comprises Kekaha Kai State Park. At one time you had to hike over a few miles of unmarked, rocky trail to get here, which kept many people out. Now, a newly paved road leads to Kua Bay, and while locals are pretty unhappy about it, this beach is still relatively uncrowded compared to others. It's easy to understand why area residents would be so protective. This is one of the most beautiful bays you will ever see—the water is crystal clear, deep aquamarine, and peaceful in summer. Rocky shores on either side keep the beach from getting too windy in the afternoon. The surf here can get very rough in winter. ⊠*Hwy. 19, north of mile marker 88* ☞*No facilities.*

★ **Makalawena.** Makalawena is a long white crescent, dotted with little coves and surrounded by dunes and trees. The sand is powdery fine, the water is perfect, and the place is deserted. If it weren't so hard to get to, this would be the unanimous choice for best beach on the island.

BEACH SAFETY

Hawai'i's world-renown, beautiful beaches can be extremely dangerous at times due to large waves and strong currents—so much so that the state rates wave hazards using three signs: a yellow square (caution), a red stop sign (high hazard) and a black diamond (extreme hazard). Signs are posted and updated three times daily or as conditions change.

Visiting beaches with lifeguards is strongly recommended, and you should only swim when there's a normal caution rating. Never swim alone or dive into unknown water or shallow breaking waves. If you're unable to swim out of a rip current, tread water and wave your arms in the air to signal for help.

Even in calm conditions, there are other dangerous things in the water to be aware of, including razor-sharp coral, jellyfish, eels and sharks, to name a few.

Jellyfish cause the most ocean injuries, and signs are posted along beaches when they're present. Box jellyfish swarm to Hawaii's leeward shores 9-10 days after a full moon. Portuguese Man-o-War are usually found when winds blow from the ocean onto land. Reactions to a sting are usually mild (burning sensation, redness, welts); however, in some cases they can be severe (breathing difficulties). If you are stung by a jellyfish, pick off the tentacles, rinse the affected area with water and apply ice. Seek first-aid from a lifeguard if you experience severe reactions.

According to state sources, the chances of getting bitten by a shark in Hawaiian waters are very low; sharks attack swimmers or surfers three or four times per year. Of the 40 species of sharks found near Hawai'i, tiger sharks are considered the most dangerous because of their size and indiscriminate feeding behavior (they eat just about anything at the water's surface). Tiger sharks are easily recognized by their blunt snouts and vertical bars on their sides.

Here are a few tips to reduce your shark-attack risk:

■ Swim, surf, or dive with others at beaches patrolled by lifeguards.

■ Avoid swimming at dawn, dusk, and night, when some shark species may move inshore to feed.

■ Don't enter the water if you have open wounds or are bleeding.

■ Avoid murky waters, harbor entrances, areas near stream mouths (especially after heavy rains), channels, or steep drop-offs.

■ Don't wear high-contrast swimwear or shiny jewelry.

■ Don't swim near dolphins, which are often prey for large sharks.

■ If you spot a shark, leave the water quickly and calmly; never provoke or harass a shark, no matter how small.

The Web site *www.oceansafety.soest. hawaii.edu* provides beach hazard maps for O'ahu, Maui, Kaua'i and the Big Island, as well as weather and surf advisories, listings of closed beaches, and safety tips.

Like Kua Bay, Mahai'ula and Ka'elehuluhulu, it is within Kekaha Kai State Park, but it is the most remote. You either have to rent a boat and anchor there, walk 20 minutes on a rough coastal trail over lava rock terrain, or take a brutal four-wheel-drive jaunt over the lava. (You still have to walk the last 5 to 10 minutes.) But it's worth it. Makalawena is more than just a great beach—it's a truly magical place. An afternoon here is a recipe for delirious happiness. Locals bodyboard here occasionally, but a jetty on the north end of the beach creates a calm area for swimming even when the surf's up a bit. Did we mention that there are wild goats hanging around on the trail leading to the beach? There's a freshwater pond that beats hosing off at one of those water-spigot showers at the marked public beaches. ⚠ **The walk over the lava isn't too bad if you're steady on your feet, but remember to wear sturdy shoes, pack light, and make sure you have sunscreen on before heading out, as most of the trail is exposed to direct sun.** ⊠ *Hwy. 19, between mile markers 88 and 89; if you're walking, park in lot at Kekaha Kai State Park and follow footpath along the shore* ☞ *No facilities.*

Kekaha Kai State Park. A 1.5-mi narrow, bumpy gravel road leads off Highway 19 to this recently developed beach park. Mahai'ula is to the south while Ka'elehuluhulu is to the north. The wide expanse of good sandy beach provides a lot of space here, so it doesn't feel crowded. There are high sand dunes and tidal pools for snorkeling and swimming. The sand is a salt and pepper mix of golden and black lava grains and pebbles. ⚠ **Caution is advised for rough surf and strong currents.** You can hike along a historic 4½-mi trail from one beach to the other, but be prepared for the heat and bring lots of drinking water. ⊠ *Hwy. 19, sign about 2 mi north of Keāhole–Kona International Airport marks rough road* ☎ *808/327–4958 or 808/974–6200* ☞ *Parking lot at entrance, Mahai'ula: Toilets, picnic area; Ka'elehuluhulu: No facilities.*

KAILUA-KONA

There are a few good sandy beaches in the area near Kailua-Kona town. However, the coastline is generally rugged black lava rock, so don't expect long stretches of wide golden sand. The beaches near Kailua-Kona get lots of use by local residents and visitors will enjoy them, too. Excellent snorkeling and scuba diving, good swimming, kayaking, and other water sports are easy to find. The beaches here are listed from north to south.

Kaloko–Honokōhau National Historical Park. There are few beaches with as many old Hawaiian archaeological ruins as these three, sheltered in a 1,160-acre park near Honokōhau Harbor, just north of Kailua-Kona town. All are good for swimming. **'Ai'opio** (☞ *Toilets*), a few yards north of the harbor, is a small beach with calm, protected swimming areas (good for kids) and great snorkeling in the water near the archaeological site of Hale o Mono. **Honokōhau Beach** (☞ *No facilities*), a ¾-mi stretch with ruins of ancient fishponds, is also north of the harbor. At the north end of the beach, a historic trail leads *mauka* (toward the mountains) across the lava to a pleasant freshwater pool

SUN SAFETY

Hawai'i's weather—seemingly never-ending warm, sunny days with gentle trade winds—can be enjoyed year-round with good sun sense. Because of Hawai'i's subtropical location, the length of daylight here changes little throughout the year. The sun is particularly strong, with a daily UV average of 14. Visitors should take extra precaution to avoid sunburns and long-term cancer risks due to sun exposure.

The Hawai'i Dermatological Society recommends these sun safety tips:

■ Plan your beach, golf, hiking, and other outdoor activities for the early morning or late afternoon, avoiding the sun between 10 am and 4 pm when it's the strongest.

■ Apply a broad-spectrum sunscreen with a sun protection factor (SPF) of at least 15. Hawai'i lifeguards use sunscreens with an SPF of 30. Cover areas that are most prone to burning like your nose, shoulders, tops of feet and ears. And don't forget to use sun protection products on your lips.

■ Apply sunscreen at least 30 minutes before you plan to be outdoors and reapply every two hours, even on cloudy days. Clouds scatter sunlight so you can still burn on an overcast day.

■ Wear light, protective clothing, such as a long-sleeve shirt and pants, broad-brimmed hat, and sunglasses.

■ Stay in the shade whenever possible—especially on the beach—by using an umbrella. Remember that sand and water can reflect up to 85 percent of the sun's damaging rays.

■ Children need extra protection from the sun. Apply sunscreen frequently and liberally on children over six months of age and minimize their time in the sun. Sunscreen is not recommended for children under six months.

called Queen's Bath. A Hawaiian settlement until the 19th century, the area is being developed as a cultural and historical site. **'Alula** (☞*No facilities*) is a slip of white sand at the south end of the harbor, a short walk over lava to the left of the harbor entrance. The park, which is still undergoing development, seeks to preserve early Hawaiian archaeological resources including *heiau* (an ancient Hawaiian place of worship), house platforms, fishponds, petroglyph rock etchings, and more. The park's wetlands provide refuge to a number of waterbirds, including the endemic Hawaiian stilt and coot. For information about the park, visit its headquarters, a 5- to 10-minute drive away. ✉*74-425 Keal-*

The calm Kailua Bay is an excellent spot for rowing, snorkeling, and swimming.

akehe Pkwy., off Hwy. 19 ☎*808/329–6881* ⊕*www.nps.gov* ⊙*Park road gate 8* AM*–3:30* PM ☞*Toilets, food concession, parking lot.*

Old Kona Airport State Recreation Area. The unused runway—great for jogging—is still visible above this palm-tree-lined beach at Kailua Park, a popular place to picnic, beachcomb, and sunbathe. It's especially busy on weekends. The generally rocky shoreline has a few small pocket coves of white sand with safe entry to the water and tide pools for children, but for adults it's better for snorkeling than swimming. Conditions are best here on calmer days. An offshore surfing break known as Old Airport is popular with local surfers. ⊠*North end of Kuakini Hwy., Kailua-Kona* ☎*808/327–4958 or 808/974–6200* ☞*Toilets, showers, picnic tables, parking lot.*

☺ **Kailua Bay & Kamakahonu Beach.** Kids will especially enjoy this small pocket beach where they can play in the sand, ride waterbikes, paddle kayaks, and splash in the calm water. Fronting the King Kamehameha's Kona Beach Hotel and next to Kailua Pier, this little crescent of white sand is the only beach in downtown Kailua-Kona. Protected by the harbor, the calm water makes this a perfect spot for kids; for adults it's a great place for a swim and a lazy beach day. The water is surprisingly clear for being surrounded by an active pier. Snorkeling can be good, especially if you move south from the beach. There's a kiosk with snorkeling and kayaking equipment rentals. ■ TIP➔ **A little family of sea turtles likes to hang out next to the seawall, so keep an eye out.** On a small peninsula protecting the beach is the reconstructed Ahuʻena Heiau, the recognized temple of King Kamehameha the Great, who spent the last years of his life here at Kamakahonu. ⊠ *Ali'i Dr.* ☞ *Toilets available on the adjacent boat pier.*

White Sands, Magic Sands, or Disappearing Sands Beach. Towering coconut trees provide some shade and lend a touch of tropical beauty to this pretty little beach park, which may well be the Big Island's most intriguing stretch of sand. A migratory beach of sorts, it goes away in winter and returns in summer: Winter waves wash away the small white-sand parcel. In summer it re-forms; you'll know you've found it when you see the body- and board surfers. Though not really a great beach, this is a popular summer hangout for young locals. ⊠ *Ali'i Dr., 4½ mi south of Kailua-Kona* ☎ *808/961–8311* ☞ *Lifeguard, toilets, showers, food concession, parking lot.*

Kahalu'u Beach Park. Snorkelers can actually hand-feed the unusually tame reef fish at this spot, although we advise against it—certain human foods may not kill them, but fish fed by humans become dependent on easy feedings and start to lose their survival instincts. Don't even get us started on the folks who think it's okay to feed candy to the fish. Kahalu'u was a favorite of King Kalākaua, whose summer cottage is on the grounds of the neighboring Outrigger Keauhou Beach Resort. The salt-and-pepper beach is a combination of white and black sand mixed with lava and coral pebbles. This is one of the Big Island's most popular swimming and snorkeling sites, thanks to the fringing reef that helps keep the waters calm. But outside the reef there are very strong rip currents, so caution is advised. ■ TIP→ **Experienced surfers find good waves to ride beyond the reef, and scuba divers like the shore dives—shallow ones inside the breakwater, deeper ones outside.** A narrow path leads directly to the hotel's Kalanikai Bar & Grill (open daily 11 AM–4 PM), which serves beverages, sandwiches, and plate lunches. ⊠ *Ali'i Dr., 5½ mi south of Kailua-Kona* ☎ *808/961–8311* ☞ *Lifeguard, toilets, showers, food concession, picnic tables, parking lot.*

SOUTH KONA & KA'Ū

You wouldn't expect to find sparkling white-sand beaches on the rugged and rocky coasts of South Kona and Ka'ū, and you won't. What you will find is something a bit more rare and well worth the visit: black- and green-sand beaches. And there's the chance to see the endangered Hawaiian green sea turtles close up. Beaches are listed here from north to south.

Nāpō'opo'o Beach Park. There's no real beach here, but don't let that deter you—this is a great spot and a historically significant one. It's where Captain James Cook landed in late 1778 to refurbish his ships; when he returned in 1779 he was killed in a skirmish with Hawaiians. A monument marks the spot on the north end of the bay. Kealakekua Bay is surrounded by high green cliffs, so the water's usually fairly calm and clear, making it ideal for swimming. Bring a mask along, as the snorkeling in the Kealakekua Bay Underwater Marine Reserve is

ADMIRING THE MARINE LIFE

Big Island beach tidal pools and shallow reef areas are exciting places to explore and discover unique marine life. To be safe: wear protective gloves and proper footwear. Watch for any high surf activity. Avoid sharp rocks and coral heads, as cuts can be painful and get infected, and by bumping into coral you may severely damage it. Many marine creatures have natural defenses like sharp teeth, spines, stingers, and even venom. So don't pick up unknown creatures and don't stick fingers into crevices in rocks or reefs where creatures may lurk.

Another big don't? Don't feed the fish or turtles. While some human food may not harm them immediately, if wild animals get used to being fed by humans, they'll lose both the ability to forage as well as their natural wariness, which makes them easy prey for poachers.

superb. It's a great place to spot varied marine life, schools of colorful reef fish, corals, and more. This is also a great kayaking spot, and there are several shops in the villages of Honalo, Kainaliu, Kealakekua, and Captain Cook along Highway 11 that rent kayaks, in addition to snorkel gear. You can also take a snorkel, scuba, or glass-bottom boat tour from Keauhou Bay. ⚠ **An earthquake in October 2006 caused rocks and dirt from the surrounding cliff to fall into the bay. The beach is now open except for an off-limits area next to the cliff marked by orange buoys.** ⊠ *End of Nāpō'opo'o Rd., off Hwy. 11, Kealakekua Bay* ☎ *808/961–8311* ☞ *Parking lot.*

Ho'okena Beach Park. Driving south on Highway 11 from Kealakekua Bay, you'll see the sign for Ho'okena Beach Park. The road down to the quiet, out-of-the-way beach is narrow and steep, but the views are great. Plus you'll feel like you're venturing off the beaten path. By Hawaiian standards, this is an average beach (the water's nice for swimming, and there's a bit of snorkeling but nothing amazing), but that still makes it great for the rest of us. It's frequented mostly by the people from the nearby village; it's rarely crowded, except on weekends. The smallish beach, blessed with a few shade trees, is composed of black and white sand mixed with lava debris, which gives the sand an overall gray color. The bay is usually calm for swimming, snorkeling, and diving but caution is advised during high surf periods. ⊠ *2-mi*

drive down road bordered by ruins of stone wall off Hwy. 11, 23 mi south of Kailua-Kona ☎808/961–8311 ☞*Toilets, showers, picnic tables, parking lot.*

RESPECT MOTHER NATURE

Mother Nature is still creating the Big Island's beaches, thanks to its flowing lava. Although it's tempting to take a souvenir container of black, green, or golden sand, you can assist in protecting and preserving the Big Island's beaches by not removing sand. As the old slogan goes, "Take nothing but pictures, and leave nothing but footprints."

★ **Papakōlea Beach (Green Sand Beach).** Tired of the same old gold-, white-, or black-sand beach? Then how about a green-sand beach? You'll need good hiking shoes or sneakers at the very least to get to this olive-green crescent, one of the most unusual beaches on the island. It lies at the base of Pu'u o Mahana, at Mahana Bay, where a cinder cone formed during an early eruption of Mauna Loa. The greenish tint is caused by an accumulation of olivine crystals that form in volcanic eruptions. The dry, barren landscape is totally surreal. The surf is often rough and swimming is hazardous due to strong currents, so caution is advised, but a dip in the clear, turquoise water, surrounded by green sand and gray cliffs sculpted into Gaudí-like shapes by the wind, may well be the highlight of your trip. Take the road toward the left at the end of the paved road to Ka Lae (South Point) about 12 mi off Highway 11. Park at the end of the road. ⚠ **Anyone trying to charge you for parking is running a scam.** Hikers can follow the 2-mi coastal trail, which will end in a steep and dangerous descent down the cliff side on an unimproved trail. Although hikers can cross the private Hawaiian Home Lands without a permit to get to the beach, those wanting to take a 4WD vehicle along the rugged coast trail are supposed to first contact the Department of Hawaiian Home Lands in Hilo (☎808/974–4250). However, there is very rarely anyone around actually checking for permits. ■TIP➡ **There is no guarantee of open access to 4WD vehicles, and sometimes the trail is closed even to foot traffic. Though the simple gate blocking the trail is not exactly a huge deterrent, it may be locked for a good reason—dangerous surf, a rock slide—so it's a good idea to check before going around it.** ✉2½ *mi northeast of South Point, off Hwy. 11* ☞*No facilities.*

★ **Punalu'u Beach Park (Black Sand Beach).** The endangered Hawaiian green sea turtle nests in the black sand of this beautiful and easily accessible beach. You can see them feeding on the seaweed along the surf break or napping on the sand. You can even swim with the turtles; they're used to people and will swim along right next to you. (Resist the urge to touch them, though.) However, strong shoreward currents make being in the water here a hazard. Don't venture far out, and avoid going out past the boat ramp as very strong rip currents are active. ■TIP➡ **It's quite rocky in the water, even close to shore—you might want to bring a pair of reef shoes if you plan to swim.** The beach is a long black-sand crescent backed by low dunes with some rocky outcroppings at the shoreline. It's not usually a tranquil spot, though, since the turtles attract big groups of picture-snapping visitors. At its northern end, near the boat ramp, lie the ruins of Kaneʻeleʻele Heiau, an old Hawaiian temple. This area used to be a sugar port until the tidal wave of 1946 destroyed the buildings. Inland is a memorial to Henry ʻŌpūkahaʻia. In 1809, when he was 17, ʻŌpūkahaʻia swam out to a fur-trading ship in the harbor and asked to sign up as a cabin boy. When he reached New England, he entered the Foreign Mission School in Connecticut, but he died of typhoid fever in 1818. His dream of bringing Christianity to the Islands inspired the American Board of Missionaries to send the first Protestant missionaries to Hawaiʻi in 1820. ⊠ *Hwy. 11, 27 mi south of Hawaiʻi Volcanoes National Park* ☎ *808/961–8311* ☞ *Toilets, showers, food concession, grills/fire pits, parking lot.*

HILO SIDE

There are no real beaches along the jagged cliffs of the Hāmākua Coast, but there are a few surf spots and swimming holes worth an afternoon stop. These spots are rarely crowded, and they're surrounded by lush rain forest. Hilo isn't exactly known for its beautiful white beaches, but there are a few in the area that provide good swimming and snorkeling opportunities. Puna's few beaches have some unique attributes—swaths of black sand, volcano-heated springs, and a coastline that is beyond dramatic (sheer walls of lava rock dropping into the bluest ocean you've ever seen). Beaches are listed from north to south.

Kolekole Beach Park. This small beach park is a picture postcard of tropical Hawaiʻi. The Kolekole Stream meets the ocean here between ʻAkaka and Umauma Falls, just below a high bridge that crosses the gulch along Highway 19. The beach is composed of large, smooth, waterworn lava rocks. Although the shoreline is rocky, the stream is calm and great for swimming. There's even a rope swing tied to a banyan tree on the opposite side. The stream flows from the lovely tropical ʻAkaka Falls Park located about 4 mi upstream. Even though the park is only fair for beach activities, it's surrounded by vegetation and is ideal for a picnic. Local surfers like this spot in the winter. ■ TIP➔ **Where the stream meets the ocean, the surf is rough and the currents strong. Only very experienced swimmers should venture here.** ⊠ *Off Hwy. 19* ☎ *808/961–8311* ⊡ *Free* ☉ *Daily 7 AM–sunset* ☞ *Toilets, showers, picnic tables, grills, parking lot.*

Honoli'i Beach Park. There aren't many places along the east Hawai'i coastline to catch the waves when the surf's up, but this is one of the best. It's popular among the local surf crowd, and it's fun to watch the surfers paddle out to catch the waves. ■ TIP→ **The presence of surfers is not an indication that an area is safe for swimmers.** The sandy beach is minimal here, a mix of sand and coral rubble debris along the mostly rocky coast. There's limited parking beside the narrow roadside. ⊠ *1.5 mi north of Hilo on Hwy. 19* 🕿 *808/961–8311* ☞ *Toilets.*

Reeds Bay Beach Park. Safe swimming, proximity to downtown Hilo, and a freshwater-fed swimming hole called "the Ice Pond" that flows into the backwaters of Hilo Bay are the enticements of this cove. No, there really isn't ice in the swimming hole; it just feels that way on a hot sultry day. The large pond, between Hilo Seaside Hotel and Harrington's Restaurant, is a favorite of local kids who enjoy jumping into and frolicking in the chilly fresh- and saltwater mix. There is no real beach here, however. ⊠ *Banyan Dr. and Kalaniana'ole Ave., Hilo* 🕿 *808/961–8311* ☞ *No facilities.*

Onekahakaha Beach Park. A white-sand beach with a shallow, enclosed tide pool makes this a favorite for Hilo families with small children. The protected tidal pools are great places to look for Hawaiian marine life such as small fish, brittle stars, sea cucumbers, seashells, sea urchins, and more. The water is usually rough beyond the line of large boulders protecting the inner tide pools. Caution is advised in times of heavy surf. ⊠ *Kalaniana'ole Ave., 3 mi east of Hilo* 🕿 *808/961–8311* ☞ *Lifeguard, toilets, showers, picnic tables, parking lot.*

Leleiwi Beach Park and Richardson Ocean Park. There's hardly any sand here near road's end in Keaukaha, east of Hilo, but these two beaches make up one beautiful spot—laced with bays, inlets, lagoons, and pretty

THE ROAD TO THE SEA?

You may have heard whispers about another green-sand beach on the island. There is indeed a beach at end of the Road to the Sea, the entrance to which is ¼ mi before mile marker 81 on Highway 11. However, the road has been closed since 2005 and remains closed at this writing. The reasons: the road down is very rough, plus most of the surrounding land is private and the owners don't want tourists getting stuck on their property. Even if the road does reopen, it's probably not worth the effort—the better-known Green Sand Beach is much nicer and easier to get to.

3

Hilo Side
Big Island

Kolekole Beach Park
Onekahakaha Beach Park
Kapoho Tide Pools
Ahalanui Park
Honoli'i Beach Park
Leleiwi Beach Park
Reeds Bay Beach Park
Hilo
10 miles
15 km
11
130
Pāhoa
132
137

BEACHCOMBING WITH KIDS

Youngsters love to comb the beach for seashells and other treasures. Here are some beachcombing tips:

■ Find a tide chart in the local newspaper, on TV, or online to check the times of high and low tides.

■ Check out the beach with a walk at low tide. Note the high tide lines by observing the location of the debris piles.

■ Return at high tide or just after it the next morning. Begin your beach-combing at those high tide debris piles noted earlier. Bring along a

small garden trowel or rake to sift through the sand. Also bring a nylon mesh bag—a plastic bag or a small container will also work—to collect seashells.

■ Slightly rockier beaches like Kahalu'u in Kona and Punalu'u Black Sand Beach are your best bets for finding interesting and intact shells.

■ Before leaving the beach with your finds, rinse excess black or green sand out of the shells you find at the Big Island's newer and more unusual beaches—or risk the wrath of Pele when you return home.

parks. It's a peaceful setting for a lazy day at the beach; the grassy area is ideal for picnics. Rocky outcrops provide shelter for schools of reef fish, and snorkeling can be great, as turtles and dolphins frequent this area. Local kids use the small black sand pocket beach for bodyboarding. ⊠ *2349 Kalaniana'ole Ave., 4 mi east of Hilo* ☎ *808/961–8311* ⌕ *Lifeguard (on weekends), picnic tables, parking lot.*

Kapoho Tide Pools. Snorkelers will find tons of coral and the fish who feed off it in this network of tide pools at the end of Kapoho-Kai Road. This is a great place for getting close-up looks at Hawai'i's interesting marine life and reef fish. Some of the pools have been turned into private swimming pools; those closest to the ocean are open to all. The pools are usually very calm, and some are volcanically heated. It's best to come during the week, as the pools can get crowded on the weekend. Note: there is no real sandy beach here. Take the road to the end, then turn left and park. ⊠ *End of Kapoho-Kai Road, off Hwy. 13, about 9 mi southeast of Pāhoa town* ⌕ *No facilities.*

Ahalanui Park. This 3-acre beach park has a ½-acre pond—fresh spring water mixed with seawater—heated by volcanic steam. There's nothing like swimming in this geothermal pool, but the nearby ocean is rough. ■ TIP→ **The pool has had ongoing bacterial contamination problems that are typical of some ocean tidal pools in Hawai'i.** Those with skin-lesion problems, or chronic conditions like psoriasis may want to avoid the water here. Others should have no problem. Check with the lifeguard on duty, and heed all posted signs. ⊠ *Hwy. 137, 2½ mi south of junction of Hwy. 132* ☎ *808/961–8311* ⌕ *Lifeguard, toilets, showers, picnic tables, grills.*

4

Water Activities & Tours

WORD OF MOUTH

"If snorkeling and kayaking are high on your list, go to the Big Island. Have been to Maui and Kona many times and love both equally, but in my opinion the snorkeling is a little better on the Big Island. Don't miss kayaking and snorkeling in Kealakekua Bay."

— sceneisle

Updated
by Amy
Westervelt

The ancient Hawaiians, who took much of their daily sustenance from the ocean, also enjoyed playing in the water. In fact, surfing was the sport of kings. Though it's easy to be lulled into whiling away the day baking in the sun on a white, golden, black, or green sand beach, getting into and onto the water will be a highlight of your trip to the Big Island.

All of the Hawaiian Islands are surrounded by the Pacific Ocean, making them some of the world's greatest natural playgrounds. But certain experiences are even better on the Big Island: nighttime scuba diving trips to see manta rays; deep-sea fishing in Kona's fabled waters, where dozens of Pacific blue marlin of 1,000 pounds or more have been caught; kayaking among the dolphins in Kealakekua Bay; and sighting humpback whales on a whale-watching cruise. With underwater coral reefs and marine preserves harboring endemic and endangered species, such as the Hawaiian green sea turtle and the Hawaiian monk seal, plus tropical fish in a rainbow of colors, snorkelers are in paradise.

From any point on the Big Island, the ocean is never far away. With the variety of water sports that can be enjoyed—from boogie boarding and snorkeling to jet skiing and surfing—there is something for everyone. For most activities, you can rent gear and go it alone or sign up for a group excursion with an experienced guide, who can offer security as well as special insights into Hawaiian marine life and culture. Want to try surfing? You can take lessons as well.

The Kona and Kohala Coasts of west Hawai'i have the largest number of ocean sports outfitters and tour operators. They operate from the small boat harbors and piers in Kailua-Kona, Keauhou, and at the Kohala Coast resorts. There are also several outfitters in the east Hawai'i and Hilo areas.

As a general rule, the waves are gentler here than on other Islands, but there are a few things to be aware of before heading to the shore. First, don't turn your back on the ocean. It's unlikely, but if conditions are right a wave could come along and push you face-first into the sand or drag you out to sea. Conditions can change quickly, so keep your eyes open. Second, realize that ultimately you must keep yourself safe. We strongly encourage you to obey lifeguards and park rangers stationed on the beaches of the Big Island, and to heed the advice of outfitters from whom you rent equipment. It could save your trip, or even your life.

BOOGIE BOARDING & BODYSURFING

According to the movies, in the Old West there was always friction between cattle ranchers and sheep ranchers. Some will say the same situation exists between surfers and boogie boarders. Sure, there's some good-natured trash-talking between the groups, but nothing more. The truth is, boogie boarding is a blast. The only surfers who don't do it are hardcore surfing purists, and almost none of that type live on this island.

■TIP→ Novice boogie boarders should use smooth-bottom boards, wear protective clothing (or at least T-shirts), and catch shore waves only. You'll need a pair of short fins to get out to the bigger waves offshore (not recommended for newbies). As for bodysurfing, just catch a wave and make like Superman going faster than a speeding bullet.

BEST SPOTS

When conditions are right, **Hāpuna Beach State Recreation Area** (⊠*Hwy. 19, near mile marker 69*) is fabulous. The water is very calm in summer, with just enough rolling waves for bodysurfing or boogie boarding. But this beach north of Kailua-Kona isn't known as the "broken-neck capital" for nothing. Ask the lifeguards about conditions before heading into the water, and remember that if almost no one is in the water, there's a good reason for it.

Much of the sand at **White Sands, Magic Sands, or Disappearing Sands Beach Park** (⊠*Ali'i Dr., 4½ mi south of Kailua-Kona*) washes out to sea and forms a sandbar just offshore. This causes the waves to break in a way that's great for intermediate or advanced boogie boarding. No wonder the Magic Sands Bodysurfing Contest, which brings out hardcore bodysurfers each winter, is held here. This small beach can get pretty crowded. There can be nasty rip currents at high tide. ■TIP→ If you're not using fins, wear reef shoes because of the rocks.

North of Hilo, **Honoli'i Cove** (⊠*Access road off Hwy. 19, just past mile marker 4*) is the best boogie boarding–surfing spot on the east side of the island. Keep in mind that it is also one of the few good boarding spots in east Hawai'i, and boogie boarders and surfers need to share the space.

EQUIPMENT

Equipment rental shacks are located at many beaches and boat harbors, along the highway, and at most resorts. Boogie board rental rates are $10 to $12 per day and $50 to $60 per week. Ask the vendor if he'll throw in a pair of fins—some will for no extra charge.

Honolua Surf Company ⊠*75-5744 Ali'i Dr., Kona Shopping Village, Kailua-Kona* ☎*808/329–1001.*

Orchid Land Surf Shop ⊠*262 Kamehameha Ave., Hilo* ☎*808/935–1533* ⊕*www.orchidlandsurf.com.*

Pacific Vibrations ⊠*75-5702 Likana La., at Ali'i Dr., Kailua-Kona* ☎*808/329–4140.*

Snorkel Depot ⊠*75-5703 Ali'i Dr., Kailua-Kona* ☎*808/334–1919.*

Boogie boarding is popular on the Big Island.

DEEP-SEA FISHING

Along the Kona Coast you can find some of the world's most exciting "blue-water" fishing. Although July, August, and September are peak months, with the best fishing and a number of tournaments, charter fishing goes on year-round. You don't have to compete to experience the thrill of landing a Pacific blue marlin or other big-game fish. More than 60 charter boats, averaging 26 to 58 feet, are available for hire, most of them out of **Honokōhau Harbor,** north of Kailua-Kona.

For an exclusive charter, prices generally range from $350 to $700 for a half-day trip (about four hours) and $600 to $950 for a full day at sea (about eight hours). For share charters, rates range from $100 to $140 per person for a half-day and $200 for a full day. If fuel prices continue increasing, expect charter costs to rise. Most boats are licensed to take up to six passengers, in addition to the crew. Tackle, bait, and ice are furnished, but you'll usually have to bring your own lunch. You won't be able to keep your catch, although if you ask, many captains will send you home with a few fillets.

Big fish are weighed in daily at **Honokōhau Harbor's Fuel Dock.** Show up at 11 AM to watch the weigh-in of the day's catch from the morning charters, or 3:30 PM for the afternoon charters. If you're lucky, you'll get to see a "grander" weighing in at 1,000-plus pounds. A surprising number of these are caught just outside Kona Harbor. ■ TIP➔ **On Kona's Waterfront Row look for the "Grander's Wall" of anglers with their prizes.**

BOATS & CHARTERS

Before you sign up with anyone, think about the kind of trip you want. Looking for a romantic cruise? A rockin' good time with your buddies? Serious fishing in one of the "secret spots"? A family-friendly excursion? Be sure to describe your expectations so your booking agent can match you with a captain and a boat that suits your style.

Charter Locker. This company can provide information on various charter boat fishing trips and make all the arrangements—they can even book you on the luxurious *Blue Hawai'i,* which has air-conditioned staterooms for overnight trips. ⊠ *74-425 Kealakehe Pkwy., Honokōhau Harbor, Kailua-Kona* ☎ *808/326–2553* ⊕ *www.charter locker.com.*

> ## BIG ISLAND, BIG FISH
>
> Along the Kona Coast, deep-sea fishermen pursue several species of game fish. The most sought after is, of course, the Pacific blue marlin, averaging 300 to 400 pounds, though "granders" of 1,000 pounds and up are not unusual. Mid-size catches include the striped marlin (averaging 150 pounds), the black marlin (around 200 pounds), and the broadbill swordfish (up to 250 pounds). The much sought after ahi (yellowfin tuna) can range up to 300 pounds. The smaller guys, weighing in from about 20 to 50 pounds, include spearfish, sailfish, *aku* (skipjack tuna), ono (wahoo), and the prized mahimahi (dolphin fish).

Charter Services Hawai'i. This booking service represents several Kona fishing boats and can assist with all the details in arranging a charter. ☎ *808/334–1881 or 800/567–2650* ⊕ *www.konazone.com.*

Honokōhau Harbor Charter Desk. With 50 boats on the books, this place can take care of almost anyone. You can make arrangements through your hotel activity desk, but we suggest you go down to the desk at the harbor and look things over for yourself. ⊠ *74-381 Kealakehe Pkwy., Kailua-Kona* ☎ *808/329–5735 or 888/566–2487* ⊕ *www. charterdesk.com.*

Humdinger Sportfishing. This game fisher guide has more than three decades of fishing experience in Kona waters. The experienced crew are marlin specialists. The 37-foot *Humdinger* has the latest in electronics and top line rods and reels. Half-day exclusive charters begin at $550, full-day exclusives at $850. ☎ *808/936–3034 or 800/926–2374* ⊕ *www.humdinger-online.com.*

Illusions Sportfishing. Captain Tim Hicks is one of Kona's top fishing tourney producers with several years' experience. The 39-foot *Illusions* is fully equipped with galley, restrooms, an air-conditioned cabin, plus the latest in fishing equipment. Half-day exclusive charters begin at $550, full-day exclusives at $800. ☎ *808/883–0180, 808/960–7371 (cell), 800/482–3474* ⊕ *www.illusionssportfishing.com.*

Kona Charter Skippers Association. In business since 1956, this company can help arrange half-day and full-day exclusive or share charters on several boats. The *Pamela (see listing below)* is their featured boat. ⊠ *Box 806, 74-857 Iwalani Pl., Kailua-Kona* ☎ *808/329–3600 or 800/762–7546* ⊕ *www.konabiggamefishing.com.*

Pamela Big Game Fishing. This family-operated company has been in the business since 1967. The 38-foot *Pamela* is captained by either Peter Hoogs or his son. They've also got an informative Web site with information on sportfishing. Half-day exclusive charters begin at $600, full-day exclusives at $950. ☎*808/329–3600 or 800/762–7546* ⊕*www.konabiggamefishing.com.*

KAYAKING

The leeward west coast areas of the Big Island are protected for the most part from the Northeast Trade Winds, making for ideal near-shore kayaking conditions. There are literally miles and miles of uncrowded Kona and Kohala coastline to explore, presenting close-up views of stark raw lava rock shores and cliffs, lava tube sea caves, pristine secluded coves, and deserted beaches.

Ocean kayakers can get in close to shore—where the commercial snorkel and dive cruise boats can't reach. This opens up all sorts of possibilities for adventure, such as near-shore snorkeling among the expansive coral reefs and lava rock formations that teem with colorful tropical fish, Hawaiian green sea turtles, and more. You can pull ashore at a quiet cove for a picnic and a plunge into a deep turquoise pool. With a good coastal map and some advice from the kayak vendor, you can explore inland, where you might find ancient battlegrounds, burial sites, bathing ponds for Hawaiian royalty, or old villages.

Kayaking experiences can be enjoyed via a guided tour or on a self-guided paddling excursion. Either way, the kayak outfitter can brief you on recommended routes, manageable currents, and how you can help preserve and protect Hawai'i's ocean resources and coral reef system.

BEST SPOTS

The likelihood of seeing dolphins makes **Kealakekua Bay** (⊠*Bottom of Nāpō'opo'o Rd., south of Kailua-Kona*) one of the most popular kayak spots on the Big Island. The bay is usually calm, and the kayaking is not difficult—except during high surf. If you're there in the morning, you're likely to see spinner dolphins. Depending on your strength and enthusiasm, you'll cross the bay in 30–60 minutes and put in at the ancient canoe landing about 50 yards to the left of the **Captain Cook Monument.** The monument marks the landfall of Captain James Cook in 1778, the first European to visit Hawai'i. The coral around the monument itself is too fragile to land a kayak, but it makes for fabulous snorkeling.

There are several rental outfitters on Highway 11 between mile markers 110 and 113. There's also one unofficial stand at the shore, at the house

THE BIG ISLAND'S TOP THREE WATER ACTIVITIES

Tour company/ Outfitter	Length	AM/ PM	Departure Point	Adult/kid Price	Kids' Ages	Snack vs. meal	Alcoholic beverages included	Boat type	Capacity	Worth Noting
Scuba Diving										
Aloha Dive Company	2-tank boat dive	Both	Honokahau Harbor	$110	10 and up	Snack	No	Small dive boat	6	Locally owned and operated, prefer unusual sites, great for experienced divers
	Manta Ray night dive	PM	Honokahau Harbor	$85	10 and up	Snack	No	Small dive boat	6	
Dive Makai	2-tank boat dive	Both	Honokahau Harbor	$125	10 and up	Snack	No	Medium dive boat	10	In-depth briefings before dives
Jack's Diving Locker	2-tank boat dive	Both	Honokahau Harbor	$125	10 and up	Snack	No	Large dive boat	15	Best for novice and intermediate divers
	Manta Ray night dive	PM	Honokahau Harbor	$145	10 and up	Snack	No	Large dive boat	15	
Torpedo Tours	2-tank boat dive	Both	Honokahau Harbor	$110	10 and up	Meal	No	Small dive boat	10	Torpedo scooters available
	Manta Ray night dive	PM	Honokahau Harbor	$89	10 and up	Snack	No	Small dive boat	6	
Snorkeling										
Body Glove Cruises	3-4.5 hours	Both	Honokahau Harbor	$112/$72	All ages	Meal	No	Large catamaran	50	Good prices; fun for kids

Captain Zodiac	4 hours	Both	Honokahau Harbor	$93/$77	4 and up	Snack	No	Pontoon	16	Small size allows access to sea caves and unique sites.
Fair Winds	3.5-4.5 hours	Both	Keauhou Harbor	$99/$59	All ages	Meal	No	Large catamaran	50	Slide into the water; great for kids
Hula Kai	4-5 hours	Both	Keauhou Harbor	$125-$149	18 and over	Meal	Yes	Large catamaran	45	Elegant boat, full bar, delicious food, great variety of sites
Kona Boys	half day	AM	Kona Boys shop, just south of mile marker 113 on Hwy 11	$159	10 and up	Meal	No	Kayaks	2 per kayak	Great combo of kayaking and snorkeling

Whale Watching

Blue Sea Cruises	2.5 hours	PM	Kailua-Kona Pier	$65/$55	All ages	Snacks	No	Large catamaran	150	Glass bottom boat
Body Glove Cruises	3 hours	PM	Honokahau Harbor	$73/$53	All ages	Snacks	No	Large catamaran	50	Best prices
Captain Dan McSweeney's	3 hours	PM	Honokahau Harbor	$70/$60	All ages	Snack	No	Large catamaran	70	Specializes in whale watching and educational cruises
Hula Kai	3 hours	PM	Keauhou Harbor	$69	8 and up	Snacks	No	Large catamaran	45	New, high-speed boats

KAYAK SAFETY

■ Whether you're a beginner or experienced kayaker, choose appropriate water and weather conditions for your kayak excursion.

■ Ask the outfitter about local conditions and hazards, such as tides and currents.

■ Beginners should practice getting into and out of the kayak and capsizing in shallow water.

■ Before departing, secure the kayak's hatches, etc., to prevent water intake.

■ Use a line to attach the paddle to the kayak to avoid losing it.

■ Always use a life vest or jacket.

■ Wear a helmet if kayaking in and around rough water and rocks.

■ Carry appropriate amounts of water and food.

■ Don't kayak alone. Create a float plan; tell someone where you're going and when you will return.

on the corner just across from the parking lot. After you've loaded your kayak onto the roof of your car, follow the 2-mi road down the rather steep hill to the parking lot below. ■ TIP→ **There are usually local guys who will set up your kayak and get you into (and out of) the water; tips of between $5 and $10 are encouraged, expected, and appreciated.**

Ōneo Bay (⊠*Ali'i Dr., south of Kailua-Kona*) is usually quite a placid place to kayak. It's easy to get to and great for all skill levels. If you can't find a parking spot along Ali'i Drive, there's a parking lot across the street near the farmers' market.

Hilo Bay (⊠*2349 Kalaniana'ole Ave., about 4 mi east of Hilo*) is a favorite kayak spot. The best place to put in is at **Richardson's Ocean Beach Park.** Most afternoons you can share the bay with local paddling clubs. Stay inside the breakwater unless the ocean is calm (or you're feeling unusually adventurous). Conditions range from extremely calm to quite choppy.

EQUIPMENT, LESSONS & TOURS

Aloha Kayak Co. This Honalo outfitter offers guided Wet-N-Wild Kayak Snorkel/Cave Tours—a four-hour morning tour ($79 per person) and a 2½-hour afternoon version ($59 per person). Morning tour includes sandwich lunch, snacks, and cold drinks; afternoon tour includes snacks and drinks. Tours depart from Keauhou Bay. Daily kayak rental rates: single $35, double $60. ■ TIP→ **Ask about renting one of their glass kayaks, for a clear and close-up view of the marinelife below you.** ⊠*79-7428 Mamalahoa Hwy., Honalo* ☎*808/322–2868 or 877/322–1444* ⊕*www.alohakayak.com.*

Kona Boys. On the highway above Kealakekua Bay, this full-service outfitter handles kayaks, boogie boards, and related equipment. Single-seat kayaks are $47 daily, doubles $67, weekly single $150, double $275. Dive kayaks with a well for an air tank are also available. The Boys also lead a guided trip to Kealakekua that includes kayaking, snorkeling, and hiking around a lava rock point (½-day starting at $159 per person, includes lunch, snacks, and drinks), a Sunset Kayak & Snorkel Tour for $125 per person, as well as customized overnight camping–kayaking trips to Miloliʻi, Pololū, or our favorite, Waipiʻo Valley. ⊠ *79-7539 Mamalahoa Hwy., Kealakekua* ☎ *808/328–1234* ⊕ *www. konaboys.com.*

Ocean Safari's Kayak Adventures. On the guided 3½-hour morning Sea Cave Tour that begins in Keauhou Bay, you can visit lava tube sea caves along the coast, then swim ashore for a snack. The kayaks are on the beach, so you don't have to hassle with transporting them. The cost is $64 per person. A two-hour Early Riser Dolphin Quest Tour leaves at 7 AM on Tuesdays. It's $35 per person. Kayak daily rental rates are single $25, double $40. ⊠ *End of Kamehameha III Rd., Kailua-Kona* ☎ *808/326–4699* ⊕ *www.oceansafariskayaks.com.*

DOLPHINS AT REST

Kealakekua Bay is a designated marine refuge where the dolphins return to rest after feeding. Kayakers occasionally pursue the dolphins in an aggressive way. Because of the actions of a few, some environmental activists are working to close the bay to all kayakers. Those who charge after dolphins may be videotaped and have complaints filed against them (as well as suffer the ephemeral but very real consequences of behaving without the aloha spirit). If you behave in a calm, nonthreatening manner, the dolphins are likely to come to you.

PARASAILING

Parasailing, gliding on the winds with a parachute while being pulled behind a power boat, is a relaxing and thrilling experience. If you can handle heights, you'll revel in the experience of being suspended in air while soaring above Kailua Bay. The water is so clear you can almost see the ocean floor. And no swimming is required; takeoffs and landings are from the back of the boat.

UFO Parasail. This is the sole parasailing outfitter in Kona. The parasailing adventures run across Kailua Bay and along the Kona Coast in rides up to 800 feet high for bird's-eye views and real thrills (an optional "freefall" that stops short of the water recreates the rush of a parachute descent). A power boat and winch provide dry takeoffs and landings; parasailors can "fly" alone or in tandem. Though the flight is short, the boat ride takes about one hour. Rates: standard 400 feet, 7 minutes, $60; deluxe 800 feet, 10 minutes, $70; non-flyers boat ride only, $30. ⊠ *55-5669 Aliʻi Dr., Kailua-Kona* ☎ *1–888/359–4836 or 808/325–5836* ⊕ *www.ufoparasailing.com.*

SAILING

For old salts and novice sailors alike, there's nothing like a cruise on the Kona or Kohala coasts of the Big Island. Calm waters, serene shores, and the superb scenery of Mauna Kea, Mauna Loa, and Hualālai, the Big Island's primary volcanic peaks, make for a great sailing adventure. You can drop a line over the side and try your luck at catching dinner, or grab some snorkel gear and explore when the boat drops anchor in one of the quiet coves and bays. A cruise may well be the most relaxing and adventurous part of a Big Island visit.

Maile Charters. Ralph Blancato and Kalia Potter offer unique around-the-Islands sailing adventures that range from half-day excursions to five-day journeys to Maui, Moloka'i, or Lāna'i. Private cabins and hot showers keep you comfortable, and island-style meals keep you satisfied. Fees start at $890 for six passengers for a half-day charter to $5,950 for five days with a maximum of four adult passengers. The price includes use of water sports equipment and food can be ordered ahead of time and purchased for an additional fee. ⊠*Kawaihae Harbor, Kawaihae* ☏*800/726–7245* ⊕*www.adventuresailing.com.*

SCUBA DIVING

The Big Island's underwater world is the setting for a dramatic diving experience. With generally calm waters, vibrant coral reefs and rock formations, and plunging underwater drop-offs, the Kona and Kohala coasts provide some great scuba diving. There are also some good dive locations in east Hawai'i, not far from the Hilo area. Divers will find much to occupy their time, including marine reserves teeming with unique Hawaiian reef fish, Hawaiian green sea turtles, an occasional and rare Hawaiian monk seal, and even some feisty Hawaiian spinner dolphins. On special night dives to see manta ray, divers descend with bright underwater lights that attract plankton, which in turn attracts these otherworldly creatures. The best spots to dive are listed in order from north to south; all are on the west coast.

BEST SPOTS

Hāpuna Beach State Recreation Area (⊠*Hwy. 19, near mile marker 69*) in Kohala can be a good shore dive. Just south of the state park is **Puako** (⊠*Puako Rd., off Hwy. 19*). Public access to the beach from Puako Road provides easy entry to some fine reef diving. Deep chasms, sea caves, rock arches, and more abound with varied marine life.

The water is usually very clear at **Pawai Bay Marine Reserve** (⊠*Just north of Old Kona Airport Beach Park, at the beginning of Kuakini Hwy.*). This bay near Kailua-Kona has numerous underwater sea caves, arches, and rock formations, plus lots of marine life. It can be busy with snorkel boats but is an easy dive spot. **Plane Wreck Point,** off Keāhole Point, is for expert divers only. Damselfish, fantail, and filefish hover around in the shadows.

HAWAI'I'S MANTA RAYS

Manta rays, one of Hawai'i's most fascinating marine life species, can be seen on some nighttime diving excursions along the Kona and Kohala Coasts. They are generally harmless to divers and don't normally attack people. If you don't want to get wet, head to the beach fronting the Mauna Kea Beach Hotel on the Kohala Coast, where each evening, visitors gather under the lights to watch manta rays feed in the shallows.

■ The manta ray (*manta birostris*), called the devil fish by some, is known as *hahalua* by Hawaiians.

■ Its wing-like fins, reaching up to 20 feet wide, allow the ray to glide through the water like a bird gliding through air.

■ The manta ray uses the two large flap-like lobes extending from its eyes to funnel food to its mouth. It eats microscopic plankton, small fish, and tiny crustaceans.

■ The manta ray, closely related to the shark, can weigh more than 3,000 pounds.

■ Its skeleton is made of cartilage, not bone.

■ A female ray gives birth to one or two young at a time; pups can be 45 inches long and weigh 20 pounds at birth.

One of Kona's best night dive spots is **Manta Village** (⊠*Off the Sheraton Keauhou Bay Resort at Keauhou*). A booking with a scuba/snorkel night dive operator is required for the short boat ride to the area. If you're a diving or snorkeling fanatic, it's well worth it for the experience of seeing the manta rays.

Dive boats come to **Pu'uhonua O Hōnaunau** (*Place of Refuge* ⊠*Rte. 160, about 20 mi south of Kailua-Kona* ⊕*www.nps.gov/puho*) for the steep drop-offs and dramatic views. You can also get in the water from the shore on the north end.

EQUIPMENT, LESSONS & TOURS

There are quite a few good dive shops on the Kona Coast. Most are happy to take on all customers, but a few focus on specific types of trips. Trip prices vary, depending on whether you're already certified and whether you're diving from a boat or from shore. Instruction with PADI, SDI, or TDI certification in three to five days costs $600–$850. Most instructors rent out dive equipment and snorkel gear, and many rent underwater cameras. A few organize otherworldly manta-ray dives at night or whale-watching cruises in season.

★ **Aloha Dive Company.** Native-born Hawaiian and PADI master dive instructor Mike Nakachi, together with wife Buffy (a registered nurse and PADI dive instructor), and Earl Kam (a videographer and PADI dive master) have been instructing since 1990. Although they'll take anybody, they're biased in favor of experienced divers who want unique locations and know how to take care of themselves in deep water. Their boat is fast enough to take you places other companies can't reach. They're fun people with great attitudes and operate the only true *kamā'aina*

The Kona Coast's relatively calm waters and colorful coral reefs are excellent for scuba diving.

(Hawai'i born-and-raised) outfitter around. Rates begin at $85 for a manta ray night dive and go up to $200 for a three-tank remote dive. ☎808/325–5560 or 800/708–5662 ⊕*www.alohadive.com.*

★ **Dive Makai.** Mainland transplants Mike and Kimberly Henshaw took over the Dive Makai operation from longtime owner Tom Shockley in 2005, but Tom still answers the phone most of the time and heads out on the boat when he can. Far more than a standard-issue trip, a dive with these guys is an educational experience. They take pride in fully debriefing passengers about the spots they're visiting and what they can expect to see there, plus plenty of interesting and quirky facts about the local marine life and reefs. Mike worked with the National Marine Fisheries Service as a biologist in the Marine Mammal Division once upon a time and is happy to share his extensive knowledge with divers. He's also a fantastic instructor and guide, patient and helpful, and always on the lookout to lead his divers to a delightful marine discovery. Rates start at $120 for a two-tank day dive or manta-ray night dive and go up to $300 for a three-tank adventure that takes divers towards the newer canyons formed on the ocean floor closer to the volcano. ☎808/329–2025 ⊕*www.divemakai.com.*

★ **Jack's Diving Locker.** The best place for novice and intermediate divers (certified to 60 feet), Jack's Diving Locker has trained and certified tens of thousands of divers since opening in 1981. The company has two boats that can each take 12 divers. It does a good job looking out for customers and protecting the coral reef. Before each charter the dive master briefs divers on various options and then everyone votes on where to go. Jack's also runs the biggest dive shop on the island and has classrooms and a dive pool for beginning instruction. ■TIP→ **Kona's best dive bargain for newbies is the introductory shore dive from Kailua Pier for $55.** ⊠75-5813 Ali'i Dr., Kailua-Kona ☎800/345–4807 or 808/329–7585 ⊕www.jacksdivinglocker.com.

★ **Torpedo Tours.** Mike and Nikki Milligan specialize in small groups, which means you'll spend more time diving and less time hanging out on the boat waiting to dive. Two-tank afternoon dives run $110, one-tank manta ray dives are $89, or you can combine the two and do a late afternoon dive plus a manta ray dive for a very reasonable $130. Torpedo Tours will take snorkelers along with divers, and provides its namesake torpedo scooters to both for free. The scooters allow both divers and snorkelers to cover more ground with less kicking, and are a fun novelty to test out. ⊠Honokōhau Harbor, Na Pali Kai II boat, 74-425 Kealakehe Pkwy., Kailua-Kona ☎808/938–0405 ⊕www.torpedoours.com.

SNORKELING

A favorite pastime on the Big Island, snorkeling is perhaps one of the easiest and most enjoyable water activities for visitors. By ducking underwater, you'll see lava rock formations, sea arches, sea caves, and coral reefs teeming with colorful tropical fish. While the Kona and Kohala coasts have more beaches, bays, and quiet coves to snorkel, the east side around Hilo and at Kapoho are also great places to get in the water.

If you don't bring your own equipment, you can easily rent all the gear needed from a beach activities vendor, who will happily provide directions to the best sites for snorkeling in the area. For access to deeper water and assistance from an experienced crew, you can opt for a snorkel cruise. Excursions generally range from two to five hours; be sure you know what equipment and food is included. Kona Boys, *in kayaking above*, lead combined kayaking, snorkeling, and hiking tours.

BEST SPOTS

★ **Kealakekua Bay** (⊠*Bottom of Nāpō'opo'o Rd., south of Kailua-Kona*) is, hands down, the best snorkel spot on the island, with fabulous coral reefs around the Captain Cook monument and generally calm waters. Besides, you'll probably get to swim with dolphins. Overland access is difficult, so you can opt for one of several guided snorkel cruises or kayak across the bay to get to the monument. ■TIP→ **Be on the lookout for kayakers who might not notice you swimming beneath them, and stay on the ocean side of the orange buoys near the cliffs.**

The snorkeling just north of the boat launch at **Pu'uhonua O Hōnaunau** (*Place of Refuge* ⊠*Rte. 160, about 20 mi south of Kailua-Kona* ⊕*www.nps.gov/puho*) is almost as good as Kealakekua Bay, and it's much easier to reach. It's also a popular scuba diving spot.

White Sands, Magic Sands, or Disappearing Sands Beach Park (⊠ *Ali'i Dr., 4½ mi south of Kailua-Kona*) is a great place for beginning and intermediate snorkelers. In winter it's also a good place to see whales.

Since ancient times, the waters around **Kahalu'u Beach Park** (⊠ *Ali'i Dr., 5½ mi south of Kailua-Kona*) have been a traditional net fishing area. The swimming is good, and the snorkeling is even better. You'll see angelfish, parrotfish, needlefish, pufferfish, and a lot more. ■ TIP➔**Stay inside the breakwater and don't stray too far, as dangerous and unpredictable currents swirl outside the bay.**

Kapoho Tide Pools (⊠ *End of Kapoho-Kai Rd., off Hwy. 137*) has the best snorkeling on the Hilo side. Fingers of lava from the 1960 flow (that destroyed the town of Kapoho) jut into the sea to form a network of tide pools. Conditions near the shore are excellent for beginners, and challenging enough farther out for experienced snorkelers.

EQUIPMENT, LESSONS & TOURS

★ **Body Glove Cruises.** This operator is a good choice for families, particularly if at least one member is a certified diver and the rest want to snorkel. Kids love the waterslide and the high dive platform, and parents appreciate the reasonable prices. The 51-foot catamaran sets off from the Kailua Pier daily for a 4½-hour dive and snorkel cruise, which includes breakfast and a buffet lunch; the three-hour afternoon cruise includes snacks and drinks. Snorkelers pay $66–$105 per adult and $44–$65 per child. Scuba divers pay the snorkel rate plus $57–$67 per person with or without gear. ⊠ *Kailua Pier, Kailua-Kona* ☎ *808/329–4807 or 800/551–8911* ⊕ *www.bodyglovehawaii.com.*

Captain Zodiac Raft Expedition. The exciting four-hour trip on an inflatable raft takes you along the Kona Coast to explore gaping lava-tube caves, search for dolphins and turtles, and snorkel around Kealakekua Bay. The captain often throws in Hawaiian folklore and Kona history; the company started up in 1974. The morning trip departs at 8:15 AM, the afternoon at 1 PM. Adults pay $93 and kids $77. A seasonal (Dec.–Apr.) three-hour whale-watch cruise is adults $70, kids $60. ⊠ *Honokōhau Harbor, Kailua-Kona* ☎ *808/329–3199* ⊕ *www. captainzodiac.com.*

★ **Fair Wind Cruises.** This outfit offers both a 4½-hour morning and 3½-hour afternoon snorkeling excursions to Kealakekua Bay, and a luxury cruise (*Hula Kai*, see below) that sails into three different secret snorkeling spots a day. Snorkel gear is included (ask about prescription masks), but bring your own towel. On morning cruises you'll get a Continental breakfast and a barbecue lunch. These trips are great for families with small kids (lots of pint-size flotation equipment), and they provide underwater viewing devices for those who don't want to use a mask–snorkel setup. Morning cruises cost $105 for adults and $65 for kids; afternoon cruises are cheaper, but you're less likely to see dolphins in the bay. The spring–summer afternoon deluxe cruise includes a late barbecue lunch and snorkel time; adults $99, kids $59. ⊠ *78-7130 Kaleiopapa St., Keauhou Bay, Kailua-Kona* ☎ *808/322–2788 or 800/677–9461* ⊕ *www.fair-wind.com.*

Continued on page 128

SNORKELING IN HAWAI'I

The waters surrounding the Hawaiian Islands are filled with life—from giant manta rays cruising off the Big Island's Kona Coast to humpback whales giving birth in Maui's Māʻalaea Bay. Dip your head beneath the surface to experience a spectacularly colorful world: pairs of milletseed butterflyfish dart back and forth, red-lipped parrotfish snack on coral algae, and spotted eagle rays flap past like silent spaceships. Sea turtles bask at the surface while tiny wrasses give them the equivalent of a shave and a haircut. The water quality is typically outstanding; many sites afford 30-foot-plus visibility. On snorkel cruises, you can often stare from the boat rail right down to the bottom.

Certainly few destinations are as accommodating to every level of snorkeler as Hawaiʻi. Beginners can tromp in from sandy beaches while more advanced divers descend to shipwrecks, reefs, craters, and sea arches just offshore. Because of Hawaiʻi's extreme isolation, the island chain has fewer fish species than Fiji or the Caribbean—but many of the fish that are here exist nowhere else. The Hawaiian waters are home to the highest percentage of endemic fish in the world.

The key to enjoying the underwater world is slowing down. Look carefully. Listen. You might hear the strange crackling sound of shrimp tunneling through coral, or you may hear whales singing to one another during winter. A shy octopus may drift along the ocean's floor beneath you. If you're hooked, pick up a waterproof fishkey from Long's Drugs. You can brag later that you've looked the Hawaiian turkeyfish in the eye.

Picasso Triggerfish

Milletseed Butterflyfish*

Yellow Tang

Moorish Idol

Hawaiian Whitespotted Toby*

Saddleback Wrasse*

Red-lipped Parrotfish

Hawaiian Turkeyfish*

Zebra Moray Eel

Stocky Hawkfish

Green Sea Turtle (Honu)

Spotted Eagle Ray

*endemic to Hawai'i

POLYNESIA'S FIRST CELESTIAL NAVIGATORS: HONU

Honu is the Hawaiian name for two native sea turtles, the hawksbill and the green sea turtle. Little is known about these dinosaur-age marine reptiles, though snorkelers regularly see them foraging for *limu* (seaweed) and the occasional jellyfish in Hawaiian waters. Most female honu nest in the uninhabited Northwestern Hawaiian Islands, but a few sociable ladies nest on Maui and Big Island beaches. Scientists suspect that they navigate the seas via magnetism—sensing the earth's poles. Amazingly, they will journey up to 800 miles to nest—it's believed that they return to their own birth sites. After about 60 days of incubation, nestlings emerge from the sand at night and find their way back to the sea by the light of the stars.

Passengers aboard the *Atlantis VII* submarine can visit the aquatic world without getting wet.

★ **Hula Kai.** Operated by Fair Winds, the Hula Kai is the company's more luxurious, adults-only snorkel cruise—"adults-only" in a peace and quiet, wine and appetizers way, not a clothing-optional way. The swanky hydrofoil boat skims quietly over the island's waters, venturing to areas not easily accessed by the company's other boats, including the southern coast, where snorkeling is fantastic amidst the canyons and reefs. A gourmet breakfast buffet and barbecue lunch is included in the $149/person rate, and whale-watching tours are available in season. The boat also offers scuba diving, which makes it a bonus for couples in groups that have a mix of divers and snorkelers. ✉ *78-7130 Kaleiopapa St., Keauhou Bay, Kailua-Kona* ☎ *808/322–2788 or 800/677–9461* ⊕ *www.fair-wind.com.*

Snorkel Bob's. You're likely to see his wacky ads in your airline inflight magazine. The company actually delivers what it promises, and you can make reservations online before beginning your trip. Basic gear package of mask, fins, and snorkel rents for $9–$22 per week; children's equipment and prescription masks are available. ✉ *75-5831 Kahakai St., Kailua-Kona* ☎ *808/329–0770 or 800/262–7725* ⊕ *www.snorkelbob.com.*

SNUBA

Snuba—a cross between scuba and snorkeling—is a gr[eat] non-scuba divers who want to go a step beyond snorkelin[g]. [You and your] instructor dive off a raft attached to a 25-foot hose and [...] can dive as deep as 20 feet or so. This is a good way to explore reefs a bit deeper than you can get to by snorkeling. If you get frightened or need a rest, the raft is right there, ready to support you.

Snuba Big Island. Rendezvous with your instructor across from King Kamehameha's Kona Beach Hotel in Kailua-Kona for 30 minutes of instruction and a one-hour dive in Kailua Bay ($79 per person). Boat dives lasting three hours leave from Honakahou Harbor ($125 per person). You can also dive in Kealakekua Bay. The minimum age for snuba is eight, but kids four to seven can come along on the Snuba Doo program, which keeps them snorkeling safely on the surface. ☎808/326–7446 ⊕www.snubabigisland.com.

SUBMARINE TOURS

☺ **Atlantis VII Submarine.** Want to stay dry while exploring the undersea Fodor'sChoice world? Climb aboard the 48-foot *Atlantis VII* submarine anchored off ★ Kailua Pier, across from King Kamehameha's Kona Beach Hotel in Kailua-Kona. A large glass dome in the bow and 13 viewing ports on the sides allow clear views of the aquatic world more than 100 feet down. This is a great trip for kids and nonswimmers. Each one-hour voyage costs $90 for adults and $45 for children under 12. The company also operates on O'ahu and Maui. ☎808/329–6626 or 800/548–6262 ⊕www.atlantisadventures.com.

SURFING

The Big Island does not have the variety of great surfing spots found on O'ahu or Maui, but it does have decent waves and a thriving surf culture. Local kids and avid surfers frequent a number of places up and down the Kona and Kohala Coasts of west Hawai'i. Expect high surf in winter and much calmer activity during summer. The surf scene is much more active on the Kona side.

BEST SPOTS

Among the best places for experienced surfers to catch the waves is **Pine Trees** (⊠ *Off Hwy. 11 and south of the Kona Airport and the Natural Energy Lab of Hawai'i on an unimproved beach road*). Keep in mind that this is a very popular local surf spot on an island where there aren't all that many surf spots, so be very respectful. Intermediate surfers brave the rocks to get out to a popular break just slightly north of **Kahalu'u Beach Park** (⊠ *Ali'i Dr., 5½ mi south of Kailua-Kona next to Outrigger Keauhou Beach Hotel.*), out past the beach's calm lagoons and snorkelers. **Banyans** (⊠ *Ali'i Dr. near the Kona Bali Kai condos*) is another popular spot with local and experienced surfers. There's no beach here—surfers need to wade in from the rocks and start paddling. **Old Kona Airport State Recreation Area** (⊠*Kuakini Rd. at the old Kona Airport*) is also a good place for catching wave action. A couple of the island's outfitters conduct surf lessons here, as the break is far away from potentially dangerous rocks and reefs. On the east side near Hilo, try **Honoli'i Cove** (⊠*Access road off Hwy. 19, just past mile marker 4*).

WORD OF MOUTH

"From late December to mid- to late April the whales come to Hawai'i, especially the Big Island and Maui. It is one of my favorite times to be there." — Lauricelli

EQUIPMENT, LESSONS & TOURS

Hawai'i Lifeguard Surf Instructors. This certified school with experienced instructors helps novice surfers become wave riders; their surf tours take more experienced riders to Kona's top surfing spots. Though they offer a one-hour introductory lesson ($72 for a small group, $98 for private instruction), they recommend the two-hour lesson to get you ready to surf. You can try a two-hour tandem lesson on a board for two. ⊠*75-159 Lunapule Rd., Kailua-Kona* ☎*808/936–7873 or 808/324–0442* ⊕*www.surflessonshawaii.com.*

Ocean Eco Tours Surf School. This surf school emphasizes the basics of safe surfing and specializes in beginners. All lessons are taught by certified CPR-trained lifeguard instructors, and they guarantee that you will surf! If you're hooked, you can sign up for a three-lesson package for $270. ⊠*74-425 Kealakehe Pkwy., Kailua-Kona* ☎*808/324–7873* ⊕*www.oceanecotours.com.*

Orchid Land Surf Shop. The shop has a wide variety of water sports and surf equipment for sale or rent. They stock professional custom surfboards, bodyboards, and surf apparel and do repairs. ⊠*262 Kamehameha Ave., Hilo* ☎*808/935–1533* ⊕*www.orchidlandsurf.com.*

WHALE-WATCHING

Each winter, some two-thirds of the North Pacific humpback whale population (about 4,000–5,000 animals) migrate over 3,500 mi from the icy Alaska waters to the warm Hawaiian ocean to give birth to and nurse their calves. Recent reports indicate that the whale population is on the upswing—a few years ago one even ventured into the mouth of Hilo Harbor, which marine biologists say is quite rare. Humpbacks are spotted here from early December through the end of April, but other species, like sperm, pilot, and beaked whales, can be seen year-round. Most ocean tour companies offer whale outings during the season, but two owner–operators do it full time. They are much more familiar with whale behavior and you're more likely to have a quality whale-watching experience. ■ TIP→ **If you take the morning cruise, you're likely to see dolphins as well.** In addition to the outfitters listed below, **Body Glove Cruises** and **Hula Kai** (*both listed in Snorkeling, above*) offer whale-watching cruises.

Humpback whales are visible off the coast of the Big Island between December and April.

EQUIPMENT, LESSONS & TOURS

Blue Sea Cruises Inc. The *Makai*, a 46-foot double-deck catamaran, cruises along the Kona Coast twice a day on two-hour tours. The boat has all the comforts, including a snack bar and restrooms. The narrated tour covers Hawai'i's marine wildlife and the history and culture of the Islands. Sightings include spinner, spotted, and bottlenose dolphins, resident pilot whales, and seasonal humpbacks. Tours depart from Kailua Pier at 8:30 AM and include snacks and cold beverages. The 11 AM tour includes a light lunch. Rates start at $61 per person. ☎*808/331–8875* ⊕*www.blueseacruisesinc.com.*

★ **Captain Dan McSweeney's Year-Round Whale Watching Adventures.** This is probably the most experienced small operation on the island. Captain Dan McSweeney offers three-hour trips on his 40-foot boat. In addition to humpbacks in the winter, he'll show you some of the six other whale species that live off the Kona Coast year-round. Three-hour tours cost $70 per adult and $60 for kids under 12 (snacks and juices included). McSweeney guarantees you'll see a whale or he'll take you out again free. ⊠*Honokōhau Harbor, Kailua-Kona* ☎*808/322–0028* or *888/942–5376* ⊕*www.ilovewhales.com.*

CLOSE UP

Protecting the Humpback Whale

The waters around the Hawaiian Islands are one of the North Pacific humpback whales' most significant habitats: the only place in the United States coastal waters where humpbacks are known to reproduce and give birth to their young.

The Hawaiian Islands Humpback Whale National Marine Sanctuary (⊕ *www.hawaiihumpbackwhale.noaa.gov*) was established in 1997 to protect humpback whales and their habitat and to educate the public about whales and the Hawai'i marine environment. The 1,400-square-mi sanctuary includes five protected areas around the main Hawaiian Islands.

DID YOU KNOW?

■ Humpback whales are the fifth largest of the world's great whales; a mature whale can be up to 45 feet long and weigh about 42–45 tons.

■ Their top jaw has fleshy knobs called tubercles. Each tubercle has a strand of hair and many nerve endings believed to serve some sensory function.

■ Their throats have expandable pleats, allowing the animal to ingest over 500 gallons of prey and water in a single gulp. They primarily eat zooplankton and small fish.

■ Their tongues can weigh up to one ton.

■ The calves have a 10- to 12-month gestation period. On average, newborns weigh 1.5 tons and are 10–16 feet long.

■ Calves nurse on the mother's rich milk for six to eight months and grow fast, nearly doubling their length by the end of the first year.

■ Humpback whales live about 40 to 60 years.

WINDSURFING

Windsurfers will find good waters and winds in the coves and bays along the Kohala Coast. The surf is usually choppy when the wind comes up but not so much that windsurfers can't get out. Unlike surfing, windsurfing requires no paddling. Instead, you have to hang on to a sail flapping in the wind and pick up speed. Coordination and balance are crucial.

One of the best windsurfing locations on the Big Island is at **'Aaeho'omalu Beach** (⊠ *Follow Waikoloa Beach Dr. to Kings' Shops, then turn left*) in North Kohala. The beach fronts the Waikoloa Beach Marriott.

EQUIPMENT, LESSONS & TOURS

Ocean Sports & Activities. This beach concession shack fronting the Waikoloa Beach Marriott has a full line of water sports and beach equipment rentals and can arrange various tours and excursions. They offer windsurfing lessons at $60 per person and claim you'll learn how to sail in just one lesson. ⊠ *69-275 Waikoloa Beach Dr., Waikoloa* ☎ *808/886–6666 or 888/724–5234* ⊕ *www.hawaiioceansports.com.*

5

Golf, Hiking & Outdoor Activities

WORD OF MOUTH

"The black lava was all around us, the volcano was to our right, the ocean was on our left, and the moon was illuminating it all. It was a beautiful night. We could hear the ocean waves hitting the rocks, feel the wind, and see the moon and stars."

—Samsaf

Updated
by Amy
Westervelt

With the Big Island's predictably mild year-round climate, it's no wonder the lifestyle emphasis is on outdoor activities. After all, this is the home of the annual Ironman Triathlon World Championship. Whether you are an avid hiker or a beginning bicyclist, a casual golfer or a tennis buff, there are plenty of land-based activities to lure you away from the sun and surf.

You can explore by ATV, bike, helicopter, or horse, or you can put on your hiking boots and use your own horsepower. No matter how you get around, you'll be treated to breathtaking backdrops along and beyond the Big Island's 266-mi coastline. Aerial tours take in the latest eruption activity and lava flows, as well as the island's gorgeous tropical valleys, gulches, and coastal areas. Trips into the backcountry wilderness explore the rain forest, private ranch lands, coffee farms, and sugar plantation villages that give a glimpse of Hawai'i's earlier days.

Golfers will find acclaimed, championship-caliber golf courses at the Kohala coast resorts—Mauna Kea Resort, Hāpuna Beach Prince Hotel, Mauna Lani Resort, Waikoloa Resort, and Four Seasons at Hualalai, among others. And during the winter, if snow conditions allow, you can go skiing on top of Mauna Kea (elevation: 13,796 feet). It's a skiing experience unlike any other.

AERIAL TOURS

There's nothing quite like the aerial view of a waterfall that drops a couple of thousand feet into multiple pools, or seeing lava flow to the ocean, where clouds of steam billow into the air. You can get this bird's-eye view from a helicopter or a small fixed-wing aircraft. Although there have been a few cases of pilots violating flight paths and altitudes over resident communities in recent years, most operators are reputable and fly with strict adherence to FAA safety rules. How to get the best experience for your money? ■TIP→ **Before you hire a company, be a savvy traveler and ask the right questions. What kind of aircraft do they fly? Do they have two-way headsets so you can talk with the pilot? What is their safety record?**

Island Hoppers. Despite the name, this isn't a helicopter line. They fly fixed-wing three- to six-passenger Cessna aircraft from both the Hilo and Kona airports. Every seat is a window seat with panoramic views. There are three air tours, from a 50-minute Volcano Waterfall tour at $149 per person to a two-hour Full Circle Island Tour for $287. The company offers $70 off per couple for those who book in advance online. ☎808/329–0018 or 800/538–7590 ⊕ *www.hawaiiislandhoppers.com.*

okulele Airlines. In addition to regular inter-island scheduled flights, is commuter line offers a 1½-hour Circle Island Tour in a nine-passenger twin-engine aircraft. The air tour departs Kona Airport and goes er Hawai'i Volcanoes National Park, the Hilo-Hāmākua Coast, and the Kohala Coast. Rates are $299 per person; ask about senior discounts. ☎808/326–7070 or 866/260–7070 ⊕www.mokulele.com.

Paradise Helicopters. Paradise flies six-passenger Bell 470 and four-passenger Hughes-500 helicopters. Everyone has a window seat in the four-seaters, and most passengers get a window in the highly maneuverable six-passenger helicopters as well. The friendly and knowledgeable pilots communicate with passengers over two-way headsets. Paradise operates from Kona and Hilo, which is better for volcano-viewing. The 50-minute Volcano & Waterfall Adventure (from Hilo) is $185 per person; the top-of-the-line tour is a three-hour Volcanoes & Valley Adventure (from Kona) for $530 per person, including lunch. For an additional thrill and an even better view, you can choose a Doors-Off Experience from Hilo; you can literally feel the heat radiating from the lava. ⊠Hilo Airport, Kona Airport ☎808/356–1800, 808/329–6601, or 888/349–7888 ⊕www.paradisecopters.com.

Sunshine Helicopters. Ride the six-seater Astar "Black Beauties" on these exciting air tours that take in the ocean cliffs and valleys of the Kohala-Hāmākua Coast and the formations and flows of the Kīlauea Volcano. Narrated tours range from 45 minutes ($210) to two hours ($429); the longer tour covers both regions, while the shorter tour focuses on the volcano. Sunshine offers a $30 discount on fares booked online. Afterward, you can buy a DVD of your flight experience. ⊠Helipad at Hāpuna Beach Prince Hotel and Hilo Airport ☎808/882–1223 Hāpuna Beach Prince Hotel, 808/969–7501 Hilo, 800/469–3000 ⊕www.sunshinehelicopters.com.

ATV TOURS

A different way to experience the Big Island's rugged coastline and wild ranch lands is through an off-road adventure—a real backcountry experience. At higher elevations, weather can be nippy and rainy, but views can be awesome. Protective gear is provided. Generally, you have to be 16 or older to ride your own ATV, though some outfitters allow children seven and older to be passengers.

ATV Outfitters Hawai'i. These trips take in the scenic beauty of the rugged North Kohala Coast, traveling along coastal cliffs and into the forest in search of waterfalls. The ATV outfitter's three adventures are priced from $109 per person for the 1½-hour Ocean Cliff Adventure to $249 per person for the 22-mi three-hour Deluxe Rainforest & Waterfall Adventure. ATV Outfitters also offers double-seater ATVs for parents traveling with children or adults who don't feel comfortable operating their own ATV. ⊠Old Sakamoto Store, Hwy. 270, Kapa'au ☎808/889–6000 or 888/288–7288 ⊕www.outfittershawaii.com.

ATV Ranch Ride. This rugged 2½-hour ATV adventure on a working ranch takes in the Hāmākua Coast and the Waipi'o Valley: dramatic ocean cliffs, quiet forests, and remnants of Hawai'i's once-thriving sugarcane industry. Prices begin at $100 per person. ⊠*Honoka'a* ☎*808/775–7291 or 877/775–7291* ⊕*www.waipioonhorseback.com.*

Cowboys of Hawai'i ATV Rides. Riders cruise Parker Ranch to Holoholo Hill for an incomparable panorama of the ranch's 175,000 acres and thousands of cattle or follow the Mana Road, in the shadow of towering Mauna Kea. Rates for the two-hour ride begin at $95 per person. ⊠*Parker Ranch Center, 67-1435 Māmalahoa Hwy., Waimea* ☎*808/885–5006* ⊕*www.cowboysofhawaii.com.*

Kahuā Ranch ATV Rides. On this working ranch, you can ride the range, from upslope rain forest to midlevel mountain desert. Dramatic cinder cones and backcountry pastures offer scenic views. ▮**TIP→ Ride later in the day, and stay for a ranch barbecue with the family; afterwards, you can stargaze through their powerful telescope and learn how to rope.** Rates for the two-hour ride begin at $95 per person (not including dinner). ⊠*Hwy. 250, 10 mi north of Waimea* ☎*808/882–7954 or 808/882–4646* ⊕*www.kahuaranch.com.*

Waipi'o Ride the Rim. On this Waipi'o Valley ride, you'll see expansive black-sand beaches, 1,200-foot Hi'ilawe Falls, and the lush rain forest surrounding the top edge of the valley. Rates for the three-hour rim tour begin at $159 per person. ⊠*Waipi'o Valley Artworks Bldg., 48-5416 Kukuihaele Rd., Kukuihaele* ☎*808/775–1701 or 877/757–1414* ⊕*www.topofwaipio.com.*

BIKING

The Big Island's biking trails range from easy to moderate coastal rides to rugged backcountry wilderness treks that will challenge the most serious bikers. En route, bikers can soak up some of the island's storied scenic vistas and varied geography—from tropical rain forest to rolling ranch country, from high country mountain meadows to dry lava deserts. It's dry, windy, and hot on leeward coastal trails and cool, wet, and muddy in upcountry windward areas. There are long distances between towns and few services available in the Ka'ū , Puna, South Kona, and Kohala Coast areas, so bikers need to plan accordingly for weather, water, food, and lodging before setting out.

The nonprofit **Big Island Mountain Bike Association** (⊕*www.interpac.net/ ~mtbike*) has tons of information on biking the Big Island. It provides maps and detailed descriptions of rides for all ability levels. For other suggested rides, see the Web site run by **Alternative Hawai'i** (⊕*www. alternative-hawaii.com/activity/biecotrb.htm*).

BEST SPOTS

Fodor's Choice ★ *Mountain Bike* magazine voted **Kulani Trails,** south of Hilo, the best ride in the state. To reach the trailhead from the intersection of highways 11 and 19, take Highway 19 south about 4 mi, then turn right onto Stain-

CLOSE UP

Ironman & Friends

Run annually since 1978, the **Ironman Triathlon World Championship** (☎ 808/329-0063 ⊕ *www.ironmanlive.com*) is the granddaddy of them all. For about a week prior to Race Day (the third Saturday of October), Kailua-Kona takes on the air of an Olympic Village as top athletes from across the globe arrive to compete for glory and $580,000 in prize money at the world's premiere swim/bike/run endurance event. To watch these 1,700 competitors push themselves to the ultimate in this grueling event is an inspiring testament to the human spirit. The competition starts at Kailua Pier with a 2.4-mi open-water swim, immediately followed by a 112-mi bicycle ride, then a 26.2-mi marathon. The Ironman wouldn't happen without the 7,000 volunteers who donate their time and services. To volunteer, register online at the Ironman Web site.

The **Honu Half-Ironman Triathlon** (☎ 808/329-0063 ⊕ *www.honuhalfironman.com*) in early June is an Ironman "farm team event." Participants swim at Hāpuna beach, bike the Ironman course, and run on the Mauna Lani resort grounds.

Supermen/women do the Ironman. A few notches down on the difficulty scale, but still extremely challenging, is the **Manna-Man Eco-Biathlon** (☎ 808/989-3655 ⊕ *www.bigislandraceschedule.com*), held the last Sunday in March. The race occurs in and around Kealakekua Bay. You're required to either wear or carry your shoes while swimming (points are given for creative ways to keep 'em with you, and you're penalized for leaving equipment or trash anywhere on the racecourse).

How about racing on an active volcano? No, you're not trying to outrun flowing lava (which is actually not much of a challenge, given the speed at which it usually travels). The **Kīlauea Volcano Wilderness Runs** (☎ 808/985-8725 ⊕ *www.volcanoartcenter.org*) includes a marathon, 10-mi and 5-mi races, and a noncompetitive 5-mi run-walk. This July event is held completely within Hawai'i Volcanoes National Park.

For the most current race information, check out the **Big Island Race Schedule** (⊕ *www.bigislandraceschedule.com/race_links.html*).

---

back Highway and continue on 2½ mi, then turn right at the Waiakea Arboretum. Park near the gate. This technically demanding ride, which passes majestic eucalyptus trees, is for advanced cyclists.

The **Old Puna Trail** (⊠ *Trailhead: From Hwy. 130, about 3 mi south of Kea'au town, take Kaloli Rd. to Beach Rd.*) is a 10½-mi ride through the subtropical jungle in Puna, one of the island's most isolated areas. You'll start out on a cinder road, which becomes a four-wheel-drive trail. If it's rained recently, you'll have to deal with some puddles—the first few of which you'll gingerly avoid until you give in and go barreling through the rest of them for the sheer fun of it. This is a great ride for all abilities that takes about 90 minutes.

EQUIPMENT

If you want to strike out on your own, there are several rental shops in Kailua-Kona and a couple in Waimea and Hilo. Many resorts rent bicycles that can be used around the properties. Most outfitters listed can provide a bicycle rack for your car. All offer reduced rates for rentals longer than one day.

Bike Works. This branch operation of Hawaiian Pedals caters to more advanced bicyclists and Ironman wannabes with its rentals of deluxe road bikes and full-suspension mountain bikes, starting at $40 a day. ⊠ *Hale Hana Centre, 74-5583 Luhia St., Kailua-Kona* ☎ *808/326–2453* ⊕ *www.hpbikeworks.com.*

Cycle Station. This shop, which has a variety of bikes to rent, from road sport to racing bikes, hybrids to tandems, will also deliver to and pick up at hotels. They have trailers for toddlers. Daily rentals range from $20 for a hybrid to $35 for a road or mountain bike. ⊠ *73-5619 Kauhola St. #105, Kailua-Kona* ☎ *808/327–0087* ⊕ *www.cyclestationhawaii.com.*

Hawaiian Pedals. For those who prefer comfort over speed, Hawaiian Pedals rents seven-speed cruiser, hybrids, and basic mountain bikes starting at $15 for five hours. Full day rental rates begin at $20. ⊠ *Kona Inn Shopping Village, 75-5744 Ali'i Dr., Kailua-Kona* ☎ *808/329–2294* ⊕ *www.hpbikeworks.com.*

Mid Pacific Wheels. This downtown Hilo bike shop carries a full line of bikes and related accessories. They also rent mountain bikes for exploring the Hilo and east Hawai'i area. Rental rates are $20 per day. They can provide information on best places to go, what to see, do, and experience on a self-guided bike tour. ⊠ *1133C Manono St., Hilo* ☎ *808/935–6211.*

GOING WITH A GUIDE

Orchid Isle Bicycling. This is the only outfitter on the west side of the island currently offering daily bicycle tours. Geared to cyclists of varying abilities, options range from challenging 3,500-foot climbs up Kohala Mountain to downhill-only rides that end with a swim. Tours, which last from four to eight hours and cover 8 to 55 mi, start at $100 per person. The outfitter also runs deluxe seasonal "Tour de Paradise" vacation packages including hotels, some meals, and all gear for $1,895 and up per person for four to six days of cycling. ☎ *808/327–0087 or 800/219–2324* ⊕ *www.orchidislebicycling.com.*

Volcano Bike Tours. A relatively new operation, Volcano Bike Tours takes visitors on a three- to four-hour bike ride through the rain forests and past the craters of Volcanoes National Park on a mostly downhill route. After cruising through the volcanoes, the tour ends at the Volcano Winery for a tasting at one of the most unique wineries in the country. The $130 tour includes all equipment, an interpretive guide, lunch, beverages, and a support van that drives alongside riders in case anyone tires out early. ☎ *888/934–9199.* ⊕ *www.bikevolcano.com.*

TIPS FOR THE GREEN

Golf is golf, and Hawai'i is part of the United States, but island golf nevertheless has its own quirks. Here are a few tips to make your golf experience in the Islands more pleasant.

■ Wear sunscreen, even in December. We recommend a minimum SPF of 30 and that you reapply on the 10th tee.

■ Stay hydrated. Spending four-plus hours in the sun and heat means you'll perspire away considerable fluids and energy.

■ All resort courses and many daily fee courses provide rental clubs. In many cases, they're the latest lines from Titleist, Ping, Callaway, and the like. This is true for both men and women, as well as left-handers, which means you don't have to schlep clubs across the Pacific.

■ Pro shops at most courses are well-stocked with balls, tees, and other accoutrements, so even if you bring your own bag, it needn't weigh a ton.

■ Come spikeless—very few Hawai'i courses still permit metal spikes.

■ Resort courses, in particular, offer more than the usual three sets of tees, sometimes four or five. So bite off as much or little challenge as you like. Tee it up from the tips and you'll end up playing a few 600-yard par-5s and see a few 250-yard forced carries.

■ In theory, you can play golf in Hawai'i 365 days a year. But there's a reason the Hawaiian islands are so green. Better to bring an umbrella and light jacket and not use them than to not bring them and get soaked.

■ Unless you play a muni or certain daily fee courses, plan on taking a cart. Riding carts are mandatory at most courses and are included in the green fees.

GOLF

For golfers, the Big Island is a big deal—starting with Mauna Kea, which opened in 1964 and remains one of the state's top courses. (That course had to close temporarily due to damage incurred during the 2006 earthquake, but is scheduled to reopen in 2009.) Black lava and deep blue sea are the predominant themes on the island. In the roughly 40 mi from the Kona Country Club out to the Mauna Kea Resort, nine courses are sculpted into sunny seaside lava, with four more in the hills above. Indeed, most of the Big Island's best courses are concentrated along the Kona Coast, statistically the sunniest spot in the Hawaiian archipelago. Vertically speaking, although the majority of courses are seaside or at least at sea level, three are located above 2,000 feet, another at 4,200 feet. This is significant because in Hawai'i temperatures drop by three degrees for every 1,000 feet of elevation gained.

Green Fees: Green fees listed here are the highest course rates per round on weekdays for U.S. residents. Courses with varying weekend rates are noted in the individual listings. (Some courses charge non–U.S. residents higher prices.) ■ TIP→ **Discounts are often available for resort guests and for those who book tee times on the Web, as well as for those willing to**

play in the afternoon instead of the morning. Twilight fees are also usually offered; call individual courses for information.

★ **Big Island Country Club.** Set 2,000 feet above sea level on the slopes of Mauna Kea, the Big Island Country Club is rather out of the way but well worth the drive. Pete and Perry Dye (1997) created a gem that plays through an upland woodlands—more than 2,500 trees line the fairways. On the par-5 15th, a giant tree in the middle of the fairway must be avoided with the second shot. Five lakes and a meandering natural mountain stream mean water comes into play on nine holes. The most dramatic is on the par-3 17th, where the Dyes created a knockoff of his infamous 17th at the TPC at Sawgrass. ☒ *71-1420 Māmalahoa Hwy., Kailua-Kona* ☎ *808/325–5044* ⛳ *18 holes. 7034 yds. Par 72. Green Fee: $143* ⛳ *Facilities: Driving range, putting green, golf carts, rental clubs, pro shop, lessons.*

Hāmākua Country Club. The typical modern 18-hole golf course requires at least 250 acres. The 9-hole, par-33 public Hāmākua course requires just 19. Compact is the word, and with several holes crisscrossing, this is BYO Hard Hat. Holes run up and down a fairly steep slope (a product of Hawai'i's plantation era) overlooking the ocean. There is no clubhouse or other amenities, and the 9th green is square, but for $15 bucks, whaddaya want? ☒ *Hwy. 19, 41 mi north of Hilo, Honoka'a* ☎ *808/775–7244* ⛳ *9 holes. 2520 yds. Par 33. Green Fee: $15* ⛳ *Facilities: Putting green, golf carts, pull carts.*

Hilo Municipal Golf Course. Hilo Muni is living proof that you don't need a single sand bunker to create a challenging course. Trees and several meandering creeks are the danger here. Despite the lack of bunkers, the course, which offers views of Hilo Bay from most holes, has produced many of Hawai'i's top players over the years. Taking a divot reminds you that you're playing on a dormant volcano—the soil is dark black crushed lava. ☒ *340 Haihai St., Hilo* ☎ *808/959–7711* ⛳ *18 holes. 6325 yds. Par 71. Green Fee: $29 weekdays, $34 weekends* ⛳ *Facilities: Driving range, putting green, golf carts, pull carts, rental clubs, pro-shop, lessons, restaurant, bar.*

★ **Hualālai Resort.** Named for the volcanic peak that is the target off the first tee, the Nicklaus Course at Hualālai is semiprivate, open only to guests of the adjacent Four Seasons Resort Hualālai. From the forward and resort tees, this is perhaps Jack Nicklaus's most friendly course in Hawai'i, but the back tees play a full mile longer. The par-3 17th plays across convoluted lava to a seaside green, and the view from the tee is so lovely, you may be tempted to just relax on the koa bench and enjoy the scenery. ☒ *100 Ka'ūpūlehu Dr., Kohala Coast* ☎ *808/325–8480* ⊕ *www.fourseasons.com/hualalai* ⛳ *18 holes. 7117 yds. Par 72. Green Fee: $250* ⛳ *Facilities: Driving range, putting green, golf carts, pull carts, rental clubs, pro shop, lessons, restaurant, bar.*

In Search of Birdies, Eagles & Whales

Breathtaking scenery is to be expected on Hawai'i golf courses—as it is everywhere around the tropical archipelago—but many golfers are surprised at the variety of fauna to be seen among the verdant flora during a round.

Fortunately, this being Hawai'i, there are no snakes, no man-eating mammals, not a single critter that poses a golfer any threat. But many do offer oohs and ahhs. The most dramatic by far are humpback whales. From late November through April, these two-ton cetaceans call Hawai'i home. Whether they're spouting, slapping tails on the surface, or leaping completely free of the sea and landing with a tremendous splash, humpbacks are a delightful distraction.

Among the Big Island courses from which golfers have reported sighting whales: Hāpuna, Mauna Lani, Waikoloa, and Kona CC.

While whales almost always induce a "wow," dolphins almost always elicit a smile. Make a double-bogey, see a pod of dolphins leaping past, and it's like the double never happened. Dolphins have been spotted from each of the aforementioned courses.

Lucky golfers, and those with good eyes, may also see sea turtles bobbing just outside the shore break or Hawaiian monk seals sunning on a beach. While seeking birdies and eagles on the course, golfers can also do some colorful—and significant—bird-watching. Significant because Hawai'i leads the United States in species extinctions, and several members of the federal

endangered species list can be seen on island golf courses. They include the Hawaiian goose (nēnē), Hawaiian duck (koloa), Hawaiian coot, and Hawaiian stilt (as well as the monk seal). In particular, the nēnē, the state bird, finds a happy home on lakes at Hāpuna.

Feathered friends range from the bright red American cardinal, seen throughout the islands, to the bright yellow saffron finch, seen primarily at Kona CC and at seaside resorts along the Kona Coast. At Hāpuna, wildlife biologists credit the creation of new courses for increasing bird habitat and the number of birds. The number of new species doubled here, including the Hawaiian owl (pueo). The pueo is important in Hawai'i, where it was a totem of the ancient Hawaiian religion and today remains an 'aumakua, family deity, for some native Hawaiians. The Waimea CC on the Big Island has been certified as an Audubon Cooperative Sanctuary for its resident population of wild turkeys. The golden plover is seen on many courses while it winters over on the Big Island after spending its summer in Alaska. Like the humpback whale, the golden plover migrates back and forth each year between Alaska and Hawai'i.

A final wildlife note: no threats to health and well-being here, but there are some conniving thieves. At many courses, mynah birds, the most human of birds, have been known to steal a sandwich left in a cart while the owner is hitting a shot between bites. Golfers beware, and protect your lunch.

★ **Kona Country Club.** This venerable country club offers two very different tests with the aptly named Ocean and Ali'i Mountain courses. The Ocean Course (William F. Bell, 1967) is a bit like playing through a coconut plantation, with a few remarkable lava features—such as

Most of the Big Island's top golf courses are located on the sunny Kona Coast.

the "blowhole" in front of the par-4 13th, where seawater propelled through a lava tube erupts like a geyser. The Ali'i Mountain Course (front nine, William F. Bell, 1983; back nine, Robin Nelson and Rodney Wright, 1992) plays a couple of strokes tougher than the Ocean and is the most delightful split personality you may ever encounter. Both nines share breathtaking views of Keauhou Bay, and elevation change is a factor in most shots. The most dramatic view on the front nine is from the tee of the par-3 5th hole, one of the best golf vistas in Hawai'i. The green seems perched on the edge of the earth, with what only seems to be a sheer 500-foot drop just beyond the fringe. The back nine is links-style, with less elevation change—except for the par-3 14th, which drops 100 feet from tee to green, over a lake. The routing, the sight lines and framing of greens, and the risk-reward factors on each hole make this one of the single best nines in Hawai'i. ⊠ *78-7000 Ali'i Dr., Kailua-Kona* ☎ *808/322–2595* ⊕ *www.konagolf. com* 🏌 *Ocean Course: 18 holes. 6806 yds. Par 72. Green Fee: $160. Mountain Course: 18 holes. 6673 yds. Par 72. Green Fee: $145* ☞ *Facilities: Driving range, putting green, golf carts, rental clubs, lessons, restaurant, bar.*

Mākālei Country Club. Set on the slopes of Hualālai, at an elevation of 2,900 feet, Mākālei is one of the rare Hawai'i courses with bent-grass putting greens, which means they're quick and without the grain associated with bermuda greens. Former PGA Tour official Dick Nugent (1994) designed holes that play through thick forest and open to provide wide ocean views. Elevation change is a factor on many holes, especially the par-3 15th, with the tee 80 feet above the green. In addition to fixed natural obstacles, the course is home to a number of wild peacocks and turkeys, which can make for an entertaining game. After noon, green fees dip drastically. ✉72-3890 Hawai'i Belt Rd., Kailua-Kona 🕾808/325–6625 ⚲18 holes. 7041 yds. Par 72. Green Fee: $99 ☞Facilities: Driving range, putting green, golf carts, rental clubs, pro shop, lessons, restaurant.

Fodor's Choice **Mauna Lani Resort.** Black lava flows, ★ lush green turf, white sand, and the Pacific's multihues of blue define the 36 holes at Mauna Lani. The South Course includes the par-3 15th across a turquoise bay, one of the most photographed holes in Hawai'i. But it shares "signature hole" honors with the 7th. A long par-3, it plays downhill over convoluted patches of black lava, with the Pacific immediately to the left and a dune to the right. The North Course plays a couple of shots tougher. Its most distinctive hole is the 17th, a par-3 with the green set in a lava pit 50 feet deep. The shot from an elevated tee must carry a pillar of lava that rises from the pit and partially blocks your view of the green. ✉68-1310 Mauna Lani Dr., Kohala Coast 🕾808/885–6655 ⊕www.maunalani.com ⚲North Course: 18 holes. 6601 yds. Par 72. Green Fee: $205. South Course: 18 holes. 6436 yds. Par 72. Green Fee: $210 ☞Facilities: Driving range, putting green, golf carts, rental clubs, pro shop, lessons, restaurant, bar.

Volcano Golf & Country Club. Located just outside Volcanoes National Park—and barely a stout drive from Halema'uma'u Crater—Volcano is by far Hawai'i's highest course. At 4,200 feet elevation, shots tend to fly a bit farther than at sea level, even in the often cool, misty air. Because of the elevation and climate, Volcano is one of the few Hawai'i courses with bent-grass putting greens. The course is mostly flat, and holes play through stands of Norfolk pines, flowering *lehua* trees, and multitrunk *hau* trees. The uphill par-4 15th doglegs through a tangle of *hau*. ✉Pi'i Mauna Dr. off Hwy. 11, Volcanoes National Park 🕾808/967–7331 ⊕www.volcanogolfshop.com ⚲18 holes. 6106 yds. Par 72. Green Fee: $63.50 mornings, $51 after noon ☞Facilities: Driving range, putting green, golf carts, rental clubs, restaurant, bar.

Fodor's Choice **Waikoloa Beach Resort.** Robert Trent Jones Jr. built the Beach Course at ★ Waikoloa (1981) on an old flow of crinkly 'a'ā lava, which he used to create holes that are as artful as they are challenging. The third tee, for instance, is set at the base of a towering mound of lava. The par-5 12th plays through a chute of black lava to an ocean-side green, the blue sea on the right coming into play on the second and third shots. At the

King's Course at Waikoloa (1990), Tom Weiskopf and Jay Morrish built a very links-esque track. It turns out lava's natural humps and declivities remarkably replicate the contours of seaside Scotland. But there are a few island twists—such as seven lakes. This is "option golf" as Weiskopf and Morrish provide different risk-reward tactics on each hole. Beach and King's have separate clubhouses. **Beach Course:** ✉ *1020 Keana Pl., Waikoloa* ☎ *808/886–6060* ⊕ *www.waikoloagolf.com* ⚑ *18 holes. 6566 yds. Par 70. Green Fee: $195* ⌘ *Facilities: Driving range, putting green, golf carts, rental clubs, lessons, restaurant, bar.* **Kings' Course:** ✉ *600 Waikoloa Beach Dr., Waikoloa* ☎ *808/886–7888* ⊕ *www.waikoloagolf.com* ⚑ *18 holes. 6594 yds. Par 72. Green Fee: $195* ⌘ *Facilities: Driving range, putting green, golf carts, rental clubs, lessons, restaurant, bar.*

> ### SAVING THE BEST FOR LAST
>
> Among golf's great traditions is the 19th Hole. No matter how the first 18 go, the 19th is sure to offer comfort and cheer, not to mention a chilled beverage. Many of the courses on the Kohala Coast offer a bit of history with excellent fare. At Hāpuna, Arnie's features numerous photos and drawings celebrating Palmer's career. At Mauna Lani, the 19th hole overlooks the South Course's first and 18th holes and the North Course's 18th. At the Kona CC, the restaurant attracts non-golfers for lunch and dinner, offering good fare and views of the Ocean Course and Keauhou Bay. Cheers!

Waikoloa Village Golf Course. Robert Trent Jones Jr., the same designer who created some of the most expensive courses on the Kohala coast, designed this little gem, which is 20 minutes from the coast, in 1972. Though not affiliated with the resorts, the Waikoloa Village course is the site of the annual Waikoloa Open, one of the most prestigious tournaments in Hawai'i. Holes run across rolling hills with sweeping mountain and ocean views. ✉ *68-1792 Melia St., Waikoloa* ☎ *808/883–9621* ⊕ *www.waikoloa.org* ⚑ *18 holes. 6230 yds. Par 72. Green Fee: $80* ⌘ *Facilities: Driving range, putting green, golf carts, rental clubs, lessons, restaurant, bar.*

HIKING

Meteorologists classify the world's weather into 13 climates. Ten are here on the Big Island, and you can experience as many of them as you like. The ancient Hawaiians blazed trails across their archipelago, and many of these paths can still be used today. Part of the King's Trail at 'Anaeho'omalu winds through a field of lava rocks covered with prehistoric carvings called petroglyphs, meant to communicate stories of births, deaths, marriages, and other family events. Plus, the serenity of remote beaches, such as Papakōlea Beach (Green Sand Beach), is accessible only to hikers.

For information on all Big Island's state parks, contact the **Department of Land and Natural Resources, State Parks Division** (✉ *75 Aupuni St., Hilo*

96720 ☎808/974–6200 ⊕*www.*
hawaiistateparks.org).

BEST SPOTS

At **Kekaha Kai (Kona Coast) State Park**
(⊠*Hwy. 19, sign about 2 mi north
of Keāhole–Kona International
Airport marks rough road*), two
1½-mi-long unpaved roads lead to
the Mahai'ula Beach and Kua Bay
sections of the park. Connecting
the two is the 4½-mi Ala Kahakai
historic coastal trail. Midway, a
hike to the summit of Pu'u Ku'ili,
a 342-foot-high cinder cone, offers
an excellent view of the coastline.
It's dry and hot with no drinking
water, so be sure to pack sunscreen
and bottled water.

The **Kealakekua Bay and Captain Cook Monument Trail** (⊠*Trailhead
just off Hwy. 11 at Captain Cook town on Nāpō'opo'o Rd. to Kealakekua Bay*) is one of Kona's more popular moderately difficult hikes.
About 100 yards from the turnoff, the steep, loose gravel and dirt trail
descends several hundred feet across old lava flows. There are some
steep switchbacks. Shade along the upper section gives way to sun
where the trail opens to lava fields. Nearer to the bay, the trail passes
through old Hawaiian village ruins and by the Captain Cook Monument, a tall white obelisk on the spot where the famed navigator was
killed in 1779 in a dispute with native Hawaiians. The bay is the site of
the Kealakekua Underwater Marine Reserve and is popular with divers
and snorkelers. The 2½-mi hike is about a three-hour round trip. The
hike back up is steep and tiring, so allow plenty of time. Park along the
road. Bring sunscreen, hat, water, and food.

Hawai'i Volcanoes National Park (⊠*Near Volcano Village, Hwy. 11, 30
mi south of Hilo* ☎808/985–6000 ⊕*www.hawaii.volcanoes.national-
park.com*) is perhaps the Big Island's premier hiking center. The 150 mi
of trails provide close-up views of fern and rain-forest environments,
cinder cones, steam vents, lava fields, and current lava flow activity.
Day hikes range from easy to moderately difficult, and from one or two
hours to a full day. For a bigger challenge, consider an overnight or
multiday backcountry hike with a stay in a park cabin. To do so, you
must first obtain a free permit at the Kīlauea Visitor Center. Just outside the park's entrance in Volcano, the Volcano Art Center (⊕www.
volcanoartcenter.org) guides visitors on a free one-hour nature hike of
its Naiulani trail every Monday morning at 8:30 AM. The guided walk
educates visitors about the flora and flauna of volcanic rain forests, and
the cultural and therapeutic uses of various plants, herbs, and flowers
in Hawaiian life. *For more on Hawai'i Volcanoes National Park, see
highlighted feature in the Exploring chapter.* **Muliwai Trail** (⊠*Trailhead
is on the west side of Waipi'o Valley, at the end of Hwy. 240 at the*

Continued on page 150

HAWAI'I'S PLANTS 101

Hawai'i is a bounty of rainbow-colored flowers and plants. The evening air is scented with their fragrance. Just look at the front yard of almost any home, travel any road, or visit any local park and you'll see a spectacular array of colored blossoms and leaves. What most visitors don't know is that the plants they are seeing are not native to Hawai'i; rather, they were introduced during the last two centuries as ornamental plants, or for timber, shade, or fruit.

Hawai'i boasts nearly every climate on the planet, excluding the two most extreme: arctic tundra and arid desert. The Islands have wine-growing regions, cactus-speckled ranchlands, icy mountaintops, and the rainiest forests on earth.

Plants introduced from around the world thrive here. The lush lowland valleys along the windward coasts are predominantly populated by non-native trees including yellow- and red-fruited **guava**, silvery-leafed **kukui**, and orange-flowered **tulip trees**.

The colorful **plumeria flower**, very fragrant and commonly used in lei making, and the giant multicolored **hibiscus flower** are both used by many women as hair adornments, and are two of the most common plants found around homes and hotels. The umbrella-like **monkeypod tree** from Central America provides shade in many of Hawai'i's parks including Kapiolani Park in Honolulu. Hawai'i's largest tree, found in Lahaina, Maui, is a giant **banyan tree**. Its canopy and massive support roots cover about two-thirds of an acre. The native **o'hia tree**, with its brilliant red brush-like flowers, and the **hapu'u**, a giant tree fern, are common in Hawai'i's forests and are also used ornamentally in gardens and around homes.

Bougainvillea

Guava

Monkeypod

Banyan

Ohia Lehua *

Tulip Tree

Plumeria

Pandanus

Hibiscus

Anthurium

Kukui Tree

Hapu'u

*endemic to Hawai'i

DID YOU KNOW?

Over 2,200 plant species are found in the Hawaiian Islands, but only about 1,000 are native. Of these, 282 are so rare, they are endangered. Hawai'i's endemic plants evolved from ancestral seeds arriving on the islands over thousands of years as baggage on birds, floating on ocean currents, or drifting on winds from continents thousands of miles away. Once here, these plants evolved in isolation creating many new species known nowhere else in the world.

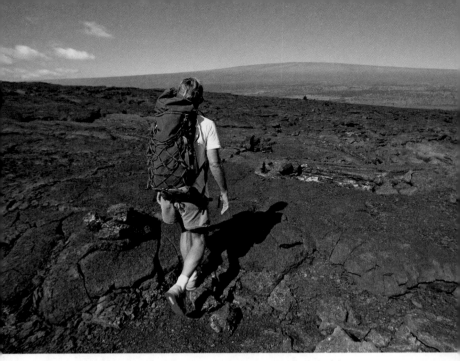

Volcanoes National Park's 150 mi of trails offer easy to moderately difficult day hikes.

bottom of the valley ☎*808/974–4221* ⊕*www.hawaiitrails.org*) begins in the Big Island's most famous valley. On the west side of mystical Waipi'o, the Muliwai trail leads to the back of the valley, then switchbacks up through a series of gulches, and finally emerges into Eden-like Waimanu Valley. Only very experienced hikers should attempt the full, 18-mile trail, but the first piece of it offers a great peak at Waipi'o. For those interested in a backcountry adventure, completing the trail can span two to three days of backpacking and camping, which requires camping permits from the Division of Forestry and Wildlife in Hilo.

Onomea Bay Trail (✉*Follow signs to 4-mi scenic loop off highway Hwy. 19, turn left onto Old Hawaiian Belt Rd., trail starts just before Botanical Garden* ⊕*www.hawaiitrails.org*) is a short but beautiful trail packed with stunning views of the cliffs, bays, and gulches of the Hamakua coast on the east side of the island. The trail is just under a mile and fairly easy, with access down to the shore if you want to dip your feet in, although we don't recommend trying to swim in the rough waters here. One word of warning: unless you pay the $15 entry fee to the Botanical Garden, entering its gates (which is easy to do even by accident off the trail), will send one of their guards running after you to nicely but firmly point you back to the free trail.

GOING WITH A GUIDE

To get to some of the best trails and places, it's worth going with a skilled guide. Costs range from $95 to $165, and some hikes include picnic meals or refreshments and gear, such as binoculars, ponchos, and walking sticks. The outfitters mentioned here also offer customized adventure tours.

Hawai'i Forest & Trail. Expert naturalist guides take you to 500-foot Kalopa Falls in North Kohala, through the 4,000-year-old craters at Mount Hualālai (the volcano that created all those lava fields along the coast), and on bird-watching expeditions throughout the island. In addition to its other expeditions, the company offers tours in Pinzgauers (Austrian all-terrain vehicles) that are perfect for groups, especially those that include off-road junkies. It offers tours into lava tubes and through normally inaccessible areas of Hawai'i Volcanoes National Park as well, and its two Kohala waterfall tours (one in a Pinzgauer, the other on foot) include cool swims in streams and pools fed by the waterfalls. ☎808/331–8505 or 800/464–1993 ⊕www.hawaii-forest.com.

Hawaiian Walkways. Hawaiian Walkways conducts several tours—a Kona Cloud Forest botanical walk, waterfall hikes, coastal adventures, a hike on the "saddle" road between Mauna Kea and Mauna Loa, and jaunts through Hawai'i Volcanoes National Park—as well as custom-designed trips. ☎808/775–0372 or 800/457–7759 ⊕www.hawaiian-walkways.com.

> ### HIKING HAWAI'I'S TRAILS
>
> ■ Trails on the eastern or windward sides of the islands are often wet and muddy, making them slippery and unstable, so wear good hiking shoes or boots.
>
> ■ Bring along a cell phone, but be aware that service is spotty on the island.
>
> ■ Don't eat any unknown fruits or plants.
>
> ■ Darkness comes suddenly here, so carry a flashlight if there's a chance you'll be out after sunset.

HORSEBACK RIDING

With its *paniolo* (cowboy) heritage and the ranches it spawned, the Big Island is a great place for equestrians. Riders can gallop through green pastures, ride to Kealakekua Bay to see the Captain Cook Monument, or saunter into Waipi'o Valley for a taste of old Hawai'i.

King's Trail Rides. Riders take a two-hour excursion to the Captain Cook Monument in Kealakekua Bay for snorkeling. All your gear is provided, except for fins and reef walkers. It costs $135–$150 per person, with lunch. ✉81-6420 Mamalahoa Hwy. (Hwy. 11), Kealakekua ☎808/323–2388 or 808/345–0616 ⊕www.konacowboy.com.

Na'alapa Stables. This company is a good bet, especially for novice riders. The horses are well trained, and the stable is well run. Rides through the Waipi'o Valley cross freshwater streams and pass a black-sand beach. Na'alapa also offers open-range and horse-drawn wagon rides on the historic Kahua Ranch in North Kohala. Rides to Waipi'o depart twice a day, Monday through Saturday, 9:30 AM and 1 PM, from Waipi'o Valley Artworks; Kahua Ranch rides depart twice daily

Hawaiian Cowboys?

When British Captain George Vancouver gave King Kamehameha a gift of cattle in the 1790s, he probably didn't anticipate the chain of events he would set in motion. The cattle, which were allowed to roam free, multiplied. Within a few years there were thousands of wild cattle on the island. In the early 1800s, when the young sailor John Palmer Parker jumped ship and settled in Hawai'i, he was appointed a wild cattle hunter to control the herds, which were a nuisance to many people. Parker soon began trading the meat, tallow, and hides with visiting ships. He married a high chief's daughter and gradually expanded his lands, eventually establishing Parker Ranch. Thus was born the big country cattle industry.

In the mid-1800s, *vaqueros* (Spanish-Mexican cowboys) were brought to the Big Island to help control the wild cattle. They also taught the fine art of cowboying to the Hawaiians. The *paniolos* (Hawaiian for cowboys) taught the natives how to ride horses and rope cattle and the other skills a cowboy needed. Today's Hawai'ian *paniolos* are a product of that cross-cultural experience.

from the ranch at 8:30 AM and 1 PM. Rates for a 2½-hour ride begin at $89 per person for both locations. ⊠ *Off Hwy. 240, Kukuihaele* ☎ *808/775–0419* ⊕ *www.naalapastables.com.*

Waipi'o Ridge Stables. Two different rides around the rim of Waipi'o Valley are offered—a 2½-hour trek for $85 and a 5-hour hidden-waterfall adventure (with swimming) for $165. Riders meet at Waipi'o Valley Artworks. ⊠ *Off Hwy. 240, Kukuihaele* ☎ *808/775–1007 or 877/757–1414* ⊕ *www.waipioridgestables.com.*

Waipi'o on Horseback. Not many outfits venture into the green jungle of the floor of the Waipi'o Valley. Waipi'o on Horseback takes you to an authentic taro farm. Rides, which depart twice daily, Monday through Saturday, from the Last Chance Store, cost $78. ⊠ *Last Chance Store, off Hwy. 240, Kukuihaele* ☎ *877/775–7291 or 808/775–7291* ⊕ *www. waipio.homestead.com.*

SKIING

Where else but Hawai'i can you surf, snorkel, and snow ski on the same day? In winter, the 13,796-foot Mauna Kea (Hawaiian for "white mountain") has snow at higher elevations—and along with that, skiing. No lifts, no manicured slopes, no faux-Alpine lodges, no après-ski nightlife—but the chance to ski some of the most remote (and let's face it, unlikely) runs on earth. Some people even have been known to use boogie board as sleds, but we don't recommend it. As long as you're up there, fill your cooler with the white stuff for a snowball fight on the beach with local kids.

Ski Guides Hawai'i. So you're an experienced skier but didn't pack your gear on a tropical Hawaiian vacation? Christopher Langan of

Mauna Kea Ski Corporation is the only licensed outfitter providing transportation, guide services, and ski equipment on Mauna Kea. Snow can fall from Thanksgiving through June, but the most likely months are February and March. This isn't Sun Valley; the runs are fairly short, and hidden lava rocks and other dangers abound. Langan

charges $450 per person for a daylong experience that includes refreshments, lunch, ski or snowboard equipment, guide service, transportation from Waimea, and four-wheel-drive shuttle back up the mountain after each ski run. He also offers a $250 mountain ski service without the frills and ski or snowboard rentals. ⌂ *Box 1954, Kamuela96743* ☎ *808/885–4188, 808/884–5131 off-season* ⊕ *www.skihawaii.com.*

TENNIS

Many of the island's resorts allow nonguests to play for a fee. They also rent rackets, balls, and shoes. On the Kohala Coast, try the Fairmont Orchid Hawai'i, the Hilton Waikoloa Village, and Waikoloa Beach Marriott. In Kailua-Kona there's the Ohana Keauhou Beach Resort, King Kamehameha's Kona Beach Hotel, and the Royal Kona Resort.

Contact the **County of Hawai'i Department of Parks and Recreation** (⊠ *25 Aupuni St., Hilo96720* ☎ *808/961–8311* ⊕ *www.hawaii-county.com/ directory/dir_parks.htm*) for information on all public courts.

In Kailua-Kona, you can play for free at the **Kailua Playground** (⊠ *75-5794 Kuakini Hwy., Kailua-Kona* ☎ *808/886–1655*). Tennis courts are available at **Old Kona Airport State Recreation Area** (⊠ *North end of Kuakini Hwy., Kailua-Kona* ☎ *808/327–4958 or 808/974–6200*).

On the Hilo side, there's a small fee to play on the eight courts (three lighted for night play) at **Hilo Tennis Stadium** (⊠ *Ho'olulu County Park, Pi'ilani and Kalanikoa Sts., Hilo* ☎ *808/961–8720*).

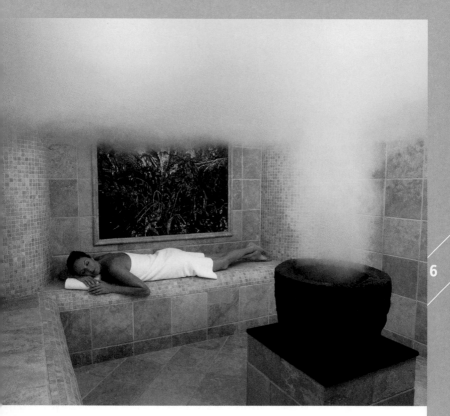

Shops & Spas

WORD OF MOUTH

"Not sure if you are in Hilo on a Saturday—but we enjoyed the tent market—nice souvenirs (coconut-shell purses), fresh flowers, and some fresh produce as well."

—Miss_Maple

6

Join, Ask, Share. www.fodors.com/forums/

By Amy
Westervelt

Residents like to complain that there isn't a lot of great shopping on the Big Island, but unless you're searching for winter coats or high-tech toys, you can find plenty to deplete your pocketbook.

Dozens of shops in Kailua-Kona offer a range of souvenirs from far-flung corners of the globe and plenty of local coffee and foodstuffs to take home to everyone you left behind. Housewares and artworks made from local materials (lava rock, minerals, koa, and milo wood) fill the shelves of small boutiques and galleries throughout the island. Upscale shops in the resorts along the Kohala Coast carry high-quality clothing and accessories, as do a few boutiques scattered around the island. Galleries and gift shops, many showcasing the work of local artists, fill historic buildings in Waimea and North Kohala, and many of the island's former sugar plantation towns have been turned into charming art communities, with local artists selling their wares directly from their studios. Hotel shops generally offer the most attractive and original resort wear but, as with everything else at resorts, the prices run higher than elsewhere on the island.

High prices are entirely too common at the island's resort spas, but a handful of truly unique experiences are worth every penny. Beyond the resorts, the Big Island is also home to independent massage therapists and day spas that offer similar treatments for lower prices, albeit usually in a slightly less luxurious atmosphere. In addition to the obvious relaxation benefits of any spa trip, the Big Island's spas have done a fantastic job incorporating local traditions and ingredients into their menus. Massage artists work with coconut or *kokui* (candlenut) oil, hot stone massages are conducted with lava stones, and ancient healing techniques such as *lomi lomi*—a massage technique that combines firm, constant movement and traditional chants—are a staple at every island spa.

SHOPS

In general, stores and shopping centers on the Big Island open at 9 or 10 AM and close by 6 PM. Hilo's Prince Kūhiō Shopping Plaza stays open until 9 PM on weekdays. In Kona, most shops in shopping plazas that are geared to tourists also remain open until 9 PM. Big outlets such as KTA Superstore are open until midnight.

KOHALA

SHOPPING CENTERS
Kawaihae Harbor Center. This harborside shopping plaza houses a dive shop, a bathing-suit store, restaurants, and art galleries, including the Harbor Gallery. ⊠ *Hwy. 270, Kawaihae.*

King's Shops at Waikoloa Village. Here you can find fine stores such as Under the Koa Tree, with its upscale gift items crafted by artisans, along with high-end outlets such as DFS Galleria and Louis Vuitton and several other specialty resort shops and boutiques. At the other end of the spectrum, there are also a couple of convenience stores here, but the prices are stiff. ⊠*250 Waikoloa Beach Dr., Waikoloa* ☎*808/886–8811.*

The Shops at Mauna Lani. A relatively new complex including everything from restaurants (Tommy Bahama's Tropical Café, Ruth's Chris Steakhouse, and a new branch of the popular Kenichi sushi restaurant) to clothing (Tommy Bahama's and A'ama Sports) to high-end housewares (Oasis), galleries (Lahaina Galleries), jewelry stores, even a nail salon and a lingerie shop. ⊠*68-1330 Mauna Lani Dr., Kohala Coast* ☎*808/885–9501* ⊕*www.shopsatmaunalani.com.*

Waikoloa Queen's Marketplace. Another large shopping complex on the Kohala Coast, this one houses several clothing shops, a jewelry store, gallery, gift shops, and a casual bar and grill. The most hotly anticipated addition to this relatively new complex is a 20,000-square-foot gourmet grocery store, which will likely come with the high prices you'd expect in this neighborhood. The Marketplace butts up against a new performing arts center and a landscaped network of "Cultural Gardens." ⊠*201 Waikoloa Beach Dr., Waikoloa* ☎*877/924–6562* ⊕*www.waikoloabeachresort.com.*

ARTS & CRAFTS

Elements Jewelry & Fine Crafts. The Old Nanbu Hotel, built in 1898, is a must-see on any stop in North Kohala. While you're there, check out John Flynn's beautiful store. In the front window Flynn creates exquisite jewelry like delicate silver leis and gold waterfalls. The shop also showcases carefully chosen gifts, including unusual ceramics and glass. ⊠*54-3885 Akoni Pule Hwy., Kapa'au* ☎*808/889–0760.*

Gallery at Bamboo. Inside the Bamboo Restaurant, one of the Island's favorite eateries, this gallery seduces visitors with elegant koa-wood pieces such as rocking chairs and writing desks. It also has a wealth of gift items such as boxes, jewelry, and Hawaiian wrapping paper. ⊠*Hwy. 270, Hāwī* ☎*808/889–1441.*

BOOKSTORES

Kohala Book Shop. In the historic Old Nanbu Hotel, the state's largest used-book store contains one of the most complete Hawaiian and Pacific collections. There are also some rare first editions. ⊠*54-3885 Akoni Pule Hwy., Kapa'au* ☎*808/889–6400.*

CLOTHING & SHOES

A'ama Surf and Sport. The new Kohala coast location of the popular Kona surf shop carries the groovy mix of surf and street that it's known for, as well as a fantastic assortment of bathing suits. ⊠*68-1330 Mauna Lani Dr., Kohala Coast* ☎*808/885–7879.*

As Hawi Turns. This North Kohala shop, in the historic 1932 Toyama Building, adds a sophisticated touch to resort wear with items made of hand-painted silk. There are vintage and secondhand treasures as well. ✉*Akoni Pule Hwy., Hāwī* ☎*808/889–5023.*

Persimmon. A darling little boutique stocked with trendy women's clothing from lines such as Ella Moss, Kenzie, Three Dots, Rebecca Beeson, and Matty M, also carries lingerie from Mary Green, and fantastic purses imported from Indonesia. Other gift items include funky stationery and cards, and candles. The Hāwī location tends to carry more casual items, while the Waikoloa location offers more dresses. ✉*55-3435 Akoni Pule Hwy., Suite 9, Hāwī* ☎*808/889–1050* ✉*201 Waikoloa Beach Dr., Waikoloa* ☎*808/895–4898.*

FLOWERS & LEIS

Na Pua O Kohala. At this popular North Kohala flower shop, you can order leis or let owner Johanna Bard help you create a memorable bouquet. She'll ship your selections for you. ✉*55-3413 Akoni Pule Hwy., Hāwī* ☎*808/889–5541 or 877/889–5571.*

GALLERIES

Ackerman Fine Art Gallery. Painter Gary Ackerman; his wife, Yesan; and their daughter, Camille, have a fine and varied collection of gifts for sale in their side-by-side gallery and gift shop near the King Kamehameha statue. ✉*54-3878 Akoni Pule Hwy., Kapaʻau* ☎*808/889–5971.*

Nanbu Gallery. Here you can admire the paintings of owner Patrick Sweeney, along with the work of glass artist Robinson Scott and other island artists. ✉*54-3885 Akoni Pule Hwy., Kapaʻau* ☎*808/889–0997.*

Rankin Gallery. Watercolorist and oil painter Patrick Louis Rankin showcases his own and other local artists' work in his shop in a restored old plantation store (the Wo On Store), next to the Chinese community and social hall, the Tong Wo Society, on the way to Pololū Valley. ✉*53-4380 Akoni Pule Hwy., Kapaʻau* ☎*808/889–6849.*

Swerdlow Art Gallery. This is a great little gallery with Swerdlow's studio in the back and unique, beautiful paintings and prints in the front. Swerdlow also showcases the work of other local artists, offering everything from paintings to prints and etched glass, plus a range of gift items and interesting home objets dʻart. ✉*54-3862 Akoni Pule Hwy., Kapaʻau* ☎*808/889–0002.*

WAIMEA

SHOPPING CENTERS

Parker Ranch Center. With a snazzy ranch-style motif, this shopping hub includes a supermarket, coffee shop, natural foods store, and some clothing boutiques. The Parker Ranch Store and Parker Ranch Visitor Center and Museum are also here, and the Kahilu Center next door hosts plays and musical entertainment most nights. ✉*67-1185 Māmalahoa Hwy., Waimea.*

Parker Square. Browse around boutiques here and in the adjacent **High Country Traders,** where you may find hand-stitched Hawaiian quilts, antiques, or local artworks. ✉ *65-1279 Kawaihae Rd., Waimea* ☎ *808/331–1000.*

Waimea Center. This standard strip mall has a handful of fast-food restaurants, a grocery store, video store, gift shop, and a travel agency. It's highly useful if you're passing through Waimea and need to pick up a few things along the way. ✉ *65-1158 Māmalahoa Hwy., Waimea.*

ARTS & CRAFTS

Dan DeLuz's Woods. Master bowl-turner Dan DeLuz creates works of art from 50 types of exotic wood grown on the Big Island. The shop features a variety of items—from picture frames to jewelry boxes—made from koa, monkeypod, mango, kiawe, and other fine local hardwoods. Dan's wife, Mary Lou, operates the Koa Shop Kaffee restaurant next door. There's another branch south of Hilo in Kurtistown. ✉ *64-1013 Māmalahoa Hwy., Waimea* ☎ *808/885–5856* ✉ *Hwy. 19, Kurtistown* ☎ *808/968–6607.*

Gallery of Great Things. It's not just a cleverly named boutique. At this Parker Square shop, you might fall in love with the Ni'ihau shell lei ranging from $150 to $7,000. More affordable are koa mirrors and other high-quality artifacts from around the Pacific basin. ✉ *65-1279 Kawaihae Rd., Waimea* ☎ *808/885–7706.*

Harbor Gallery. For fine art, furniture, and decorative pieces made with koa and other native woods, be sure to stop here. Though it also carries some of the usual ocean scene schlock, Harbor has one of the better and more unique selections of art on the island. The gallery is next to Harbor Grill. ✉ *Kawaihae Harbor Center, Hwy. 270, Kawaihae* ☎ *808/882–1510* ⊕ *www.harborgallery.biz.*

KAILUA-KONA

SHOPPING CENTERS

Coconut Grove Marketplace. Just south of Kona Inn Shopping Village, this meandering labyrinth of airy buildings hides coffee shops, boutiques, ethnic restaurants, and an exquisite gallery. At night locals gather here to watch the outdoor sand volleyball games held in the middle of the marketplace or grab a couple of beers at the sports bar. ✉ *75-5795–75-5825 Ali'i Dr.* ☎ *808/326–2555.*

Crossroads Shopping Center. Shopping in Kailua-Kona has begun to go the way of mainland cities—this complex includes both a Safeway and a Wal-Mart. ■TIP→ This is also where you'll find Kona Natural Foods, one of the best whole foods stores on the island, and Mana Korean BBQ, a cheap, fast, and tasty mixed-plate favorite. Borders, Jamba Juice, and a second location of A'ama Surf & Sports are right across the street. ✉ *75-1000 Henry St.* ☎ *808/329–4822.*

Kaloko Industrial Park. Developed for local consumers, this shopping plaza has outlets such as Costco Warehouse and Home Depot. It can be useful for practical purchases (food from Costco can be a good deal if you're staying in a condo for a week or more) and the occasional

Continued on page 164

ALL ABOUT LEIS

Leis brighten every occasion in Hawai'i, from birthdays to bar mitzvahs to baptisms. Creative artisans weave nature's bounty—flowers, ferns, vines, and seeds—into gorgeous creations that convey an array of heartfelt messages: "Welcome," "Congratulations," "Good luck," "Farewell," "Thank you," "I love you." When it's difficult to find the right words, a lei expresses exactly the right sentiments.

WHERE TO BUY THE BEST LEIS

Florists **Na Pua O Kohala** (54-3760 Akoni Pule Hwy., Kapa'au, 808/885-5541); **Honopua Farm** (Waimea, 808/885-4148); **Hawai'i Tropicals** (71 Banyan Dr., Hilo, 808/961-5575); **Elegant Flowers and Gifts** (68-1845 Waikoloa Rd., Waikoloa Village, 808/883-0225). Lei stands at the Kona and Hilo airports sell a surprisingly nice assortment of leis at reasonable prices. KTA, Safeway, and Costco also sell leis, but they tend to stick to "basics" like plumeria, orchid or tuberose.

LEI ETIQUETTE

■ To wear a closed lei, drape it over your shoulders, half in front and half in back. Open leis are worn around the neck, with the ends draped over the front in equal lengths.

■ Pīkake, ginger, and other sweet, delicate blossoms are "feminine" leis. Men opt for cigar, crown flower, and ti leaf, which are sturdier and don't emit as much fragrance.

■ Leis are always presented with a kiss, a custom that supposedly dates back to World War II when a hula dancer fancied an officer at a U.S.O. show. Taking a dare from members of her troupe, she took off her lei, placed it around his neck, and kissed him on the cheek.

■ You shouldn't wear a lei before you give it to someone else. Hawaiians believe the lei absorbs your *mana* (spirit); if you give your lei away, you'll be giving away part of your essence.

ORCHID

Growing wild on every continent except Antarctica, orchids—which range in color from yellow to green to purple—comprise the largest family of plants in the world. There are more than 20,000 species of orchids, but only three are native to Hawai'i—and they are very rare. The pretty lavender vanda you see hanging by the dozens at local lei stands has probably been imported from Thailand.

MAILE

Maile, an endemic twining vine with a heady aroma, is sacred to Laka, goddess of the hula. In ancient times, dancers wore maile and decorated hula altars with it to honor Laka. Today, "open" maile leis usually are given to men. Instead of ribbon, interwoven lengths of maile are used at dedications of new businesses. The maile is untied, never snipped, for doing so would symbolically "cut" the company's success.

'ILIMA

Designated by Hawai'i's Territorial Legislature in 1923 as the official flower of the island of O'ahu, the golden 'ilima is so delicate it lasts for just a day. Five to seven hundred blossoms are needed to make one garland. Queen Emma, wife of King Kamehameha IV, preferred 'ilima over all other leis, which may have led to the incorrect belief that they were reserved only for royalty.

PLUMERIA

This ubiquitous flower is named after Charles Plumier, the noted French botanist who discovered it in Central America in the late 1600s. Plumeria ranks among the most popular leis in Hawai'i because it's fragrant, hardy, plentiful, inexpensive, and requires very little care. Although yellow is the most common color, you'll also find plumeria leis in shades of pink, red, orange, and "rainbow" blends.

PĪKAKE

Favored for its fragile beauty and sweet scent, pīkake was introduced from India. In lieu of pearls, many brides in Hawai'i adorn themselves with long, multiple strands of white pīkake. Princess Kaiulani enjoyed showing guests her beloved pīkake and peacocks at Āinahau, her Waikīkī home. Interestingly, pīkake is the Hawaiian word for both the bird and the blossom.

KUKUI

The kukui (candlenut) is Hawai'i's state tree. Early Hawaiians strung kukui nuts (which are quite oily) together and burned them for light; mixed burned nuts with oil to make an indelible dye; and mashed roasted nuts to consume as a laxative. Kukui nut leis may not have been made until after Western contact, when the Hawaiians saw black beads from Europe and wanted to imitate them.

surprise gift item (you don't have to tell them you got it at the Hawai'i Costco). ⊠*Off Hwy. 19 and Hina Lani St., near Kona Airport.*

Keauhou Shopping Center. About 5 mi south of Kailua-Kona, the stores and boutiques here include KTA Superstore, Longs Drugs, and Alapaki's Hawaiian Gifts, along with Kenichi Pacific, a great sushi restaurant; a multiplex movie theater; and Peaberry & Galette, the only hip café on the island. ⊠*78-6831 Ali'i Dr.* ☎*808/322–3000.*

King Kamehameha Shopping Mall. Just around the corner from the King Kamehameha Hotel, this outdoor mall includes a wine market and bar, a couple of quality clothing stores, and a popular Internet café. ⊠*75-5626 Kuakini Hwy.*

Kona Marketplace. On the *makai* side of Ali'i Drive in the heart of Kailua-Kona, extending for an entire block along Kailua Bay, the village is crammed with boutiques selling bright beach wraps and knickknacks. The marketplace, whose tenants seem to change almost annually, is across the street from Tacos El Unico, one of the few authentic Mexican food joints on the island. ⊠*75-5744 Ali'i Dr.* ☎*808/329–6573.*

Makalapua Center. Just north of Kona, off Highway 19, islanders find bargains at Kmart and island-influenced clothing, jewelry, and housewares at the large Macy's, along with one of the island's largest movie theaters. ⊠*Kamakaeha Ave. at Hwy. 19, south of Kailua-Kona.*

ARTS & CRAFTS

Alapaki's Hawaiian Gifts. For hula instruments, intricate feather headbands, and other original art, look no further than this popular shop. ⊠*Keauhou Shopping Center, 78-6831 Ali'i Dr.* ☎*808/322–2007.*

★ **Antiques and Orchids.** Housed in a great old green building with white trim along Highway 11, this shop lives up to its name, offering shoppers a well-selected collection of antiques and Hawaiiana, interspersed with orchids of various colors and varieties. ⊠*King Kamehameha's Kona Beach Hotel, 81-6224 Māmalahoa Hwy.* ☎*808/323–9851.*

Hōlualoa Gallery. In the little coffee town of Hōlualoa, this is one of several excellent galleries that crowd the narrow street. It carries stunning raku (Japanese lead-glazed pottery). ⊠*76-5921 Māmalahoa Hwy., Hōlualoa* ☎*808/322–8484.*

★ **Made on the Big Island.** This place is geared to cruise-ship passengers with little time on their hands. It's one-stop shopping for traditional island gifts. You can find quite a few treasures here, such as koa boxes and bonsai trees that may be exported. ⊠*King Kamehameha's Kona Beach Hotel, 75-5660 Palani Rd.* ☎*808/326–4949.*

CLOTHING & SHOES

'A'ama Surf & Sport. This boutique has some cool button-ups for men, along with cropped pants in a variety of fabrics and cute swimsuits for women (many from the Salinas beachwear label). There's a second location on Henry, across the street from the Crossroads Shopping Center, and a new, third location on the Kohala coast at the Shops at Mauna Lani. ⊠*75-5741 Kuakini Hwy.* ☎*808/326–7890* ⊠*75-*

1002 Henry St. ☎*808/326–7890*
⊕*www.aamasurf.com.*

Flamingo's. Stop by this little shop to browse vintage clothing and antique jewelry. ✉*Kona Inn Shopping Village, 75-5744 Ali'i Dr.* ☎*808/329–4122.*

★ **Hilo Hattie.** The west coast outlet of the well-known clothier matches his-and-her aloha wear and carries a huge selection of casual clothes, slippers, jewelry, and souvenirs. ■TIP→ **Call for free transportation from nearby hotels.** ✉*75-5597 Palani Rd., Kopiko Plaza, Kailua-Kona* ☎*808/329–7200.*

ISN'T IT GOOD, HAWAIIAN WOO

That pretty wood with th grain you see in shops around the island is koa wood, one of the few species native to Hawai'i (even the palm tree was a transplant). It's expensive and you're not likely to find a good deal on it no matter how hard you look. Why? Koa wood is now protected under a moratorium and you must have a permit to harvest it. Supply, demand, you get the drift.

6

Honolua Surf Company. Surfer chic, compliments of Roxy, Volcom, and the like: This is a great place to look for a bikini or board shorts or to pick up a cool, casual T-shirt. Their second location, just across the walkway, focuses on women's clothing, with a large assortment of bathing suits and sundresses. ✉*Kona Inn Shopping Village* ☎*808/329–1001.*

Island Salsa. You'll find plenty of tropical toppers and gift items, as well as cute souvenir T-shirts, at this little shop. ✉*Kona Inn Shopping Village, 75-5744 Ali'i Dr.* ☎*808/329–9279.*

★ **Kimura's Lauhala Shop.** Men can pick up an authentic *lau hala* hat here for some stylish sun protection. ✉*Māmalahoa Hwy., Hōlualoa* ☎*808/324–0053.*

Miss M. Kealakekua is home to the first high-end designer boutique on the Big Island, a prayer answered for locals who had been forever complaining that they couldn't find "cool" clothes anywhere. Though the original owner has moved on, and the store has changed its name (it was formerly Sirena), Miss M. still carries squeal-worthy contemporary clothing from designers like Carlos Miele, Barbara Bui, and Catherine Malandrino. If these names are familiar, we don't need to tell you to expect high prices. ✉*79-7491 Māmalahoa Hwy., Kealakekua* ☎*808/322–3900.*

★ **My Best Friend's Closet.** The airy and modern My Best Friend's Closet seems more like a boutique you'd find in Santa Monica than on the Big Island. The large shop offers the island's widest selection of stylish women's clothing that can't be classified as surfer duds or resortwear. Although there are a handful of other boutiques on the island, this new beauty offers both the best selection *and* the best prices. The shop is tucked into the side of the Kona Marketplace, on the same side of the street, but across the alleyway from Pancho & Lefty's and Fujimama's, ✉*75-5725 Ali'i Dr., Kailua-Kona* ☎*808/329–2002.*

Paradise Found. In the upcountry town of Kainaliu, as well as in two of Kailua-Kona's shopping centers, this reputable spot carries contemporary silk and rayon clothing. ⊠*Māmalahoa Hwy. 11, Kainaliu* ☎*808/322–2111* ⊠*Lanihau Center, 75-5595 Palani Rd., Kailua-Kona* ☎*808/329–2221* ⊠*Keauhou Shopping Center, 78-6831 Ali'i Dr., Kailua-Kona* ☎*808/324–1177.*

FOOD

Kailua Candy Company. The chocolate here is made with locally grown cacao beans from the Original Hawaiian Chocolate Factory, and most truffles and candies incorporate other local ingredients as well (passion fruit truffles—yum!). Of course, tasting is part of the fun. Through a glass wall you can watch the chocolate artists at work. ⊠*In the Koloko Industrial Area, Kamanu and Kauholo Sts., Kailua-Kona* ☎*808/329–2522.*

Kona Wine Market. This popular wine market carries both local and imported varietals, along with a selection of fine cheeses and other gourmet food products, Hawaiian gifts and products (macadamia nuts, coffee, etc.), and the best selection of cigars and tobacco products on the island. As an added bonus, they'll deliver wine and any of their gourmet food products to your hotel or condo. Their Mixx bar is a somewhat recent addition to the Kailua-Kona nightlife scene (not that it really qualifies as a "scene"), and with live music and happy hour deals it has become popular fast. ⊠*King Kamehameha Mall, 75-5626 Kuakini Hwy.* ☎*808/329–9400* ⊕*www.konawinemarket.com.*

♻ **Sweet Ohana Candy Factory.** You can spot the bright pink building of this locally owned sweets shop from miles away. Sweet Ohana makes its own delicious taffy and chocolates with no hydrogenated oils or wax. In the tradition of old-fashioned candy stores, it smells absolutely heavenly inside, and it has a 1950s-style soda fountain and café that serves shakes, malts, ice cream sodas, and a limited breakfast and lunch menu. It's a fun stop for kids as well as a wireless hot spot for the laptop-toting crowd. ⊠*Kuakini Hwy., Kailua-Kona* ☎*808/329–9676* ⊕*www.sweetohanacandy.com.*

GALLERIES

Kona Arts Center. There's an entire community of artists at work in this complex; feel free to drop in if the doors are open. ⊠*Māmalahoa Hwy., Hōlualoa.*

MARKETS

Ali'i Gardens Marketplace. More a flea market than a farmers' market, this cluster of about 50 vendor stalls has beautiful tropical flowers, jewelry, clothing, produce, coffee, and even 'ukuleles. It's open Wednesday to Sunday, 9 AM until 5 PM. ⊠*75-6129 Ali'i Dr., 1½ mi south of Kona Inn Shopping Village, Kailua-Kona* ☎*808/334–1381* ⊕*www.aliigardens.com.*

Keauhou Farmers' Market. Less obvious than the others in its location 5 mi south of Kailua-Kona, this market is packed most Saturdays (8 AM–noon) for good reason: live music, plus local produce (much of it organic, some of it experimental), honey, goat cheese, meat, seafood, flowers, coffee, macadamia nuts, and more. ✉78-6831 Ali'i Dr., Kailua-Kona.

Kona Inn Farmers' Market. This low-key farmers' market is filled with produce, coffee, and macadamia nuts from around the region. It's held in the parking lot of the Kona Inn Shopping Village on Wednesday and Saturday from 7 AM until 3 PM. ✉75-7544 Ali'i Dr., park at Kona Inn Shopping Village parking lot, Kailua-Kona.

Kona International Market. The new kid on the block, housed in an open-air facility, has attracted vendors away from a lot of other island markets to sell flowers, local produce, Hawaiian crafts, clothes, and random collectibles. It's open Tuesday through Sunday, from 9 AM to 5 PM, and includes both farmers' market vendor stalls and proper stores—it's great one-stop shopping for all your souvenirs. ✉On Luhia St., in Kailua-Kona's Old Industrial Area.

HILO

SHOPPING CENTERS

6

Hilo Shopping Center. This rather dated shopping plaza has several air-conditioned shops tending to the practical needs of the locals, as well as a salon and a few restaurants. Great cookies, cakes, and baked goodies are at Lanky's Pastries. There's plenty of free parking. ✉Kekuanaoa St. at Kīlauea Ave., Hilo.

Prince Kūhiō Shopping Plaza. Hilo's most comprehensive mall, Prince Kūhiō Shopping Plaza is where you can find Macy's for fashion, Safeway for food, and Longs Drugs for just about everything else, along with several other shops and boutiques. ✉111 E. Puainako St., at Hwy. 11, Hilo ☎808/959–3555.

Waiakea Center. Here you can find a Borders Books & Music, Island Naturals health food store, and a Wal-Mart. If all the shopping makes you hungry, there's also a food court and one of the island's best restaurants, Hilo Bay Foods, tucked away in the corner. ✉Maka'ala St. and Kanoelehua Ave., across from Prince Kūhiō Shopping Plaza, at Hwy. 11, Hilo ☎808/792–7225.

ARTS & CRAFTS

Most Irresistible Shop. This place lives up to its name by stocking unique gifts from around the Pacific, be it coconut-flavored butter or whimsical wind chimes. ✉256 Kamehameha Ave. ☎808/935–9644 ✉Prince Kūhiō Shopping Plaza, 111 E. Puainako St., at Hwy. 11, Hilo ☎808/959–6515.

BOOKSTORES

Basically Books. This shop stocks one of Hawai'i's largest selections of maps and charts, including topographical and relief maps. It also has Hawaiiana books, with great choices for children. ✉160 Kamehameha Ave., Hilo ☎808/961–0144 or 800/903–6277.

CLOTHING & SHOES

★ **Hilo Hattie.** The east coast outlet of the well-known clothier is slightly smaller than its Kailua-Kona cousin, but still offers plenty of the same his-and-her aloha wear, casual clothes, slippers, jewelry, and souvenirs. ⊠*Prince Kūhiō Shopping Plaza, 111 E. Puainako St., Hilo* ☎*808/961–3077.*

Hoaloha. If you're driving north from Hilo, take time to browse through this shop and pick up a colorful *pareu* (beach wrap). ⊠*Last Chance Store, off Hwy. 240, Kukuihaele* ☎*808/775–0502.*

★ **Sig Zane Designs.** This acclaimed boutique sells distinctive island wearables with bold colors and motifs. ⊠*114 Kamehameha Ave., Hilo* ☎*808/935–7077* ⊕*www.sigzane.com.*

FLOWERS & LEIS

Fuku-Bonsai Cultural Center. In addition to selling and shipping miniature *brassaia lava* plantings and other bonsai plants, this place on the way to Volcano has interesting exhibits of different ethnic styles of pruning. ⊠*Olaʻa Rd., Kurtistown* ☎*808/982–9880.*

FOOD

★ **Big Island Candies.** This chocolate factory lets you tour and taste before you buy. ⊠*585 Hinano St., Hilo* ☎*808/935–8890.*

Hilo Coffee Mill. In addition to a fantastic coffee farm tour, the Hilo Coffee Mill sells coffee from a variety of local producers, along with locally made baked goods, candies, artwork, and gifts. ⊠*17-995 Volcano Road, between mile markers 12 and 13, Mountain View* ☎*808/968–1333* ⊕*www.hilocoffeemill.com.*

HOME DECOR

Dragon Mama. Step into this popular downtown Hilo spot to find authentic Japanese fabrics, futons, and antiques, along with a limited but elegant selection of clothing, sleepwear, and slippers for women. ⊠*266 Kamehameha Ave., Hilo* ☎*808/934–9081.*

Etsʻko. You'll find Japanese tea sets, exquisite ceramics, and affordable bamboo ware here. ⊠*35 Waiānuenue Ave., Hilo* ☎*808/961–3778.*

MARKETS

★ **Hilo Farmers' Market.** The farmers here sell a profusion of tropical flowers, high-quality produce, and macadamia nuts. This colorful, open-air market—the most popular in the state—opens for business Wednesday and Saturday from 6:30 AM to 2:30 PM. ⊠*Kamehameha Ave. and Mamo St., Hilo.*

★ **Panaewa Hawaiian Homestead Farmers' Market.** The best thing here is the fresh fish, but there are also the usual farmers' market produce vendors 8 AM–5 PM every day on the sidewalk in front of the Hilo Wal-Mart. ✉*325 Makaala St., Hilo.*

HĀMĀKUA COAST

ARTS & CRAFTS

Glass from the Past. The best place to stop for a quirky gift or just to poke around a truly unique store chock full of a colorful assortment of old bottles, plus antiques, vintage clothing, and ephemera. ✉*28-1672 Old Māmalahoa Hwy., #A, Honomū* ☎*808/963–6449.*

Kama'aina Woods. A great little shop in charming Honoka'a, and the only place in Hawai'i (possibly in the world) where you can pick up your very own set of "Huli Hands," salad tongs shaped like hula hands and made from koa wood. If the Huli Hands don't catch your eye, the koa-wood bowls surely will. ✉*Off Hwy. 19, Honoka'a* ☎*808/775–7722* ⊕*www.hulihands.com.*

GALLERIES

Waipi'o Valley Artworks. In this remote gallery you can find finely crafted wooden bowls, koa furniture, paintings, and jewelry—all made by local artists, plus a great little café where you can pick up a sandwich or ice cream before descending into the valley. ✉*Off Hwy. 240, Kukuihaele* ☎*808/775–0958.*

Woodshop Gallery. This pleasant surprise in Honomū, run by local artists Peter and Janette McLaren, showcases their woodwork and photography collections along with beautiful ceramics, woodwork, photography, glass, and fine art from other Big Island artists. The McClarens also serve up sandwiches and ice cream to hungry tourists from nearby 'Akaka Falls. ✉*28-1692 Old Government Rd., Honomū* ☎*808/963–6363* ⊕*www.woodshopgallery.com.*

SPAS

The Big Island's spa directors have done their homework and produced menus full of "only in Hawai'i" treatments well worth a holiday splurge. Local specialties include *lomi lomi* massages, hot lava stone massages, and scrubs and wraps that incorporate plenty of coconut, orchids, ginger, and macadamia nuts. Expect to also find Swedish and deep tissue massages and, at some spas, Thai massage. And in romantic Hawai'i, couples can be pampered side by side in a variety of offerings. ■TIP→ *Lomi lomi* **massage can be a little too close to deep tissue massage for some, but most** *kahune* **(practitioners) are happy to adjust the pressure to your needs.** The only full-service spas on the Big Island are associated with the resorts on the west coast. With the exception of the Four Seasons Spa at Hualālai, the resort spas are open to anyone. In fact, many of the hotels outsource management of their spas, and there is

GROWN WITH ALOHA

The Big Island is home to more farmers' markets than most cities, each offering a different range of goods, but all providing at the very least a good place to pick up fresh produce while you're in town (especially helpful if you're staying in a condo). Not surprisingly, locally grown mango, papaya, pineapple, passion fruit, coconut, and guava are available in abundance at great prices, but you can also find delicious avocados, organic peppers, fantastic goat cheese, and, of course, coffee.

Hawai'i's farmers are experimenting with hundreds of varieties of avocados and citrus, and with exotic fruits such as poha berries, bilimbi, and mamey sapoy. If you come across unfamiliar fruits, try them—particularly the sweet, fluffy pulp inside the yard-long ice cream bean. Because of government restrictions, these fruits generally can't leave the island, so this is your only chance to sample them.

The markets located in Kailua-Kona and Hilo are listed under the corresponding shopping sections; the following markets are scattered about the Big Island. You might happily stumble upon them as you explore the coasts.

ON THE KONA SIDE

Hawaiian Homesteaders Association Farmers' Market. Check out the crafts sold here in the Kuhio Hale Building before you head to Waimea's more expensive stores. Produce, flowers, plants, and baked goods are also available. Open 7 AM to noon every Saturday.

Ka'u Farmers' Market. On a trip to the South Point, stock up on local produce and handmade baked goods at this market held at the Na'alehu Theater every Saturday, 8 AM to noon.

Under the Banyans Farmers' Market. Fresh produce, seasonal fruit, plants, and craft items are sold at this market way up north in the village of Hāwī. It's open Saturdays from 7:30 AM until 1 PM.

ON THE HILO SIDE

Downtown Honok'a Farmers' Market. This good old-fashioned farmers' market in the midst of a charming old plantation town is a good stop during a drive up the Hāmākua Coast. It begins at 8 AM on Saturdays.

The following markets are all south of Hilo.

Kea'au Village Farmers' Market. Fresh local farm produce featuring super-sweet corn and flowers daily from 7 AM to 5 PM; on Fridays, vendors also sell handmade Hawaiian arts and crafts.

Maku'u Farmers' Market. There's food and produce here, but what differentiates it from the rest are the Hawaiian crafts, plants, jewelry, shells, ethnic and recycled clothing, records/CDs, and books. It's along the Kea'au/Pāhoa Highway, Sundays 8 AM to noon.

Pāhoa Village Farmers' Market. A great market, held in a large, covered outdoor space with local produce, prepared foods, coffee, clothing, and live music 9 AM to 3 PM every Sunday.

Volcano Village Farmers Market. A favorite on the east side of the island. Local produce, flowers, prepared foods, baked goods, and an occasional clothing swap, in the Cooper Center, every Sunday 8:30–11 AM.

Hawaiian Healing

The Hawaiians have held healers in high regard since ancient times, and many of their old traditions still hold sway, even in the fanciest of resort spas. Every spa on the island blends some aspect of local culture and ingredients into its menu, from traditional Hawaiian standbys like *lomi lomi* massage and *kukui* (candlenut) oil to lesser-known ancient rituals like *opu huli* (literally "stomach turn"), an abdominal massage that is great for gastritis, jet lag, or menstrual cramps. There are also Hawaiian versions of popular therapies: imagine a hot stone massage done with lava rocks and warm coconut oil. Following are a few of our favorite Hawaiian healing rituals and the best places to experience them firsthand:

Lomi lomi **massage:** This traditional form of massage is intended to relieve physical *and* emotional stress. Our favorite is administered by the *kahune* (specialists) of the Spa Without Walls at the Fairmont Orchid, on the beach.

Healing waters: For their healing rituals, the ancient Hawaiians often used Coconut Island, in Hilo, because of the restorative powers of its spring waters. You can visit any time for free. On the Kona side of the island, Mamalahoa Hot Tubs provides a slightly more modern experience with luxurious soaks in beautiful wooden tubs.

La'au Lapa'au: Ancient Hawaiian herbal medicine is utilized to great effect these days in a number of fine skin treatments, like the Alo Lani treatment at the Four Seasons Spa Hualālai, which includes a warm kukui and coconut back and neck massage and a soothing facial massage treatment utilizing *noni* juice, known throughout the islands for its healing powers.

no difference in price for guests and nonguests, although guests have the added bonus of receiving in-room services.

★ **Hale Ho'ōla Spa in Volcano.** Those staying in Volcano or Hilo now have quick and easy access to the body treatments, massages, and facials available at the resort spas on the other side of the island—and at far more reasonable prices. Hale Ho'ōla's menu includes more local ingredients and traditional Hawaiian treatments than any other spa on the island, including a handful of very traditional Hawaiian massages, such as *lomi hula,* which is lomi lomi massage choreographed to hula music; *la'au hamo,* which blends lomi lomi with traditional Hawaiian healing herbs and plant extracts; and *Pō'pōkāpa'i,* which is a divine blend of hot stone massage and la'au hamo that incorporates lomi lomi massage with warm compresses filled with healing herbs. Facials and body scrubs incorporate the usual suspects—ginger, coconut, and macadamia nut—but also some unexpected surprises such as taro, locally grown vanilla, and volcanic clay that works wonders in the form of a facial mask. ⊠ *11-3913 7th St., Mauna Loa Estates, Volcano* ☎ *808/756–2421* ⊕ *www.halehoola.net* ☞ *$75 60-min lomi lomi massage; $150 half-day packages. Services: aromatherapy, body scrubs and wraps, facials, massages.*

Ho'ōla Spa at the Sheraton Keauhou Bay. The Sheraton Keauhou Bay occupies one of the prettier corners of the island, with an unbeatable view from most parts of the hotel. That being the case, it's too bad that the Ho'ōla Spa fails to truly take advantage of its location. Although there are plenty of windows with pretty views of the bay, the spa lacks the outdoor treatment areas other island spas are known for. Still, the spa menu includes a variety of locally influenced treatments, and the warm lava-rock massage is a little slice of heaven. The packages are an excellent deal, combining several services for far less than you would pay à la carte. For couples, the spa offers an ocean-side massage that takes place on a balcony overlooking the water, followed by a dip in a whirlpool bath. ⊠*78-128 Ehukai St., Kailua-Kona* ☎*808/930–4900* ⊕*www. sheratonkeauhou.com* ☞*$110 50-min lomi lomi massage; $215–$345 half-day packages. Hair salon, hot tub, sauna, steam room. Services: aromatherapy, body scrubs and wraps, facials, massages, waxing.*

Kalona Salon & Spa at the Outrigger Keauhou Beach Resort. This spa is a great place to get a massage or body treatment for much less than you'd likely pay at the big resorts. Though not quite as nice as the bigger facilities, it's simple and clean, on the ocean, and staffed with well-trained therapists. The spa offers facials using its own line of products made from island ingredients. Be careful if you have sensitive skin. ⊠*78-6740 Ali'i Dr., Kailua-Kona* ☎*808/322–3441 or 800/462–6262* ⊕*www.outrigger.com* ☞*$85 50-min lomi lomi massage; $115–$220 half-day packages. Services: facials, massage.*

★ **Kohala Sports Club & Spa at the Hilton Waikoloa Village.** The orchids that run riot in the rain forests of the Big Island suffuse the signature treatments at the Kohala Sports Club & Spa. By the end of the Orchid Isle Wrap, you're completely immersed in the scent and in bone-deep relaxation. The island's volcanic character is also expressed in several treatments, as well as in the design of the lava-rock soaking tubs. Locker rooms are outfitted with private changing rooms for the modest, and a wealth of beauty and bath products. The extensive hair and nail salon could satisfy even Bridezilla with its updo consultations and luxe pedicure stations. The nearby ocean-side cabanas are the perfect venue for a massage on the beach. The fitness center is well-equipped, but group classes that roam across the beautifully manicured resort grounds—like tai chi on the lawn or walking meditation at Buddha Point—are much more appealing. ⊠*Hilton Waikoloa Village, 425 Waikoloa Beach Dr., Kohala Coast* ☎*808/886–2828 or 800/445–8667* ⊕*www.kohalaspa. com* ☞*$135 50-min lomi lomi massage; $399–$431 half-day packages. Hair salon, hot tubs (indoor and outdoor), sauna, steam room. Gym with: cardiovascular machines, free weights, weight-training equipment. Services: acupuncture, aromatherapy, body scrubs and wraps, facials, hydromassage, massage. Classes and programs: body sculpting, fitness analysis, personal training, Pilates, Spinning, step aerobics, tai chi, yoga.*

★ **Mamalahoa Hot Tubs and Massage.** Tucked into a residential neighborhood above Kealakekua, this little gem is a welcome alternative to the large resort spas. Soaking tubs are made of the finest quality wood,

INDEPENDENT CONTRACTORS

Sometimes all you want is a good massage, preferably on the beach—no high prices, herbal tea, or aromatherapy required. Following are a few of our favorite local practitioners. They work by appointment only.

An Ocean Front Therapeutic Massage. Let the marvelous Bea work out your kinks as you listen to the ocean just a few feet away. This is not on the beach, but it is oceanfront, with an ocean view and windows open, so it's pretty darn close. ⊠ *Kona Inn Shopping Village, Suite 250, Kailua-Kona* ☎ *808/329–8912* ☞ *$80 60-min massage.*

Healing Arts Alliance. If you're a deep tissue fan, look no farther than Scott Miller. Specializing in rolfing and deep tissue massage, Scott is also a licensed acupuncturist with several years' experience. His colleague, Lynn Vrooman, does gentler *lomi lomi* massages for those who prefer a gentler touch. ⊠ *103 Kalakaua St., Hilo* ☎ *808/934–7030* ☞ *Scott: $50 60-min deep tissue massage. Lynn: $50 90-min lomi lomi massage.*

Pilates and Movement Centre of Kona. Although best paired with a yoga or Pilates session, Laura Crittendon's lomi lomi is tough to beat. ⊠ *75-5995 Kuakini Hwy., Suite 900, Kona* ☎ *808/329–3211* ⊕ *www.konapilates.com* ☞ *$75 60-min massage.*

tropical plants and flowers abound, and each tub is enclosed in its own little gazebo, with portholes in the roof for your stargazing pleasure. Tastefully laid out and run, there's no seedy "hot tub party" vibe here, just a pleasant soak followed by, if you like, an hour-long massage. Mamalahoa offers *lomi lomi,* Swedish, deep tissue, and a Hawaiian hot stone massage performed with lava rocks collected from around the island. In addition to its secret hideaway ambience, Mamalahoa's prices are lower than any other spa on the island. ⊠ *Kealakekua, south of Kailua-Kona* ☎ *808/323–2288* ⊕ *www.mamalahoa-hottubs.com* ☞ *$30 60-min soak; $85 30-min soak plus 60-min lomi lomi, Swedish, or deep tissue massage; $135 30-min soak plus 90-min hot stone massage* ☉ *By appointment only. Open Wed.–Sat. noon–8* PM.

★ **Mandara Spa at the Waikoloa Beach Marriott Resort.** Overlooking the hotel's main pool with a distant view of the ocean, Mandara offers a very complete if not unique spa menu, with more available facial options than you'll find at the island's other spas. Mandara operates spas throughout the world and on a number of cruise lines, and they are managing this one for Marriott, using Elemis and La Therapie products in spa and salon treatments. The spa menu contains the usual suspects—*lomi lomi,* a variety of facials, scrubs, and wraps—but they do incorporate local ingredients where appropriate (lemon and ginger in the scrubs, warm coconut milk in the wraps), and the new facilities, designed in a style that combines 20th-century modern American with traditional Asian motifs, are beautiful. ⊠ *69-275 Waikoloa Beach Dr., Kohala Coast* ☎ *808/886–8191* ⊕ *www.mandaraspa.com* ☞ *$115 50-min lomi lomi massage; $215–$400 half-day packages. Hair salon, steam room. Gym with: cardiovascular machines, free weights, weight-*

training equipment. Services: *aromatherapy, body scrubs and wraps, facials, massage.*

Mauna Lani Spa. If you're looking for a one-of-a-kind experience, this is your destination. Most treatments take place in outdoor, bamboo-floor *hales* (houses) surrounded by lava rock. Incredible therapists offer a mix of the old standbys (*lomi lomi* massage, moisturizing facials) and innovative treatments, many of which are heavily influenced by ancient traditions and incorporate local products. One exfoliating body treatment is self-administered in one of the outdoor saunas—a great choice for people who aren't too keen on therapists seeing them in their birthday suits. Watsu therapy takes place in an amazing pool filled and heated by the adjacent lava tube, with help from solar panels overhead. Meant to re-create the feeling of being in a womb, the hour-long therapy is essentially an underwater massage. You feel totally weightless, thanks to some artfully applied weights and the buoyancy of the warm salt water. It's a great treatment for people with disabilities that keep them from enjoying a traditional massage. The aesthetic treatments on the menu incorporate high-end products from Epicuran and Emminence, so a facial will have a real and lasting therapeutic effect on your skin. The spa also offers a full regimen of fitness and yoga classes, as well as more mainland-style procedures like Botox and Restylane injections. ⊠*Mauna Lani Resort, 68-1400 Mauna Lani Dr., Kohala Coast* ☎*808/885–6622* ⊕*www.maunalani.com* ☞*$135 50-min lomi lomi massage; $275–$425 half-day packages. Hair salon, hot tubs (indoor and outdoor), sauna, steam room. Gym with: cardiovascular machines, free weights, weight-training equipment. Services: aquatic therapy, baths, body wraps, Botox, facials, massage, Restylane, scrubs. Classes and programs: aerobics, kickboxing, personal training, Pilates, Spinning, weight training, yoga.*

Paul Brown Salon & Spa at the Hāpuna Beach Prince Hotel. It's not unusual for locals to drive an hour each way to get their hair cut here. Paul Brown has been in the business for 30 years, and he now has three locations in Hawai'i. Hair is still the specialty, but it's not just a salon. The full-service spa—nicely designed to let in lots of light—has an extensive menu of massages, facials, and body treatments. The well-run facility also has a trained practitioner who administers expert acupuncture treatments. It's the best place for waxing. You can use the gym at the Hāpuna Golf Course's clubhouse, accessible via a free shuttle. ⊠*62-100 Kauna'oa Dr., Kohala Coast* ☎*808/880–1111 or 800/882–6060* ⊕*www.princeresortshawaii.com* ☞*$115 50-min lomi lomi massage; $240–$380 half-day package. Hair salon, sauna, steam room. Services: acupuncture, body wraps, facials, massage. Classes and programs: aerobics, yoga.*

The Spa at Hualālai. The Spa at Hualālai is for the exclusive use of Four Seasons Resort guests, so you can sign everything to your room and never have a problem booking a treatment. Though it can feel like a New York spa dropped onto a tropical island, the Spa at Hualālai does include outdoor massage *hales*, which affords more of a Hawaiian experience. The therapists are also top-notch, and a real effort has

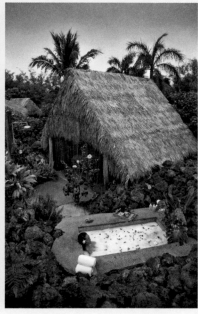

Mauna Lani Spa

been made to incorporate local traditions and ingredients like honey, kokui nuts, and coconut into spa treatments. ⊠*100 Ka'ūpūlehu Dr., Ka'ūpūlehu/Kona* ☎*808/325–8000* ⊕*www.fourseasons.com* ☞*$120 50-min massage; $145 body scrub; $120 facials. Hair salon, outdoor hot tubs, sauna, steam room. Gym with: cardiovascular machines, free weights, weight-training equipment. Services: body treatments, facials, massage. Classes and programs: personal training, Pilates, Spinning, tai chi, yoga.*

★ **Spa Without Walls at the Fairmont Orchid Hawai'i.** This is possibly the best massage spa on the island, partially due to its setting—massage tables face either the ocean or a waterfall. Though most people will probably opt for the ocean, both settings are absolutely peaceful. There are other great treatments as well, including facials, fragrant herbal wraps, and coffee and vanilla scrubs, but the massages are the best thing going. ⊠*Fairmont Orchid Hawai'i, 1 N. Kanikū Dr., Kohala Coast* ☎*808/885–2000* ⊕*www.fairmont.com* ☞*$155 45-min lomi lomi massage; $285–$295 half-day packages. Sauna, steam room. Gym with: cardiovascular machines, free weights, weight-training equipment. Services: baths, body wraps, facials, massage, scrubs. Classes and programs: aquaerobics, guided walks, meditation, personal training, yoga.*

7

Entertainment & Nightlife

WORD OF MOUTH

"The Big Island is about Hawaiian history, culture, etc., an experience which has nothing to do with miniature golf courses and extensive nightlife. Both Kailua-Kona and Hilo fold up their sidewalks precisely at ten (well, nine actually) and people who live there are not seen again."

—fdecarlo

By Amy
Westervelt

If you're the sort of person who doesn't come alive until after dark, you might be a little lonely on the Big Island.

Blame it on the plantation heritage. People did their cane-raising in the morning. Still, there are a few lively bars on the island, a handful of great local playhouses, half a dozen or so movie houses (including those that play foreign and independent films), and plenty of musical entertainment to keep you occupied. And let's not forget the lū'aus. These fantastic dance and musical performances are combined with some of the best meals on the island and are plenty of fun for the whole family.

ENTERTAINMENT

DINNER CRUISES & SHOWS

★ **Captain Beans' Polynesian Dinner Cruise.** Sometimes called "the booze cruise," this is the ever-popular standby in sunset dinner cruises. You can't miss it—as the sun sets, look out over the water and you'll see a big gaudy boat with distinctive orange sails. This cruise is corny, and dinner is nothing special, but it's an experience, with unlimited drinks and a Hawaiian show. This is for adults only. ⊠ *Kailua Pier, Kailua-Kona* ☎ *808/329–2955 or 800/831–5541* ⊕ *www.robertshawaii.com* ⊉ *$60* ☉ *Tues.–Sun. at 5:15.*

★ **Hawaiian Sunset Pūpū Cruise and Dolphin Adventure.** Blue Sea Cruises offers a classed-up alternative to the booze cruise, with soothing Hawaiian music, elegant pūpūs, and tropical juices and cocktails. It's focus is on the sunset and the scenery, and the chance to see spinner dolphins (and whales from November to May). ⊠ *Kailua Pier, Kailua-Kona* ☎ *808/331–8875* ⊕ *www.blueseacruisesinc.com* ⊉ *$60* ☉ *Tues.–Sun., check in at 4:40* PM.

LŪ'AU & POLYNESIAN REVUES

KOHALA COAST & WAIKOLOA **Fairmont Orchid.** The Fairmont's "Gathering of the Kings Polynesian Feast" is the most recent addition to the Kohala coast lū'au scene and offers the most entertainment bang for your resort buck. The show is slickly produced and well choreographed, incorporating both traditional and modern dance and choreography as well as beautiful costumes. The meal offers more variety than most, with options representing all of the early Hawaiian settlers, including those from New Zealand, Hawaii, Tahiti, and Samoa. ⊠ *1 N. Kaniku Dr., Kohala Coast* ☎ *808/885–2000* ⊕ *www.fairmont.com/orchid* ⊉ *$99* ☉ *Fri. at 6.*

Hilton Waikoloa Village. The Hilton seats 400 people outdoors at the Kamehameha Court, where the acclaimed Polynesian group Tihati performs a lively show. A buffet dinner provides samplings of Hawaiian food as well as fish, beef, and chicken to appeal to all tastes. ⊠ *425 Waikoloa Beach Dr., Waikoloa* ☎ *808/886–1234* ⊕ *www.hiltonwaikoloavillage.com* ⊉ *$80* ☉ *Fri. at 6.*

★ **Kona Village Resort.** In its utter isolation, the lū'au here is one of the most authentic and traditional on the Islands. As in other lū'au, activities include the steaming of a whole pig in the *imu* (ground oven). The Wednesday night show focuses solely on Hawaiian traditions and music, while Friday night incorporates Polynesian dancing, music, and traditions as well. The dancing, done on a stage over a lagoon,

> ## WORD OF MOUTH
>
> "A lot of Hawaiians do vacation at Kona Village for the Polynesian ambience.... Also, this is a very good place to see a luau, which is held on [Wednesday and] Friday nights."
>
> —Flying Maltese

is magical. On Wednesday, the lū'au stage gives way to Hawaiian cowboys, or paniolo, for cowboy tales and a tasty barbecue. ⊠*Queen Ka'ahumanu Hwy., 6 mi north of Kona International Airport, Kailua-Kona* ☎*808/325–5555 or 808/325–4273* ⊕*www.konavillage.com* ☜*$84, includes one cocktail* ⊗*Wed. and Fri. from 5; walking tour at 5:30, imu ceremony at 6:30, dinner at 7, show at 8.*

Waikoloa Beach Marriott. At this celebration, entertainment includes a Samoan fire dance as well as songs and dances of various Pacific cultures. Traditional Hawaiian dishes are served alongside more familiar fare. ⊠*69-275 Waikoloa Beach Dr., Waikoloa* ☎*808/886–6789* ⊕*www.marriott.com* ☜*$75, including open bar* ⊗*Wed. and Sun. 5–8:30.*

King Kamehameha's Kona Beach Hotel. Witness the royal court arrive by canoe at the Island Breeze Lū'au, a beachfront event, which includes a 22-item buffet, an open bar, and a show. ⊠*75-5660 Palani Rd., Kailua-Kona* ☎*808/326–4969 or 808/329–8111* ⊕*www.islandbreezeluau.com* ☜*$70* ⊗*Tues.–Thurs. and Sun. 5:30–8:30.*

Royal Kona Resort. This resort lights lū'au torches for a full Polynesian show and a Hawaiian-style oceanfront buffet three times a week. ⊠*75-5852 Ali'i Dr., Kailua-Kona* ☎*808/329–3111 Ext. 4* ⊕*www.konaluau.com* ☜*$68* ⊗*Mon., Wed., Fri., and Sat. at 5.*

Sheraton Keauhou Bay. A recent addition to the Big Island's lū'au scene, Kamaha'o—The Wondrous Myths of Hawai'i—adds a little Cirque du Soleil to the traditional Hawaiian formula, mixing Hawaiian language, storytelling, and traditional hula with modern dance and acrobatics to create a highly entertaining theatrical display. And the open bar doesn't hurt either. ⊠*75-5852 Ali'i Dr., Kailua-Kona* ☎*808/930–4900* ⊕*www.sheratonkeauhou.com* ☜*$80* ⊗*Mon., Wed., Fri., and Sat. at 5.*

FESTIVALS

There is a festival dedicated to just about everything on the Big Island. Some of them are small community affairs, but a handful of film, food, and music festivals provide quality entertainment for visitors and locals alike. The following is a list of our favorites:

Roasted Pigs, Poi & Hula: the Lū'au Explained

Large parties have always been a part of Hawaiian culture. In ancient times they were referred to as *aha-aina* (gathering for a meal). In the 1800s, King Kamehameha II broke the entrenched *kapu* (a system of social rules and taboos) by dining with women. That single action abolished the kapu system entirely, lifting the ban not only on men and women eating together but also on what types of food women could eat. Subsequent large feasts included everyone in the community sharing the same food, and the word lū'au was chosen to describe these new gatherings.

Lū'au actually referred to the edible leaves of a young taro plant, which were used to wrap various foods before placing them in the *imu* (an oven dug into the ground). Taro is still incorporated into the modern-day lū'au in the form of *poi* (pounded taro root)—usually the one thing left virtually untouched on every guest's plate. Let's just say it's an acquired taste.

If you think the modern-day version of the lū'au is large and extravagant, keep in mind that the Hawaiian royal lū'au blew today's parties out of the water. King Kalakaua, known as the "Merry Monarch" for his love of parties and dance (Hilo's annual hula festival is named after him), invited more than 1,500 guests to his 50th birthday lū'au, and fed them in shifts of 500.

Black & White Night. This lovely annual outdoor party is in downtown Hilo. The stores stay open late, the sidewalks are dotted with live jazz bands, and everyone dresses in black and white, some in shorts and tees and others in gowns and tuxes, to enter the "Best Dressed" contest. ☎ *808/933–9772* ⊙ *Early Nov.*

Chinese New Year. Hilo throws a big free party complete with live music, food, drums, and fireworks downtown to commemorate this holiday every year. There's a smaller celebration along Ali'i Drive in Kona as well. ☎ *808/933–9772* ⊙ *Feb.*

Kona Brewers Festival. At this great annual party, roughly 30 breweries and 25 restaurants offer samples and live music, fire dancers, and fashion shows. ☎ *808/331–3033* ⊕ *www.konabrewersfestival.com* ⊙ *Early Mar.*

Kona Coffee Cultural Festival. The oldest food festival in Hawai'i brings together a variety of events over a 10-day period, but our favorite is the coffee recipe cooking contest. Coffee chili is one of the best things you've never tasted. ⊕ *www.konacoffeefest.com* ⊙ *Early Nov.*

★ **Merrie Monarch Festival.** The mother of all Big Island festivals, the Merrie Monarch celebrates all things hula and completely overtakes Hilo for one fantastic weekend a year. The largest event of its kind in the world honors the legacy of King David Kalākaua, Hawai'i's last king and the man responsible for reviving a lot of the fading Hawaiian traditions including the hula (of which he was a big fan). The festival is staged at the spacious Edith Kanaka'ole Stadium during the first week following Easter Sunday. Hula *hālau* (schools) compete in various classes of ancient and modern dance styles. ■ TIP➔ **You need to reserve accommo-**

dations and tickets up to a year in advance. If you're planning on being in Hilo during this time of year but not attending the festival, know that most accommodations will be booked about a year out and plan accordingly. ☎808/935–9168 ⊕*www.merriemonarchfestival.org* ☉*Apr.*

A Taste of the Hawaiian Range Food and Agricultural Festival. Since 1995, this culinary event has been giving locals and visitors a taste of what the Island's best chefs and farms have to offer, from grass-fed beef and bison to organic produce, cheese, chocolates, and coffee. ☎808/322–4892 ⊕*www.ctahr.hawaii.edu/taste* ☉*Early Oct.*

FILM

Aloha Spirit Film Festival. This independent film festival, held in mid-September, screens cutting-edge documentaries, shorts, and feature films from throughout the islands. Screenings and festivities are held at the Aloha Theatre in Kainaliu and the Sheraton Keauhou Bau just south of Kailua-Kona.

Louis Vuitton Hawai'i International Film Festival. Showing throughout the Islands and in Hilo (Palace Theater) and Kainaliu (Aloha Theatre) on the Big Island, this festival has been blazing trails in the exhibition of Asian and Pacific feature films since 1981. It runs for about 10 days in late October. ⊕*www.hiff.org*.

KONA SIDE **Keauhou 7 Cinemas.** This is a splendid seven-theater complex, and there are several pre- or post-movie food options in the center. ⊠*Keauhou Shopping Center, 78-6831 Ali'i Dr.* ☎808/324–7200.

Makalapua Stadium Cinemas. The 10-screen theater has stadium seating and digital surround sound. ⊠*Makalapua Ave., next to Kmart* ☎808/327–0444.

HILO First-run films are shown on the nine screens of the state-of-the-art **Prince Kūhiō Stadium Cinemas** (⊠*Prince Kūhiō Plaza, 111 E. Puainako St.* ☎808/959–4595). **Kress Cinemas** (⊠*174 Kamehameha Ave.* ☎808/961–3456) shows first-run films and the occasional art-house flick on four screens in a pretty Art Deco building. **Honoka'a People's Theater** (⊠*Mamane St., Honoka'a* ☎808/775–0000) screens selected art films during the week and more mainstream films on weekends.

Palace Theatre. After decades of being closed, the 1925 theater has been beautifully restored and now shows not-so-recently released movies. The price is right: the first show of the day is only 50¢. ⊠*38 Haili St., Hilo* ☎808/934–7010.

THEATER

Aloha Angel Performing Arts Center. Local talent stages musicals and Broadway plays at this charming old plantation center near Kailua-Kona. ⊠*Aloha Angel Theatre Café, 79-7384 Māmalahoa Hwy., Kainaliu* ☎808/322–2122.

★ **Kahilu Theatre.** For legitimate theater, the little town of Waimea is your best bet. The Kahilu Theater hosts regular internationally acclaimed performances, interspersed with a variety of top-notch music acts. In a recent season, Chick Corea, Laurie Anderson, and Pink Martini shared

Continued on page 186

MORE THAN A FOLK DANCE

Hula has been called "the heartbeat of the Hawaiian people" and also "the world's best-known, most misunderstood dance." Both are true. Hula isn't just dance. It is storytelling. No words, no hula.

Chanter Edith McKinzie calls it "an extension of a piece of poetry." In its adornments, implements, and customs, hula integrates every important Hawaiian cultural practice: poetry, history, genealogy, craft, plant cultivation, martial arts, religion, protocol. So when 19th century Christian missionaries sought to eradicate a practice they considered depraved, they threatened more than just a folk dance.

With public performance outlawed and private hula practice discouraged, hula went underground for a generation, to rural villages. The fragile verbal link by which culture was transmitted from teacher to student hung by a thread. Even increasing literacy did not help because hula's practitioners were a secretive and protected circle.

As if that weren't bad enough, vaudeville, Broadway, and Hollywood got hold of the hula, giving it the glitz treatment in an unbroken line from "Oh, How She Could Wicky Wacky Woo" to "Rock-A-Hula Baby." Hula became shorthand for paradise: fragrant flowers, lazy hours. Ironically, this development assured that hundreds of Hawaiians could make a living performing and teaching hula. Many danced 'auana (modern form) in performance; but taught kahiko (traditional), quietly, at home or in hula schools.

Today, 30 years after the cultural revival known as the Hawaiian Renaissance, language immersion programs have assured a new generation of proficient—and even eloquent—chanters, songwriters, and translators. Visitors can see more, and more authentic, traditional hula than at any other time in the last 200 years.

Like the culture of which it is the beating heart, hula has survived.

Lei *po'o*. Head lei. In kahiko, greenery only. In 'auana, flowers.

Face emotes appropriate expression. Dancer should not be a smiling automaton.

Shoulders remain relaxed and still, never hunched, even with arms raised. No bouncing.

Eyes always follow leading hand.

Lei. Hula is rarely performed without a shoulder lei.

Arms and hands remain loose, relaxed, below shoulder level—except as required by interpretive movements.

Traditional hula skirt is loose fabric, smocked and gathered at the waist.

Hip is canted over weight-bearing foot.

Knees are always slightly bent, accentuating hip sway.

Kupe'e. Ankle bracelet of flowers, shells, or—traditionally—noise-making dog teeth.

In kahiko, feet are flat. In 'auana, they may be more arched, but not tiptoes or bouncing.

Speak or Sing

Moon or Sun

Grass Shack or House

Mountains or Heights

Love or Caress

At backyard parties, hula is performed in bare feet and street clothes, but in performance, adornments play a key role, as do rhythm-keeping implements.

In hula kahiko (traditional style), the usual dress is multiple layers of stiff fabric (often with a pellom lining, which most closely resembles *kapa*, the paperlike bark cloth of the Hawaiians). These wrap tightly around the bosom but flare below the waist to form a skirt. In pre-contact times, dancers wore only kapa skirts. Monarchy-period hula is performed in voluminous Mother Hubbard mu'umu'u or high-necked muslin blouses and gathered skirts. Men wear loincloths or, for monarchy period, white or gingham shirts and black pants—sometimes with red sashes.

In hula 'auana (modern), dress for women can range from grass skirts and strapless tops to contemporary tea-length dresses. Men generally wear aloha shirts, but sometimes grass skirts over pants or even everyday gear. (One group at a recent competition wore wetsuits to do a surfing song!)

SURPRISING HULA FACTS

■ Grass skirts are not traditional; workers from Kiribati (the Gilbert Islands) brought this custom to Hawai'i.

■ In olden-day Hawai'i, *mele* (songs) for hula were composed for every occasion—name songs for babies, dirges for funerals, welcome songs for visitors, celebrations of favorite pursuits.

■ Hula *ma'i* is a traditional hula form in praise of a noble's genitals; the power of the *ali'i* (royalty) to procreate gave *mana* (spiritual power) to the entire culture.

■ Hula students in old Hawai'i adhered to high standards: scrupulous cleanliness, no sex, daily cleansing rituals, certain food prohibitions, and no contact with the dead. They were fined if they broke the rules.

WHERE TO WATCH

■ **Brown's Beach House** at the Fairmont Orchid. Hula dancers perform nightly on a moonlit grassy knoll.

■ **Kamaha'o "The Wondrous Myths of Hawai'i."** The island's most talented dancers perform in this weekly lū'au production at the Sheraton Keauhou.

■ **Merrie Monarch Festival.** The king of all hula festivals, held annually the first Thursday after Easter Sunday in Hilo. Tickets are hard to get so book as early as possible.

■ **Volcano Center & Volcanoes National Park Na Mea Hawai'i Hula Kahiko.** A series of free public performances takes place outdoors facing Halema'uma'u crater, the sacred home of the volcano goddess Pele.

SLACK KEYS & 'UKULELES

It's easy to forget that Hawai'i has its own music until you step off a plane on the Islands—and then there's no escaping it. It's a unique blend of the strings and percussion favored by the early settlers and the chants and rituals of the ancient Hawaiians. Hawaiian music today includes Island-devised variations on acoustic guitar—slack key and steel guitar—along with the 'ukulele (a small, four-string guitar about the size of a violin), and vocals that have evolved from ritual chants to more melodic compositions.

This is one of the few folk music traditions in the United States that is fully embraced by the younger generation, with no prodding from their parents or grandparents. More than half the radio stations on the Big Island play solely Hawaiian music, and concerts performed by Island favorites like Makana are filled with fans of all ages.

The best way to get an introduction to the music is to attend one of the annual festivals: The free **Annual Hawai'i Slack Key Guitar Festival** (July) features a handful of greats performing throughout the day at the Sheraton Keauhou Bay; the **Annual 'Ukulele and Slack Key Guitar Institute** (November) at the Kahilu Theatre in Waimea takes it one step further, providing both a variety of concerts and workshops for those interested in learning to play the instruments; and the **Annual Big Island Hawaiian Music Festival** (July) at the UH Hilo Performing Arts Center is a weekend full of slack key, steel guitar, and 'ukulele madness.

Or, you can catch live performances most nights at one of a handful of local bars and clubs, including **Mixx Bar and Bistro, Huggo's on the Rocks,** or the **Kona Brewing Company** in Kailua-Kona, and **Cronie's Bar and Grill** in Hilo.

the calendar with modern dance performances, plays, and traditional Hawaiian dance shows. ⊠ *Parker Ranch Center, 67-1185 Māmalahoa Hwy., Waimea* ☎ *808/885–6868* ⊕ *www.kahilutheatre.org.*

University of Hawai'i at Hilo Theater. A full concert series of varied performances, acts, musical groups, and plays is held from September through May each year. ⊠ *200 W. Kawili St., Hilo* ☎ *808/974–7310.*

★ **Volcano Art Center.** Annual and special performances of Hawaiian music and dance, as well as theatre performances, are hosted by this local art center. People drive here from all over the island for some of their Hawaiian music concerts. ⊠ *Volcano House Hotel, adjacent to the Kīlauea Visitors Center, Hawai'i Volcanoes National Park* ☎ *808/967–8222* ⊕ *www.volcanoartcenter.org.*

NIGHTLIFE

KOHALA DISTRICT

BARS

Honu Bar. This elegant spot at the Mauna Lani Bay Hotel & Bungalows has a nice dance floor for weekend revelry. Delicious appetizers, imported cigars, and fine cognacs make this a popular gathering spot on the Kohala Coast. ⊠68-1400 Mauna Lani Dr., Kohala Coast ☎808/885–6622.

Malolo Lounge. A favorite after-work spot for employees from the surrounding hotels, this lounge in the Hilton Waikoloa Village offers decent live music (usually jazz), friendly bartenders, and a pool table. ⊠425 Waikoloa Beach Dr., Waikoloa ☎808/886–1234.

Polo Bar. This wood-paneled watering hole in the Fairmont Orchid Hawai'i has a huge lānai and a great view. Bartenders are great, and service is impeccable. The crowd's not rowdy, so it's a great place for an early evening cocktail or an after-dinner port. ⊠1 N. Kanikū Dr., Kohala Coast ☎808/885–2000.

KAILUA-KONA

BARS

Kona Brewing Company. Still very popular, the Kona Brewery has been a local favorite practically since it opened. Good food, good local beer (go for the sampler and try them all), and an outdoor patio with nightly live music acts make sure it stays that way. ⊠75-5629 Kuakini Hwy. ☎808/334–2739 ⊕www.konabrewingco.com.

Mixx Bar and Bistro. Kailua-Kona's first and only wine bar, adjacent to the Kona Wine Market, Mixx is also the only air-conditioned bar in Kona, but it's got a few other things going for it as well—namely good food, stiff and inventive cocktails, and live music nightly on their outdoor patio. ⊠*King Kamehameha Mall, 75-5626 Kuakini Hwy.* ☎*808/329–7334* ⊕*www.konawinemarket.com.*

Oceans Sports Bar & Grill. A somewhat recent addition to Kona, and a popular gathering place, this sports bar in the back of the Coconut Grove Marketplace has a pool table and an outdoor patio, along with the dozens of TVs you'd expect at a sports bar. This place really gets hopping on the weekends and on its weekly karaoke nights. ⊠*Coconut Grove Marketplace, 75-5811 Ali'i Dr., Kailua-Kona* ☎*808/327–9494.*

CLUBS

Huggo's on the Rocks. Jazz, country, and even rock bands perform at this popular restaurant, so call ahead to find out what's on. Outside, people often dance in the sand to Hawaiian songs. The crowd skews to slightly older and better behaved than Lulu's across the street. ⊠*75-5828 Kahakai Rd., at Ali'i Dr., Kailua-Kona* ☎*808/329–1493.*

Lulu's. On weekends, the young crowd gyrates until late in the evening to hot dance music—hip-hop, R&B, and rock—spun by a professional DJ. ⊠*75-5819 Ali'i Dr., Kailua-Kona* ☎*808/331–2633.*

HILO

BARS

Cronie's Bar & Grill. A sports bar and hamburger joint by day, Cronie's is a local favorite when the lights go down, with a packed bar and a steady schedule of live local bands. ⊠*11 Waianuenue Ave, Hilo* ☎*808/961–9666.*

Flipside Too. The crowd can get a little rowdy here, especially on weekends, but that's sort of the point. With tons of cheap and exotic drinks like the large green Midori-filled "Exorcist," a pool table, free karaoke, electronic darts, and pinball machines, not to mention plenty of friendly locals, Flipside Too has a well-deserved rep as a fun place to grab a drink any night of the week. ⊠*94 Mamo St.* ☎*808/961–0057.*

Shooter's Bar & Grill. Another sports bar-turned-nightclub: Come for the game, stay for the late-night live music and drunken karaoke. ⊠*121 Banyan Dr., Hilo* ☎*808/969–7069.*

Where to Eat

WORD OF MOUTH

"Moco loco: double yum! Tried several places and Cafe 100
won hands down. I might start making them at home now."
—SoloAlex

WHERE TO EAT PLANNER

Eating Out Strategy

Where should we eat? With dozens of island eateries competing for your attention, it may seem like a daunting question. But our expert writers and editors have done most of the legwork—the 80-plus selections here represent the best eating experience this island has to offer. Search "Best Bets" for top recommendations by price, cuisine, and experience.

With Kids

Little ones are welcome almost everywhere on the kid-friendly Big Island; the exceptions are a small handful of fine-dining restaurants that cater to adults. The majority of restaurants feature a kid's menu, and many have toys and gimmicks, from coloring kits to spotlights on local marine life, to keep kids entertained.

Smoking

Smoking is prohibited in all Hawai'i restaurants and bars.

Reservations

Though it's rare to find a restaurant completely booked on the Big Island, a select few are sticklers about reservations. If you're booking a special occasion dinner, call ahead just in case, or check with your hotel concierge.

What to Wear

There isn't a single place on the Big Island that requires formal attire. The general rule is anything goes, although there are a handful of restaurants (Pahui'a at the Four Seasons, the CanoeHouse at the Mauna Lani, and Batik at Mauna Kea) where you might feel out of place in your beach clothes.

Hours & Prices

Though it might seem at first glance like the Big Island's dining scene consists of either very high-end restaurants or divey holes-in-the-wall, there is in fact a fairly large middle ground of quality restaurants that cater both to local and visiting families, and new places are cropping up all the time. Prices are generally higher than on the mainland, mostly because the cost of living is higher here in general, and because restaurants have to import a good portion of their raw materials, though there is an increasing emphasis on locally sourced food.

Tipping is similar here to elsewhere in the country: 15%–20% of the bill or $1 per drink at a bar. Bills for large parties generally include an 18% tip, as do bills at some resort restaurants, so be sure to check your bill before leaving extra.

WHAT IT COSTS AT DINNER				
¢	$	$$	$$$	$$$$
Under $10	$10–$17	$18–$26	$27–$35	Over $35
Restaurant prices are for a main course at dinner, excluding 4.7% excise tax.				

BEST BETS FOR BIG ISLAND DINING

Where can I find the best food the island has to offer? Fodor's writers and editors have selected their favorite restaurants by price, cuisine, and experience in the lists below. In the first column, the Fodor's Choice properties represent the "best of the best" across price categories. You can also search by area for excellent eats—just peruse our complete reviews on the following pages.

FODOR'S CHOICE

Bamboo, $$, p. 197

Brown's Beach House, $$$, p. 195

Ke'ei Café, $$, p. 214

Merriman's, $$$, 205

Pahui'a, $$$$, p. 196

By Price

Ba-Le, p. 209

Big Island Grill, p. 209

Café 100, p. 218

U-Top-It, p. 208

The Coffee Shack, 213

Kona Brewing Company, p. 206

Manago Hotel, p. 213

Merriman's Market Café, p. 194

Uko Taco, p. 198

$$

Café Pesto, p. 193

Harrington's, p. 217

Hilo Bay Café, p. 217

Jackie Rey's Ohana Grill, p. 211

O's Bistro, p. 212

$$$

Donatoni's at Hilton Waikoloa, p. 193

Fujimamas, p. 212

Huggo's, p. 212

Kenichi Pacific, p. 210

$$$$

Alan Wong's Hualalai Grille, p. 195

Chef Daniel's Seafood Café, p. 205

The Grill at the Fairmont Orchid, p. 197

Hale Samoa at Kona Village Resort, p. 195

Kamuela Provision Company, p. 196

By Cuisine

HAWAIIAN

Alan Wong's Hualalai Grille, $$$$

Hilo Bay Café, $$

Jackie Rey's Ohana Grill, $$

Manago Hotel, $

Pahui'a, $$$$

PLATE LUNCH

Ba-Le, ¢

Blane's Drive-In, ¢, p. 218

Big Island Grill, ¢

Café 100, ¢

Kona Mix Plate, ¢, p. 209

SUSHI

Kenichi Pacific, $$$

Norio's Sushi Bar, $$$, p. 194

Sushi Rock, $$, p. 194

Wasabi's, $$, p. 210

By Experience

MOST KID-FRIENDLY

Bubba Gump Shrimp Company, $, p. 205

Ken's House of Pancakes, $, p. 218

Manago Hotel, $

The Seaside Restaurant, $$, p. 220

U-Top-It, ¢

MOST ROMANTIC

Hale Samoa, $$$$

Harrington's, $$

Huggo's, $$$

Ke'ei Café, $$

Pahui'a, $$$$

BEST VIEW

Brown's Beach House, $$$$

Bubba Gump Shrimp Company, $

The Coffee Shack, $

Harrington's, $$

Huggo's, $$$

8

By Amy
Westervelt

Between star chefs and an influx of quality local farms, the Big Island restaurant scene has been heating up in the last couple of years. In the past it used to be a pleasant surprise for visitors to discover a gourmet meal on the island; now food writers from national magazines are praising the chefs of the Big Island for their ability to turn the local bounty into inventive blends of the island's cultural heritage. The Big Island has become a destination for vacationing foodies who are drawn by rave reviews and the reputations of some world-renowned chefs.

Hotels along the Kohala Coast have long invested in celebrated chefs who know how to make a meal memorable, from inventive entrées to spot-on wine pairings. But great food on the Big Island doesn't begin and end with the resorts. A handful of cutting-edge chefs have retired from the fast-paced hotel world and opened up their own small bistros closer to the farms in Upcountry Waimea. And, as the old plantation towns transform into youthful arts communities, unique and wonderful restaurants have cropped up in Hāwī, Kainaliu, and on the east side of the island in Hilo. Though the larger, gourmet restaurants (especially those at the resorts) tend to be very pricey, there are still "ono grindz" (Hawaiian slang for tasty local food) to be found at budget prices throughout the island, from greasy plate lunch specials to reasonably priced organic fare at a number of cafés and health food markets. Less populated areas like Kaʻū, the Hāmākua Coast, and Puna offer limited choices for dinner, but usually at least one or two spots that do a decent plate lunch, and a handful of excellent bakeries.

In addition to the individual restaurants, events such as the Great Waikoloa Food, Wine & Music Fest at the Hilton Waikoloa Village, the Kona Coffee Cultural Festival at the Outrigger Keauhou, and Cuisines of the Sun at the Mauna Lani Bay Hotel draw hundreds of guests to starlit open-air dinners celebrating the bounty of the isle's land and waters. Island tourism bureaus have also made an effort as of late to promote agritourism, and it has turned into a booming new business. Farm tours afford visitors the opportunity to meet with and learn from the local farmers and tour a variety of organic farms. Some tours conclude with a meal comprised of items sourced from the same farms. From goat farms churning creamy, pungent goat cheese to Waimea farms planting row after row of bright tomatoes to small aquaculture operations, visitors can see exactly where their next meal will come from and taste the difference that local, fresh, and organic production can make.

KOHALA COAST

CHINESE

$$ ✕**Grand Palace Chinese Restaurant.** A reasonably priced alternative in a land of hotel dining, this restaurant offers dishes from most regions, including such standards as egg foo yung, wonton soup, chicken with snow peas, and beef with broccoli. More adventurous dishes include sautéed local seafood, lobster, and sizzling shrimp with garlic sauce. Etched-glass panels with cherry wood frames and ornate floral carpets make it feel more upscale than your typical Chinese take-out restaurant. ✉*King's Shops at Waikoloa Village, 250 Waikoloa Beach Dr., Kohala Coast* ☎*808/886–6668* ▭*AE, DC, MC, V.*

ECLECTIC

$$ ✕**Waikoloa Beach Grill.** Although on resort grounds (the first tee of the Waikoloa Beach golf course, to be exact), the Waikoloa Beach Grill is independently owned and operated by two accomplished chefs, Stephen Tabor (grill master) and David Brown (bread and pastries). The menu is literally all over the map, with well-done French classics such as the Coquille St. Jacques (a shellfish casserole baked with cream sauce and sprinkled with browned bread crumbs), traditional and tasty Indian curries, nicely grilled American steaks, and the best Bloody Marys on the island. Desserts are delicious and made fresh daily—the pies are outstanding, as is the cheese plate. Lunch includes entrée-size salads and huge sandwiches and burgers served on homemade bread. It's great value, especially given the skyrocketing rates of the surrounding establishments. ✉*69-1022 Keana Pl., Waikoloa* ☎*808/886–6131* ▭*AE, D, MC, V.*

ITALIAN

$$ ✕**Café Pesto.** This branch of Café Pesto, in the quaint harbor town of Kawaihae, is just as popular as its sibling in Hilo. Exotic pizzas (with chili-grilled shrimp, shiitake mushrooms, and cilantro crème fraîche, for example), Asian-inspired pastas and risottos, and fresh seafood reflect the ethnic diversity of the island. Local microbrews and a full-service bar make this a good place to end the evening, and the lounge-y bar area with sofas and comfy chairs is a great place to grab a drink while you're waiting for a table. ✉*Kawaihae Harbor Center, Hwy. 270, Kawaihae* ☎*808/882–1071* ⊕*www.cafepesto.com* ▭*AE, D, DC, MC, V.*

$$$ ✕**Donatoni's at the Hilton Waikoloa Village.** This romantic restaurant overlooking the boat canal resembles an Italian villa and serves scrumptious dishes with the subtle sauces of northern Italy. From mahimahi with marinated artichokes to fettuccine with Hawaiian lobster, the kitchen sets out to please, although some may find the pasta prices tough to justify. If you're here with companions, order a mix of entrées and pastas to get a good sampling of what the imported Italian chef can do. Be sure to look over the Italian wine and champagne list. ✉*425 Waikoloa Beach Dr., Kohala Coast* ☎*808/886–1234* ▭*AE, D, DC, MC, V* ☾*No lunch.*

JAPANESE

$$$$ ✕**Hakone Steakhouse & Sushi Bar at the Hāpuna Beach Prince Hotel.** It's hard not to start whispering in this tranquil and graceful restaurant. Choose from exquisite Japanese sukiyaki, shabu-shabu (thin slices of

8

beef cooked in broth), and the selections at the elaborate sushi bar. The broad selection of sake (try a sakitini, a martini made with sake) is guaranteed to enliven your meal. The best time to visit is on a Friday or Saturday night when the restaurant serves a great dinner buffet. ✉*Hāpuna Beach Prince Hotel, 62-100 Kauna'oa Dr., Kohala Coast* ☎*808/880–3192* ▭*AE, D, DC, MC, V* ◷*No lunch.*

$$$ ✕**Norio's Sushi Bar & Restaurant.** Norio's is great, but it's very pricey for sushi and there are sushi restaurants of equal or higher caliber with lower prices in Kona (Kenichi Pacific), or north of Kohala in Hāwī (Sushi Rock). Still, if you're staying at one of the resorts nearby and don't feel like taking a 30- to 40-minute drive for food, Norio's is a solid choice. Sashimi and sushi are lovingly prepared with the freshest possible fish (both from the ocean and from the numerous aqua farms on the island). The flounder, 'ahi, and abalone are not to be missed. Some equally delicious hot dishes include baked sea scallops and miso butterfish. The assortment of tropical drinks is tasty, as is the sinfully good chocolate fondue, served with an assortment of tropical fruits. ✉*Fairmont Orchid Hawai'i, 1 N. Kaniku Dr., Kohala Coast* ☎*808/885–2000* ▭*AE, D, DC, MC, V* ◷*Closed Tues. and Wed. No lunch.*

$$ ✕**Sushi Rock.** In Hāwī's funky Without Boundaries, Sushi Rock isn't big on ambience—its narrow dining room is brightly painted and casually decorated with various Hawaiian and Japanese knickknacks—but hungry locals and visiting couples flock here not for the decor but some of the island's freshest raw fish. In addition to lots of new-wave California-style rolls and a terrific Hawaiian-style ceviche, the menu includes a variety of cooked seafood, noodle dishes, and salads. Everything is plated beautifully and served either at the sushi bar, at one of the handful of indoor tables in the restaurant's narrow dining room, or on the covered back patio. There's also a full bar. ✉*55-3435 Akoni Pule Hwy., Hāwī* ☎*808/889–5900* ▭*AE, DC, MC, V* ◷*No lunch.*

MEDITERRANEAN

$ ✕**Merriman's Market Café.** From Peter Merriman, one of Hawai'i's star chefs, comes a more affordable alternative to his upscale Waimea and Maui restaurants. The simple but delicious Mediterranean-influenced menu includes a variety of pasta dishes, tasty appetizers, and some of the island's best salads. Its huge patio has quickly become a favorite for locals and visitors alike, which means you could have a bit of a wait for a table. ✉*King's Shops at Waikoloa Village, 250 Waikoloa Beach Dr., Kohala Coast* ☎*808/886–1700* ▭*AE, MC, V.*

MEXICAN

$$ ✕**Tres Hombres Beach Grill.** The food is decent, if a bit pricey, but what you come here for are the marvelous margaritas. They're in all sorts of tropical flavors, including *liliko'i* (passion fruit). Lunch is the usual Mexican combination platters (tacos, enchiladas, chiles rellenos) as well as burgers and sandwiches. Dinner entrées include fresh fish, killer fajitas, bean-and-rice combinations, and steaks. ✉*Kawaihae Harbor Center, Hwy. 270, Kawaihae* ☎*808/882–1031* ▭*MC, V.*

MODERN HAWAIIAN

$$$$ ✗**Alan Wong's Hualalai Grille at the Four Seasons Resort Hualalai.** The market-driven menu changes regularly here, but expect the sort of fusion fare you'd find in a top-notch New York or San Francisco restaurant. The added bonus is that you can sit outside and enjoy balmy breezes. If *moi*, favored by Hawaiian

royalty, is on the menu, go for it; other standouts include the grilled kalua pork and cheese sandwiches with Waimea tomato soup, Wong's take on traditional Hawaiian poke (ahi sashimi mixed with onions, avocado, and ponzu sauce), and soy braised short ribs. Prices seem reasonable for the quality of the food and the location, and you could easily make a meal out of a selection of *pūpū*. The wine list is extensive and well-chosen, and servers are knowledgeable and helpful. ⊠*Four Seasons Resort Hualālai, 100 Kaʻūpūlehu Dr., North Kona Coast* ⚑*Reservations essential* ▤*AE, DC, MC, V* ⊗*Closed Wed., Fri., and 1st wk in Dec.*

$$$$ ✗**Brown's Beach House at the Fairmont Orchid Hawaiʻi.** This waterfront

Fodor'sChoice wonder is well worth the splurge—the menu is inventive (but not too

★ inventive), and the wine list is excellent. Though you can order steak here, the seafood is really where it's happening. Their crab-crusted ono is a little piece of heaven, sitting on clouds of wasabi mashed potatoes. Leave room for dessert; the sweets change regularly, but they're always worth the indulgence. Local musicians play nightly on the grassy knoll outside. ⊠*Fairmont Orchid Hawaiʻi, 1 N. Kanikū Dr., Kohala Coast* ☎*808/885–2000* ▤*AE, D, DC, MC, V* ⊗*No lunch.*

$$$ ✗**Coast Grille at Hāpuna Beach Prince Hotel.** This is a beautiful spot, with high ceilings and a lānai overlooking the ocean. It offers a well-rounded seafood menu, including loads of fresh oysters and creative Pacific Rim dishes like pan-seared *opah* (moonfish) in cardamom sauce and, when available, delicate farm-raised moi. However, the kitchen and the service have been slipping of late, and with entrées prices just as high as they are at nearby resort restaurants, you might want to opt for one of these better neighbors instead. If you're in the mood for an early dinner (before 6:30 PM), however, Coast Grille has a selection of very reasonably priced three-course prix-fixe meals; the reasonable price, combined with the views, make up for the average food. ⊠*Hāpuna Beach Prince Hotel, 62-100 Kaunaʻoa Dr., Kohala Coast* ☎*808/880–3192* ▤*AE, D, DC, MC, V* ⊗*No lunch.*

$$$$ ✗**Hale Samoa at Kona Village Resort.** Formal and romantic, this Kona Village restaurant has a magical atmosphere, especially at sunset. In a Samoan setting with screens and candles, you can feast on five-course prix-fixe dinners that change daily. Specialties may include sautéed abalone raised at the aqua-farm up the street, papaya-and-coconut bisque, duck stuffed with andouille sausage, or wok-charred prime strip loin. Reservations can be made only on the day you dine. ⊠*Kona Village Resort, Hwy. 19, 12 mi north of Kailua-Kona, North Kona Coast* ☎*808/325–5555* ⚑*Reservations essential* ▤*AE, DC, MC, V* ⊗*Closed Wed., Fri., and 1st wk in Dec.*

8

$$$$ ✕**Kamuela Provision Company at the Hilton Waikoloa Village.** Quiet guitar music, tables set along a breezy lānai, and a sweeping view of the Kohala coast are the perfect accompaniments to the elegant yet down-to-earth Hawai'i regional cuisine. The lānai offers the best seats in the house—get there by 5:30 if you want to score a seat for the sunset. Popular are the bouillabaisse with *nori crostini* and the Parker Ranch rib-eye steak with green peppercorn sauce. This is a great place to sip cocktails—the adjacent Wine Bar makes for a romantic evening in itself, with an appetizer menu, outstanding dessert menu, and more than 40 labels available by the glass. ⊠*Hilton Waikoloa Village, 425 Waikoloa Beach Dr., Kohala Coast* ☎*808/886–1234* ⊟*AE, D, DC, MC, V* ☾*No lunch.*

$$$$
Fodor'sChoice
★
✕**Pahui'a at the Four Seasons Resort Hualālai.** *Pahui'a* means "aquarium," so it's fitting that a 9- by 4-foot aquarium in the entrance casts a dreamy light through this exquisite restaurant. Presentation is paramount, and the food tastes as good as it looks. Asian-influenced dishes stand out for their layers of flavor. Don't miss the three sashimi and three caviar appetizers, or the crispy whole *moi* served with Asian slaw, black beans, and sweet chili-lime vinaigrette. In keeping with the island-wide trend, the restaurant is featuring special prix-fixe dinner menus that change seasonally and focus on local produce, meats, and fish. Breakfasts are superb; the lemon ricotta pancakes are so good they should be illegal. Reserve a table on the patio and you may be able to spot whales while dining. ⊠*Four Seasons Resort Hualālai, 100 Ka'ūpūlehu Dr., North Kona Coast 96740* ☎*808/325–8000* ⊟*AE, D, DC, MC, V* ☾*No lunch.*

$$$ ✕**Roy's Waikoloa Bar & Grill.** Roy's is part of a chain, and it's located in a strip mall. If either of those things turns you off immediately, skip it—there are as good or better meals to be had elsewhere on the island. If, however, you're looking for consistently decent food and you're staying nearby, you could do worse. And if you're looking for a light meal, you can easily fill up on the enormous selection of great appetizers, and the extensive wine-by-the-glass list offers good pairing options. Be forewarned that the place tends to get noisy. ⊠*King's Shops at Waikoloa Village, 250 Waikoloa Beach Dr., Kohala Coast* ☎*808/886–4321* ⊕*www.roysrestaurant.com* ⊟*AE, D, DC, MC, V.*

$$$$ ✕**Tommy Bahama's Tropical Café.** It's funny that a chain known for its "Hawaiian-ness" would start in California and then one day end up in Hawaii, but that is Tommy Bahama's story. Located in the Shops at Mauna Lani, in an open-air space above the Tommy Bahama store, the restaurant does a good job of making guests forget they're in a shopping center. And the food is decent, although derivative of other menus on the island. The macadamia-crusted *opakapaka* (Pacific red snapper) is a standout. Some of the best items, and best values, on the menu are actually in the appetizer section—the *poke* is outstanding—and salad list, which includes a fresh take on a roasted beet and spinach salad with hearts of palm and a *lilikoi* (passion fruit) –infused dressing. Desserts are decadent and great for sharing. ⊠*68-1330 Mauna Lani Dr., #102* ☎*808/881–8686* ⚶*Recommended Casual* ⊟*AE, D, MC, V.*

PACIFIC RIM

$$ **Fodor's Choice** **★** **✕ Bamboo Restaurant.** It's out of the way, but the food at this spot in the heart of Hāwī is good and the service and ambience have a Hawaiian–country flair. Creative entrées feature fresh island fish prepared several ways. The Thai-style fish, for example, combines lemongrass, Kaffir lime leaves, and coconut milk; it's best washed down with a passion-fruit margarita or passion-fruit iced tea. Bamboo accents, bold local artwork, and an old unfinished wooden floor make the restaurant cozy. Local musicians entertain on Friday and Saturday night. ⊠ *Hwy. 270, Hāwī* ☎ *808/889–5555* ═ *MC, V* ☺ *Closed Mon. No dinner Sun.*

$$$$ **✕ CanoeHouse at the Mauna Lani Bay Hotel & Bungalows.** Although the open-air, beachfront setting is stunning, the CanoeHouse is starting to lose some ground to the other resort restaurants in the food department. It was among the first on the island to offer Pacific Rim fusion, and it still does it well, but the menu seems unoriginal now that fusion is a mainstay at most resort restaurants—it focuses on meat or seafood paired with sauces influenced by foreign cuisines and made with local fruits and vegetables. Shanghai lobster is the standout, and the fresh fish is always cooked to perfection. The wine list is also great, and the location makes the price tag worth it on clear evenings, even with better restaurants a few miles away. ⊠ *Mauna Lani Bay Hotel & Bungalows, 68-1400 Mauna Lani Dr., Kohala Coast* ☎ *808/885–6622* ═ *AE, D, DC, MC, V.*

SEAFOOD

$$ **✕ Kawaihae Harbor Grill & Seafood Bar.** This little restaurant is always packed—there's something about the crisp green-and-white 1850s building, along with the scent of fresh local seafood being sautéed with garlic, that draws people in. The food downstairs at the Harbor Grill is a bit more than some want to pay for basics like grilled mahimahi and fish-and-chips, but the Seafood Bar, upstairs in a separate structure that also dates from the 1850s, serves a dynamite and fairly well-priced bar menu with sandwiches and *pūpū* (appetizers), and a good lunch as well. The upstairs area is also a bit more fun and casual than downstairs; it's been a hot spot since it opened in 2003. ⊠ *Kawaihae Harbor, Hwy. 270, Kawaihae* ☎ *808/882–1368* ═ *MC, V.*

STEAK

$$$$ **✕ The Grill at the Fairmont Orchid Hawai'i.** Set back from the beach, the Grill is a martini-and-filet-mignon kind of place. The menu is heavier on meats (leaving the seafood to the nearby Brown's Beach House), and you'd be hard-pressed to find a better steak on the island. The service is impeccable, the wine list superb, and the macadamia-nut pie may be the best dessert we've ever had. Be prepared to pay high, fancy steakhouse prices. Open-air seating is available, and the tables are still close enough to the ocean to catch the breeze. ⊠ *Fairmont Orchid Hawai'i, 1 N. Kanikū Dr., Kohala Coast* ☎ *808/885–2000* ⌲ *Reservations essential* ═ *AE, D, DC, MC, V.*

$$$$ **✕ Ruth's Chris Steakhouse.** Located in the Shops at Mauna Lani complex, the new Hawai'i location of the popular Louisiana steak-house chain serves the same sizzling steaks and heaping sides the restaurant is known for throughout the country. They claim to have vegetarian

8

options, but Ruth's Chris is a true steak house in every way and as such is best suited to meat lovers. Steaks come sizzling; tasty, unhealthy classic sides, which are á la carte, include creamed spinach, broccoli with cheddar cheese, and potatoes au gratin. ⊠ *68-1330 Mauna Lani Dr., Kohala Coast* ☎*808/887–0800* ☰*AE, D, MC, V* ⊗*No lunch.*

WAIMEA

ECLECTIC

$$ ✕ **Tante's Bar & Grill.** You fully expect to see Hawaiian *paniolos* sauntering up to the bar here—and it's not unheard of. Tante's is the John Wayne version of an elegant dining room with plenty of steaks and ribs on the menu to satisfy even the hungriest cowpoke at prices that won't break the bank. And of course, since this is Hawai'i after all, expect to see multicultural dishes rubbing elbows with cowboy classics. Locals flock here for fantastic Filipino dishes like pork *adobo* (slow-cooked pork simmered in garlic, oil, and vinegar) and chicken *lau lau* (ground chicken with spices and taro, wrapped in ti leaf and steamed). ⊠ *67-1185 Māmalahoa Hwy., G-138, Parker Ranch Center, Hwy. 19* ☎*808/885–8942* ⊠*75-5693 Ali'i Dr., Kona* ☎*808/329–4488* ☰*MC, V.*

GERMAN

$$$ ✕ **Edelweiss.** An authentic German *gasthaus* right in the middle of Hawai'i, Edelweiss is an anomaly. Fear not if you don't see anything you want on the menu; your server will rattle off 15 to 20 daily specials without batting an eye. The rack of lamb is always good, and anything ending in "schnitzel," "brat," or "braten" is a safe bet. Soup (which often sounds weird but turns out to be a real treat), salad, and coffee or tea are included in dinner prices. The wine list is decent, but c'mon, get the Hefeweizen. You won't have room for dessert with the size of their portions, but you're not missing much. If you're a potato pancake fan, call two days ahead and the kitchen will whip up a batch for you. Dinner is pretty consistently good here, but lunch is almost as consistently disappointing. ⊠*Hwy. 19, Waimea* ☎*808/885–6800* ⚶*Reservations essential* ☰*MC, V* ⊗*Closed Sun. and Mon. and Sept.*

ITALIAN

$ ✕ **Solimene's.** A simple spot in one of Waimea's strip malls, Solimene's sponge-painted yellow walls and Italian villa murals are pleasant if not overly beautiful. Stick with the tasty thin crust pizzas, and you won't be disappointed. Pasta dishes are underwhelming, although nightly specials ranging from eggplant parmigiana to meatball subs tend to be quite good. For dessert, although you might be tempted by the tiramisu, the chocolate hazelnut ice cream is the way to go. ⊠*65-1158 Māmalahoa Hwy. in the Waimea Shopping Center* ☎*808/887–1313* ☰*MC, V* ⊗*Closed Mon. No dinner Sun.*

MEXICAN

$ ✕ **Tako Taco.** Everyone in Waimea and beyond is heralding the reopening of Tako Taco, one of the best Mexican restaurants on the island. Housed in a small, brightly painted hut, Tako Taco feels more like a mainland burrito joint than an island Mexican food restaurant, and its

Continued on page 204

LŪʻAU: A TASTE OF HAWAIʻI

The best place to sample Hawaiian food is at a backyard lūʻau. Aunts and uncles are cooking, the pig is from a cousin's farm, and the fish is from a brother's boat.

But even locals have to angle for invitations to those rare occasions. So your choice is most likely between a commercial lūʻau and a Hawaiian restaurant.

Most commercial lūʻau will offer you little of the authentic diet; they're more about umbrella drinks, laughs, spectacle, and fun. Expect to spend some time and no small amount of cash.

For greater authenticity, folksy experiences, and rock-bottom prices, visit a Hawaiian restaurant (most are in anonymous storefronts in residential neighborhoods). Expect rough edges and some effort negotiating the menu.

In either case, much of what is known today as Hawaiian food would be as foreign to a 16th-century Hawaiian as risotto or chow mien. The pre-contact diet was simple and healthy–mainly raw and steamed seafood and vegetables. Early Hawaiians used earth ovens and heated stones to cook seafood, taro, sweet potatoes, and breadfruit and seasoned their food with sea salt and ground kukui nuts. Seaweed, fern shoots, sweet potato vines, coconut, banana, sugarcane, and select greens and roots rounded out the diet.

Successive waves of immigrants added their favorites to the ti leaf-lined table. So it is that foods as disparate as salt salmon and chicken long rice are now Hawaiian—even though there is no salmon in Hawaiian waters and long rice (cellophane noodles) is Chinese.

AT THE LŪ'AU: KĀLUA PORK

The heart of any lū'au is the *imu*, the earth oven in which a whole pig is roasted. The preparation of an imu is an arduous affair for most families, who tackle it only for special occasions or at Thanksgiving, when many Islanders prefer to imu their turkeys. Commercial lū'au operations have it down to a science, however.

THE ART OF THE STONE

The key to a proper imu is the *pohaku*, the stones. Imu cook by means of long, slow, moist heat released by special stones which can withstand a hot fire without exploding. Many Hawaiian families treasure their imu stones, keeping them in a pile in the back yard and passing them on through generations.

PIT COOKING

The imu makers first dig a pit about the size of a refrigerator, then lay down *kiawe* (mesquite) wood and stones, and build a white-hot fire that is allowed to burn itself out. The ashes are raked away, and the hot stones covered with banana and ti leaves. Well-wrapped in leaves and a net of chicken wire, the pig is lowered onto the leaf-covered stones. *Laulau* may also be placed inside. The whole is topped with more leaves, wet burlap sacks, and a canvas tarp, and left to steam for the better part of a day.

OPENING THE IMU

This is the moment everyone waits for: The imu is unwrapped like a giant present and the imu keepers gingerly wrestle out the steaming pig. When it's unwrapped, the meat falls moist and smoky-flavored from the bone, looking and tasting just like Southern-style pulled pork, but without the barbecue sauce.

WHICH LŪ'AU?

Fairmont Orchid. Blends modern and traditional music with stories of the kings of Hawai'i, Tahiti, Samoa, and New Zealand. Foods from all four cultures are served.

Sheraton Keauhou. Fantastic show blends modern lighting and aesthetic with traditional myths and dances. Open bar and full buffet are bonuses.

Kona Village. The imu ceremony and tradional show make this a long-time island favorite. In addition to the pig, they put fresh fish in the imu—delicious.

MEA ʻAI ʻONO.
GOOD THINGS TO EAT.

LAULAU
Steamed meats, fish, and taro leaf in ti-leaf bundles: fork-tender, a medley of flavors; the taro resembles spinach.

LOMI LOMI SALMON
Salt salmon in a piquant salad or relish with onions, tomatoes.

POI (DON'T CALL IT LIBRARY PASTE.)
Islanders are beyond tired of jokes about poi, a paste made of pounded taro root.

Consider: The Hawaiian Adam is descended from *kalo* (taro). Young taro plants are called "keiki"—children. Poi is the first food after mother's milk for many Islanders. ʻAi, the word for food, is synonymous with poi in many contexts.

Not only that, we like it. "There is no meat that doesn't taste good with poi," the old Hawaiians said.

But you have to know how to eat it: with something rich or powerfully flavored. "It is salt that makes the poi go in," is another adage. When you're served poi, try it with a mouthful of smoky kālua pork or salty lomi lomi salmon. Its slightly sour blandness cleanses the palate. And if you don't like it, smile and say something polite. (And slide that bowl over to a local.)

Laulau

Lomi Lomi Salmon

Poi

8

E HELE MAI ʻAI! COME AND EAT!

Hawaiian restaurants tend to be inconveniently located in well-worn storefronts with little or no parking, outfitted with battered tables and clattering Melmac dishes, open odd (and usually limited) hours and days, and often so crowded you have to wait. But they personify aloha, invariably run by local families who welcome tourists who take the trouble to find them.

Many are cash-only operations and combination plates are a standard feature: one or two entrées, a side such as chicken long rice, choice of poi or steamed rice and—if the place is really old-style—a tiny portion of coarse Hawaiian salt and some raw onions for relish.

Most serve some foods that aren't, strictly speaking, Hawaiian, but are beloved of kamaʻāina, such as salt meat with watercress (preserved meat in a tasty broth), or *akubone* (skipjack tuna fried in a vinegar sauce).

Our two favorites: **Kanaka-Kava and Kūhiō Grille.**

MENU GUIDE

Much of the Hawaiian language encountered during a stay in the Islands will appear on restaurant menus and lists of lūʻau fare. Here's a quick primer.

ʻahi: *yellowfin tuna.*

aku: *skipjack, bonito tuna.*

ʻamaʻama: *mullet; it's hard to get but tasty.*

bento: *a box lunch.*

chicken lūʻau: *a stew made from chicken, taro leaves, and coconut milk.*

haupia: *a light, pudding-like sweet made from coconut.*

imu: *the underground ovens in which pigs are roasted for lūʻau.*

kālua: *to bake underground.*

kaukau: *food. The word comes from Chinese but is used in the Islands.*

kimchee: *Korean dish of pickled cabbage made with garlic and hot peppers.*

Kona coffee: *coffee grown in the Kona district of the Big Island.*

laulau: *literally, a bundle. Laulau are morsels of pork, chicken, butterfish, or other ingredients wrapped with young taro leaves and then bundled in ti leaves for steaming.*

lilikoʻi: *passion fruit, a tart, seedy yellow fruit that makes delicious desserts, juice, and jellies.*

lomi lomi: *to rub or massage; also a massage. Lomi lomi salmon is fish that has been rubbed with onions and herbs; commonly served with minced onions and tomatoes.*

lūʻau: *a Hawaiian feast; also the leaf of the taro plant used in preparing such a feast.*

lūʻau leaves: *cooked taro tops with a taste similar to spinach.*

mahimahi: *mild-flavored dolphinfish, not the marine mammal.*

mai tai: *potent rum drink with orange and lime juice, from the Tahitian word for "good."*

malasada: *a Portuguese deep-fried doughnut without a hole, dipped in sugar.*

manapua: *dough wrapped around diced pork or other fillings.*

manō: *shark.*

niu: *coconut.*

ʻōkolehao: *a liqueur distilled from the ti root.*

onaga: *pink or red snapper.*

ono: *a long, slender mackerel-like fish; also called wahoo.*

ʻono: *delicious; also hungry.*

ʻopihi: *a tiny shellfish, or mollusk, found on rocks; also called limpets.*

pāpio: *a young ulua or jack fish.*

pohā: *Cape gooseberry. Tasting a bit like honey, the pohā berry is often used in jams and desserts.*

poi: *a paste made from pounded taro root, a staple of the Hawaiian diet.*

poke: *chopped, pickled raw tuna or other fish, tossed with herbs and seasonings.*

pūpū: *Hawaiian hors d'oeuvre.*

saimin: *long thin noodles and vegetables in broth, often garnished with small pieces of fish cake, scrambled egg, luncheon meat, and green onion.*

sashimi: *raw fish thinly sliced and usually eaten with soy sauce.*

tī leaves: *a member of the agave family. The fragrant leaves are used to wrap food while cooking and removed before eating.*

uku: *deep-sea snapper.*

ulua: *a member of the jack family that also includes pompano and amberjack. Also called crevalle, jack fish, and jack crevalle.*

Where to Eat on the Kohala Coast & Waimea

Alan Wong's Hualalai Grille
at the Four Seasons Resort
Hualalai 1
Bamboo Restaurant 21
Brown's Beach House
at the Fairmont
Orchid Hawai'i 15
Café Pesto 18
CanoeHouse at the Mauna
Lani Bay Hotel &
Bungalows 11
Chef Daniel's Seafood
Café 23
Coast Grille at Hapuna
Beach Prince Hotel 16
Donatoni's at the
Hilton Waikoloa Village ... 4

Edelweiss 24
Grand Palace Chinese
Restaurant 7
The Grill at the Fairmont
Orchid Hawai'i 10
Hakone Steakhouse &
Sushi Bar at the Hapuna
Beach Prince Hotel 17

Hale Samoa at
Kona Village Resort 3
Huli Sue's BBQ & Grill ... 29
Kamuela Provision
Company at the Hilton
Waikoloa Village 5
Kawaihae Harbor Grill
& Seafood Bar 19
Merriman's 25

Merriman's Market Café ... 8
Norio's Sushi Bar
& Restaurant 14
Pahu'a at the Four Seasons
Resort Hualalai 2
Roy's Waikoloa Bar & Grill .. 9
Ruth's Chris Steakhouse ... 13
Solimene's 26

Sushi Rock 22
Tako Taco 27
Tante's Bar & Grill 28
Tommy Bahama's
Tropical Café 12
Tres Hombres
Beach Grill 20
Waikoloa Beach Grill 6

authentic food makes it hugely popular with both locals, who line up for to-go orders, and visitors who snag one of the plastic booths and eat in. With a focus on fresh ingredients, Tako Taco whips up awesome tacos, burritos, Mexican salads, enchiladas, rellenos, and seriously *ono* (Hawaiian slang for "tasty") quesadillas fresh to order. The tomatillo pineapple salsa is the bee's knees, and they're also now serving top-shelf margaritas, both classic and flavored—strawberry, mango, or *lilikoi* (passion fruit)—along with local beers and wine. ⊠*64-1066A Mamalahoa Hwy.* ☎*808/887–1717* ▭*MC, V.*

MODERN HAWAIIAN

$$$$ ✕**Chef Daniel's Seafood Café.** Formerly known as Daniel Thiebaut's, the seafood café still features the creations of respected local chef Thiebaut in a quaint little yellow building that once housed the historic Chock In Store, which catered to the ranching community beginning in 1900. The store's redwood countertop now serves as one long community dining table. Collectibles abound, such as antique porcelain pieces. The French-Asian menu includes an amazing appetizer of sweet-corn crab cake with a lemongrass, coconut, and lobster sauce. Other signature dishes include Hunan-style rack of lamb served with eggplant compote, and Big Island goat cheese. ⊠*65-1259 Kawaihae Rd., Waimea* ☎*808/887–2200* ▭*AE, D, DC, MC, V* ⊗*closed for lunch.*

$ ✕**Huli Sue's BBQ and Grill.** Owned and operated by the same folks that run the fantastic and popular Fujimamas restaurant in Kailua-Kona, Huli Sue's serves large portions of updated Hawaiian classics in a casual little restaurant along the highway between Waimea and Honoka'a. The barbe-cue menu, which includes your choice of meat (classics like ribs, pork roast, brisket) with one of four sauces, is melt-in-your-mouth delicious. The menu includes many other options, including a baked potato stuffed with your choice of meat, cilantro sour cream, and Fontina cheese, a variety of curry dishes, and a handful of fantastic appetizers, such as the chicken sausage cakes with cilantro pesto and the crab, smoked pepper, onion, and Fontina quesadilla. Salads, with produce from a nearby farm, are great, too. ⊠*64-957 Māmalahoa Hwy. (Hwy. 11)* ☎*808/885–6268* ▭*MC, V.*

$$$ ✕**Merriman's.** This is the signature restaurant of Peter Merriman, one of
Fodor's Choice the pioneers of Hawai'i regional cuisine. Merriman's is the home of the
★ original wok-charred 'ahi, usually served with buttery Wainaku corn. If you prefer meat, try the Kahuā Ranch lamb, raised to the restaurant's specifications, or the prime Kansas City Cut steak, grilled to order. The wine list includes 22 selections poured by the glass, and the staff is refreshingly knowledgeable. For true foodies, Merriman's now offers a farmers' market tour—four hours spent browsing around local ranches and food stands, culminating in a fantastic five-course meal using produce and meat bought throughout the day. ⊠*'Opelo Plaza, 65-1227 'Opelo Rd., Waimea* ☎*808/885–6822* ⟓*Reservations essential* ▭*AE, MC, V.*

KAILUA-KONA

AMERICAN

$ ✕**Bubba Gump Shrimp Company.** Okay, it's a chain, and a chain that centers around a Tom Hanks movie, no less. Get over it. For starters,

CLOSE UP

Green Hawai'i: Farm Tours

As local ingredients continue to play a more prominent role on Big Island menus, chefs and farmers are working together to support a burgeoning ag-tourism industry in Hawai'i. Several local farms have cropped up over the past few years to make specialty items that cater to the island's gourmet restaurants. The **Hawai'i Island Goat Dairy** produces specialty cheese; lone beekeeper Richard Spiegel of **Volcano Island Honey Co.** produces a rare and delicious honey now available not only in local restaurants but on the shelves of high-end stores like Neiman Marcus; and the **Hāmākua Heritage Farm** has turned mowed down koa forests into a safe haven for gourmet mushrooms. While a handful of farms—like **Mountain Thunder,** which produces 100% organic Kona coffee, and **Hawaiian Vanilla Vineyards,** which is cultivating vanilla from orchids growing wild on the Hāmākua Coast—are open to

the public and offer free tours, others have opted instead to offer limited tours through group operators. Chef Peter Merriman has put together a tour with **Hawai'i Forest and Trail** (⊕ *www.hawaii-forest.com/adv-farm-tour.html* for booking information) that includes stops at **Kahua Ranch,** a working cattle ranch at 3,000 feet in the Kohala Mountains, and **Honopua Farm,** where organic vegetables, lavender, and cut flowers are grown. The tour finishes up at Merriman's Restaurant where the group is treated to a five-course dinner prepared from the local ingredients they have just seen growing. The **Big Island Farm Bureau** has also tried to encourage local farming and ag-tourism through the creation of **Hawai'i AgVentures,** a new organization that schedules farm visits (to either a single or multiple farms) for interested parties (see ⊕ *www.hawaiiagventures.com* for more information).

it has one of the largest oceanfront patios on the island. And the food's not bad, once you get past the silly names. Anything with popcorn shrimp in it is good, and the "Run Chicken Run" salad (a combination of chicken, Gorgonzola cheese, walnuts, and cranberries) is the perfect size for lunch. Too bad they're no longer doing breakfast—they used to be one of the best in town for it. ✉ *75-5776 Ali'i Dr., Kailua-Kona* ☎ *808/331–8442* ▤*MC, V.*

¢ ✕**Harbor House.** This open-air restaurant on the docks at Kona's busy harbor is one of the best spots on the island for fresh fish, and a fun place to grab a beer and a bite after a long day fishing, surfing, or diving. The fish is probably a few hours off the boat—if that. It's nothing fancy—an old wooden bar, and dozens of plastic tables and chairs scattered about the covered patio—but Harbor House is a local favorite for fresh fish sandwiches and a variety of fried fish-and-chip combos. The icy schooners of Kona Brewing Company ale don't hurt, either. ✉ *74-425 Kealakehe Pkwy., Ste. 4, Honokohau Harbor* ☎ *808/326–4166* ▤*MC, V.*

$ ✕**Kona Brewing Company & Brewpub.** This large and cheery spot with a huge outdoor patio features an excellent and varied menu including pulled-pork quesadillas, gourmet pizzas, and a killer spinach salad with Gorgonzola cheese, macadamia nuts, and strawberries. Go for the beer tasting menu—your choice of four of their eight available microbrews

Where to Eat on the Kona Coast

KONA COAST

Alula & Honokōhau

Kona International Airport

Kailua-Kona

KAILUA-KONA

NORTH KONA

SOUTH KONA

Pu'uhonua o Hōnaunau National Historic Park

Kahalu'u Beach

White Sands Beach

KEAUHOU

Kailua Bay

Kalaoa

Kealakekua Bay

Kealakekua Bay

Hōlualoa

Honalo

Kainaliu

Kealakekua

Captain Cook

Nāpo'opo'o

Ke'ei

Hōnaunau

Keōkea

Keōkea

Keōlia

Ho'okena

Hu'upuloa

Miloli'i

Okoe Bay

Kaunā Point

Pōhue Bay

Hawai'i Belt Rd.

(Māmalahoa Hwy.)

Queen Ka'ahumanu Hwy.

Ali'i Drive

Ali'i Drive

Kuakini Hwy.

Kamehameha III Rd.

0   2 miles
0   3 km

Adriana's 4
Aloha Angel Cafe 6
Ba-Le 38
Bangkok House Thai Restaurant 34
Big Island Grill 23
Boston Basil's 31

Bubba Gump Shrimp Company 24
The Coffee Shack 1
Don the Beachcomber at the Royal Kona Resort ... 17
Fish Hopper 26
Fujimamas 25
Harbor House 8

Huggo's 21
Jackie Rey's Ohana Grill 16
Kai at the Sheraton Keauhou Bay 10
Kanaka Kava 18
Kē'ei Café 5
Kenichi Pacific 11

Kona Brewing Company & Brewpub 33
Kona Inn Restaurant 30
Kona Mix Plate 36
La Bourgogne 15
Los Habaneros 12
Mahina Pizza 28
Manago Hotel 3

Mi's Italian Bistro 2
Mixx Bistro 35
O's 14
Pancho & Lefty's 29
Peaberry & Galette 13
Pine Tree Café 9
Quinn's Almost By the Sea 32

Restaurant Hayama 37
Tacos El Unico 27
Teshima's 7
Thai Rin Restaurant 20
U-Top-It 19
Wasabi's 22

in miniature glasses that add up to about two regular-size mugs for the price of one. ⊠*75-5629 Kuakini Hwy., just past Palani intersection on right, Kailua-Kona* ☎*808/329–2739* ⊟*MC, V.*

$$$ ✕**Kona Inn Restaurant.** This historic open-air restaurant offers some of the best, unobstructed ocean views on the island. It's a great place to have a mai tai and some appetizers while watching the sunset, or to enjoy a tasty calamari or ono sandwich and a salad at lunch. Dinner is also available, but the entrées are less than stellar and for the prices there are better options once the sun disappears. ⊠*75-5744 Ali'i Dr., Kailua-Kona* ☎*808/329–4455* ⊟*AE, MC, V.*

¢ ✕**Quinn's Almost By the Sea.** Okay, Quinn's is a bit of a dive. That said, it does have a few things going for it—some of the best ono sandwiches on the island, for example. It's open until 11 PM, later than any other restaurant in Kailua-Kona (except Denny's). If time gets away from you on a drive to South Point, Quinn's is awaiting your return with a cheap beer and a basket of excellent calamari. You can also have a beer at the funky bar filled with fishermen. ⊠*75-5655A Palani Rd., Kailua-Kona* ☎*808/329–3822* ⊟*MC, V.*

¢ ✕**U-Top-It.** Tucked behind the shops and cafés of the Coconut Grove Marketplace, U-Top-It is a local favorite breakfast joint. Opened by a former Kona Village resort chef, all dishes at U-Top-It are built upon the restaurant's terrific taro pan crepes, which guests can choose to top with any combination of over 100 different toppings ranging from straightforward fruit or egg combinations to more unusual toppings. At lunchtime, try pairing one of the crepes with beef or chicken teriyaki. ⊠*75-5799 Ali'i Dr., Coconut Grove Market Pl.* ☎*808/329–0092* ⊟*MC, V* ⊗*Closed Mon.*

CAFÉ

$ ✕**Mixx Bistro.** Kona never knew it needed a wine bar until it got Mixx, but now the town would seem strange without it. In addition to their fantastic wine and cheese delivery service, Mixx serves up a tasty menu of bistro-inspired *pūpū* (appetizers) ranging from super healthy plates of sautéed veggies and tofu to what they claim are "the Island's best fries." They also offer a handful of entrée options, including steak frites and a whole crab or lobster served with drawn butter. And then of course there's the cheese plate. And the wine. *Sigh.* Live music keeps the patio lively most nights and Sunday afternoons. ⊠*75-5626 Kuakini Hwy., in the King Kamehameha Center* ☎*808/329–7334* ⊕*www. konawinemarket.com* ⊟*MC, V.*

FRENCH

$$$ ✕**La Bourgogne.** A genial husband-and-wife team owns this relaxing, country-style bistro with dark-wood walls and private, romantic booths. The traditional French menu has classics such as escargots, beef with a cabernet sauvignon sauce, rack of lamb with roasted garlic and rosemary, and a less-traditional venison with a pomegranate glaze. Call well in advance for reservations. ⊠*77-6400 Nālani St., Kailua-Kona* ☎*808/329–6711* ⚑*Reservations essential* ⊟*AE, D, DC, MC, V* ⊗*Closed Sun. and Mon. No lunch.*

$ ✕**Peaberry & Galette.** This little creperie is a welcome addition to the neighborhood. It serves Illy espresso, excellent sweet and savory crepes, and rich desserts like lemon cheesecake and chocolate mousse that are made fresh daily. It's got a cool, urban-café vibe, and is a nice place to hang for a bit if you're waiting for a film at the theater next door, or just feel like taking a break from paradise to sip a decent espresso and flip through the latest *W.* ✉ *Keauhou Shopping Center, 78-6740 Makolea St., Kailua-Kona* ☎ *808/322–6020* 🍴 *MC, V.*

HAWAIIAN

¢ ✕ **Ba-Le.** Comparable to Kona Mix Plate in terms of prices, food quality, and street cred, Ba-Le serves a great plate lunch. It also has tasty Vietnamese-influenced food, such as their popular croissant sandwiches stuffed with mint, lemongrass, sprouts, and your choice from a variety of Vietnamese-style meats. *Pho* (Vietnamese noodle soup) is another great option, especially if you have the misfortune of catching an island cold. There are 20 other shops throughout the state, but it's Hawaiian-owned and operated, so the place doesn't feel like a chain. ✉ *Kona Coast Shopping Center, 74-5588 Palani Rd., Kailua-Kona* ☎ *808/327–1212* 🍴 *No credit cards.*

¢ ✕ **Big Island Grill.** This typical, local Hawaiian restaurant looks like an old coffee shop or a Denny's—it's dark and nondescript inside, with booths along the walls and basic tables with bingo hall chairs in the middle of the room. Local families love it for the huge portions of pork chops, chicken *katsu,* and an assortment of grilled or pan-seared fish specialties at very reasonable prices. It has been popular with locals since it opened a few years back and there's sometimes a wait for a table. "Biggie's" also serves a great breakfast—the prices and portions make this a good place to take large groups or families. ✉ *75-5702 Kuakini Hwy.* ☎ *808/326–1153* 🍴 *MC, V* ☽ *Closed Sun.*

$ ✕ **Kanaka Kava.** A popular local hangout, and not just because da kava makes you mellow. Their *pūpū* rock! Fresh poke, smoky, tender bowls of pulled kālua pork, and healthy sautéed veggies are available in fairly large portions for less than you'll pay anywhere else on the island. Seating is at a premium, but don't be afraid to share a table and make friends. ✉ *75-5803 Ali'i Dr., Space B6, in the Coconut Grove Market Pl.* ☎ *808/883–6260* 🍴 *MC, V.*

¢ ✕ **Kona Mix Plate.** Don't be surprised if you find yourself rubbing elbows with lots of hungry locals at this inconspicuous Kona lunch spot. The antithesis of a tourist trap, this casual island favorite with fluorescent lighting and wooden tables is all about the food. Try the teriyaki chicken, shrimp tempura, or *katsu*—a chicken breast fried with bread crumbs and served with a sweet sauce. ✉ *341 Palani St., Kailua-Kona* ☎ *808/329–8104* 🍴 *No credit cards* ☽ *Closed Sun.*

$ ✕ **Pine Tree Café.** Located next to Matsuyama's market in the new Kohanaiki buisness park along Hwy. 11, north of Kona, Pine Tree is filling the giant void left by Sam Choy's closing up shop. The menu is on a dry erase board on the wall and consists of local classics such as Huli Huli Chicken and Loco Moco alongside new inventions like the shrimp curry bisque with corn bread. The fresh fish plate is always great, and all meals are served with fries or rice and that macaroni, potato, and tuna salad concoction that you only get in Hawaii. Portions are huge and prices are low, which keeps locals coming back. ✉ *Kohanaiki Plaza, 73-4354 Māmalahoa Highway (Hwy. 11)* ☎ *808/327–1234* 🍴 *No credit cards.*

ITALIAN

$ ✕**Boston Basil's.** This tiny traditional trattoria serves solid, family-style Italian food and great pizzas at very good prices. The atmosphere is the same you'll find at hundreds of Italian restaurants in the U.S.—the tablecloths are checkered, the candles are in Chianti bottles, there's spaghetti on the menu, and it always feels a little hot and greasy inside. That said, you can't beat the location on Ali'i Drive in downtown Kailua-Kona, right across the street from the ocean. ✉75-5707 Ali'i Dr., Kailua-Kona ☎808/326–7836 ▭MC, V.

$ ✕**Mahina Pizza.** Locals are ecstatic to see Mahina's, a favorite pizza joint in town a few years back, reopen in the Kona Inn Shopping Village. Upstairs, above the shops, Mahina's serves up some of the tastiest pies on the island (from the usual pepperoni, sausage, and mushroom combos to a great "Garden of Eden" vegetarian option) accompanied by cool ocean breezes and pleasant "downtown" Kona views. It is not uncommon for the owner to close up shop to go paddling, so call ahead to make sure they're open. ✉75-5744 Ali'i Dr., in the Kona Inn Shopping Village ☎808/326–1577 ▭MC, V.

> **[CON]FUSION**
>
> What is referred to as "Hawai'i cuisine" is most often a blend of several Pacific Rim and Asian cuisines, along with a few European influences. The Islands are home to large populations of Japanese, Chinese, Portuguese, Thai, Vietnamese, Korean, and Filipino immigrants, and each group has brought a little bit of home with them. This explains why a "traditional Hawaiian" restaurant will include everything from teriyaki to chicken katsu to pork adobo and Portuguese sausage on the menu. We still can't figure out how Spam got involved.

JAPANESE

$$$ ✕**Kenichi Pacific.** With its black-lacquer tables and lipstick-red banquettes, Kenichi's seems a little out of place in this small strip mall. The location keeps many tourists from finding it, even though it's been open for several years now. This is where everyone in Kailua-Kona goes when they feel like splurging on top-notch sushi. It's a little on the pricey side, but it's worth it. The sashimi is so fresh it melts in your mouth, and the signature rolls are inventive and tasty. For vegetarians, the Austin roll—asparagus tempura—is fish-free and delicious. ✉Keauhou Shopping Center, 78-6831 Ali'i Dr., Kailua-Kona ☎808/322–9140 ▭No credit cards.

$$ ✕**Restaurant Hayama.** Tucked into Kopiko Plaza, just below Long's, this local favorite for quality Japanese fare goes beyond sushi. Hayama serves traditional Japanese specialties like sukiyaki, teriyaki, shabu-shabu, and *udon* noodles, all made from quality local ingredients. Sushi is available as well, but only traditional *nigiri*, slices of raw fish layered with wasabi and rice, and sashimi. Lunch specials are a great deal, and dinner specials provide a three-course dinner for two for $40. Despite its strip mall location, Hayama manages to pull off a Zen vibe that matches the quiet and attentive, albeit slow, service. ✉75-5660 Kopiko St., D1 ☎808/331–8888 ▭MC, V.

$$ ✕**Wasabi's.** A tiny little place tucked into the back of the Coconut Plaza on Ali'i, Wasabi's five little tables tend to be occupied by the west side's Japanese population, here for some of the best sashimi on the island. Prices may seem steep, but the fish is of the highest quality. Fans of Americanized sushi rolls will find the familiar California and spicy tuna rolls here, along with a few unique inventions. And for those who will never be hip to the raw fish thing, teriyaki, *udon,* and sukiyaki options abound. ⊠*75-5803 Ali'i Dr., Coconut Grove Market Pl.* ☎*808/326–2352* ▭*MC, V.*

MEXICAN

¢ ✕**Los Habaneros.** A surprising find in the corner of this shopping mall, next to the movie theater, Habaneros serves up tasty, fresh, and fast Mexican food for low low prices. Our favorites are usually the day's specials, which can be anything from enchilada plates to homemade sopes and chiles rellenos. Their giant burritos are also a solid pick, stuffed with meat, beans, cheese, and all the fixings. ⊠*Phase II, Keauhou Shopping Center* ☎*808/324–4688* ▭*MC, V* ⊘*Closed Sun.*

$ ✕**Pancho & Lefty's.** Across the street from the Kona Village Shopping Center, Pancho & Lefty's is a typical Tex-Mex place—great for nachos and margaritas (watch out, they pour 'em strong) on a lazy afternoon. Some of the items on the menu are expensive, and some of the combos are described exactly the same way in other sections of the menu for less, so read carefully. ⊠*75-5719 Ali'i Dr., Kailua-Kona* ☎*808/326–2171* ▭*MC, V.*

¢ ✕**Tacos El Unico.** An array of authentic soft-taco choices (beef and chicken, among others), burritos, quesadillas, and great homemade tamales. Order at the counter, take a seat outside at one of a dozen yellow tables with blue umbrellas, and enjoy all the good flavors served up in those red plastic baskets. ⊠*Kona Marketplace, 75-5729 Ali'i Dr., Kailua-Kona* ☎*808/326–4033* ▭*No credit cards.*

MODERN HAWAIIAN

$$ ✕**Jackie Rey's Ohana Grill.** Uphill from downtown Kailua-Kona, this bright green open-air restaurant is a popular lunch destination, and increasingly crowded for dinner as well, thanks to the chef's fantastic poke, perfectly prepared local seafood dishes, and a few juicy meat standouts, including Korean-style short ribs and a delicious blackened prime rib. At lunchtime, the fresh fish sandwiches with wasabi mayo and the chicken sandwich with avocado and Swiss are both excellent combinations of flavors, and the fries are crisped to perfection. On the lighter side, inventive salads like the Angie salad, with candied walnuts, papaya, Maui onions, dried cranberries, and blue cheese, keep it healthy but flavorful. ⊠*Pottery Terrace, 75-5995 Kuakini Hwy., Kailua-Kona* ▭*MC, V.*

PACIFIC RIM

$$ ✕**Don the Beachcomber at the Royal Kona Resort.** The "original home of the Mai Tai," Don the Beachcomber also offers a great oceanfront breakfast buffet and has recently become a popular local spot for lunch, thanks to delicious ahi sandwiches and addictive sweet-potato fries. Though dinners may seem a bit pricey for this hotel, the location and surprising quality of the food are worth the markup. Try any of the nightly seafood specials or the Huli Huli chicken, and save room for

8

the Molten Lava cake. ⊠*75-5852 Aliʻi Dr., in the Royal Kona Resort* ☎*808/329–3111* ▭*AE, D, MC, V.*

$$$ ✕ **Fish Hopper.** The new Hawaii location of the popular Monterey, California restaurant has an expansive menu, with inventive fresh fish specials alongside the fish-and-chips and clam chowder the original restaurant is known for. The owners spent serious time and money renovating the old and funky Ocean View Inn, and the restaurant itself is lovely—lots of koa wood, Hawaiian art, and an open-air floor plan that takes advantage of the ocean view. The food is decent, but may not feel worth the price. However, the wine list is outstanding, and there are frequent bottle specials, so this is a great spot for wine and appetizers with a view. It's also currently the only ocean-view restaurant in town to serve breakfast. ⊠*75-5683 Aliʻi Dr.* ☎*808/326–2002* ▭*AE, D, MC, V.*

$$$ ✕ **Fujimamas.** A fantastic new addition to the Kona dining scene, Fujimamas serves up tasty fusion dishes like shiitake sirloin with wasabi mashed potatoes, pan-seared salmon on a curried corn pancake, and a positively addictive "Thai Caesar salad" that is big enough to share. Unless it's a rare chilly night, opt to sit outside on the patio, surrounded by bamboo and colorful artwork, while sipping a passion-fruit cocktail. ⊠*75-5719 Aliʻi Dr., Kailua-Kona* ☎*808/327–2125* ▭*AE, D, MC, V* ⊗ *Closed Mon.*

$$$ ✕ **Huggo's.** This is the only restaurant in town with prices and atmosphere comparable to the splurge restaurants at the Kohala-coast resorts. Open windows extend out over the rocks at the ocean's edge, and at night you can almost touch the manta rays drawn to the spotlights. Relax with a cocktail for two and feast on fresh local seafood; the catch changes daily, and the nightly chef's special is always a good bet. **Huggo's on the Rocks,** next door, is a great outdoor bar with a floor of sand; it's become Kailua-Kona's hot spot for drinks and live music on Friday nights. ⊠*75-5828 Kahakai Rd., off Aliʻi Dr., Kailua-Kona* ☎*808/329–1493* ▭*AE, D, DC, MC, V.*

$$ ✕ **Kai at the Sheraton Keauhou Bay.** Aside from the lobby, this restaurant is the best-looking part of the Sheraton Keauhou Bay, with a prime view facing the Bay. The enormous windows are left open most of the time, making it feel almost like an outdoor restaurant. The menu is limited, but each entrée is good, from the fresh local fish to the brined and roasted hormone-free chicken. Everything is prepared with that fusion of Pacific Rim and Continental that makes up Hawaiian cuisine. The seared ʻahi appetizer is not to be missed. Breakfast is a good bet as well; very reasonable, great buffet, and the view during the daytime is just about perfect. ⊠*78-128 Ehukai St., Kailua-Kona* ☎*808/930–4900* ▭*AE, MC, V.*

$$ ✕ **O's Bistro.** Probably the best restaurant you'll ever find in a strip mall. Chef Amy Ferguson-Ota combines Southwestern flavors with Hawaiʻi regional cuisine and a touch of French cooking. There are noodles of all types, in all shapes, from all ethnic backgrounds—be they as delicate spring rolls, as a crisp garnish to an exquisite salad, or as orecchiette in Ota's updated tuna casserole with wok-seared spiced ʻahi and shiitake cream. ⊠*Crossroads Shopping Center, 75-1129 Henry St., Kailua-Kona* ☎*808/329–9222* ▭*AE, D, DC, MC, V.*

THAI

$$ ✕**Bangkok House Thai Restaurant.** It may not look like much, with its small, dark interior and tired carpets, but Bangkok House is the local go-to for good Thai food. One of few Thai restaurants on the island to add enough spice to their sauces, Bangkok serves up tasty curries, satays, and soups, along with a random assortment of Chinese entrées. The huge menu can actually be a bit overwhelming (there are over 100 options) but the Rainbow salad, panang curry, and spring rolls are all standouts. Make sure to save room for homemade lychee ice cream. ✉ *75-5626 Kuakini Hwy., in the King Kamehameha Mall* ☎ *808/329–7764* ▤ *MC, V.*

$ ✕**Thai Rin Restaurant.** The Thai owner at this old-timer in Aliʻi Sunset Plaza is likely to take your order, cook it, and bring it to your table himself. The restaurant is small, with about 10 tables total, but bright and clean, with plenty of windows, white tablecloths, light blue walls, and various bits of Thai artwork and knickknacks spread throughout. The menu includes five curries, a green-papaya salad, and a popular platter that combines spring rolls, satay, beef salad, and *tom yum* (lemongrass soup). ✉ *75-5799 Aliʻi Dr., Kailua-Kona* ☎ *808/329–2929* ▤ *AE, D, DC, MC, V.*

SOUTH KONA

AMERICAN

$ ✕**Aloha Angel Cafe.** With an emphasis on healthy, organic fare, this friendly café adjacent to the Aloha Theatre serves tasty, mostly good-for-you options on a lānai overlooking Kealakekua Bay and the orchards above it. Choose from an assortment of egg dishes and pastries in the morning, burgers, fish sandwiches, and salads for lunch, and pasta, grilled fish, or steak for dinner, all at very reasonable prices. For dessert, save room to sample selections from the café's killer pastry case. The only problem here is that service is glacially slow—even the locals complain, so you know it's bad; plan on chilling out on their veranda, taking in the views for awhile. ✉ *79-7384 Māmalahoa Hwy., Kainaliu* ☎ *808/322–3383* ▤ *MC, V.*

$ ✕**The Coffee Shack.** There's really no flaw to this place. The view is stunning, the service is excellent even when it's busy (which is most of the time), and the eggs Benedict and hot Reuben sandwich are the best on the island. Breads and pastries are all homemade, and the coffee is strong and tasty. On your way to nowhere in particular, stop by for a Hawaiian smoothie, an iced honey mocha latte, or homemade lūʻau bread—all worth a detour. In the evening, enjoy gourmet pizza and an amazing sunset view. ✉ *83-5799 Māmalahoa Hwy.* ☎ *808/328–9555* ▤ *MC, V.*

$ ✕**Manago Hotel.** About 20 minutes south of Kailua-Kona, Manago is a time-warp experience. A vintage neon sign identifies the hotel, and Formica tables, ceiling fans, and venetian blinds add to the flavor of this film-noir spot. The T-shirts (which are great souvenirs for friends at home) brag that the hotel has the best pork chops in town, and it's not false advertising. The fresh fish is excellent as well, especially ono and butterfish. Unless you request otherwise, the fish is all sautéed with a tasty house butter-soy sauce concoction. Meals come with rice for the table and an assortment of side dishes that changes from time to time, but usually includes a macaroni, potato, and tuna salad, and some sort of braised tofu and sautéed veggie dish. ✉ *82-6155 Māmalahoa Hwy., Captain Cook* ☎ *808/323–2642* ▭ *D, DC, MC, V* ⊘ *Closed Mon.*

ECLECTIC

$$ ✕ **Ke'ei Café.** This beautiful restaurant is in a plantation-style building

Fodor's Choice

★ 15 minutes south of Kona. Delicious dinners with Brazilian, Asian, and European flavors utilize fresh ingredients provided by local farmers. Try the Thai red curry or wok-seared 'ahi accompanied by a selection from the extensive wine list. The owners are Brazilian, so the *caipirinhas* are outstanding if you're tired of mai tais. ✉ *Hwy. 11, ½ mi south of Kainaliu, Hōnaunau* ☎ *808/328–8451* ⟐ *Reservations essential* ▭ *MC, V* ⊘ *Closed Sun. and Mon.*

ITALIAN

$$ ✕ **Mi's Italian Bistro.** A welcome newcomer to the Kainaliu dining scene, Mi's is a classed-up, white tablecloth establishment in a tiny strip mall on the mountain (mauka) side of Hwy. 11. The restaurant's husband-and-wife owners prepare homemade pastas and focaccia daily. Daily specials are always delicious and usually include a lasagna, focaccia, and risotto option. The homemade herb cheese ravioli are rich and delicious, and even the salad options are a notch above, with ingredients such as candied macadamia nuts, roasted beets, and sautéed haricots verts. Homemade desserts are worth saving room for, particularly the banana rum flambé. ✉ *81-6372 Māmalahoa Hwy., Kainaliu* ☎ *808/323–3880* ▭ *MC, V.*

JAPANESE

$ ✕ **Teshima's.** Come here for the most authentic Japanese cuisine on the island. Locals show up at this small, neighborhood restaurant whenever they're in the mood for fresh sashimi, puffy shrimp tempura, or *hekka* (beef and vegetables cooked in an iron pot) at a reasonable price. Teshima's doesn't look like much, inside or out, but it's been crowded since 1929 for a reason. You might also want to try a *teishoku* (tray) of assorted Japanese delicacies, or the popular bento box lunch. The service is laid-back and friendly. The restaurant is 15 minutes south of Kailua-Kona. ✉ *Māmalahoa Hwy., Honalo* ☎ *808/322–9140* ▭ *No credit cards.*

MEXICAN

¢ ✕ **Adriana's.** A tiny little hole in the wall housed in a small shopping center, you could easily miss Adriana's if you don't happen to catch their homemade sign down on the highway pointing the way. It's worth

---

WORD OF MOUTH

"Just returned from 16 days in the Big Island. A few recommendations from this trip…Ke'ei Cafe in Kainaliu—the food is fresh and delicious. Service is sometimes a little ragged—we always make an early reservation (6 pm) so we're there before they get really busy. We have never been disappointed."

—Martym

keeping an eye out. The restaurant's owner and namesake serves up home-cooked El Salvadoran food—generally very similar to Mexican food, except with slightly fewer chilies. Adriana's handmade tamales are incredible, and no other spot on the island has a salsa bar to compete with this one. ⊠ *Kealakekua Ranch Center* ☎ *808/217–7405* ⊟ *No credit cards* ⊗ *Closed weekends.*

VOLCANO

AMERICAN

$ ✕**Lava Rock Café.** This is a decent place to grab a sandwich or a coffee and check your e-mail before heading to the Volcano. (Lava Rock also serves dinner, but service tends to be less than stellar, especially for tourists.) Dishes range from chicken salad to New York steak, beverages from cappuccino to wine. Though it's not perfect, Lava Rock is a good place to stop if you want to take a picnic into the park: once inside, the park's concessionaires sell bland, overpriced food, and within Volcano Village there are no other fast and tasty deli options. ⊠ *Old Volcano Hwy., behind Kīlauea General Store, Volcano* ☎ *808/967–8526* ⊗ *No dinner Sun.* ⊟ *MC, V.*

$ ✕**Volcano Golf & Country Club.** This restaurant does not feel much like a country club—it's simple and not at all fancy with oak tables filled with local old-timers talking story and chowing down on greasy local favorites. Locals love this spot for its large portions and classic breakfasts: ordering the breakfast burger (with fried egg, cheese, and your choice of meat) and a cup of local coffee is the way to go. If it's lunchtime, you can't beat the burgers. ⊠ *Pi'i Mauna Dr., off Hwy. 11, Volcano* ☎ *808/967–8228* ⊗ *No dinner* ⊟ *MC, V.*

CONTINENTAL

$$$ ✕**Kīlauea Lodge.** Chef Albert Jeyte combines contemporary trends with traditional cooking styles from the Mainland, France, and his native Hamburg, Germany. Entrées include venison, duck à l'orange with an apricot-mustard glaze, and authentic *hasenpfeffer* (braised rabbit) served with Jeyte's signature sauerbraten. The coconut-crusted brie appetizer is huge, melty, and absolutely delicious. Built in 1937 as a YMCA camp, the restaurant still has the original "Friendship Fireplace" made from stones from around the world. The roaring fire, koa-wood tables, and warm lighting make the sunny main building feel like a lodge. ⊠ *Old Volcano Hwy., Volcano* ☎ *808/967–7366* ⊟ *AE, MC, V* ⊗ *No lunch.*

ITALIAN

$$ ✕🍴**Kiawe Kitchen.** Everyone around here says the same thing: "Kiawe has awesome pizza, but it's a little expensive for pizza." And it's true— the wood-fired pizza at this warm and pretty Italian eatery, with red walls and wood floors, has a perfect thin crust and an authentic Italian taste, but you have to be prepared to spend around $15 on a typical pie. Food options are limited in this area, though. Go for it. ⊠ *19-4005 Old Volcano Rd., Volcano* ☎ *808/967–7711* ⊟ *MC, V* ⊗ *Closed Wed.*

8

Where to Eat on Hilo Side & Volcano

Bears' Coffee **11**

Big Island Pizza **16**

Blane's Drive-In **10**

Café 100 .... **12**

Café Pesto **15**

Happy Valley
Seafood Restaurant **18**

Harrington's **21**

Hilo Bay Café **7**

Ken's House of Pancakes .. **9**

Kiawe Kitchen **4**

Kīlauea Lodge **3**

Kūhiō Grille **8**

Lava Rock Café **1**

Luquin's Mexican
Restaurant **6**

Naung Mai **13**

Pescatore **14**

Reuben's Mexican
Restaurant **19**

Royal Siam **22**

The Seaside Restaurant
& Aqua Farm **20**

Sombat's Fresh
Thai Cuisine **23**

Thai Thai Restaurant **5**

Uncle Billy's **17**

Volcano Golf
& Country Club **2**

THAI

$ ✕**Thai Thai Restaurant.** The food is authentic, and the prices are reasonable at this little Volcano Village find. A steaming-hot plate of curry or a dish of pad thai noodles is the perfect antidote to a chilly day on the volcano. The chicken satay is excellent—the peanut dipping sauce the perfect match of sweet and spicy. Be careful when you order, as "medium" is more than spicy enough even for hard-core chili addicts. The service is warm and friendly, and the dining room is pleasant, with white tablecloths, Thai art, and a couple of silk wall hangings. ✉19-4084 Old Volcano Rd., Volcano ☎808/967–7969 ⊘No lunch ⊟MC, V.

HILO & PUNA

AMERICAN

$$ ✕**Harrington's.** Harrington's is one of the few restaurants in Hilo with real staying power, and it's got a lot of things going for it—a charming location on Reed's Bay with a great view, super-fresh seafood options, tender farm-raised beef, and a popular happy hour. You can't go wrong with either the catch of the day served in a tangy citrus-wasabi beurre blanc or the peppercorn steak. The garlic-laced Slavic steak is a specialty of the house. For lunch try the Harrington's burger, served with cream-cheese aioli. ✉135 Kalaniana'ole Ave., Hilo ☎808/961–4966 ⊟MC, V.

$$ ✕**Hilo Bay Café.** What this eatery lacks in setting—it's in a strip mall that contains Office Max and Wal-Mart—it makes up for with modern decor and fantastic food. When in season, the out-of-this-world heirloom tomato salad puts any mainland variation to shame. The vegan offerings, which range from garlic fries to potpie, are good enough to seduce meat-eaters. Other excellent options include cheese fondue, pepper steak, roasted chicken breast stuffed with pine nuts and garlic cream cheese, and any of the salads (the beet salad is a standout). Prices are exceedingly reasonable given the quality of the food. ✉315 Makaala St., Hilo ☎808/935–4939 ⊟AE, DC, MC, V.

CHINESE

$$ ✕**Happy Valley Seafood Restaurant.** Don't let the name fool you. Though Hilo's best Chinese restaurant does specialize in seafood (the salt-and-pepper prawns are fantastic), they also offer a wide range of other Cantonese treats, including the sizzling lamb platter, salt-and-pepper pork, Mongolian beef or chicken, and vegetarian specialties like garlic eggplant and crispy green beans. The food is good, portions are large, and the price is right, but don't come here expecting any ambience—this is a funky and cheap Chinese restaurant, with a few random pieces of artwork tacked up here and there. ✉1263 Kilauea Ave., Ste. 320 ☎808/933–1083 ⊟MC, V.

8

$ ✕ **Bears' Coffee.** A favorite Hilo breakfast spot, much loved for their
☺   fresh-fruit waffles and tasty morning coffee. Service can be a little slow,
but where are you running off to anyway? For lunch they serve up
huge deli sandwiches and decent entrée-size salads. In keeping with its
name, the little diner is full of stuffed bears, ceramic bears, even bear
wallpaper—it's a little much, but the kids will like it. ✉*106 Keawe St.*
☎*808/935–0708* ▭*No credit cards.*

$ ✕ **Ken's House of Pancakes.** For years this 24-hour coffee shop between
the airport and the hotels along Banyan Drive has been a gathering
place for Hilo residents. As its name implies, Ken's serves good pancakes, but there are about 180 other tasty local specialties and American diner–inspired items from which to choose. Wednesday is prime
rib night. ✉*1730 Kamehameha Ave., Hilo* ☎*808/935–8711* ▭*AE,
D, DC, MC, V.*

¢   ✕ **Blane's Drive-In.** With a vast menu second only to Ken's House of
Pancakes, Blane's serves up everything from standard hamburgers to
chicken *katsu.* There's a mean plate lunch with tons of fresh fish for
only $7. The slow-cooked homemade chili and sticky white rice is a
meal in itself, and costs less than $3. At one point it was a real drive-in,
with car service. Now, customers park, order at the window and then
eat either at one of the few picnic tables provided or in their cars, or
take their food to go. ✉*217 Wainuenue Ave., Hilo* ☎*808/969–9494*
▭*No credit cards.*

¢   ✕ **Café 100.** This popular local restaurant is famous for its tasty *loco
moco,* prepared in more than a dozen ways, and its dirt-cheap breakfast and lunch specials. (You can stuff yourself for $3 if you order
right.) If you're looking for a salad, keep walking. The word restaurant,
or even café, is used liberally here—you order at a window and eat your
plate lunch on one of the outdoor benches provided—but you come
here for the food and prices, not the ambience. ✉*969 Kīlauea Ave.,
Hilo* ☎*808/935–8683* ▭*No credit cards.*

$ ✕ **Kūhiō Grille.** There's no ambience to speak of, and water is served in
unbreakable plastic, but if you're searching for local fare—that eclectic
and indefinable fusion of ethnic cuisines—Kūhiō Grille is a must. Sam
Araki serves a 1-pound *laulau* (a steamed bundle of taro leaves and
pork) that is worth the trip. This diner at the edge of Hilo's largest mall
opens at 6 AM. ✉*Prince Kūhiō Shopping Plaza, 111 E. Puainako St.,
at Hwy. 11* ☎*808/959–2336* ▭*AE, MC, V.*

$$ ✕ **Uncle Billy's.** Uncle Billy's is pure Hawaiian kitsch—right out of 1930s
Hollywood—but the thatch roofs, tinkling capiz-shell wind chimes,
and Tahitian-print curtains add to the fun, as does a free nightly hula
show. The show and the ambience are the reasons to visit; the food is
so-so. Choose from mahimahi meunière, teriyaki chicken, and local
specialties. ✉*Hilo Bay Hotel, 87 Banyan Dr., Hilo* ☎*808/935–0861*
▭*AE, D, DC, MC, V* ☽*No lunch.*

CLOSE UP

The Plate Lunch Tradition

To experience island history first-hand, take a seat at one of Hawai'i's ubiquitous "plate lunch" eateries, and order a segmented Styrofoam plate piled with rice, macaroni salad, and maybe some fiery pickled vegetable condiment. On the sugar plantations, native Hawaiians and immigrant workers from many different countries ate together in the fields, sharing food from their kaukau kits, the utilitarian version of the Japanese *bento* lunchbox. From this melting pot came the vibrant language of pidgin and its equivalent in food: the plate lunch.

At beaches and events, you can probably see a few tiny kitchens-on-wheels, another excellent venue for sampling plate lunch. These portable restaurants are descendants of lunch wagons that began selling food to plantation workers in the 1930s. Try the deep-fried chicken *katsu* (rolled in Japanese panko flour and spices). The marinated beef teriyaki is another good choice, as is miso butterfish. The noodle soup, *saimin*, with its Japanese fish stock and Chinese red-tinted barbecue pork, is a distinctly local medley. Koreans have contributed spicy barbecue *kal-bi* ribs, often served with chili-laden kimchi (pickled cabbage). Portuguese bean soup and tangy Filipino adobo stew are also favorites. The most popular Hawaiian contribution to the plate lunch is the *laulau*, a mix of meat and fish and young taro leaves, wrapped in more taro leaves and steamed.

ITALIAN

$$ ✕**Big Island Pizza.** If spending a twenty on a large pizza is something you just can't come to grips with, steer clear of Big Island Pizza. If, on the other hand, you can rationalize paying more for a pie that's topped with things like Black Tiger shrimp, scallops, and chunks of crabmeat (the "Ali'i Feast"), then order up and get ready for a little slice of heaven. There are only have a handful of tables for eating in, but they do a brisk take-out business and also deliver to the eastern side of the island. ✉*760 Kilauea Ave.* ☎*808/934–8000* ⊕*www.bigislandpizza. com* ▤*AE, D, MC, V.*

$$ ✕**Café Pesto.** *See full review in Kohala section, above.* ✉*308 Kamehameha Ave., Hilo* ☎*808/969–6640* ▤*AE, D, DC, MC, V.*

$$ ✕**Pescatore.** With dim lights, stately high-back chairs, and dark-wood paneling, Pescatore conjures up an Italian trattoria. The food is good, but not amazing, with plenty of Italian basics such as lasagna, chicken marsala, and chicken or veal parmigiana. Lunch consists of Italian-style sandwiches; breakfast, served on weekends only, features omelets and crepes. Families love the simple pastas made to please choosy children. ✉*235 Keawe St., at Haili St., Hilo* ☎*808/969–9090* ▤*AE, D, DC, MC, V.*

MEXICAN

$ ✕**Luquin's Mexican Restaurant.** Long an island favorite for tasty, albeit greasy, Mexican grub, Luquin's is still going strong in the funky town of Pahoa. Tacos are great here (go for crispy), especially when stuffed with grilled, seasoned local fish. Chips are warm and salty, the salsa's got some kick, and the beans are thick with lard and topped with melted cheese. This is not the place to eat right before going for a

8

swim, but it's perfect after a long day of exploring. ⊠ *Main St., Pahoa* ☏ *808/965–9990* ▭ *MC, V.*

$ ✕**Reuben's Mexican Restaurant.** It's not the best Mexican food you've ever had, but if you're in Hilo and you're jonesing for some chile verde, Reuben's has got you pretty well covered. You could make a meal out of their warm chips and salsa alone, and they're known for pouring a stiff margarita. Fancy? No. Authentic? *Mas o menos* (more or less). Sometimes you just want a greasy plate of nachos and a margarita. ⊠ *336 Kamehameha Ave., Hilo* ☏ *808/961–2552* ▭ *No credit cards.*

SEAFOOD

$$ ✕**The Seaside Restaurant and Aqua Farm.** The Nakagawa family has been running this eatery since the early 1920s. The latest son to manage the place has spruced it up a bit with tablecloths and candles, but the decor is still bare-bones; however, it serves some of the freshest fish on the island. (Not a surprise, as the fish come from the restaurant's own aqua farm.) Islanders travel great distances for the fried *āholehole* (young Hawaiian flagtail). Landlubbers should try the grilled lamb chops, chicken, or prime rib. Arrive before sunset and request a table on the patio for a view of the egrets roosting around the fish ponds. ⊠ *1790 Kalaniana'ole Ave., Hilo* ☏ *808/935–8825* ▭ *AE, DC, MC, V* ⊘ *Closed Mon. No lunch.*

THAI

$ ✕**Naung Mai.** There's not much to this downtown eatery: five tables, three booths, and owner Alisa Rung Khongnok hard at work in the kitchen. It's a bit hard to find, but fresh, reasonably priced meals make it worth seeking out—it may be the best Thai food on the island. For those who like to pair spicy curry with cold beer, feel free to pick up a six-pack at the grocery store up the street. Naung Mai charges $2 for glasses. ⊠ *86 Kīlauea Ave., Hilo* ☏ *808/934–7540* ▭ *MC, V* ⊘ *Closed Sun. No lunch Wed. or Sat.*

$ ✕**Royal Siam.** A downtown Hilo fixture, this authentic Thai eatery offers little ambience. But you don't need a dramatic view when you can choose from a menu that includes five kinds of curries and plenty of stir-fried meals. The tangy stir-fried garlic shrimp with coconut milk and wild mushrooms is particularly good. ⊠ *70 Mamo St., Hilo* ☏ *808/961–6100* ▭ *AE, D, DC, MC, V* ⊘ *Closed Sun.*

$ ✕**Sombat's Fresh Thai Cuisine.** The name says it all. Sombat Parente uses only the freshest local ingredients (many of which come from his own garden) to prepare authentic and tasty Thai treats like pumpkin curry, spring rolls with lime sauce, and green papaya salad. The weekday lunch plate special is a steal ($6–$8). And if you can't leave the island without it, Sombat's infamous pad thai sauce is available to take home in jars. ⊠ *88 Kanoelehue Ave., Waiakea Kai Plaza* ☏ *808/969–9336* ⊕ *www.sombats.com* ▭ *MC, V* ⊘ *Closed Sun.*

Where to Stay

WORD OF MOUTH

"Before designating a 'central location' for the BI you first need to decide what you want to see and do. If proximity to white sand beaches and good weather are priorities, Kohala is the best choice."

—fdecarlo

WHERE TO STAY PLANNER

Hotels & Resorts

The resorts—all clustered on the Kohala Coast—are expensive, there are no two ways about it. That said, many offer free nights with longer stays (fifth or seventh night free) and often team up with airlines or consolidators to offer great package deals that may include a rental car, meals, spa treatments, golf, and other activities. Children under 17 can sometimes stay for free. Ask about specials when you book, and check their Web site as well—many resorts have Internet-only deals.

B&Bs & Inns

Bed-and-breakfasts and locally run inns are a nice halfway point between the resorts and condos, offering a bit more privacy than a resort, as well as some of the perks of hotels (breakfast and maid service), but without the extras that drive up rates at resorts.

Be sure to check the association Web sites as well as property Web sites and call to ask questions. There are still a few "B&Bs" that are really just dumpy rooms in someone's house, and you don't want to end up there.

Condos & Vacation Rentals

Condos and vacation homes are the best deal going on the island. There are hundreds to choose from in and around Kailua-Kona, dozens more dotted around the island, and more being built every day, which keeps driving rates down. You can get more space and save some money by eating in (although groceries aren't cheap on the island).

Reservations

You'll almost always be able to find a room on the Big Island, but you might not get your first choice if you wait until the last minute. Make reservations six months to a year in advance if you're visiting during the winter season (December 15 through April 15). The week after Easter Sunday, when the Merrie Monarch Festival is in full swing, all of Hilo's rooms are booked. Kailua-Kona is packed in mid-October during the Ironman World Triathlon Championship.

Prices

Generally, the farther you are from the beach, the less you'll pay. If you're willing to drive 10 to 30 minutes to get to the beach, you can find great deals. At the beach, garden view rooms are less expensive than those with an ocean view. High season is usually considered December to February and June to August.

Keep in mind that most of the resorts now charge "resort fees" for things like parking, daily newspaper service, and activities, and some condos and vacation rentals charge an additional cleaning fee. Always ask about extra fees as well as specials and discounts when you book, and look online for great package deals.

WHAT IT COSTS IN HOTELS

¢	$	$$	$$$	$$$$
Under $100	$100–$180	$181–$260	$261–$340	Over $340

Hotel prices are for two people in a standard double room in high season. Condo price categories reflect studio and one-bedroom rates.

BEST BETS FOR BIG ISLAND LODGING

odor's writers and editors have selected their favor-
te hotels, resorts, condos, vacation rentals, and B&Bs
y price and experience. Fodor's Choice properties
epresent the "best of the best" across price catego-
ies. You can also search by area for excellent places
o stay—check out our complete reviews on the fol-
owing pages.

ODOR'S CHOICE

hu Pohaku
o'omaluhia, $$$–
$$$, p. 235

ur Seasons Resort
ualālai, $$$$, p. 225

ona Village Resort,
$$$, p. 230

aianuhea, $$, p. 258

y Price

ona Tiki Hotel, p. 238

anago Hotel, p. 246

e Bay House, p. 254

ale Hualalai, p. 245

ale Ohia Cottages,
250

ona Pacific, p. 244

aimea Gardens
ottage, p. 237

$

lauea Lodge, p. 248

oyal Kona Resort,
239

Shipman House B&B,
p. 255

Vista Waikoloa, p. 235

Waterfalls Inn B&B,
p. 256

$$$

Hōlualoa Inn, p. 246

Keauhou Kona Surf &
Racquet Club, p. 242

ResortQuest Kona by
the Sea, p. 245

Sheraton Keauhou
Bay Resort, p. 239

Waikoloa Beach
Marriott, p. 232

$$$$

Fairmont Orchid
Hawai'i, p. 225

Hāpuna Beach Prince
Hotel, p. 227

Mauna Lani Bay Hotel,
p. 232

By Experience

BEST BEACH

Four Seasons Resort
Hualālai, $$$$

Hāpuna Beach Prince
Hotel, $$$$

Hilton Waikoloa
Village, $$$–$$$$,
p. 227

Kona Village Resort,
$$$$

Waikoloa Beach
Marriott, $$$

BEST HOTEL BAR

Four Seasons
Hualālai, $$$$

Hilton Waikoloa
Village, $$$–$$$$

Mauna Lani Bay Hotel,
$$$$

Royal Kona Resort, $$

Sheraton Keauhou
Bay Resort, $$$

BEST B&BS & INNS

Ahu Pohaku
Ho'omaluhia,
$$$-$$$$

Hilo Honu Inn,
$-$$, p. 254

Hōlualoa Inn, $$$

Palms Cliff House Inn,
$$$, p. 256

Waimea Garden
Cottage, $

BEST SPA

Fairmont Orchid
Hawai'i, $$$$

Hilton Waikoloa Vil-
lage, $$$-$$$$

Mauna Lani Bay Hotel,
$$$$

Waikoloa Beach Mar-
riott, $$$

MOST KID-FRIENDLY

Casa De Emdeko,
¢-$, p. 242

Dolphin Bay Hotel,
$, p. 253

Hāpuna Beach Prince
Hotel, $$$$

Hilton Waikoloa
Village, $$$-$$$

Sheraton Keauhou
Bay Resort, $$$

MOST ROMANTIC

Four Seasons Resort
Hualālai, $$$$

Hōlualoa Inn, $$$

Kona Village Resort,
$$$$

Volcano Teapot
Cottage, $, p. 251

Waianuhea, $$

9

By Amy
Westervelt

Even among locals, there is an ongoing debate about which side of the Big Island is "better," so don't worry if you're having a tough time deciding where to stay. Our recommendation? Do both. Each side of the island offers a totally different range of accommodations, restaurants, and activities.

Consider staying at one of the resorts along the Kohala Coast or in a condo in Kailua-Kona for half of your trip. Then, shift gears and check into a romantic B&B on the Hāmākua Coast or near the volcano. If you've got children in tow, opt for a vacation home or one of Hilo's family-friendly hotels. On the west coast, lounge on the pristine beaches and try some of the fine-dining restaurants; on the east, hike through rain forests, frolic in waterfalls, and go for a plate lunch.

Some locals like to say that the east is "more Hawaiian," but we argue that King Kamehameha himself made the west his last resting place, and Hawaiians have always loved the beach. Another reason to try a bit of both: your budget. You can justify splurging on a west coast resort for a few nights because you'll spend the rest of your time paying one-third that rate in the east. And although food at the resorts is very expensive (except for Kona Village, which is all-inclusive), you don't have to eat every meal there. Condos and vacation homes can be ideal for a family trip or for a group of friends looking to save money and live like a local for a week or two. Many of the homes also have private pools and/or hot tubs, lānai, ocean views, and more; you can go as budget or as high-end as you like.

If you choose a B&B, inn, or an out-of-the-way hotel, explain your expectations fully and ask plenty of questions before booking. Be clear about your travel and location needs. Some places require stays of two or three days. When booking, ask about car-rental arrangements, as many B&B networks offer discounted rates. No matter where you stay, you'll want to rent a car—preferably one with four-wheel drive. This is imperative for getting to some of the best beaches and really seeing the island.

Members of the Big Island–based **Hawai'i Island Bed & Breakfast Association** ⊕ *www.stayhawaii.com* are listed with phone numbers and rates in a comprehensive online brochure. In order to join this network, B&Bs must be evaluated and meet fairly stringent minimum requirements, including a yearly walk-through by Association officers, to maintain their membership.

Other B&B associations include **Bed & Breakfast Honolulu (Statewide)** (☎ *800/288–4666* ⊕ *www.hawaiibnb.com*) and **Hawai'i's Best Bed & Breakfasts** (☎ *808/985–7488 or 800/262–9912* ⊕ *www.bestbnb.com*).

For information on camping at county parks, including Spencer Beach Park, contact the **Department of Parks and Recreation** (⊠ *25 Aupuni St., Hilo 96720* ☎ *808/961–8311* ⊕ *www.hawaii-county.com*).

KOHALA COAST

The Kohala Coast is home to all of the Big Island's mega-resorts. One after the other, manicured lawns and golf courses, luxurious hotels, and white-sand beaches break up the long expanse of black lava rock along the northwest coast. Many visitors to the Big Island check in here and rarely leave, except to try the restaurants, spas, or golf courses at neighboring resorts. If you're looking to be pampered (for a price!) and lounge on the beach or by the pool all day with an umbrella drink in hand, this is where you need to be. That's not to say that staying in Kohala makes it difficult to see the rest of the island. On the contrary, most of the hiking and adventure tour companies on the island offer pickups at the Kohala resorts, and many of the hotels have deals with various rental car agencies so you can be as active or lazy as you like.

HOTELS & RESORTS

$$$$ ⊞ **Fairmont Orchid Hawai'i.** The Fairmont is a mega-resort in every sense of the word—huge, crowded, expensive, with grand staircases, domed ceilings, chandeliers, and marble everywhere. If you're looking for a unique, intimate experience, this is not your hotel, but with its antiques and 32 acres of beachfront gardens the Orchid provides the perfect old-school hotel experience for some. Its restaurants are also among the best on the island, with a large variety of options ranging from sushi to modern Hawaiian cuisine to an upscale steak house. A one-time $40 activity pass good for your entire stay gets you access to all sorts of classes, equipment rentals, and various other amenities. The resort also offers 2½-hour voyages aboard an authentic Polynesian double-hull sailing canoe, the *Hahalua Lele*, or "Flying Manta Ray." The "Gold Floor" of the hotel includes free breakfast and a daily wine and hors d'oeuvres hour, a deal that is useful if you can't start your day without a big breakfast—there's nearly always a wait for a table at the restaurant in the morning. **Pros:** oceanfront location, great restaurants. **Cons:** mammoth resort lacks personal feel, outdated room decor. ⊠*1 N. Kanikū Dr., Kohala Coast 96743* ☎*808/885–2000 or 800/845–9905* ⊕*www.fairmont.com* ➾*486 rooms, 54 suites* ⏶*In-room: safe, ethernet. In-hotel: 4 restaurants, bars, golf courses, tennis courts, pool, gym, spa, beachfront, water sports, children's programs (ages 5–12), no-smoking rooms* ☐*AE, D, DC, MC, V.*

$$$$ ⊞ **Four Seasons Resort Hualālai.** Beautiful views everywhere, polished
⟳ wood floors, brand-new furnishings and linens in warm earth and cool
Fodor'sChoice white tones, and Hawaiian artwork make Hualālai a peaceful retreat.
★ Ground-level rooms have outdoor garden showers. Bungalows are large and cozy, with down comforters and spacious slate-floor bathrooms. One of the five pools, called King's Pond, is a brackish pond with loads of fish and two manta rays that guests have the opportunity to feed daily. The main infinity pool looks like something out of an ad for an expensive liquor—it's long and peaceful, surrounded by cabanas and palm trees with a clear view to the ocean beyond. The on-site Hawaiian Cultural Center honors the grounds' spiritual heritage, and the sports club and spa offer top-rate health and fitness options. Hualālai's golf course hosts the Senior PGA Tournament of Champi-

9

Four Seasons Resort Hualālai

ons. Despite its quiet luxury, the resort is also super kid-friendly, with a great activities program, and a few pool options for families. The downside is that despite valiant efforts to the contrary, the Four Seasons doesn't feel much like Hawai'i; add to that the number of guests who will be squawking on their cell phones next to you at the pool (despite the sign reading NO CELL PHONES), and you can see why some folks avoid this place. Still, it is beautiful, the restaurants are fantastic (the infamous Alan Wong operates the Hualālai Grill and Pahui'a serves up the best beachfront Sunday brunch on the island), the rooms are more than comfortable, and the service is definitely of Four Seasons quality. **Pros:** beautiful location, island's best restaurants. **Cons:** can be noisy poolside, doesn't feel Hawaiian. ⊠ *100 Ka'ūpūlehu Dr.* ⌂*Box 1269, Kailua-Kona 96745* ☎*808/325–8000, 800/819–5053, or 888/340–5662* ⊕*www.fourseasons.com* ↝*243 rooms, 31 suites* ⚘*In-room: safe, DVD, ethernet. In-hotel: 3 restaurants, room service, bars, golf course, tennis courts, pools, gym, spa, beachfront, children's programs (ages 5–12), laundry service, airport shuttle, no-smoking rooms* ▤*AE, DC, MC, V.*

$$$$ ⏣**Hāpuna Beach Prince Hotel.** Often more reasonably priced than its
ᐰ neighbors, thanks to a variety of ongoing discount options, the Hāpuna Beach Prince is no less luxurious and happens to be sitting on a corner of the best beach on the island. Initially designed with business travelers in mind, rooms at the Hāpuna Prince are spacious, with large marble bathrooms and plenty of in-room amenities. However, the generous rooms and beachfront location have turned the hotel into more of a family vacation destination than a business hotel, which means that couples seeking a romantic getaway might be disappointed by the number of kids playing Marco Polo at the pool. Still, the place is large enough to escape from other guests if you so desire, and the staff is exceedingly helpful. The golf course, designed by Arnold Palmer and Ed Seay, has topped many a "best courses" list and was recently named one of the most women-friendly courses in the world (what that means, we're still trying to figure out). A hiking trail and a frequent shuttle connect Hāpuna with its sister hotel, the Mauna Kea Beach Hotel, with access to yet another great beach. **Pros:** extra-large rooms, full or partial ocean views from most rooms, direct access to one of island's best beaches. **Cons:** tons of kids around the pool can make it noisy, restaurant standards have been slipping lately. ⊠ *62-100 Kauna'oa Dr., Kohala Coast 96743* ☎*808/880–1111 or 800/882–6060* ⊕*www.princeresortshawaii.com* ↝*314 rooms, 36 suites* ⚘*In-room: refrigerator, ethernet. In-hotel: 5 restaurants, bars, golf course, tennis courts, pool, gym, spa, beachfront, children's programs (ages 5–12), no-smoking rooms* ▤*AE, D, DC, MC, V.*

$$$–$$$$ ⏣**Hilton Waikoloa Village.** Dolphins chirp in the lagoon; a pint-size
ᐰ daredevil zooms down the 175-foot waterslide; a bride poses on the grand staircase; a fire-bearing runner lights the torches along the seaside path at sunset—these are some of the scenes that may greet you at this 62-acre playground of a resort. Shaded pathways lined with a multimillion-dollar Pacific Island art collection connect the three tall buildings; Swiss-made trams and Disney-engineered boats shuttle

WHERE TO STAY ON THE KOHALA COAST & WAIMEA

Property Name	Worth Noting	Cost $	Pools	Beach	Golf Course	Tennis Courts	Gym	Spa	Children's Programs	Rooms	Restaurants	Other	Location
Hotels & Resorts													
❾ Fairmont Orchid Hawai'i	Massages on the beach	479–849	1	yes	yes	10	yes	yes	5–12	540	4	shops	South Kohala
⭐ ❶ Four Seasons Hualālai	King's Pond snorkeling	695–735	5	yes	yes	8	yes	yes	5–12	274	3		North Kona
⑫ Hāpuna Beach Prince	Fantastic beach	350–560	1	yes	yes	13	yes	yes	5–12	350	5		South Kohala
❸ Hilton Waikoloa Village	Dolphin Quest program	259–409	3	yes	yes	8	yes	yes	5–12	1297	10	shops	Waikoloa
⭐ ❷ Kona Village Resort	2 lū'au options	590–1200	2	yes		3	yes	yes	6–17	125	2	no A/C	North Kona
❿ Mauna Lani Bay Hotel	Renowned golf & spa	395–850	1	yes	yes	16	yes	yes	5–12	350	8		South Kohala
❹ Waikoloa Beach Marriott	Great deal for location	289–499	1	yes	yes	6	yes	yes	5–12	545	1		Waikoloa
⑱ Waimea Country Lodge	Includes breakfast	110–130								21		no A/C	Waimea
Condos & Vacation Rentals													
⑮ Aloha Vacation Cottages	Private, close to beach	135–145								2		no A/C	Waimea
⑪ Mauna Lani Point, Islands	Waterfall pool	395–750	1		priv.					61		kitchens	South Kohala
❺ Outrigger Fairway Villas	Infinity pool, gym	239–555	1				yes			80		kitchens	Waikoloa
❻ Outrigger Kolea	Infinity pool, kids pool	450–550	2				yes			70		kitchens	Waikoloa
❼ ResortQuest Shores	Great package deals	295–410	1			2	yes			75		kitchens	Waikoloa
❽ Vista Waikoloa	2 lānai per unit	180–300	1			1	yes			70		kitchens	Waikoloa
⑯ Waimea Gardens Cottage	Mountainside stream	140–160								3		kitchens	Waimea
B&Bs & Inns													
⑲ Aaah, The Views!	Streamside, those views	105–175								4		kitchens	Waimea
⭐ ⑭ Ahu Pohaku Ho'omaluhia	Eco-resort	225–400								9		no A/C, no phone, no TV	North Kohala
⑬ Hale Ho'onanea	Great deal	110–140								3		no A/C	Kawaihae
⑰ Jacaranda Inn	Good breakfast, big rooms	159–225, cottage 450								9		no A/C	Waimea
⑳ Mana Ranch	Mauna Kea views	85–130								3			Waimea

Where to Stay
on the Kohala Coast
& Waimea

NORTH
KOHALA

SOUTH
KOHALA

NORTH
KONA

Pololū Beach

Makapala

Kapaʻau

Hāwī

Māhukona

Mahukona Beach Park

Spencer Beach Park

Hapuna Beach

Kauna'oa Beach

Puakō

Lahuipuna

Anaeho'omalu Bay

Kiholo Bay

Kekaha Kai State Park

Kona International Airport

Alula & Honokōhau

Kailua-Kona

Hōlualoa

Kalaoa

Huʻehuʻe Ranch

Huālalai
(8,271 ft.)

Puʻuanahulu

Waikoloa

Kawaihae

Waimea
(Kamuela)

Waipiʻo

Honokaʻa

KOHALA MOUNTAINS

Kohala Mountain Rd.

Akoni Pull Hwy.

Kawaihae Rd.

Queen Kaʻahumanu Hwy.

Waikoloa Rd.

(Mamalahoa Hwy.)

(Mamalahoa Hwy.)

Hawaiʻi Belt Rd.

Saddle Rd.

240

190

250

270

19

19

11

190

1 2

3 – 8

9 – 11

12

13

14

15 18

19

20

2 miles

3 km

0

0

those weary of the long hallways and meandering paths. In another nod to Disney, employees access the various areas of the resort via underground tunnels. The stars of **Dolphin Quest** (☎800/248–3316 ⊕*www.dolphinquest.org*) are the resort's pride and joy; reserve in advance for an interactive learning session. Though there's no ocean beach, there is a seaside trail to 'Anaeho'omalu Bay, aka A-Bay, one of the island's most pleasant beaches. An artificial sand beach borders the 4-acre resort lagoon. Modern rooms in neutral tones have private lānai and are large enough to accommodate the families that flock here. In addition to the resort's assortment of restau-

WORD OF MOUTH

"We have been to the Four Seaons Hualālai three times. We were there last summer…. the hotel was just a shade less than it had been before. Could this be because of the new ownership? I don't know. Anyway I will say that Hualālai is still the best hotel/resort I have ever visited. The grounds, rooms, restaurants, amenities are just fabulous. I would go back in a heartbeat anytime if possible. I do not think there is another hotel anywhere in Hawaii that is equal to Four Seasons Hualālai."

—judibur

rants, the nearby King's Shops and Queen's Marketplace offer further options plus a small grocery store for picnic provisions. Be sure to leave your room with plenty of time before any appointment, or you'll learn to appreciate the size of this place as you sprint past the tram. ■TIP→ **Brides-to-be, take note: this is one-stop shopping, as the resort has a wedding-planning office, cakes, flowers, photography, and even fireworks and a "Just Married" boat ride.** **Pros:** a kid's idea of paradise, lots of restaurant and activity options. **Cons:** gigantic, crowded, and often noisy; restaurants are pricey. ⊠*425 Waikoloa Beach Dr., Waikoloa 96738* ☎*808/886–1234 or 800/445–8667* ⊕*www.hiltonwaikoloavillage.com* ⇗*1,240 rooms, 57 suites* ⚲*In-room: safe, refrigerator, ethernet. In-hotel: 10 restaurants, room service, bars, golf courses, tennis courts, pools, gym, spa, beachfront, water sports, children's programs (ages 5–12), laundry facilities, laundry service, no-smoking rooms* ⊟*AE, D, DC, MC, V.*

$$$$
Fodor'sChoice
★
Kona Village Resort. The most Hawaiian of the Kohala Coast resorts, Kona Village was one of the first, and it makes a real effort to keep modern life at bay. Without phones, televisions, or radios, the Kona Village is in a time warp—the perfect place for couples or families to get away from it all in their own thatch-roof *hale* (house) near the resort's sandy beach. Built on the grounds of an ancient Hawaiian village, the bungalows reflect styles of South Seas cultures—Tahitian, Samoan, Maori, Fijian, or Hawaiian. The extra-large Royal rooms have private hot tubs. Some of the bungalows are oceanfront, some nestled in a rain-forest-like setting of ponds and gardens, and no matter where your hale is and how crowded the resort is, you'll feel like this is your own little hideaway. The other bonus about Kona Village that sets it apart from many of the other resorts is that it tends to attract repeat customers for decades, and it retains its staff for equally as long, which breeds a very comfortable vibe around the resort. The beach

Kona Village Resort

Ahu Pohaku Ho'omaluhia Hawaii Island Eco Retreat

here is small, but idyllic, with sea turtles nesting in the sand around a calm, turquoise bay. Rates include all meals, an authentic Polynesian Wednesday- or Friday-night lūʻau, grounds tours, tennis, sports activities, and rides in the resort's glass-bottom boat. The resort's ocean program has recently been expanded to include sea kayaking, scuba diving on a new boat that can accommodate up to six divers, and

snorkeling excursions. ■TIP→ Children's programs are not available in May or September, which are designated "adults-only" months, so if you're planning a honeymoon to Hawaiʻi and want to stay at Kona Village, May or September is a good choice. **Pros:** detached bungalows afford ultimate privacy, sea turtles nest on the resort's private beach, all meals and many activities included. **Cons:** somewhat isolated location, no phones in rooms. ⊠*Queen Kaʻahumanu Hwy., Box 1299, Kailua-Kona 96745* ☎*808/325–5555 or 800/367–5290* ⊕*www.konavillage.com* ↩*125 bungalows* ⌂*In-room: no a/c, no phone, no TV. In-hotel: 2 restaurants, bars, tennis courts, pools, gym, spa, beachfront, children's programs (ages 6–17), airport shuttle* ☰*AE, DC, MC, V.*

$$$$ ⊡**Mauna Lani Bay Hotel & Bungalows.** A Kohala Coast classic, popular with honeymooners and anniversary couples for decades, the elegant Mauna Lani is still one of the most beautiful resorts on the island. The open-air lobby has ceilings near the stratosphere, ocean views, and a constant, pleasant breeze. The vast majority of the large, recently renovated rooms have ocean views, and all have a large lānai. The resort is known for its two spectacular golf courses and award-winning spa. Though the resort's Canoe House restaurant has been highly acclaimed for years and makes for a beautiful dining experience (open air, right on the beach, tons of beautiful koa wood and candlelight), none of the Mauna Lani restaurants really qualify as phenomenal— but not to worry, Tommy Bahama's and Ruth's Chris Steakhouse have opened up in The Shops at Mauna Lani, the Fairmont's restaurants are right next door, and several others await within a 10-mi radius of the hotel. **Pros:** beautiful design, award-winning spa, each room has a large private lānai. **Cons:** so-so restaurants, lacks kid-friendly features. ⊠*68-1400 Mauna Lani Dr., Kohala Coast 96743* ☎*808/885–6622 or 800/367–2323* ⊕*www.maunalani.com* ↩*335 rooms, 10 suites, 5 bungalows* ⌂*In-room: safe, refrigerator, DVD, Wi-Fi. In-hotel: 8 restaurants, bars, golf courses, tennis courts, pool, gym, spa, beachfront, children's programs (ages 5–12), public Internet, no-smoking rooms* ☰*AE, D, DC, MC, V.*

$$$ ⊡**Waikoloa Beach Marriott.** The most affordable resort on the Kohala Coast, the Waikoloa Beach Marriott covers 15 acres and encompasses ancient fishponds, historic trails, and petroglyph fields. All of the Marriott's rooms, some of them very recently completed, have low-slung, sleek modern beds framed with dark wood that contrasts nicely with bright white linens and Hawaiian art in a rainbow of tropical colors. The oversize cabana rooms overlook the lagoon. Dining is not the hotel's strong suit, but the Waikoloa Beach Grill, plus the tons of restaurants at the King's Shops, Queen's Marketplace, and the next-door Hilton, offer plenty of choices within walking distance. The hotel's Mandara Spa offers a full range of treatments in a spacious new wellness center. Bordering the white-sand beach of ʻAnaehoʻomalu Bay, the hotel has a range of ocean activities, including wedding-vow renewals on a catamaran. **Pros:** great location at a great price, brand new hotel, well-designed interiors. **Cons:** no stand-out restaurants, nothing particularly Hawaiian about it. ✉69-275 Waikoloa Beach Dr., Waikoloa 96738 ☎808/886–6789 or 800/688–7444 ⊕www.marriott.com ➷523 rooms, 22 suites ⌂In-room: refrigerator, ethernet. In-hotel: restaurant, bars, golf courses, tennis courts, pool, gym, spa, beachfront, children's programs (ages 5–12), laundry facilities, no-smoking rooms ▤AE, D, DC, MC, V.

> ## FOR MEMBERS ONLY
>
> A handful of members-only clubs offer discounts on lodging, activities, and meals on the Big Island. **American Automobile Association** (⊕ www.aaa.com) discounts are available at most hotels. **Hideaways** (⊕ www.hideaways.com) offers stellar deals on condo rentals at Mauna Lani Point, ResortQuest Shores at Waikoloa, and Vista Waikoloa. Their annual fee of $185 entitles members to free travel-planning services, room upgrades, discounts on lodging and meals, and special perks at locations throughout the world.

CONDOS & VACATION RENTALS

Along the Kohala Coast, most of the available condos are associated with the resorts and can be booked through the resort reservations desk. There are, however, a couple of nearby housing developments that have vacation homes for rent. Most owners let a local property management company do the work, but some prefer to handle it themselves, through Web sites like Vacation Rental By Owner ⊕www.vrbo.com. Nothing in this area will be bad in terms of proximity to the beach, restaurants, airport, and good weather, but double-check that the home is located on the coast and not in North Kohala (North Kohala is beautiful, but wetter and more rain-forest-like than the coast). Be sure to ask about things like parking, pools, and cleaning deposits.

$$$$ 🏨 **Mauna Lani Point Villas and The Islands of Mauna Lani Condominiums.** Surrounded by the emerald greens of a world-class ocean-side golf course, spacious two-story suites at Islands of Mauna Lani offer a private, independent home away from home. The privately owned units, individually decorated according to the owners' tastes, have European cabinets and oversize soaking tubs in the main bedrooms. The pool has a little waterfall. The Mauna Lani Point villas are closer to the beach, which means they're priced a little higher, but an ocean view from the lānai of most units may be worth it. A number of celebrities have booked vacations here to escape the media glare—depending on the package you get, some of the villas even come with a personal butler. Whether you choose to stay closer to the golf course at Mauna Lani Point, or to the beach at Mauna Lani Terrace, you're just a few steps away from the Mauna Lani Bay Hotel and Bungalows, where you have access to golf, tennis, spa facilities, and restaurants. **Pros:** privacy, but with access to resort amenities; soaking tubs; extra-large units. **Cons:** can get very pricey, a bit farther from restaurants. ☒ *68-1050 Mauna Lani Point Dr., Kohala Coast 96743* ☎ *808/885–5022 or 800/642–6284* ⊕ *www.classicresorts.com* ✆ *61 units* ♿ *In-room: kitchen (some). In-hotel: pool* ▤ *AE, DC, MC, V.*

$$$–$$$$ ⛉ **Outrigger Fairway Villas at Waikoloa.** Large and comfy town houses just off the fairway of the Hilton Waikoloa golf course are a short walk from 'Anaeho'omalu Bay. The Fairway Villas, designed to mimic plantation-era homes, are decorated with rattan furniture and cozy earth tones. Unlike most of the other condominium complexes, there is a uniformity to the Fairway Villas—units are individually owned, but all are managed by Outrigger, which means they are all decorated and laid out similarly. The villas have their own infinity pool and hot tub and a small gym right next to the pool. Guests do not have access to the fitness or pool facilities at the neighboring Hilton Waikoloa Village, but they are welcome at the spa, restaurants, shops, and grounds. **Pros:** good location for beach and golf, infinity pool, kid friendly. **Cons:** don't have complete use of resort facilities, no 1-bedroom units. ☒ *Waikoloa Beach Resort, 69-200 Pohakulana Pl., Waikoloa 96738* ☎ *808/886–0036* ⊕ *www.outrigger.com* ✆ *80 units* ♿ *In-room: kitchen. In-hotel: pool, gym, laundry facilities* ▤ *AE, D, DC, MC, V.*

$$$$ ⛉ **Outrigger Kolea at Waikoloa.** The latest upscale condo development to join the Waikoloa Beach Resort, Kolea is aiming to capture the very high-end crowd dominated by the condos associated with the Mauna Lani and Four Seasons. These brand-new condos are impeccably furnished and turned out, views from each unit's lānai are spectacular, and the complex is closer to the beach than any of the others in this area. Kolea also offers far more amenities than the average condo complex, with both an infinity pool and a kids' pool at their oceanside Beach Club, a fitness center, and a lava-rock hot tub. **Pros:** high design, close to beach, resort amenities. **Cons:** overpriced, not very kid-friendly. ☒ *Waikoloa Beach Resort, 69-289 Waikoloa Beach Dr., Waikoloa 96738* ☎ *808/886–0036* ⊕ *www.outrigger.com* ✆ *70 units* ♿ *In-room: kitchen. In-hotel: pools, hot tub, gym* ▤ *AE, D, DC, MC, V.*

$$–$$$$ ⛉ **ResortQuest Shores at Waikoloa.** Villas with red-tile roofs are set amid landscaped lagoons and waterfalls at the edge of the championship Waikoloa Village Golf Course. The spacious villas and condo units—the ground floor and upper floor are available separately—are privately owned, so furnishings vary from unit to unit. Sliding glass doors open onto large lānai. Picture windows look out onto rolling green fairways. All units have complete kitchens with washer-dryers, and come with maid service. Check the Web site for deals; separate rates are quoted for online booking, and they often advertise specials exclusively on their Web site. ResortQuest also offers a variety of air-inclusive packages, which can be a great deal. **Pros:** good prices, great location, fully self-sufficient condos with maid service. **Cons:** no access to resort amenities, fee for Internet access. ✉ *69-1035 Keana Pl., Waikoloa 96738* ☎ *808/886–5001 or 800/922–7866* ⊕ *www.resort-questhawaii.com* ⇴ *75 units* ♿ *In-room: kitchen, ethernet. In-hotel: tennis courts, pool, gym, laundry facilities* ▭ *AE, D, DC, MC, V.*

$$ 🏨 **Vista Waikoloa.** Older and more reasonably priced than most of the condo complexes along the Kohala Coast, the two-bedroom, two-bath Vista condos offer ocean views and a great value for this part of the island. All are large and well appointed, with two lānai per unit, plus they are walking distance to A-Bay, the King's Shops at Waikoloa, and the restaurants and amenities of the Hilton Waikoloa, and within short driving distance of the airport, other resorts, and a variety of Big Island sights. **Pros:** centrally located, reasonably priced, very large units. **Cons:** hit or miss on decor because each unit is individually owned, some owners charge (refundable) security deposits. ✉ *Waikoloa Beach Resort, 69-1010 Keana Pl., Waikoloa 96738* ☎ *808/886-3594* ⊕ *www.waikoloarentals.com* ⇴ *70 units* ♿ *In-room: kitchen. In-hotel: tennis court, pool, gym, laundry facilities* ▭ *AE, MC, V.*

> ## CONDO COMFORTS
>
> There are fewer stores and take-out options on the Kohala Coast than elsewhere on the island, but, as the condos are all associated with resorts, most of your needs will be met. If you require anything not provided by the management, the **King's Shops at Waikoloa Village** (✉ *250 Waikoloa Beach Dr., Waikoloa* ☎ *808/886–8811*) is the place to go. There are a small grocery store, a liquor store, and a couple of decent takeout options. It's not exactly cheap, but you're paying for the convenience of not having to drive into town.

B&BS & INNS

$$$–$$$$ 🏨 **Ahu Pohaku Ho'omaluhia Hawaii Island Eco Retreat.** Ahu Pohaku is set

above the cliffs of North Kohala near Pololu valley. As the name implies, it has plenty of "green" credentials: the retreat generates its own solar power, uses a water catchment tank, and grows almost all of its own food. Beautiful hardwood floors are built from sustainably harvested woods, and rooms take advantage of natural light and ventilation to keep energy usage low. Surrounded by 60 acres, 20 of which are a dedicated conservation area, the retreat feels both luxurious and completely hidden from the world. Rooms are large and bright, with ocean views and brightly colored walls. Most have private balconies, and all are equipped with large bathrooms that include both soaking tubs and showers. The retreat will add a full-service spa in late 2008, but in the meantime offers guests massage appointments, yoga and hula classes, and an assortment of nature adventures in the Kohala area. A van shuttles guests to and from the airport, into nearby Kapa'au or Hāwī, or out to the beaches. Three meals a day are prepared from the retreat's garden supply, augmented by additions from local farms. Ahu Pohaku's owners even make their own creamy and delicious goat cheese. **Pros:** stunning location, new and beautiful construction with no expense spared, eco-friendly. **Cons:** not within walking distance of restaurants, no pool, off the beaten path. ✉ *Follow signs off Hwy. 270 in Kapa'au, North Kohala*

9

96719 ☎*808/889–6336* ⊕*www.hawaii-island-retreat.com* ➦*9 rooms* ⌂*In-room: no a/c, no phone, no TV. In-hotel: restaurant, no elevator, no-smoking rooms* ⊟*AE, MC, V.*

$ ⊞**Hale Ho'onanea.** A comfortable home with three detached guest suites, this 3-acre property in the Kohala Estates lives up to the English translation of its name, "House of Relaxation." From its bluff above the ocean you can watch the sun rise over Mauna Kea and set over the Pacific, and view the sparkling beauty of Hawai'i's night sky. It's minutes away from dining and shopping at Waimea and the attractions of the Kohala Coast as well. The rooms are comfortable and spacious, if not terribly beautiful; the views and grounds make up for what the rooms lack, as does the price in this neck of the woods (less than half the nightly rate of the Kohala Coast resorts). Continental breakfast is included. There's a two-night minimum if you book less than a week in advance; a $25 fee applies to single-night bookings made within seven days of arrival. **Pros:** detached suites for maximum privacy, panoramic ocean views from private lānai, good price for the neighborhood. **Cons:** not within walking distance to restaurants, no pool. ⊠*Kohala Estates, 59-513 Ala Kahua Dr., Kawaihae 96743* ☎*808/882–1653 or 877/882–1653* ⊕*www.houseofrelaxation.com* ➦*3 suites* ⌂*In-room: no a/c, kitchen* ⊟*MC, V.*

WAIMEA

Though it seems a world away, Waimea is only about a 15- to 20-minute drive from the Kohala Coast resorts, which means it takes roughly the same amount of time to get to the Island's best beaches from Waimea as it does from Kailua-Kona. Yet, few visitors think to book lodging in this pleasant upcountry village, where cool mornings and evenings are enjoyable after a day spent bathing in the sun. To the delight of residents and visitors, a few retired resort chefs have opened up their own little projects in Waimea. Sightseeing is easy from here, too: Mauna Kea is a short drive away, and Hilo and Kailua-Kona can be reached in about an hour. Because Waimea doesn't attract as many visitors as the coasts, you won't find as many condos and hotels, but the B&Bs in the area are superb. They also offer some of the island's best lodging deals, especially when you consider that their vantage point up in the hills affords some pretty spectacular views.

HOTELS & RESORTS

$ ⊞**Waimea Country Lodge.** In the heart of cowboy country, this modest ranch house–style lodge offers views of the green, rolling slopes of Mauna Kea. It's so quiet you forget you're close to busy Waimea. The rooms are large and clean, with Hawaiian quilts lending an authentic touch. A Continental breakfast is included in the rate, and you can charge meals at Merriman's and Paniolo Country Inn to your room. A handful of studios with kitchenettes are also available, and there are plenty of grocery stores in Waimea to stock up on provisions for the week. **Pros:** affordable, large rooms equipped with kitchenettes; charge meals to your room at one of the island's best restaurants (Merriman's). **Cons:** rooms could use some updating, no pool. ⊠*65-1210*

Lindsey Rd., Waimea ⌂Box 2559, Kamuela 96743 ☎808/885–4100 or 800/367–5004 ⊕www.castleresorts.com ⇩21 rooms ⚘In-room: no a/c, kitchen (some), ethernet. In-hotel: no-smoking rooms ▤AE, D, DC, MC, V.

CONDOS & VACATION RENTALS

$ ⌂**Aloha Vacation Cottages.** Set on several acres of North Kohala property, these two rental cottages don't look like much from the outside, but inside they are clean, comfortable, and well stocked with beach toys, towels and mats, books, cable TV, videos, you name it. The price is right, and they are just a 10-minute drive from the Kohala Coast. To fully relax during your stay, book a massage when you reserve a cottage. **Pros:** each cottage equipped with gas grill, free Wi-Fi, 10-minute drive from great beaches. **Cons:** somewhat remote location, can't walk to restaurants or stores, no pool. ⌂Box 1395, Waimea 96743 ☎877/875–1722 or 808/885–6535 ⊕www.alohacottages.net ⇩2 units ⚘In-room: no a/c, kitchen, DVD, VCR, Wi-Fi ▤MC, V.

$ ⌂**Waimea Gardens Cottage.** Charming country cottages surrounded by flowering private gardens contain surprisingly luxe suites that look like they just leapt out of a glossy magazine. One (Kohala) includes a full kitchen and the others (Waimea and the Garden Studio) a kitchenette, and all are stocked with provisions for a self-serve Continental breakfast. Both have their own private gardens, beautiful hardwood floors, and bathrooms equipped with rain-head showers and large soaking tubs. The grounds are full of birds and plant life that will make you want to move in for good. **Pros:** no detail left out, beautiful self-contained cottages, gardens, complete privacy. **Cons:** pricey for the area, requires payment in full six weeks prior to arrival. ⌂Box 520, Kamuela 96743 ☎808/885–8550 ⊕www.waimeagardens.com ⇩2 cottages, 1 studio ⚘In-room: kitchen, VCR ▤No credit cards.

B&BS

$ ⌂**Aaah, The Views!** This tranquil and pretty stream-side mountain home in upcountry Waimea is lovingly tended by owners Erika and Derek Stuart. Rooms are clean and bright, with lots of windows to enjoy the views. The Dream Room is actually an apartment, with a full kitchen, private deck, and hot tub. The house has a sauna and a yoga room (private lessons available), and an in-house massage therapist as well. This is a popular spot with couples, but is not well-suited to families with young children. **Pros:** away from it all, beautiful countryside views, on-site yoga and massage. **Cons:** not kid friendly, no pool, must drive to area restaurants and attractions. ✉66-1773 Alaneo St., off Akulani, just past mile marker 60 on Hwy. 19, Waimea 96743 ☎808/885–3455 ⊕www.aaahtheviews.com ⇩4 rooms ⚘In-room: kitchen (some), refrigerator, Wi-Fi. In-hotel: no-smoking rooms ▤No credit cards.

$$ ⌂**Jacaranda Inn.** Charming inside and out, the lavender Jacaranda Inn can be spotted from miles away. Built in 1897, the sprawling estate was once the home of the manager of Parker Ranch; it's been redecorated in hues of raspberry and lavender, with lots of koa wood accents. Most of the rooms have hot tubs. The units are booked under two separate

plans. Plan A includes daily maid service, full breakfasts, and a bottle of wine; Plan B is simpler, with Continental breakfast and less service. A separate nearby cottage that sleeps six has been recently renovated with new hardwood floors, a stone fireplace, and large outdoor hot tub. This place is a great deal, and the rooms are very comfortable. **Pros:** country charm, hot tubs in most rooms, walking distance to Waimea restaurants. **Cons:** no pool, lots of purple, pricey for the area. ⊠*65-1444 Kawaihae Rd., Waimea 96743* ☎*808/885–8813* ⊕*www.jaca-randainn.com* ➵*8 suites, 1 cottage* ⅏*In-room: no a/c, no phone, no TV. In-hotel: no-smoking rooms* ⊟*MC, V.*

$ **ɯ Mana Ranch.** A quiet and removed mountainside ranch in the shadows of Mauna Kea, Mana Ranch is an idyllic retreat. There are two rooms available in the main house and a separate "paniolo cottage" with a kitchenette, which sleeps four. Rooms are clean and comfortable, if not overly stylish, with a pleasant blend of Hawaiian accents. The spa room is a nice touch, especially with its views of Mauna Kea, and its private shower and bath come in handy if your neighbors across the hall in the main house are bathroom hogs—the two bedrooms share a bathroom. **Pros:** free Wi-Fi and in-room DVD players, enclosed outdoor hot tub with Mauna Kea views, great prices. **Cons:** shared bathrooms, somewhat tired decor. ⊠*64-5163 Mana Rd., Waimea 96743* ☎*866/399–5842* ⊕*www.manaranch.com* ➵*3 rooms* ⅏*In-room: DVD, Wi-Fi* ⊟*MC, V.*

KAILUA-KONA

Kailua-Kona, a bustling little village full of restaurants, shops, and entertainment options, has a zillion lodging options. In addition to half a dozen hotels, oceanfront Ali'i Drive is crammed with condo complexes and homes on both sides of the street, and there are several grocery stores for those who choose to go the condo or vacation home route. Kailua-Kona has three beaches, White Sands, Kahalu'u, and King Kamehameha, and each has its selling point: Kahalu'u is renowned for its snorkeling, White Sands is a local favorite that's great for bodysurfing (but the beach is small), and King Kamehameha is a small beach next to a calm marina, which makes it nice for kids. The downside to staying here is that you'll have to drive 30–45 minutes up the road to the Kohala Coast to get Hawai'i's signature long white-sand beaches. However, you'll also pay about half what you would at any of the beachfront resorts, and Kailua-Kona has a bit more local charm.

HOTELS & RESORTS

¢ **ɯ Kona Tiki Hotel.** The best thing about this three-story walk-up budget hotel, about a mile south of Kailua-Kona, is that all the units have lānai right next to the ocean. The rooms are modest but pleasantly decorated. You can sunbathe by the seaside pool, where a complimentary Continental breakfast is served. Some would call this place old-fashioned; others would say it's local, has a certain kitschy charm, and is the best deal in town, with glorious sunsets no different from those at the resorts. **Pros:** very low price, ocean-front lānai and pool, convenient location. **Cons:** older hotel in need of update, no beach, doesn't accept credit cards. ✉75-5968 Ali'i Dr., Kailua-Kona 96745 ☎808/329–1425 ⊕www.konatiki.com ⇔15 rooms ⚹In-room: no a/c, no phone, refrigerator, no TV. In-hotel: pool, no elevator ▭No credit cards.

$ ▦**Outrigger Keauhou Beach Resort.** Although it has won awards for preserving its unique history (the grounds include a *heiau*, a sacred fishpond, and a replica of the summer home of King David Kalākaua), the Outrigger Keauhou Beach Resort is not doing such a hot job at preserving the guest accommodations. That said, if you can find a good rate, this is still a good place to stay, mainly for its proximity to Kahalu'u, one of the best snorkeling beaches on the island, and its extra-large rooms. With its lower prices and larger rooms, the hotel tends to be particularly popular with families. **Pros:** large rooms, unique history, next to one of the island's best snorkeling beaches. **Cons:** restaurant has gone downhill, hotel needs a face-lift. ✉78-6740 Ali'i Dr., Kailua-Kona 96740 ☎808/322–3441 or 800/462–6262 ⊕www.outrigger. com ⇔311 rooms, 6 suites ⚹In-room: refrigerator, safe, ethernet. In-hotel: restaurant, bar, tennis courts, pool, gym, beachfront, laundry facilities, laundry service, no-smoking rooms ▭AE, D, DC, MC, V.

$$ ▦**Royal Kona Resort.** This is a great option if you're on a budget. The Royal Kona has seen better days, but the owners are finally doing a bit of renovation, and the hotel has greatly improved, as has the quality of food and service at its restaurant. The location is great, the lobby, pool, and restaurant are right on the water, and most of the hotel's large, lānai-front rooms have been recently updated from Hawaiian kitsch to a more toned-down modern take that includes neutral-tone walls, classic Hawaiian art, and bamboo headboards. The hotel is within walking distance of Kailua-Kona and across the street from numerous shops and restaurants. The weekly lū'au with Polynesian entertainment is fun and quite popular. Make sure to book online, where the rates can be as much as 50% less than the rack rates, and select rooms in the Ali'i or Lagoon tower if you'd like a recently renovated room. **Pros:** convenient location, waterfront pool, low prices. **Cons:** older hotel in need of renovation, oceanfront lagoon is often closed, staff are sometimes grumpy. ✉75-5852 Ali'i Dr., Kailua-Kona 96740 ☎808/329–3111 or 800/222–5642 ⊕www.royalkona.com ⇔452 rooms, 8 suites ⚹In-room: safe, refrigerator, dial-up. In-hotel: restaurant, bar, tennis courts, pool, gym, spa, beachfront, laundry facilities, public Internet, no-smoking rooms ▭AE, D, DC, MC, V.

$$$ ▦**Sheraton Keauhou Bay Resort & Spa.** For the big-resort style of the Kohala Coast at a less astronomical price, the Sheraton is a good bet. Longtime Big Island visitors might remember it as the old Kona Surf. Left empty for several years, the hotel still shows some of its wear and tear (in order to keep it as close to the ocean as possible, the Sheraton had to work with what they had—no demolition allowed), but the new owners have gone to great lengths to restore it to its former glory. The lobby, with floor to ceiling windows and carved marble architectural elements, is particularly stunning, and the well-designed restaurant Kai serves a limited but excellent menu. The only remnants of the old hotel in the bright and modern Sheraton rooms are the small and unim-

9

WHERE TO STAY ON THE KONA COAST

Property Name	Worth Noting	Cost $	Pools	Beach	Golf Course	Tennis Courts	Gym	Spa	Children's Programs	Rooms	Restaurants	Other	Location
Hotels & Resorts													
18 Kona Tiki Hotel	Oceanfront lānai	69–92	1							15		no A/C	Kailua-Kona
7 Manago Hotel		31–70								106	1	no A/C	Captain Cook
12 Outrigger Keauhou	Close to Kahulu'u Beach	119–250	1	yes		6	yes			317	1		Kailua-Kona
19 Royal Kona Resort	Good rates for oceanfront	145–285	1	yes		4	yes	yes		460	1		Kailua-Kona
9 Sheraton Keauhou Bay	Cool pool with slide	199–460	1	yes		2	yes	yes		521	1		Kailua-Kona
Condos & Vacation Rentals													
15 Casa de Emdeko	Oceanfront saltwater pool	95–135	2							85		kitchens	Kailua-Kona
3 Colony One at Sea Mountain	Close to Black Sand Beach	50–95	1		yes	1				74		kitchens	Ka'u
11 Keauhou Kona Club	Tennis courts, big pool	180–325	1			3				188		kitchens	Kailua-Kona
13 Kona Magic Sands	Ocean view from all units	105–155	1							37	1	kitchens	Kailua-Kona
16 Kona Nalu	Huge lānai, ocean views	225–250	1	yes						15		kitchens	Kailua-Kona
17 Kona Pacific	Ocean view from pool, BBQ	73–135	1							80		kitchens	Kailua-Kona
10 Outrigger Kanaloa at Kona	Oceanfront restaurant	229–365	3			2				166		kitchens	Kailua-Kona
14 ResortQuest Kona by Sea	Oceanfront pool	125–200	1					yes		78		kitchens	Kailua-Kona
21 Silver Oaks Guest Ranch	Working ranch	175	1							2		no A/C	Kailua-Kona
1 South Point Banyan	Deck with hot tub	185								1		no A/C	Ka'u
B&Bs & Inns													
5 Aloha Guesthouse	Eco-conscious	164–280								5			South Kona
6 Dragonfly Ranch	Exotic island treehouse	100–250					yes	yes		6			South Kona
20 Hale Hualalai	Outstanding breakfast	160								6		no A/C	Hōlualoa
8 Hōlualoa Inn	Beautiful interior	260–380	1							6		no A/C	Hōlualoa
2 Kalaekilohana	Hot breakfast, cozy linens	139–159								4		no A/C	Ka'u
4 Nancy's Hideaway	Lots of privacy	115–135								6		no A/C	Kailua-Kona

Where to Stay
on the Kona Coast

Kona International Airport

Kalaoa

NORTH KONA

Kailua-Kona

Alula & Honokōhau

KONA COAST

Hōlualoa

Honalo

Kainaliu

Kealakekua

Captain Cook

Nāpō'opo'o

Kealakekua Bay

Ke'ei

Hōnaunau

Kā'ōkea

Kealia

Pu'uhonuao Hōnaunau National Historic Park

Ho'okena

SOUTH KONA

Hawai'i Belt Rd.

Hu'upuloa

Okoe Bay

Miloli'i

Kaunā Point

Pōhue Bay

Kahuku Ranch

KA'Ū

Mamalahoa Hwy.

South Point (Ka Lae)

KAILUA-KONA

Kailua Bay

White Sands Beach

Kahalu'u Beach

Ali'i Drive

Kuakini Hwy.

Queen Ka'ahumanu Hwy.

Kamehameha III Rd.

Ali'i Drive

KEAUHOU

0 — 2 miles
0 — 3 km

pressive bathrooms. On the upside, many of the rooms have great views of the bay, and all have the Sheraton's signature Sweet Sleeper beds, which ensure a good night's sleep for all but the most insomnia-ridden guests. The big selling point for those traveling with kids is the pool, which can only be described as massive, and is one of the coolest on the island, with a slide, waterfalls, and an ocean view. The resort also has a full-service, oceanfront spa (Ho'ola), a highly acclaimed new lū'au, an oceanfront wedding area, and the Manta Ray Experience, which allows guests to view

manta rays nearly every night (provided the rays cooperate). **Pros:** fantastic pool, manta rays on view nightly, resort style at lower price. **Cons:** no beach, only one restaurant. ⊠*78-128 Ehukai St., Kailua-Kona 96740* ☎*808/930–4900* ⊕*www.sheratonkeauhou.com* ⇱*511 rooms, 10 suites* ⚫*In-room: safe, refrigerator, dial-up, Wi-Fi. In-hotel: restaurant, bar, tennis courts, pool, gym, spa, water sports, no-smoking rooms* ▤*AE, D, DC, MC, V.*

CONDOS & VACATION RENTALS

¢–$ ☖**Casa de Emdeko.** A large and pretty complex on the *makai* (oceanfront) side of Ali'i Drive, Casa de Emdeko offers a few more amenities than most condo complexes, including an on-site convenience store that makes great sandwiches, a sandy oceanfront area for sunbathing, and both fresh and saltwater pools. As with any complex, decor and maintenance of units varies depending on the owner, so be sure to view photos of the specific unit you're renting. All units have lānai, with either garden or ocean views (ocean view is a bit more expensive). **Pros:** oceanfront fresh- and saltwater pools, on-site convenience store. **Cons:** quality can be hit or miss depending on owner, some units are located close to high-traffic road. ⊠*75-6082 Ali'i Dr., Kailua-Kona 96740* ☎*808/329–2160* ⊕*casadeemdeko.org* ⇱*85 units* ⚫*In-room: kitchen. In-hotel: pools* ▤*AE, MC, V.*

$$$ ☖**Keauhou Kona Surf & Racquet Club.** This large gated complex sits right along the ocean, offering prime views from oceanfront units and the pool. Condos are large, comfortable, and very well maintained. Unlike many other complexes, Keauhou Kona has tennis courts and a very large pool. The two-story town houses are ideal for larger groups, although these are a bit more dated than the rest of the complex. **Pros:** oceanfront complex with many ocean-view units, close to harbor and golf course, tennis courts and large pool in complex. **Cons:** removed location requires drive to local restaurants, no a/c in some units. ⊠*78-6800 Ali'i Dr., Kailua-Kona 96740* ☎*800/799–5662 or 808/322–6696* ⊕*www.kksrc.com* ⇱*188 units* ⚫*In-room: no a/c (some), kitchen. In-hotel: tennis courts, pool, laundry facilities* ▤*MC, V.*

A TEMPORARY HOME IN HAWAI'I

Renting a condo or vacation house gives you much more room than the average hotel, the chance to meet more people (neighbors are usually friendly, kids always hang together at the pool), lower nightly rates, and the option of cooking or barbecuing some nights rather than eating out. When booking, remember that most are individually owned and most owners outsource the rental process to property management companies. A handful of property management and rental agencies handle the bulk of condo and vacation home rentals on the Big Island, and their Web sites are the best places to look for rentals. Following is a list of our favorites for various lodging types throughout the island. Be sure to call and ask questions before booking, even if the pictures online are *real purdy*.

Abbey Vacation Rentals (⊕www.waikoloarentals.com) has luxury condos on the Kohala Coast.

Big Island Villas (⊕www.bigislandvillas.com) lists a variety of condos attached to the Four Seasons Hualālai, Mauna Kea, and Mauna Lani resorts.

CJ Kimberly Realty (⊕www.cjkimberly.com) offers fantastic deals on some oceanfront homes and condos.

Hawaiian Beach Rentals (⊕www.hawaiianbeachrentals.com) and **Tropical Villa Vacations** (⊕www.tropicalvillavacations.com) are excellent for high-end, ocean- or beachfront homes.

Hawai'i Vacation Rentals (⊕www.vacationbigisland.com) lists several properties on the beach in Puako, a sleepy beach settlement just up the road from the Kohala coast resorts.

Keauhou Property Management (⊕www.konacondo.net) has condos along the Kona coast, just south of Kailua-Kona around Keauhou Bay.

Kolea Vacations (⊕www.koleavacations.com) lists dozens of condos at the Kolea at Waikoloa complex as well as a stunning oceanfront home on Ali'i in Kailua-Kona.

Kona Coast Vacations (⊕www.konacoastvacations.com) offers a large variety of condos on the west side of the island and wins high marks for good service.

Kona Hawai'i Vacation Rentals (⊕www.konahawaii.com) offers very affordable condos in Kailua-Kona.

Knutson and Associates (⊕www.konahawaiirentals.com) handles rentals for a wide variety of Kailua-Kona condos and oceanfront vacation homes.

Property Network (☎808/329–7977 ⊕www.hawaii-kona.com) lists and manages dozens of condo rentals in and around Kailua-Kona.

Rent Hawai'i Home (⊕www.renthawaiihome.com) offers several affordable cottage and beach house rentals, ideal for those who are staying for a while and want some room/privacy, but don't want to spend half a year's salary on a beachfront palace.

South Kohala Management (⊕www.southkohala.com) lists a wide variety of luxury Kohala Coast condos.

Vacation Rental By Owner (⊕www.vrbo.com) has homes and condos for rent all over the island.

9

$ **Kona Magic Sands.** Cradled between two small beaches, this condo complex is great for swimmers and sunbathers in summer (the sand at Magic Sands Beach washes away in winter). Units vary because they're individually owned, but all the studios are oceanfront, spacious, and light. Some units have enclosed lānai, and all have an ocean view. **Pros:** next door to popular beach, ocean view from all units. **Cons:** studios only, some units are very dated. ⊠77-6452 Ali'i Dr., Kailua-Kona 96740 ☎808/329–9393 or 800/622–5348 ⊕www.konahawaii.com/ms.htm ⇨37 units △In-room: no a/c (some), kitchen. In-hotel: pool, no elevator ☐MC, V.

$$ **Kona Nalu.** One of the nicest complexes on the ocean side of Ali'i, Kona Nalu units are large and beautifully furnished with super-sized lānai, and ocean views from all units. The pool is tiny, but they have a small sandy beach for lying in the sun, and the complex itself is small so you won't be fighting for pool room. **Pros:** extra-large units, ocean views. **Cons:** not within walking distance of stores or restaurants, sandy beach doesn't provide safe ocean entry. ⊠76-6212 Ali'i Dr., Kailua-Kona 96740 ☎808/329–6438 ⊕www.sunquest-hawaii.com ⇨15 units △In-room: kitchen. In-hotel: pool, beachfront, laundry facilities ☐MC, V.

¢–$ **Kona Pacific.** Once a hotel, the Kona Pacific gives you plenty of space. The one-bedroom units, which comfortably sleep four, are the size of two large hotel rooms, with a full kitchen and usually two bathrooms. There are ocean views from the lānai of most units and the pool. This large and well-maintained complex is just at the edge of Kailua-Kona, within walking distance of shops and restaurants. If you don't feel like cooking or barbecuing by the pool, a great Mexican food restaurant is waiting across the street with margaritas and fajitas, and a Hawaiian grill serving fresh seafood and awesome ahi sandwiches is across the street behind the complex. Note that the acceptance of credit cards varies with the unit owners. **Pros:** very large units, some with two lānai, ocean-view pool, well-maintained complex. **Cons:** some units in better shape than others, some units get noise from nearby highway. ⊠75-5865 Walua Rd., Kailua-Kona 96740 ☎808/329–6140 ⊕www.konacoastvacations.com ⇨80 units △In-room: no a/c (some), kitchen. In-hotel: pool.

$$–$$$ **Outrigger Kanaloa at Kona.** The 16-acre grounds provide a peaceful and verdant background for this low-rise condominium complex bordering the Keauhou-Kona Country Club. It's walking distance to the golf course but within a five-minute drive of the nearest beaches (Kahalu'u and White Sands). Large one-, two-, and three-bedroom apartments have koa-wood cabinetwork and washer-dryers; oceanfront villas have private hot tubs. A restaurant, The Bar and Grill at Kanaloa, serves up New American cuisine on a lovely covered outdoor patio. **Pros:** oceanfront restaurant in complex, across the street from acclaimed golf course, three pools with hot tubs. **Cons:** not within walking distance of grocery store or beach, some owners don't manage their rentals well. ⊠78-261 Manukai St., Kailua-Kona 96740 ☎808/322–9625, 808/322–2272, or 800/688–7444 ⊕www.outrigger.com ⇨166 units △In-room: no a/c (some), safe, kitchen. In-hotel: bar, tennis courts, pools, laundry facilities ☐AE, D, DC, MC, V.

$$$ ⌂**ResortQuest Kona by the Sea.** Complete modern kitchens, tile lānai, and washer-dryer units can be found in every suite of this comfortable oceanfront condo complex. Despite being near the bustling town of Kailua-Kona, this four-story place is quiet and relaxing. The nearest sandy beach is 2 mi away, but the pool is next to the ocean and many of the rooms have ocean views. Guests are lulled to sleep by the ocean nightly. Be sure to check the Web site for specials: they usually offer a fourth or fifth night free and often advertise deals only on their own Web site. **Pros:** ocean front, quiet and peaceful. **Cons:** no beach, not many kid-friendly features. ✉*75-6106 Ali'i Dr., Kailua-Kona 96740* ☎*808/327–2300 or 800/922–7866* ⊕*www.resortquesthawaii.com* ⌂*37 1-bedroom units, 41 2-bedroom units* ⌂*In-room: kitchen. In-hotel: pool, spa, laundry facilities, no-smoking rooms* ⊟*AE, D, DC, MC, V.*

CONDO COMFORTS

Crossroads Shopping Center. The Safeway here is the cleanest, largest, and best-stocked store on the island. It's right next to **Kona Natural Foods,** so you can supplement with local organic produce, and **Coldstone Creamery.** ✉*75-1000 Henry St., Kailua-Kona.*

Blockbuster. ✉*Kona Coast Shopping Center, 74-5588 Palani Rd., Kailua-Kona* ☎*808/326–7694.*

Pizza-wise, **Kona Brewing Company** is best if you're willing to go pick it up. For delivery, try **Domino's** (☎*808/329–9500).*

$–$$ ⌂**Silver Oaks Guest Ranch.** These two private cottages set on a 10-acre working ranch are one of the best deals going on the west side of the island. Five miles from the airport and from Kailua-Kona, the cottages afford total privacy, with a few more amenities than a vacation house or condo. Owners Mark and Amy drop off a welcome basket with breakfast goodies your first day, there's a washer and dryer in each unit, an outdoor pool and hot tub, great ocean views from your private deck, and the ranch is like a little petting zoo with horses, goats, and chickens throughout. Each cottage is stocked with a library of books and videos, various beach toys, backpacks, coolers, beach towels, binoculars, robes, hair dryers, and even snorkeling equipment. **Pros:** very private, deck with ocean views. **Cons:** five-night minimum stay, not within walking distance of stores or restaurants, dated decor. ✉*73-4570 Māmalahoa Hwy., just north of Kaloko Dr., Kailua-Kona 96740* ☎*877/325–2300 or 808/325–2000* ⊕*www.silveroaksranch.com* ⌂*2 cottages* ⌂*In-room: no a/c, kitchen, VCR, Wi-Fi. In-hotel: pool, laundry facilities* ⊟*MC, V.*

B&BS & INNS

$ ⌂**Hale Hualalai.** Perfect for couples, Hale Hualalai has two suites with exposed beams, hardwood floors, hot tubs, and private lānai. Perhaps the most memorable aspect of Hale Hualalai is the food—owner Lonn Armour was a professional chef for 20 years, and cooks up a breakfast that puts other B&B offerings to shame. The inn is near the artsy village of Hōlualoa. **Pros:** gourmet breakfast with Kona coffee, new and tastefully decorated house, whirlpool tubs. **Cons:** not kid friendly, removed from local beaches and restaurants. ✉ *74-4968 Māmalahoa Hwy., Hōlualoa 96725* ☎*808/326–2909* ⊕*www.hale-hualalai.com* ➪*2 suites* ⌂*In-room: no a/c, no phone, refrigerator, Wi-Fi* ⊟*No credit cards.*

$$$ ⛫**Hōlualoa Inn.** Six spacious rooms are available in this beautiful cedar home on a 40-acre coffee country estate, 4 mi above Kailua Bay and steps away from the artists' town of Hōlualoa. The Balinese suite, one of the nicest here, has wraparound windows with stunning views. A lavish breakfast includes estate-grown coffee as well as homemade breads and macadamia-nut butter. Rooftop gazebos inspire quiet, relaxing moments, and for stargazers there's a telescope. **Pros:** within walking distance to small village, well appointed with wood floors and lots of windows, panoramic views, infinity pool. **Cons:** a bit far away from beaches and restaurants, expensive for location. ✉ *76-5932 Māmalahoa Hwy.* ⌖ *Box 222, Hōlualoa 96725* ☎*808/324–1121 or 800/392–1812* ⊕*www.holualoainn.com* ➪*6 rooms* ⌂*In-room: no a/c, no TV. In-hotel: pool, no kids under 13, no-smoking rooms* ⊟*AE, D, DC, MC, V.*

$ ⛫**Nancy's Hideaway.** A few miles up the hill from Kailua-Kona, this charming cottage and studio offer modern comforts and ocean views. Each has its own entrance, a lānai, and a wet bar. The cottage stands alone; the studio is attached to the main house, but is very private. Breakfast is served in the rooms to give guests their privacy. This place is ideal for couples, but not for families with kids. **Pros:** plenty of privacy, ocean views. **Cons:** slightly inconvenient location, kids not allowed. ✉ *73-1530 Uanani Pl., Kailua-Kona 96740* ☎*808/325–3132 or 866/325–3132* ⊕*www.nancyshideaway.com* ➪*6 rooms* ⌂*In-room: no a/c, VCR. In-hotel: no kids under 13, no-smoking rooms* ⊟*MC, V.*

SOUTH KONA & KA'U

There are no resorts in this area, but there are plenty of fantastic B&Bs and inns around Kealakekua Bay and some great deals to be had on vacation condos and homes in the hills above the bay. The main attraction here *is* the bay, where kayaking and snorkeling are superb. The towns of Captain Cook and Kainaliu provide some excellent dining and shopping options, and there are dozens of coffee farms open for tours as well. You can get to the volcano in about an hour. It's a nice place to stay if you want to be out of the fray, but the drawback is that there are no beaches in this area. The "beach" by Kealakekua Bay is all rocks, although the bay is great for a swim; Kailua-Kona area beaches are a 15- to 30-minute drive, and the sandy Kohala Coast is an hour or more away.

HOTELS

¢   ⛫**Manago Hotel.** This historic hotel is a good option if you want to escape the touristy thing but still be close to everything on the island. Don't let the front TV room creep you out—you have not checked into an old folks' home. The place has an authentic Hawai'i vibe, and the restaurant is one of the best on the island. Dwight Manago—whose grandparents, Kinzo and Osame Manago, built the main building in 1917—has maintained one Japanese-style room with tatami mats and a *furo,* a traditional Japanese bath, and this is the room to book. The other rooms are nothing special, but they're clean, and those in the newer wing have great views high above the Kona Coast. **Pros:** local color, rock-bottom prices, terrific on-site restaurant. **Cons:** a bit run-down, not the best sound insulation between rooms. ✉*81-6155 Māmalahoa Hwy.* ✆ *Box 145, Captain Cook 96704* ☎*808/323–2642* ⊕*www.managohotel.com* ⇨*64 rooms, 42 with bath* ⛶*In-room: no a/c, no TV. In-hotel: restaurant, no elevator* ▤*D, MC, V.*

CONDOS & VACATION RENTALS

¢ 🏨 **Colony One at Sea Mountain.** Near the Punalu'u black sand beach, these condos have been recently renovated, and the grounds have been much improved. Though not beachfront, they are close to the beach, near enough to hear the ocean, and just a short trip (30 minutes or less) from the Volcano. **Pros:** golf course and black-sand beach next door, prime sea turtle viewing, close to volcano. **Cons:** remote location, no restaurant, beach is not great for swimming. ✉*95-789 Ninole Loop Rd., South Kona 96742* ☎*800/359–6089 or 808/939–7368* ⊕*www. landofficehawaii.com* ⇨*74 units* ⛶*In-room: kitchen, VCR (some). In-hotel: golf course, tennis court, pool, laundry facilities* ▤*MC, V.*

$$ 🏨 **South Point Banyan Tree House.** Ideal for romance, this charming little tree cottage is built into a Chinese banyan tree. The partially transparent roof is the world's greatest skylight, letting in lots of light and offering views of the beautiful tree canopy above. A wraparound deck with a hot tub provides one of the best places on the island to watch the sunset. **Pros:** secluded and romantic, interesting architecture, hot tub with a view. **Cons:** remote location, not within walking distance to grocery store or restaurants, no pool or beach. ✉*Hwy. 11 at Pinao St., Waiohinu (near South Point), 96742* ☎*715/302–8180* ⊕*www. southpointbth.com* ⇨*1 cottage* ⛶*In-room: no a/c, kitchen, VCR. In-hotel: laundry facilities* ▤*MC, V.*

B&BS & INNS

$–$$ 🏨 **Aloha Guesthouse.** In the hills above Kealakekua Bay, Aloha Guesthouse offers quiet elegance, complete privacy, and ocean views from every room. With a focus on nature, the house is furnished in earth tones. The bath products are 100% organic, and the yummy full breakfasts are as close to organic as they can muster. Common areas include a kitchenette for guests who want to cook their own meals, as well as a high-definition television, a DVD library, and a computer with high-speed Internet. **Pros:** eco-conscious, full breakfast, views of Kealakekua Bay. **Cons:** remote location, no grocery stores or restaurants within walking distance, not recommended for kids. ✉*Old Tobacco Rd., off Hwy. 11 near mile marker 104, Captain Cook 96704* ☎*808/328–8955* ⊕*www.alohaguesthouse.com* ⇨*5 rooms* ⛶*In-room: refrigerator, DVD (some), Wi-Fi. In-hotel: public Internet* ▤*AE, MC, V.*

$–$$ 🏨 **Dragonfly Ranch.** A unique, slightly hippie-ish hideaway built into the trees of Honaunau (about 10 mi south of Kealakekua Bay), the Dragonfly is not for everyone, but for some it is paradise. Dubbed an eco-retreat, this remarkable jungle tree house brings the outside in, with windows everywhere, lots of open-air sitting areas, and plants and flowers galore. The ranch doubles as a Healing Arts Center, and food is prepared from the ranch's organic garden. A labyrinth walk and *lomi lomi* massages are available, as are dolphin swims (they take you to the bay to "play respectfully with dolphins"). There's even a variety of musical instruments in the front room for anyone to play. **Pros:** unique in every way, emphasis on health, dolphin swims. **Cons:** can be a little New Agey, prices are high for location and vibe. ⚐ *Box 675, Honaunau off Hwy. 160, Captain Cook 96726* ☎*808/328–2159* ⊕*www.dragonflyranch. com* ⬎*3 rooms, 2 suites, 1 cottage* ♿*In-room: Wi-Fi* ▤*MC, V.*

$ 🏠**Kalaekilohana.** You wouldn't really expect to find a top-notch B&B in Ka'u, but just up the road from South Point, this charming yellow house offers large, comfortable private suites with beautifully restored hardwood floors, private lānai with ocean and mountain views, and big, comfy beds decked out with high-thread-count sheets and fluffy down comforters. Choose between a full hot breakfast or a Continental breakfast of local fruits and baked goods. For those anxious to get an early start on exploring the area's green- and black-sand beaches or Volcanoes National Park (a half-hour drive away), hosts Kenny Joyce and Kilohana Domingo are happy to pack a bento box to go. Guests can also look forward to a nightly cocktail hour and plenty of great advice from their hosts. The B&B prides itself on its programs and work surrounding Hawaiian cultural arts, and guests are welcome to take part in lei-making workshops and other lessons on traditional Hawaiian handicrafts. **Pros:** luxurious beds, beautifully restored house, delicious breakfast. **Cons:** strange location, no pool. ✉*94-2152 South Point Rd., Na'alehu 96772* ☎*808/939–8052* ⊕*www.kau-hawaii.com* ⬎*4 rooms* ♿*In-room: no a/c, ethernet. In-hotel: laundry facilities* ▤*MC, V.*

VOLCANO

If you are going to visit Volcanoes National Park, and we highly recommend that you do, stay the night in Volcano Village. This allows you to do the late-night lava hike—the best way to see lava—without worrying about driving an hour or more back to your condo, hotel, or B&B. Lucky for you, there are plenty of places to stay in the area, and many of them are both charming and reasonable. Volcano Village has just enough dining and shopping options to satisfy you for a day or two. From here you are also close to Hilo, the Puna region, and Punalu'u's black-sand beach, should you decide to make Volcano your home base for more than a day or two.

HOTELS & RESORTS

$–$$ 🏠**Kīlauea Lodge.** A mile from the entrance of Hawai'i Volcanoes National Park, this lodge was initially built as a YMCA camp in the 1930s. Now it is a pleasant inn, tastefully furnished with European antiques. Rooms have rich quilts and Hawaiian photographs, and some have their own wood-burning fireplaces. A charming two-bedroom cottage with a gas fireplace and a private balcony is perfect for romance. Cottages off the main property include Pi'i Mauna House, on the fairway of the Volcano Golf Course. Rates include a full hot breakfast at the

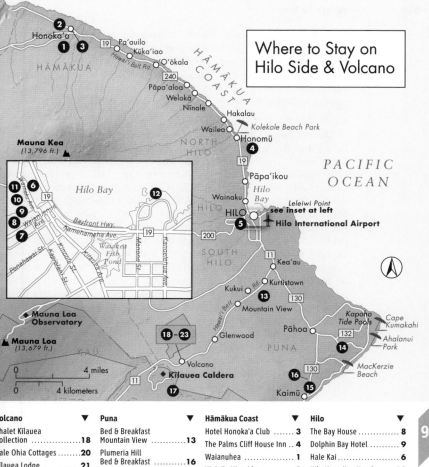

Where to Stay on Hilo Side & Volcano

9

olcano ▼

halet Kīlauea
ollection **18**

ale Ohia Cottages **20**

īlauea Lodge **21**

y Island
ed & Breakfast Inn **22**

āmakani Paio Cabins **17**

olcano Places **19**

olcano Teapot
ottage **23**

Puna ▼

Bed & Breakfast
Mountain View **13**

Plumeria Hill
Bed & Breakfast **16**

Steam Vent
Inn and Retreat **15**

Yoga Oasis **14**

Hāmākua Coast ▼

Hotel Honoka'a Club **3**

The Palms Cliff House Inn .. **4**

Waianuhea **1**

Waipi'o Wayside **2**

Hilo ▼

The Bay House **8**

Dolphin Bay Hotel **9**

Hale Kai **6**

Hilo Hawaiian Hotel **12**

Hilo Honu Inn **7**

The Inn at Kulaniapia Falls . **5**

Shipman House Bed &
Breakfast Inn **11**

Waterfalls Inn Bed &
Breakfast **10**

Lodge's restaurant, which has an excellent dinner menu as well. **Pros:** great restaurant, close to volcano, fireplaces. **Cons:** overpriced for area, limited breakfast selection. ⊠*Old Volcano Hwy., 1 mi northeast of Volcano Store* ⬧*Box 116, Volcano 96785* ☎*808/967–7366* ⊕*www.kilauealodge.com* ⇱*11 rooms, 3 cottages* &*In-room: no a/c, no TV (some). In-hotel: restaurant, no-smoking rooms* ⊟*AE, MC, V.*

B&BS AND VACATION RENTALS

¢–$$ ⊞**Chalet Kīlauea Collection.** The Collection comprises five inns and lodges and five vacation houses in and around Volcano Village; the theme rooms, suites, and vacation homes range from no-frills dorm-style bedrooms in a funky old house to a plantation mansion with its own six-person hot tub. There is a two-night minimum at all of the Chalet Kilauea properties. Although the Collection's showpiece property, the Inn at Volcano, is overpriced and slipping in quality, its remaining properties do have something to offer. The **Lokahi Lodge** ($115–$135) provides cozy rooms in a country lodge with plenty of exposed beams and wood, and comfy beds with custom-made raised wooden bed frames. A large kitchen is available for guest use, as is an on-site hot tub. Lokahi is the most recently updated of the Collection's properties. For those looking for a bit more privacy, the **Volcano Cottages** are dispersed vacation homes and cottage rentals around Volcano Village. Each of the six one-, two-, or three-bedroom rentals has a different layout and decor; our favorites are the Ohia Hideaway ($135/night) for couples or small groups, and Pele's Plantation ($225/night) for large groups. The Collection's most reasonably priced offering is the **Volcano Hale** ($55–$69 double-occupancy room), which has a communal kitchen and fireplace. **Pros:** large variety of lodging types to choose from, hot tub, fireplace. **Cons:** two-night minimum; staff and management changes frequently, which can sometimes make service suffer. ⊠*Wright Rd., Volcano 96785* ☎*808/967–7786 or 800/937–7786* ⊕*www.volcano-hawaii.com* ⇱*11 rooms, 9 suites, 5 houses* &*In-room: no a/c, no phone (some), kitchen (some). In-hotel: no-smoking rooms* ⊟*AE, D, DC, MC, V.*

$ ⊞**Hale Ohia Cottages.** A stately and comfortable Queen Anne–style mansion, Hale Ohia was built in the 1930s as a summer place for a wealthy Scotsman. The namesake Ohia cottage, large enough for a family, has a full kitchen. The 'Ihilani cottage is the cushiest of the group; built into an old water tank, it's naturally lighted, beautifully designed, and completely private. Breakfast (including homemade banana bread, macadamia nuts, and cranberries) is left in your refrigerator while you're away in the afternoon so that you can enjoy it at your leisure in the morning. This place does everything possible to make everyone from couples to families to solo travelers feel at home. **Pros:** unique architecture, hot tub, plenty of props like umbrellas and flashlights for volcano excursions. **Cons:** rooms need to be updated; property cat roams around, which could be a problem for allergic guests. ⊠*Hale Ohia Rd., off Hwy. 11, Volcano 96785* ☎*808/967–7986* ⊕*www.haleohia.com* ⇱*4 rooms, 3 cottages, 1 suite* &*In-room: no a/c, no phone, kitchen (some), refrigerator (some), Wi-Fi. In-hotel: no-smoking rooms* ⊟*MC, V.*

¢–$ 🏨 **My Island Bed & Breakfast Inn.** Gordon and Joann Morse, along with their daughter Ki'i, opened their historic home and 7-acre botanical estate to visitors in 1985. The oldest in Volcano, it was built in 1886 by the Lyman missionary family. Three rooms, sharing two baths, are in the main house. Scattered around the area are three garden apartments and five fully equipped guesthouses. You won't start the day hungry after a deluxe all-you-can-eat breakfast. **Pros:** historic home, full breakfast. **Cons:** remote location, some shared bathrooms. ✉*19-3896 Old Volcano Hwy.* ⬡*Box 100, Volcano 96785* ☎*808/967–7216 or 808/967–7110* ⬡*www.myislandinnhawaii.com* ➸*6 rooms, 3 with bath; 5 guesthouses* ⬡*In-room: no a/c, no phone (some), no TV (some). In-hotel: no-smoking rooms* ▤*MC, V.*

¢–$$ 🏨 **Volcano Places.** A collection of lovely vacation homes, the accommodations range from a simple cottage in the rain forest to a stunning Craftsman-style house with its own spa room. Many can accommodate up to eight people comfortably. All come equipped with full kitchens. **Pros:** unique architecture, rain-forest location, total privacy. **Cons:** can't always select the exact property you want, prices of more expensive units is high for the area. ⬡*Box 159, Volcano 96785* ☎*808/967–7990* ⬡*www.volcanoplaces.com* ➸*3 cottages* ⬡*In-room: kitchen, refrigerator, VCR (some)* ▤*MC, V.*

$ 🏨 **Volcano Teapot Cottage.** A near-perfect spot for couples seeking a romantic getaway, this cute red-and-white cottage is completely private. The claw-foot bathtub, hot tub, and fireplace add to the general coziness. Breakfast is included, and the restaurants in Volcano Village are nearby. **Pros:** claw-foot tub, hot tub, fireplace. **Cons:** isolated location, no credit cards accepted. ✉*19-3820 Old Volcano Hwy.* ⬡*Box 511, Volcano 96785* ☎*808/967–7112* ⬡*www.volcanoteapot.com* ➸*1 cottage* ⬡*In-room: kitchen, VCR* ▤*No credit cards.*

CABINS

¢   🏨 **Nāmakani Paio Cabins.** These A-frame cabins at the end of a long,
🕙 deserted road, look like little birdhouses. Though recently remodeled, and managed by Volcano House, the cabins are definitely for those who are into roughing it. Inexpensive and clean, each has a double bed, two bunk beds, and electric lights, but no outlets. Bring extra blankets, as it gets cold at night. Each cabin also has a grill outside, but you must bring your own firewood. A communal bathroom facility provides toilets and hot showers for all cabin guests. **Pros:** camping in Volcanoes National Park, unique design. **Cons:** cold nights with no insulation, price is high for rustic cabins. ⬡*Volcano House, Box 53, Hawai'i Volcanoes National Park, Volcano 96785* ☎*808/967–7321* ⬡*www. volcanohousehotel.com/cabins.htm* ➸*10 cabins* ⬡*In-room: no a/c, no phone, no TV* ▤*MC, V.*

9

Puna is a world apart—wild jungles, volcanically heated hot springs, and not a resort for miles around. There are, however, a handful of vacation homes and bed-and-breakfasts, most of which are a great deal due to the fact that Puna doesn't attract nearly as many visitors as other regions on the island. This is not a typical vacation spot: there are a few black-sand beaches (some of them clothing-optional), very few dining or entertainment options, and quite a few, er, interesting locals. That said, for those who want to have a unique experience, get away from everything, and like the thought of rubbing shoulders with the locals, this is the place to do it. The volcano, Hilo, and the Hāmākua Coast are all within easy driving distance, and nearby Pahoa has a few restaurants.

¢–$ ⌂ **Bed & Breakfast Mountain View.** This modern home is surrounded by rolling forest and farmland. The secluded 4-acre estate has extensive floral gardens and a fishpond. Owners Linus and Jane Chao are longtime Big Island art educators and have an art studio on the lower level where they teach classes. Some special packages include art lessons. The house itself is a virtual art gallery with varied displays in oil, acrylic, watercolor, and Oriental brush paintings. **Pros:** reasonable prices, local artist hosts, beautiful landscaping. **Cons:** rooms could use some updating, location is remote. ⊠*South Kulani Rd., Kurtistown 96760* ☎*808/968–6868 or 888/698–9896* ⊕*www.bbmtview.com* ⇆*4 rooms, 2 with shared bath* △*In-room: no a/c, no TV (some). In-hotel: laundry facilities, no kids under 5* ▤*MC, V.*

$ ⌂ **Plumeria Hill Bed & Breakfast.** A relatively new B&B near the popular steam vent caves in Opihikao in the Puna region, Plumeria Hill offers two beautiful suites, each with its own private entrance, two queen beds covered with Hawaiian quilts, and large floor-to-ceiling windows with ocean views. It doesn't get more Hawaiian than the Puna region, with its wild rain forest and reputation for outlaw locals, and Plumeria Hill's hosts do a great job of providing modern luxury amid this wilderness. The B&B also includes a massage treatment room and on-site masseuse. **Pros:** wildly beautiful location, massage therapist on-site, proximity to volcano and steam vent caves. **Cons:** remote location, only two rooms, must drive to get to nearest restaurant. ⊠*Opihikao-Kamaʻili Rd., off Hwy. 130 just past mile marker 15, Puna 96778* ☎*808/965–8810* ⊕*www.plumeriahill.com* ⇆*2 suites* △*In-room: kitchenette, no phone, DVD* ▤*MC, V* ⌐*CP.*

¢ ⌂ **Steam Vent Inn and Retreat.** Not at all luxurious, but comfortable and clean, this inn is equipped with volcanically heated showers, hot tubs, and a pond. Massage and reflexology are also available, and a clothing-optional black-sand beach is five minutes away. For those on a budget, single-person huts with small kitchenettes are available for only $25 a night. Nicer rooms in the main house are a bit more, but still very reasonable. **Pros:** dirt cheap, volcanically heated water, close to steam vent caves. **Cons:** very rustic, too hippie-ish for some. ⊠*13-3775 Kalapana Hwy., Puna 96778* ☎*808/965–8800* ⇆*10 rooms* △*In-room: no a/c, no phone (some), kitchen (some), no TV* ▤*No credit cards.*

¢–$ ⌂ **Yoga Oasis.** This center, on 26 tropical acres, has a bit of a commune feel. With its exposed redwood beams, Balinese doorways, and imported art, Yoga Oasis draws those who seek relaxation and rejuvenation, and perhaps a free yoga lesson or two. A 1,600-square-foot state-of-the-art yoga and gymnastics space, with 18-foot ceilings, crowns this friendly retreat. You're close to hot springs and black-sand beaches, and the volcano is a 45-minute drive away. Bathrooms are shared. **Pros:** daily yoga, focus on relaxation, very low prices. **Cons:** remote location, shared bathrooms in the main building. ⊠*Pohoiki Rd.* ⌂ *Box 1935, Pāhoa 96778* ☎*808/965–8460 or 800/274–4446* ⊕*www.yogaoasis.org* ⇆*5 rooms with shared bath, 4 bungalows, 1 cottage* ⌂*In-room: no a/c, no phone, no TV. In-hotel: laundry service, no-smoking rooms* ⊟*MC, V.*

HILO

Hilo is the wetter, more lush eastern side of the Big Island, which means if you stay here you'll be close to waterfalls and rain-forest hikes, but not to a warm, dry, white-sand beach. Though Hilo had the wind knocked out of its sails a bit when sugar left the islands over a decade ago, it has gotten back on its feet in the last couple of years and is experiencing something of a revival. Locals, driven farther and farther east by development in the west, have taken a greater interest in Hilo; signs of that interest are showing in new restaurants, restored buildings, and a handful of clean and pleasant parks. Hilo has a few decent hotels, but none of the high-end resorts that are the domain of the west. So, get into the groove at one of Hilo's fantastic B&Bs. Most have taken over lovely historic homes and serve breakfast comprised of ingredients from their backyard gardens. The volcano is only a 30- to 40-minute drive, as are the sights of the Puna region. The beaches, unfortunately, are at least an hour's drive.

HOTELS & RESORTS

$ **Dolphin Bay Hotel.** A glowing lava flow sign marks the office and bespeaks owner John Alexander's passion for the volcano. Stunning lava pictures adorn the common area, and Alexander is a great source of information for visiting the park and for exploring the back roads of Hilo. Units in the 1950s-style motor lodge are modest, but they are clean and inexpensive. Coffee and fresh fruit are offered daily. Four blocks from Hilo Bay, in a residential area called Pu'ue'o, the hotel borders a verdant 2-acre Hawaiian garden with jungle trails and shady places to rest. Guests of the hotel return repeatedly, and it's ideal for families who seek a home base. **Pros:** great value, extremely helpful and pleasant staff, rates go down every night you stay. **Cons:** located along a busy road; basic, motel-style rooms. ⊠*333 'Iliahi St., Hilo 96720* ☎*808/935–1466* ⊕*www.dolphinbayhotel.com* ⇆*13 rooms, 4 1-bedroom units, 1 2-bedroom unit* ⌂*In-room: no a/c, no phone, kitchen, no TV* ⊟*MC, V.*

$-$$ **Hilo Hawaiian Hotel.** Though it does show its age and some of the rooms are in dire need of a refresh, this older hotel, with large bay-front rooms offering spectacular views of Mauna Kea and Coconut Island, is one of the most pleasant lodgings on Hilo Bay. Streetside rooms overlook the golf course. Most accommodations have private lānai, and kitchenettes are available in some one-bedroom suites. Views of the bay are showcased in the Queen's Court dining room, and the Wai'oli Lounge has entertainment Thursday through Saturday. **Pros:** Hilo Bay views, private lānai, large rooms. **Cons:** rooms sorely in need of renovation, prices high for quality of rooms. ⊠*71 Banyan Dr., Hilo 96720*

9

☎808/935–9361, 800/367–5004 from mainland, 800/272–5275 inter-island ⊕www.castleresorts.com ⬯286 rooms, 6 suites ⚘In-room: kitchen (some), refrigerator, dial-up. In-hotel: restaurant, bar, pool, laundry facilities, no-smoking rooms ▭AE, D, DC, MC, V.

B&BS & VACATION RENTALS

$ ⊞**The Bay House.** Overlooking Hilo Bay and just steps away from the "Singing Bridge" into Hilo's historic downtown area, this small, quiet B&B is pleasantly decorated, with comfy beds and private lānai. An outdoor hot tub on the cliff offers excellent views of the bay below. A Continental breakfast buffet is provided with fresh fruits, breads, and coffee from the area—guests are invited to take what they want from the buffet back to their lānai for a more private breakfast. **Pros:** cliffside hot tub, Hilo Bay views. **Cons:** no hot breakfast, books up fast. ⊠42 Pukihae St, Hilo 96720 ☎888/235–8195 or 808/961–6311 ⊕www.bayhouse hawaii.com ⬯3 rooms ⚘In-room: no a/c, Wi-Fi ▭AE, MC, V.

$ ⊞**Hale Kai.** On a bluff above Hilo Bay, this 5,400-square-foot modern home is 2 mi from downtown Hilo. Four impeccable rooms with patios have been freshly painted and spruced up by new owners Maria Macias and Ricardo Zepeda, as has the private loft, which is ideal for families. All rooms have grand ocean views and are within earshot of lapping waves. Fresh flowers add a warm, European touch. Maria and Ricardo serve a full hot breakfast every morning on an outdoor deck or in the kitchen's bay-window dining area. **Pros:** delicious hot breakfast, panoramic views, privacy. **Cons:** removed from town, no kids allowed. ⊠111 Honoliʻi Pali St., Hilo 96720 ☎808/935–6330 ⊕www.halekai hawaii.com ⬯4 rooms, 1 suite ⚘In-hotel: pool, laundry service, no kids under 16, no-smoking rooms ▭No credit cards.

$–$$ ⊞**Hilo Honu Inn.** A charming old Craftsman home lovingly restored by a friendly and hospitable couple from North Carolina, the Hilo Honu offers quite a bit of variety. Its three rooms range from the small and reasonably priced Honu's Nest to the large and luxurious Samurai Suite. The Honu's Nest provides fantastic views of the sunrise over Hilo Bay from the comforts of a large, comfy bed. The larger Bali Hai Suite has a sitting room and a window seat that looks out on tree ferns, orchids, and anthuriums. Upstairs, the entire second floor is the Samurai Suite, furnished with traditional tatami mats and beautiful antiques imported from Japan. The suite also includes a large stone soaking tub for two and a beautiful sun porch that looks out over all of Hilo and the bay beyond. Breakfast is delicious and usually includes a variety of homemade baked goods. **Pros:** beautifully restored home, spectacular Hilo Bay views, delicious breakfast. **Cons:** only three rooms, not walking distance to downtown Hilo. ⊠465 Haili St., Hilo 96720 ☎808/935–4325 ⊕www.hilohonu.com ⬯3 rooms ⚘In-room: no a/c, refrigerator, DVD, VCR, Wi-Fi. In-hotel: no kids under 6 ▭AE, MC, V.

$ ⊞**The Inn at Kulaniapia Falls.** The Inn at Kulaniapia has wonderful views both of Hilo Bay and a magnificent 120-foot waterfall that tumbles into a 300-foot-wide swimming pond. The Pagoda, a private guesthouse with a kitchen and living room, sleeps four adults and two children for $175 a night. The only drawbacks are the slightly tacky decor and less than amazing service. The spa has a menu of eight different massages.

LODGING ALTERNATIVES

HOME EXCHANGES

If you would like to exchange your home for someone else's, join a home-exchange organization, which will send you its updated listings of available exchanges for a year and will include your own listing in at least one of them. It's up to you to make specific arrangements.

Exchange Clubs **HomeLink USA** (✉ *2937 NW 9th Terrace, Wilton Manors, FL 33311* ☎ *954/566–2687 or 800/638–3841* ⊕ *www.homelink. org*); $75 yearly for a listing and online access; $45 additional to receive directories. **Intervac U.S.** (✉ *30 Corte San Fernando, Tiburon, CA 94920* ☎ *800/756–4663* ⊕ *www. intervacus.com*); $128 yearly for a listing, online access, and a catalog; $68 without catalog.

HOSTELS

No matter what your age, you can save on lodging costs by staying at hostels. In some 4,500 locations in more than 70 countries around the world, Hostelling International (HI), the umbrella group for a number of national youth-hostel associations, offers single-sex, dorm-style beds and, at many hostels, rooms for couples and family accommodations. Membership in any HI national hostel association, open to travelers of all ages, allows you to stay in HI-affiliated hostels at member rates; one-year membership is about $28 for adults (C$35 for a two-year minimum membership in Canada, £15 in the U.K., A$52 in Australia, and NZ$40 in New Zealand); hostels charge about $10–$30 per night. Members have priority if the hostel is full; they're also eligible for discounts around the world, even on rail and bus travel in some countries.

Organizations **Hostelling International–USA** (✉ *8401 Colesville Rd., Suite 600, Silver Spring, MD 20910* ☎ *301/495–1240* ⊕ *www.hiusa.org*).

Local Resources **Hilo Bay Hostel** (✉ *101 Waianuenue Ave., 96720* ☎ *808/933–2771* ⊕ *www.hawaii hostel.net*). **Holo Holo Inn** (✉ *19-4036 Kalani Honua Rd., Volcano Village 96785* ☎ *808/967–7950* ⊕ *www.enable.org/holoholo*). **Hotel Honoka'a Club** (✉ *45-3480 Māmane St., Box 247, Honoka'a 96727* ☎ *808/775–0678 or 800/808–0678* ⊕ *www.hotel honokaa.com*). **Koa Wood Hale Inn** (✉ *75-184 Ala Ona Ona St., Kailua-Kona 96740* ☎ *808/329–9663* ⊕ *www.alternative-hawaii.com/ affordable/kona.htm*).

All in all, this place is a good deal for those who aren't expecting four-star accommodations. **Pros:** waterfalls on property, good value. **Cons:** tacky decor, some complain of poor service. ⌂ *Box 11338, Hilo 96721* ☎ *808/935–8088 or 888/838–6373* ⊕ *www.waterfall.net* ⌷ *4 rooms* ⌂ *In-room: no a/c. In-hotel: no-smoking rooms* ☐ *AE, MC, V.*

$$ ⛨ **Shipman House Bed & Breakfast Inn.** You'll have a choice between three rooms in the "castle"—the turreted main house dating from 1899—or two rooms in a separate cottage. The B&B is on 5½ verdant acres on Reed's Island; the house is furnished with antique koa and period pieces, some dating from the days when Queen Lili'uokalani came to tea. On Tuesday night, an authentic hula school practices Hawai'i's ancient dances in the house. Barbara (part of the Shipman family) and her husband Gary are friendly hosts with a vast knowledge of the area and the rest of the

island; they're also excellent cooks, which means you should try absolutely everything at breakfast. **Pros:** great home cooking, historic home, friendly and knowledgeable local hosts. **Cons:** chock-full of antiques, not a great spot for kids. ✉ *131 Kaʻiulani St., Hilo 96720* ☎ *808/934–8002 or 800/627–8447* ⊕ *www.hilo-hawaii.com* ⬗ *3 rooms, 2 cottage rooms* ⬗ *In-room: no a/c, no phone, refrigerator, no TV. In-hotel: no kids under 16, no-smoking rooms* ⊟ *AE, MC, V.*

$$ 🏨 **Waterfalls Inn Bed & Breakfast.** This elegant old family home is in the exclusive Reed's Bay neighborhood, just a few blocks from downtown Hilo. Relaxation is the key here. Bounded on two sides by tropical streams and forest, there's no noise except the gentle gurgle of the stream. The 1916-era home has been carefully restored, retaining the original light fixtures, fine ʻōhiʻa wood flooring, antique furniture, and some original bath fixtures; some of the rooms include large whirlpool tubs. You'll find lots of room to unwind in the expansive glassed-in lānai. Breakfast (George always whips up a warm and wonderful treat) is served in the large dining room. Business travelers enjoy easy access to town, government offices, and the University of Hawaiʻi at Hilo. There's a $20 additional fee for one-night stays. **Pros:** gourmet breakfasts, Jacuzzi tubs, restored historic home. **Con:** fee for single-night stays. ✉ *240 Kaʻiulani St., Hilo 96720* ☎ *808/969–3407* ⊕ *www. waterfallsinn.com* ⬗ *4 suites* ⬗ *In-room: no a/c, refrigerator, DVD, VCR, Wi-Fi. In-hotel: no elevator, no kids under 6* ⊟ *AE, MC, V.*

HĀMĀKUA COAST

One of the most beautiful stretches of coastline in the world, the Hāmākua Coast is an ideal spot for those seeking peace, tranquillity, and beautiful views, which is why it tends to be a favorite with honeymooners. A half dozen or so über-romantic B&Bs dot the coast, each with its own personality and views. As with Hilo, the beaches are an hour's drive away or more, so most visitors spend a few nights here and a few closer to the beaches on the west coast. A handful of vacation homes provide an extra level of privacy for couples, groups, or families, but the nearest grocery store is 15 mi up the road in either Hilo or Waimea.

¢   🏨 **Hotel Honokaʻa Club.** This bargain hotel is 45 minutes from Hilo and close to Waipiʻo Valley. Rustic rooms range from lower-level dormitory-style units—bring your own sleeping bag—to upper-story rooms with private baths, ocean views, and a complimentary Continental breakfast. **Pros:** historic hotel in historic town, close to Waipio Valley, low prices. **Cons:** funky old hotel in need of an update, somewhat remote location. ✉ *45-3480 Māmane St., Box 247, Honokaʻa 96727* ☎ *808/775–0678 or 800/808–0678* ⊕ *www.hotelhonokaa.com* ⬗ *13 rooms, 5 dorm-style rooms* ⬗ *In-room: no a/c, no phone, no TV (some), Wi-Fi. In-hotel: restaurant, no-smoking rooms* ⊟ *MC, V.*

$$$ 🏨 **The Palms Cliff House Inn.** This handsome Victorian-style mansion, 15 mi north of Hilo, is perched on the sea cliffs 150 feet above the crashing surf of the tropical Hāmākua Coast. You can pick tropical fruit and macadamia nuts from the gardens of the 3½-acre estate. Indi-

Waianuhea

vidually decorated rooms have private lānai. Suites include double hot tubs (the one in Room 8 is by the window with a stunning view of the coast), but there's also a communal hot tub in the garden. A husband-and-wife team serves breakfast with pride on the veranda overlooking the cliffs; meals generally include fresh-baked muffins, locally grown fruit, a warm egg or meat dish (they always ask about food allergies or dietary restrictions ahead of time), and, of course, fantastic local coffee. Dinner is available on request. They can help you plan activities, including hula lessons. **Pros:** stunning views, terrific breakfast, comfortable rooms with every amenity. **Cons:** service is erratic, remote location means you have to drive to restaurants. ⊠ *28-3514 Māmalahoa Hwy., Honomū 96728* ☎ *808/963–6076* ⊕ *www.palmscliffhouse.com* ⌂ *2 rooms, 6 suites* & *In-room: no a/c (some), safe, DVD, dial-up. In-hotel: no kids under 12, no-smoking rooms, no elevator* ☐ *AE, D, DC, MC, V.*

$$
Fodor'sChoice
★

🏨 **Waianuhea.** Waianuhea defines Hawaiian country elegance. Fully self-contained, this gorgeous country home sits in a forested area on the Hāmākua Coast. The four guest rooms and large suite have tasteful color schemes and lavish furnishings, complete with extra pillows, fluffy down comforters, and soaking tubs, and there is contemporary artwork throughout. The large common room with its stunning ocean views and lava-rock fireplace is a big attraction, especially at the wine tasting and hors d'oeuvres hour each evening. Stroll the flower garden and fruit orchards. The house has solar-electric power. **Pros:** eco-friendly hotel, hot and healthy breakfast, beautiful views. **Cons:** very remote location, unreliable phone and Internet access. ⊠ *45-3503 Kahana Dr., Honoka'a 96727* ☎ *888/775–2577 or 808/775–1118* ⊕ *www. waianuhea.com* ⌂ *4 rooms, 1 suite* & *In-room: no a/c, DVD. In-hotel: public Internet, no-smoking rooms* ☐ *AE, D, MC, V.*

$–$$
🏨 **Waipi'o Wayside.** Nestled amid the avocado, mango, and kukui trees of a plantation estate, this serene inn provides a retreat close to the Waipi'o Valley. Jacqueline Horne has given each room its own character with, for example, rare Chinese antiques or patchwork quilts. A sprawling garden has an orchid-covered deck and a little gazebo has hammocks to help you indulge your lazy side. Many of the rooms have ocean views and some also have skylights. Breakfast includes fresh fruit from the estate, locally grown coffee, granola, yogurt, and muffins. **Pros:** close to Waipio, authentic Hawaiian feel, hammocks with views. **Cons:** remote location, no hot breakfast. ⊠ *Waipi'o Valley Rd., Hwy. 240, Honoka'a 96727* ☎ *808/775–0275 or 800/833–8849* ⊕ *www. waipiowayside.com* ⌂ *5 rooms* & *In-room: no a/c, no phone, no TV, dial-up. In-hotel: no-smoking rooms* ☐ *MC, V.*

HAWAIIAN VOCABULARY

Although an understanding of Hawaiian is by no means required on a trip to the Aloha State, a *malihini,* or newcomer, will find plenty of opportunities to pick up a few of the local words and phrases. Traditional names and expressions are widely used in the Islands. You're likely to read or hear at least a few words each day of your stay.

With a basic understanding and some uninhibited practice, anyone can have enough command of the local tongue to ask for directions and to order from a restaurant menu. One visitor announced she would not leave until she could pronounce the name of the state fish, the *humuhumunukunukuāpua'a.*

Simplifying the learning process is the fact that the Hawaiian language contains only eight consonants—*H, K, L, M, N, P, W,* and the silent *'okina,* or glottal stop, written '—plus one or more of the five vowels. All syllables, and therefore all words, end in a vowel. Each vowel, with the exception of a few diphthongized double vowels such as *au* (pronounced "ow") or *ai* (pronounced "eye"), is pronounced separately. Thus *'Iolani* is four syllables (ee-oh-la-nee), not three (yo-la-nee). Although some Hawaiian words have only vowels, most also contain some consonants, but consonants are never doubled.

Pronunciation is simple. Pronounce *A* "ah" as father; *E* "ay" as in weigh; *I* "ee" as in marine; *O* "oh" as in no; *U* "oo" as in true.

Consonants mirror their English equivalents, with the exception of *W.* When the letter begins any syllable other than the first one in a word, it is usually pronounced as a *V. 'Awa,* the Polynesian drink, is pronounced "ava," *'ewa* is pronounced "eva."

Almost all long Hawaiian words are combinations of shorter words; they are not difficult to pronounce if you segment them. *Kalaniana'ole,* the highway running east from Honolulu, is easily understood as *Kalani ana 'ole.* Apply the standard pronunciation rules—the stress falls on the next-to-last syllable of most two- or three-syllable Hawaiian words—and Kalaniana'ole Highway is as easy to say as Main Street.

Now about that fish. Try *humu-humu nuku-nuku āpu a'a.*

The other unusual element in Hawaiian language is the *kahakō,* or macron, written as a short line (‾) placed over a vowel. Like the accent (´) in Spanish, the kahakō puts emphasis on a syllable that would normally not be stressed. The most familiar example is probably *Waikīkī.* With no macrons, the stress would fall on the middle syllable; with only one macron, on the last syllable, the stress would fall on the first and last syllables. Some words become plural with the addition of a macron, often on a syllable that would have been stressed anyway. No Hawaiian word becomes plural with the addition of an *S,* since that letter does not exist in the language.

What follows is a glossary of some of the most commonly used Hawaiian words. Hawaiian residents appreciate visitors who at least try to pick up the local language.

'a'ā: rough, crumbling lava, contrasting with *pāhoehoe,* which is smooth.
'ae: yes.
aikane: friend.
āina: land.
akamai: smart, clever, possessing savoir faire.
akua: god.
ala: a road, path, or trail.
ali'i: a Hawaiian chief, a member of the chiefly class.
aloha: love, affection, kindness; also a salutation meaning both greetings and farewell.

'ānuenue: rainbow.

'a'ole: no.

'apōpō: tomorrow.

'auwai: a ditch.

auwē: alas, woe is me!

'ehu: a red-haired Hawaiian.

'ewa: in the direction of 'Ewa plantation, west of Honolulu.

hala: the pandanus tree, whose leaves (*lau hala*) are used to make baskets and plaited mats.

hālau: school.

hale: a house.

hale pule: church, house of worship.

ha mea iki or **ha mea 'ole:** you're welcome.

hana: to work.

haole: ghost. Since the first foreigners were Caucasian, *haole* now means a Caucasian person.

hapa: a part, sometimes a half; often used as a short form of *hapa haole,* to mean a person who is part-Caucasian.

hau'oli: to rejoice. *Hau'oli Makahiki Hou* means Happy New Year. *Hau'oli lā hānau* means Happy Birthday.

heiau: an outdoor stone platform; an ancient Hawaiian place of worship.

holo: to run.

holoholo: to go for a walk, ride, or sail.

holokū: a long Hawaiian dress, somewhat fitted, with a yoke and a train. Influenced by European fashion, it was worn at court, and at least one local translates the word as "expensive mu'umu'u."

holomū: a post–World War II cross between a *holokū* and a mu'umu'u, less fitted than the former but less voluminous than the latter, and having no train.

honi: to kiss; a kiss. A phrase that some tourists may find useful, quoted from a popular hula, is *Honi Ka'ua Wikiwiki:* Kiss me quick!

honu: turtle.

ho'omalimali: flattery, a deceptive "line," bunk, baloney, hooey.

huhū: angry.

hui: a group, club, or assembly. A church may refer to its congregation as a *hui* and a social club may be called a *hui.*

hukilau: a seine; a communal fishing party in which everyone helps to drive the fish into a huge net, pull it in, and divide the catch.

hula: the dance of Hawai'i.

iki: little.

ipo: sweetheart.

ka: the. This is the definite article for most singular words; for plural nouns, the definite article is usually *nā.* Since there is no *S* in Hawaiian, the article may be your only clue that a noun is plural.

kahuna: a priest, doctor, or other trained person of old Hawai'i, endowed with special professional skills that often included prophecy or other supernatural powers; the plural form is kāhuna.

kai: the sea, saltwater.

kalo: the taro plant from whose root *poi* (paste) is made.

kamā'aina: literally, a child of the soil; it refers to people who were born in the Islands or have lived there for a long time.

kanaka: originally a man or humanity, it is now used to denote a male Hawaiian or part-Hawaiian, but is occasionally taken as a slur when used by non-Hawaiians. *Kanaka maoli,* originally a full-blooded Hawaiian person, is used by some native Hawaiian rights activists to embrace part-Hawaiians as well.

kāne: a man, a husband. If you see this word on a door, it's the men's room. If you see *kane* on a door, it's probably a misspelling; that is the Hawaiian name for the skin fungus tinea.

kapa: also called by its Tahitian name, *tapa,* a cloth made of beaten bark and usually dyed and stamped with a repeat design.

kapakahi: crooked, cockeyed, uneven. You've got your hat on *kapakahi.*

kapu: keep out, prohibited. This is the Hawaiian version of the more widely known Tongan word *tabu* (taboo).

kapuna: grandparent; elder.

kēia lā: today.

keiki: a child; *keikikāne* is a boy, *keiki-wahine* a girl.

kona: the leeward side of the Islands, the direction (south) from which the *kona* wind and *kona* rain come.

kula: upland.

kuleana: a homestead or small plot of ground on which a family has been installed for some generations without necessarily owning it. By extension, *kuleana* is used to denote any area or department in which one has a special interest or prerogative. You'll hear it used this way: If you want to hire a surfboard, see Moki; that's his *kuleana.*

lā: sun.

lamalama: to fish with a torch.

lānai: a porch, a balcony, an outdoor living room. Almost every house in Hawai'i has one. Don't confuse this two-syllable word with the three-syllable name of the island, Lāna'i.

lani: heaven, the sky.

lau hala: the leaf of the *hala,* or pandanus tree, widely used in handicrafts.

lei: a garland of flowers.

limu: sun.

lolo: stupid.

luna: a plantation overseer or foreman.

mahalo: thank you.

makai: toward the ocean.

malihini: a newcomer to the Islands.

mana: the spiritual power that the Hawaiian believed inhabited all things and creatures.

manō: shark.

manuwahi: free, gratis.

mauka: toward the mountains.

mauna: mountain.

mele: a Hawaiian song or chant, often of epic proportions.

Mele Kalikimaka: Merry Christmas (a transliteration from the English phrase).

Menehune: a Hawaiian pixie. The *Menehune* were a legendary race of little people who accomplished prodigious work, such as building fishponds and temples in the course of a single night.

moana: the ocean.

mu'umu'u: the voluminous dress in which the missionaries enveloped Hawaiian women. Now made in bright printed cottons and silks, it is an indispensable garment. Culturally sensitive locals have embraced the Hawaiian spelling but often shorten the spoken word to "mu'u." Most English dictionaries include the spelling "muumuu."

nani: beautiful.

nui: big.

ohana: family.

'ono: delicious.

pāhoehoe: smooth, unbroken, satiny lava.

Pākē: Chinese. This *Pākē* carver makes beautiful things.

palapala: document, printed matter.

pali: a cliff, precipice.

pānini: prickly pear cactus.

paniolo: a Hawaiian cowboy, a rough transliteration of *español,* the language of the Islands' earliest cowboys.

pau: finished, done.

pilikia: trouble. The Hawaiian word is much more widely used here than its English equivalent.

puka: a hole.

pupule: crazy, like the celebrated Princess Pupule. This word has replaced its English equivalent in local usage.

pu'u: volcanic cinder cone.

waha: mouth.

wahine: a female, a woman, a wife, and a sign on the ladies' room door; the plural form is *wāhine.*

wai: freshwater, as opposed to saltwater, which is *kai.*

wailele: waterfall.

wikiwiki: to hurry, hurry up (since this is a reduplication of *wiki,* quick, neither W is pronounced as a V).

Note: Pidgin is the unofficial language of Hawai'i. It is a Creole language, with its own grammar, evolved from the mixture of English, Hawaiian, Japanese, Portuguese, and other languages spoken in 19th-century Hawai'i, and it is heard everywhere.

Big Island of Hawai'i Essentials

PLANNING TOOLS, EXPERT INSIGHT, GREAT CONTACTS

There are planners and there are those who, excuse the pun, fly by the seat of their pants. We happily place ourselves among the planners. Our writers and editors try to anticipate all the issues you may face before and during any journey, and then they do their research. This section is the product of their efforts. Use it to get excited about your trip to Big Island of Hawai'i, to inform your travel planning, or to guide you on the road should the seat of your pants start to feel threadbare.

GETTING STARTED

We're really proud of our Web site: Fodors.com is a great place to begin any journey. Scan Travel Wire for suggested itineraries, travel deals, restaurant and hotel openings, and other up-to-the-minute info. Check out Booking to research prices and book plane tickets, hotel rooms, rental cars, and vacation packages. Head to Talk for on-the-ground pointers from travelers who frequent our message boards. You can also link to loads of other travel-related resources.

▮ RESOURCES

ONLINE TRAVEL TOOLS

For more information on the Big Island of Hawai'i, visit ⊕*www.bigisland.org*, the Web site of the Big Island Visitors Bureau. Other sites to check out include ⊕*www.kohalacoastresorts.com*, the Kohala Coast Resort Association Web site; ⊕*www.destinationkonacoast.com* for information on Kailua-Kona; ⊕*www.downtownhilo.com*, for information on the historical town of Hilo; ⊕*www.gohawaii.com*, the official Web site of the Hawai'i Visitors & Convention Bureau; ⊕*www.bestplaceshawaii.com* for the Hawai'i State Vacation Planner; and ⊕*www.ehawaii.gov*, the state's official Web site, for all information on the destination. The Hawai'i Department of Land and Natural Resources, ⊕*www.state.hi.us/dlnr* has information on hiking, fishing, and camping permits and licenses; online brochures on hiking safety and mountain and ocean preservation; and details on volunteer programs. For an online guide to the island's state parks, visit ⊕*www.hawaii-county.com/parks/pdf/CampingInformation.pdf*. You can also get online maps and directions for more than 15 hiking trails on the island at ⊕*www.hawaiitrails.org*, the Web site of "Nā Ala Hele," the State of Hawai'i Trail and Access Program. If you're planning on spending time at any of the four national parks on the Big Island, visit ⊕*www.nps.*

gov, the Web site of the National Parks Service. Sponsored by the Hawai'i Tourism Authority, ⊕*www.travelsmarthawaii.com* offers tips on everything from packing to flying.

Safety Transportation Security Administration (*TSA;* ⊕ *www.tsa.gov*).

Time Zones Timeanddate.com (⊕ *www.timeanddate.com/worldclock*) can help you figure out the correct time anywhere in the world.

Weather Accuweather.com (⊕ *www.accuweather.com*) is an independent weather-forecasting service with especially good coverage of hurricanes. **Weather.com** (⊕ *www.weather.com*) is the Web site for the Weather Channel.

Other Resources CIA World Factbook (⊕ *www.odci.gov/cia/publications/factbook/index.html*) has profiles of every country in the world. It's a good source if you need some quick facts and figures.

VISITOR INFORMATION

Before you go, contact the Big Island Visitors Bureau to request a free official vacation planner with information on accommodations, transportation, sports and activities, dining, arts and entertainment, and culture. Take a virtual visit to the Big Island on the Web, which can be helpful in planning your vacation. The site also has a calendar section that allows you to see what local events coincide with your visit.

The Hawai'i Island Chamber of Commerce has links to dozens of museums, attractions, bed-and-breakfasts, and parks on its Web site. Volcano Art Center offers a host of activities at Kīlauea, including classes and workshops, music, dance, and theater performances, art shows, and volcano runs, which you may want to participate in while on the island.

Contacts Big Island Visitors Bureau (☎ *808/961–5797, 800/648–2441 for vacation planner and brochures ⊕ www.bigisland. org*). **Hawai'i Island Chamber of Commerce** (☎ *808/935–7178 ⊕ www.gohilo.com*). **Volcano Art Center** (☎ *866/967–7565 or 808/967–7565 ⊕ www.volcanoartcenter.org*).

■ THINGS TO CONSIDER

GEAR

Hawai'i is casual: sandals, bathing suits, and comfortable, informal clothing are the norm. In summer synthetic slacks and shirts, although easy to care for, can be uncomfortably warm.

One of the most important thing to tuck into your suitcase is sunscreen. Hats and sunglasses offer important sun protection, too. Both are easy to find in island shops, but if you already have a favorite packable hat or sun visor, bring it with you. All major hotels in Hawai'i provide beach towels.

As for clothing in the Hawaiian Islands, there's a saying that when a man wears a suit during the day, he's either going for a loan or he's a lawyer trying a case. Only a few upscale restaurants require a jacket for dinner. The *aloha* shirt is accepted dress in Hawai'i for business and most social occasions. Shorts are acceptable daytime attire, along with a T-shirt or polo shirt. There's no need to buy expensive sandals on the mainland—here you can get flip-flops for a couple of dollars and off-brand sandals for $20. Golfers should remember that many courses have dress codes requiring a collared shirt; call courses you're interested in for details. If you're not prepared, you can pick up appropriate clothing at resort pro shops.

If you're visiting in winter, bring a sweater or light- to medium-weight jacket. A polar fleece pullover is ideal, and makes a great impromptu pillow.

If your vacation plans include Hilo, especially during the spring and winter months, you'll want to pack a folding umbrella and light raincoat. And if you'll be exploring Hawai'i Volcanoes National Park, make sure you pack appropriately as weather ranges from hot and dry along the shore to cool and rainy at the summit. Good boots are recommended if you'll be hiking or camping in the Park.

TRIP INSURANCE

What kind of coverage do you honestly need? Do you need trip insurance at all? Take a deep breath and read on.

We believe that comprehensive trip insurance is especially valuable if you're booking a very expensive or complicated trip (particularly to an isolated region) or if you're booking far in advance. Who knows what could happen six months down the road? But whether or not you get insurance has more to do with how comfortable you are assuming all that risk yourself.

Comprehensive travel policies typically cover trip-cancellation and interruption, letting you cancel or cut your trip short because of a personal emergency, illness, or, in some cases, acts of terrorism in your destination. Such policies also cover evacuation and medical care. Some also cover you for trip delays because of bad weather or mechanical problems as well as for lost or delayed baggage. Another type of coverage to look for is financial default—that is, when your trip is disrupted because a tour operator, airline, or cruise line goes out of business. Generally you must buy this when you book your trip or shortly thereafter, and it's only available to you if your operator isn't on a list of excluded companies.

Trip Insurance Resources

INSURANCE COMPARISON SITES		
Insure My Trip.com	800/487–4722	www.insuremytrip.com
Square Mouth.com	800/240–0369	www.quotetravelinsurance.com
COMPREHENSIVE TRAVEL INSURERS		
Access America	866/807–3982	www.accessamerica.com
CSA Travel Protection	800/873–9855	www.csatravelprotection.com
HTH Worldwide	610/254–8700 or 888/243–2358	www.hthworldwide.com
Travelex Insurance	888/457–4602	www.travelex-insurance.com
Travel Guard International	715/345–0505 or 800/826–4919	www.travelguard.com
Travel Insured International	800/243–3174	www.travelinsured.com
MEDICAL-ONLY INSURERS		
International Medical Group	800/628–4664	www.imglobal.com
International SOS	215/942–8000 or 713/521–7611	www.internationalsos.com
Wallach & Company	800/237–6615 or 504/687–3166	www.wallach.com

Expect comprehensive travel insurance policies to cost about 4% to 7% of the total price of your trip (it's more like 12% if you're over age 70). A medical-only policy may or may not be cheaper than a comprehensive policy. Always read the fine print of your policy to make sure that you are covered for the risks that are of most concern to you. Compare several policies to make sure you're getting the best price and range of coverage available.

BOOKING YOUR TRIP

Unless your cousin is a travel agent, you're probably among the millions of people who make most of their travel arrangements online. But have you ever wondered just what the differences are between an online travel agent (a Web site through which you make reservations instead of going directly to the airline, hotel, or car-rental company), a discounter (a firm that does a high volume of business with a hotel chain or airline and accordingly gets good prices), a wholesaler (one that makes cheap reservations in bulk and then re-sells them to people like you), and an aggregator (one that compares all the offerings so you don't have to)? Is it truly better to book directly on an airline or hotel Web site? And when does a real live travel agent come in handy?

▌ ONLINE

You really have to shop around. A travel wholesaler such as Hotels.com or Hotel-Club.net can be a source of good rates, as can discounters such as Hotwire or Priceline, particularly if you can bid for your hotel room or airfare. Indeed, such sites sometimes have deals that are unavailable elsewhere. They do, however, tend to work only with hotel chains (which makes them just plain useless for getting hotel reservations outside of major cities) or big airlines. Also, with discounters and wholesalers you must generally prepay, and everything is nonrefundable. And before you fork over the dough, be sure to check the terms and conditions, so you know what a given company will do for you if there's a problem and what you'll have to deal with on your own.

▌TIP➔ To be absolutely sure everything was processed correctly, confirm reservations made through online travel agents, discounters, and wholesalers directly with your hotel before leaving home.

Booking engines like Expedia, Travelocity, and Orbitz are actually travel agents, albeit high-volume, online ones. And airline travel packagers like American Airlines Vacations and Virgin Vacations—well, they're travel agents, too. But they may still not work with all the world's hotels.

An aggregator site will search many sites and pull the best prices for airfares, hotels, and rental cars from them. Most aggregators compare the major travel-booking sites such as Expedia, Travelocity, and Orbitz; some also look at airline Web sites, though rarely the sites of smaller budget airlines. Some aggregators also compare other travel products, including complex packages—a good thing, as you can sometimes get the best overall deal by booking an air-and-hotel package.

▌ WITH A TRAVEL AGENT

If you use an agent—brick-and-mortar or virtual—you'll pay a fee for the service. And know that the service you get from some online agents isn't comprehensive. For example Expedia and Travelocity don't search for prices on budget airlines like jetBlue, Southwest, or small foreign carriers. That said, some agents (online or not) *do* have access to fares that are difficult to find otherwise, and the savings can more than make up for any surcharge.

A knowledgeable brick-and-mortar travel agent can be a godsend if you're booking a cruise, a package trip that's not available to you directly, an air pass, or a complicated itinerary including several overseas flights. What's more, travel agents that specialize in a destination may have exclusive access to certain deals and insider information on things such as charter flights. Agents who specialize in types of travelers (senior citizens, gays and lesbians, naturists) or types of trips (cruises, luxury travel, safaris) can also be invaluable.

Online Booking Resources

AGGREGATORS

Kayak	www.kayak.com	also looks at cruises and vacation packages.
Mobissimo	www.mobissimo.com	
Qixo	www.qixo.com	also compares cruises, vacation packages, and even travel insurance.
Sidestep	www.sidestep.com	also compares vacation packages and lists travel deals.
Travelgrove	www.travelgrove.com	also compares cruises and packages.

BOOKING ENGINES

Cheap Tickets	www.cheaptickets.com	a discounter.
Expedia	www.expedia.com	a large online agency that charges a booking fee for airline tickets.
Hotwire	www.hotwire.com	a discounter.
lastminute.com	www.lastminute.com	specializes in last-minute travel the main site is for the U.K., but it has a link to a U.S. site.
Luxury Link	www.luxurylink.com	has auctions (surprisingly good deals) as well as offers on the high-end side of travel.
Onetravel.com	www.onetravel.com	a discounter for hotels, car rentals, airfares, and packages.
Orbitz	www.orbitz.com	charges a booking fee for airline tickets, but gives a clear breakdown of fees and taxes before you book.
Priceline.com	www.priceline.com	a discounter that also allows bidding.
Travel.com	www.travel.com	allows you to compare its rates with those of other booking engines.
Travelocity	www.travelocity.com	charges a booking fee for airline tickets, but promises good problem resolution.

ONLINE ACCOMMODATIONS

Hotelbook.com	www.hotelbook.com	focuses on independent hotels worldwide.
Hotel Club	www.hotelclub.net	good for major cities worldwide.
Hotels.com	www.hotels.com	a big Expedia-owned wholesaler that offers rooms in hotels all over the world.
Quikbook	www.quikbook.com	offers "pay when you stay" reservations that let you settle your bill at checkout, not when you book.

OTHER RESOURCES

Bidding For Travel	www.biddingfortravel.com	a good place to figure out what you can get and for how much before you start bidding on, say, Priceline.

A top-notch agent planning your trip may get you a room upgrade or a resort food and beverage credit; the one booking your cruise may arrange to have a bottle of champagne chilling in your cabin when you embark. And complain about the surcharges all you like, but when things don't work out the way you'd hoped, it's nice to have an agent to put things right.

■TIP➔ Remember that Expedia, Travelocity, and Orbitz are travel agents, not just booking engines. To resolve any problems with a reservation made through these companies, contact them first.

If this is your first visit to the Big Island, a travel agent or vacation packager specializing in Hawai'i can be extremely helpful in planning a memorable vacation. Not only do they have knowledge of the destination, but they can save you money by packaging the costs of airfare, hotel, activities, and car rental. In addition, many of the Hawai'i travel agents may offer added values or special deals when you book a package with them. The Hawai'i Visitors & Convention Bureau provides a list of member travel agencies and tour operators.

Agent Resources American Society of Travel Agents (☎ 703/739–2782 ⊕ www.astanet.com).

Hawai'i Travel Agents AA Vacations (☎ 800/321–2121 ⊕ www.aavacations.com). **AAA Travel** (☎ 800/436–4222 ⊕ www.aaa.com). **All About Hawaii** (☎ 800/274–8687 ⊕ www.allabouthawaii.com). **Continental Airlines Vacations** (☎ 800/301–3800 ⊕ www.covacations.com). **Delta Vacations** (☎ 800/654–6559 ⊕ www.deltavacations.com). **Flying Dutchmen Travel** (☎ 800/514–5194 ⊕ www.flyingdutchmentravel.com). **Funjet Vacations** (☎ 888/558–6654 ⊕ www.funjet.com). **Hello Hawai'i** (☎ 800/809–9844 ⊕ www.hellohawaii.com). **Incredible Journey Travel** (☎ 888/729–6899 ⊕ www.incredible-journey.net). **Travel Hawai'i** (☎ 888/373–2422 ⊕ www.travel-hawaii.com). **United Vacations**

(☎ 800/699–6122 ⊕ www.unitedvacations.com).

▌ AIRLINE TICKETS

Most domestic airline tickets are electronic; international tickets may be either electronic or paper. With an e-ticket the only thing you receive is an e-mail receipt citing your itinerary and reservation and ticket numbers. The greatest advantage of an e-ticket is that if you lose your receipt, you can simply print out another copy or ask the airline to do it for you at check-in. You usually pay a surcharge (up to $50) to get a paper ticket, if you can get one at all.

Check local and community newspapers when you're on the Big Island for deals and coupons on interisland flights, should you wish to visit neighboring islands. go! Airlines, Hawaiian Airlines, Island-Air, Mokulele Airlines and PW Express offer regular service between the islands. In addition to offering very competitive rates and online specials, all have free frequent-flier programs which will entitle you to rewards and upgrades the more you fly. Be sure to compare prices offered by all of the interisland carriers. If you are somewhat flexible with your dates and times for island-hopping, you should have no problem getting a very affordable round-trip ticket.

nterisland Carriers **go! Airlines**
(☎888/435–9462 ⊕www.iflygo.com). **Hawaiian Airlines** (☎800/367–5320 ⊕www.
hawaiianair.com). **IslandAir** (☎800/652–6541
⊕www.islandair.com). **Mokulele Airlines**
(☎808/326–7070 ⊕www.mokuleleairlines.
com). **PW Express** (☎888/866–5022 ⊕www.
flypwx.com).

CHARTER FLIGHTS

In addition to its regular service between
the Big Island and Maui, Mokulele Airlines also provides charter service from
the Kona airport to Maui, Moloka'i and
Lāna'i. In business since 1998, the Kona-
based company also offers air tours of the
Big Island. Pacific Wings offers a variety
of charter options at the Hilo, Kamuela, and Kona airports and also serves
Lāna'i, Maui, Moloka'i, and O'ahu. Services include premiere (same-day depar-
tures on short notice), premium (24-hour
notice), priority (48-hour notice), group,
and cargo/courier. The company also has
a frequent-flier program. The cost of a
round-trip between Honolulu and Kamuela purchased in advance through the
company's Web site is about $600.

Paragon Air offers 24-hour private charter service to and from the Hilo, Kamuela,
and Kona airports. In business since 1980,
the company prides itself on its perfect
safety record and has served a number of
celebrities including Bill Gates, Michael
Douglas, and Kevin Costner, among others. You can arrange a customized tour
of the Big Island or neighboring islands,
as well as air service from any airport in
Hawai'i. Charter prices start at $475.

Charter Companies Mokulele Airlines
(☎808/326–7070 ⊕www.mokuleleairlines.
com). **Pacific Wings** (☎888/575–4546
⊕www.pacificwings.com). **Paragon Air**
(☎800/428–1231 ⊕www.paragon-air.com).

▌RENTAL CARS

Should you plan to do any sightseeing
on the Big Island, it is best to rent a car
due to the size of the island. With more
than 260 mi of coastline—and attractions as varied as the Hawai'i Volcanoes
National Park, 'Akaka Falls State Park,
and Pu'ukoholā Heiau National Historic
Site—ideally you should split up your
stay between the east and west coasts of
the island. Even if all you want to do is
relax at your resort, you may want to hop
in the car to check out one of the island's
popular restaurants.

While on the Big Island, you can rent anything from an econobox to a Ferrari to a
motor home. Rates are usually better if
you reserve though a rental agency's Web
site. It's wise to make reservations far in
advance and make sure that a confirmed
reservation guarantees you a car, especially if visiting during peak seasons or
for major conventions or sporting events.
It's not uncommon to find several car
categories sold out during major events
on the island like the Merrie Monarch
Festival in Hilo in April or the Ironman
Triathlon World Championship in Kailua-Kona in October. ▌TIP➔ If you're
planning on driving to the 13,796-foot summit of Mauna Kea for stargazing, you'll need
a four-wheel drive vehicle. Harper Car and
Truck Rental, with offices in Hilo and
Kona, is a good source for 4x4 vehicles.

For some, renting an RV or motor home
might be an appealing way to see the
island. Harper's has motor homes available and Imua Camper Company rents
out Volkswagon Westfalia camping vans.
And if exploring the island on two wheels
is more your speed, Kona Harley-David-
son rents motorcycles.

Rates begin at about $25 to $35 a day
for an economy car with air-conditioning,
automatic transmission, and unlimited
mileage. This does not include the airport
concession fee, general excise tax, rental
vehicle surcharge, or vehicle license fee.

Car Rental Resources

AUTOMOBILE ASSOCIATIONS		
American Automobile Association	☎ 315/797–5000	⊕ www.aaa.com
National Automobile Club	☎ 650/294–7000	⊕ www.thenac.com; CA residents only
LOCAL AGENCIES		
AA Aloha Cars-R-Us	☎ 800/655–7989	⊕ www.hawaiicarrental.com
Discount Hawaii Car Rentals	☎ 888/292–3307	⊕ www.discounthawaiicarrental.com
Harper Car and Truck Rental (Big Island)	☎ 800/852–9993	⊕ www.harpershawaii.com
Hawaiian Discount Car Rentals	☎ 800/882–9007	⊕ www.hawaiidrive-o.com
Imua Camper Company		⊕ www.imua-tour.com
Kona Harley-Davidson	☎ 866/326–9887	⊕ www.hawaiiharleyrental.com
MAJOR AGENCIES		
Alamo	☎ 800/462–5266	⊕ www.alamo.com
Avis	☎ 800/331–1212	⊕ www.avis.com
Budget	☎ 800/527–0700	⊕ www.budget.com
Hertz	☎ 800/654–3131	⊕ www.hertz.com
National Car Rental	☎ 800/227–7368	⊕ www.nationalcar.com
Thrifty	☎ 800/847–4389	⊕ www.thrifty.com

When you reserve a car, ask about cancellation penalties and drop-off charges should you plan to pick up the car in one location and return it to another. Many rental companies in Hawai'i offer coupons for discounts at various attractions that could save you money later on in your trip.

In Hawai'i you must be 21 years of age to rent a car and you must have a valid driver's license and a major credit card. Those under 25 will pay a daily surcharge of $15–$25. Request car seats and extras such as GPS when you book. Hawai'i's Child Restraint Law requires that all children three years and younger be in an approved child safety seat in the backseat of a vehicle. Children ages four to seven must be seated in a rear booster seat or child restraint such as a lap and shoulder belt. Car seats and boosters range from $5 to $8 per day.

In Hawai'i, a valid mainland driver's license is valid for rental for up to 90 days.

Since the road circling the Big Island is mostly two lanes, be sure to allow plenty of time to return your vehicle so that you can make your flight. Traffic can be bad during morning and afternoon rush hour, especially in the Kona area. Give yourself about 3½ hours before departure time to return your vehicle.

CAR-RENTAL INSURANCE

Everyone who rents a car wonders whether the insurance that the rental companies offer is worth the expense. No one—including us—has a simple answer. It all depends on how much regular insurance you have, how comfortable you are with risk, and whether or not money is an issue.

If you own a car and carry comprehensive car insurance for both collision and liability, your personal auto insurance will probably cover a rental, but read your policy's fine print to be sure. If you don't have auto insurance, then you should probably buy the collision- or loss-damage waiver (CDW or LDW) from the rental company. This eliminates your liability for damage to the car. Some credit cards offer CDW coverage, but it's usually supplemental to your own insurance and rarely covers SUVs, minivans, luxury models, and the like. If your coverage is secondary, you may still be liable for loss-of-use costs from the car-rental company (again, read the fine print). But no credit-card insurance is valid unless you use that card for *all* transactions, from reserving to paying the final bill.

■ TIP→ Diners Club offers primary CDW coverage on all rentals reserved and paid for with the card. This means that Diners Club's company—not your own car insurance—pays in case of an accident. It doesn't mean that your car-insurance company won't raise your rates once it discovers you had an accident.

You may also be offered supplemental liability coverage; the car-rental company is required to carry a minimal level of liability coverage insuring all renters, but it's rarely enough to cover claims in a really serious accident if you're at fault. Your own auto-insurance policy will protect you if you own a car; if you don't, you have to decide whether you are willing to take the risk.

U.S. rental companies sell CDWs and LDWs for about $15 to $25 a day; supplemental liability is usually more than $10 a day. The car-rental company may offer you all sorts of other policies, but they're rarely worth the cost. Personal accident insurance, which is basic hospitalization coverage, is an especially egregious rip-off if you already have health insurance.

■ TIP→ You can decline the insurance from the rental company and purchase it through a third-party provider such as Travel Guard (⊕ www.travelguard.com)—$9 per day for $35,000 of coverage. That's sometimes just under half the price of the CDW offered by some car-rental companies.

■ VACATION PACKAGES

Packages *are not* guided excursions. Packages combine airfare, accommodations, and perhaps a rental car or other extras (theater tickets, guided excursions, boat trips, reserved entry to popular museums, transit passes), but they let you do your own thing. During busy periods packages may be your only option, as flights and rooms may be sold out otherwise. Packages will definitely save you time. They can also save you money, particularly in peak seasons, but—and this is a really big "but"—you should price each part of the package separately to be sure. And be aware that prices advertised on Web sites and in newspapers rarely include service charges or taxes, which can up your costs by hundreds of dollars.

■ TIP→ Some packages and cruises are sold only through travel agents. Don't always assume that you can get the best deal by booking everything yourself.

Each year consumers are stranded or lose their money when packagers—even large ones with excellent reputations—go out of business. How can you protect yourself? First, always pay with a credit card; if you have a problem, your credit-card company may help you resolve it.

Second, buy trip insurance that covers default. Third, choose a company that belongs to the United States Tour Operators Association, whose members must set aside funds to cover defaults. Finally, choose a company that also participates in the Tour Operator Program of the American Society of Travel Agents (ASTA), which will act as mediator in any disputes. You can also check on the tour operator's reputation among travelers by posting an inquiry on one of the Fodors.com forums.

About half of the visitors to the Big Island travel on package tours. All of the wholesalers specializing in Hawai'i offer a range of packages from the low to the high end. Because of the volume of business they do, wholesalers typically have great deals. Combine that with their knowledge of the destination and wholesale packages to the Big Island make a lot of sense. However, shop around and compare before you book to make sure you are getting a good deal.

Organizations American Society of Travel Agents (*ASTA* ☎ *703/739–2782 or 800/965–2782* ⊕ *www.astanet.com*). **United States Tour Operators Association** (*USTOA* ☎ *212/599–6599* ⊕ *www.ustoa.com*).

Hawai'i Tour Operators American Express Vacations (☎ *800/528–4800* ⊕ *www.americanexpressvacations.com*). **Apple Vacations** (☎ *800/517–2000* ⊕ *www.applevacations.com*). **Classic Vacations** (☎ *800/635–1333* ⊕ *www.classicvacations.com*). **Creative Leisure** (☎ *800/413–1000* ⊕ *www.creativeleisure.com*). **Pleasant Holidays** (☎ *800/742–9244* ⊕ *www.pleasantholidays.com*).

■ TIP→ **Local tourism boards can provide information about lesser-known and small-niche operators that sell packages to only a few destinations.**

▌GUIDED TOURS

Guided tours are a good option when you don't want to do it all yourself. You travel along with a group (sometimes large, sometimes small), stay in prebooked hotels, eat with your fellow travelers (the cost of meals sometimes included in the price of your tour, sometimes not), and follow a schedule. But not all guided tours are an if-it's-Tuesday-this-must-be-Belgium experience. A knowledgeable guide can take you places that you might never discover on your own, and you may be pushed to see more than you would have otherwise.

Tours aren't for everyone, but they can be just the thing for first-time travelers to the Big Island or those who enjoy the group traveling experience. Whenever you book a guided tour, find out what's included and what isn't. A "land-only" tour includes all your travel (by bus, in most cases) in the destination, but not necessarily your flights to and from or even within it. Also, in most cases prices in tour brochures don't include fees and taxes. And remember that you'll be expected to tip your guide (in cash) at the end of the tour.

Globus has three Hawai'i itineraries that include the Big Island, one of which is an escorted cruise on Norwegian Cruise Lines' *Pride of America* that includes one day each in Kona and Hilo. Tauck Travel and Trafalgar offer several land-based Hawai'i itineraries that include two to three nights on the Big Island, depending on the tour. Both companies offer similar itineraries. Tauck offers seven- and 11-night multi-island tours with two and three nights on the Big Island, respectively, including a "Magical Hawai'i" trip for families. Trafalgar has seven-, nine-, 10-, and 12-night multi-island tours with two nights on the Big Island. In all cases, visits to Hawai'i Volcanoes National Park are included.

EscortedHawaiiTours.com, owned and operated by Atlas Cruises & Tours, sells more than a dozen Hawai'i trips ranging from seven to 12 nights operated by various guided tour companies including Globus, Tauck, and Trafalgar.

Recommended Companies **Atlas Cruises & Tours** (☎ 800/942–3301 ⊕ www.escorted hawaiitours.com). **Globus** (☎ 866/755–8581 ⊕ www.globusjourneys.com). **Tauck Travel** (☎ 800/788–7885 ⊕ www.tauck.com). **Trafalgar** (☎ 866/544–4434 ⊕ www.trafalgar.com).

SPECIAL-INTEREST TOURS

ADVENTURE STUDY

Want to discover the incredible geologic treasures of Kīlauea Volcano? If so, you'll want to book a tour with Volcano Discovery, a company founded by volcanologist Tom Pfeiffer and photographer Tobias Schorr in Germany in 2005. Along with Hawai'i geologic specialist Philip Ong, who lives on the Big Island, the company offers exciting expeditions for travelers who want to get an up-close look at Kīlauea. "Heartbeat of the Earth" is a 13-night study and walking tour where participants will spend four days learning all about Kīlauea Volcano, followed by further exploration of the island's many other natural highlights. "Kīlauea Volcano" is a five-night study tour of the geologic features of this amazing volcano. These tours can be scheduled at any time of the year for groups ranging from two to eight people. In addition, the company usually offers a fixed-date hiking and geology tour of the Big Island.

Contact **Volcano Discovery** (☎ 011/49–2241–2080175 [Germany] ⊕ www.volcano discovery.com).

ART

Whether you want to learn about Hawaiian arts, history and culture; astronomy, ecology or botany; or the geology of the Hawaiian volcanoes, Volcano Art Center can design a program for your group that utilizes the talents of local artists, scientists, performers, historians, park rangers, storytellers and guides. You choose the length of the vacation and the Art Center staff packages all of the components including transportation, accommodations, meals, field trips, hikes, demonstrations, entertainment, classes and lectures. The Art Center also features workshops and performances throughout the year that you may want to incorporate into your vacation.

Contact **Volcano Art Center** (☎ 866/967–7565 ⊕ www.volcanoartcenter.org).

BIKING

If you're a bicycling enthusiast, you've got exciting options on the Big Island. Bicycle Adventures has a seven-day Hawai'i tour and a six-day budget tour. You'll ride about 45 mi per day. Priced at about $2,900 per person, the Hawai'i tour incorporates biking, hiking, snorkeling, sailing, and whale-watching. The budget tour is priced at about $2,100 per person, and accommodations are in moderately priced hotels; only biking, hiking, and snorkeling are included. Both tour prices include accommodations, meals, snacks, maps, van support, guide, activity fees and park admissions, taxes, and gratuities. Bicycle rental, pre- or post-lodging, and singles supplements are extra.

WomanTours has a seven-night bike tour for women only that circumnavigates the entire island. Included in the $2,190 per person price are seven nights' accommodations (some triple occupancy rooms), some meals (five breakfasts, a picnic lunch, five dinners, and snacks), van support, and trained guides. Rental bikes and upgrades to single or double rooms are available for an additional cost.

Airfare must be purchased separately for these bike tours.

■TIP➔ Most airlines accommodate bikes as luggage, provided they're dismantled and boxed.

Contacts **Bicycle Adventures** (☎ *800/443–6060* ⊕ *www.bicycleadventures.com*). **WomanTours** (☎ *800/247–1444* ⊕ *www.womantours.com*).

BIRD-WATCHING

Hawai'i boasts more than 150 species of birds that live in the Hawaiian Islands. Field Guides has a three-island, 11-day guided bird-watching trip that focuses on endemic landbirds and specialty seabirds. While on the Big Island, birders will visit Hawai'i Volcanoes National Park, Hakalau Preserve and Mauna Kea to see forest birds including the Hawaiian hawk, Oma'o (Hawaiian thrush), nēnē (Hawaiian goose), Hawai'i Creeper, and the spectacular 'Akihi po'olā'au. Participants might also get a glimpse of the rare Palila, the only finch-like Hawaiian honeycreeper that remains on the main islands. The trip costs about $4,200 per person and includes accommodations, meals, ground transportation, interisland air, an eight-hour pelagic boat trip, and guided bird-watching excursions. Travelers must purchase their own airfare from/to their gateway city.

Victor Emanuel Nature Tours has two nine-day trips that include the Big Island. The guide for both tours is Bob Sundstrom, a skilled birder with a special interest in birdsong who has been leading birding tours in Hawai'i and other destinations since 1989. "Kaua'i and Hawai'i" is the theme of the March birding trip. Birders will see indigenous Hawaiian birds including the 'Amakihi, 'Apapane, 'Elepaio, and the comical scarlet 'I'iwi, as well as endemic birds such as the Ōma'o, Palila, and 'Ākepa honey creepers. Participants in the "Fall Hawai'i" birding trip will visit O'ahu, Kaua'i, and the Big Island in October. Birders will spend two nights at the Volcano House which is perched alongside the Kīlauea Caldera. "Kaua'i and Hawai'i" costs about $3,300/person and "Fall Hawai'i" is priced at about $4,000/person. Both trips include accommodations, meals, interisland air, ground transportation, and guided excursions. Travelers must purchase their own airline ticket from/to their gateway city.

Contacts **Field Guides** (☎ *800/728–4953* ⊕ *www.fieldguides.com*). **Victor Emanuel Nature Tours** (☎ *800/328–8368* ⊕ *www.ventbird.com*).

CULTURE

Elderhostel, a nonprofit educational travel organization which has been leading all-inclusive learning adventures around the world for more than 20 years, offers several land-only cultural and educational tours. *Big Island of Hawai'i: History, Volcanoes and Marine Life* is a 14-night tour presented in association with Lyman Mission House and Museum and the University of Hawaii-Hilo. You'll spend five nights in Hilo, five nights at Hawai'i Volcanoes National Park, and four nights in Kona learning about Hawaiian history, geology, star navigation, language, arts and crafts, and medicine from local cultural historians. You'll visit Rainbow and 'Akaka Falls, Waipi'o, orchid and macadamia nut factories, Pu'uhonua O Hōnaunau National Historic Park, Hulihe'e Palace, and Moku'aikaua Church—and you'll walk through rain forests, lava, and petroglyph fields. Visits to beaches and free time also are included. The cost of this tour starts at $2,631 per person and includes accommodations, meals, ground transportation, and admission fees.

"Big Island of Hawai'i Odyssey: Earth, Sky and Sea" is an 11-night tour designed for children ages nine to 12 accompanied by an adult. Highlights include Hawaiian storytelling, an astronomy presentation at the Onizuka Visitor Center at Mauna Kea, horseback riding in Waimea, and a hike to a black-sand beach, among others. Prices start at $1,956 per person.

The Big Island also is included in several multi-island tours; check out the Elderhostel Web site for information.

Contacts **Elderhostel** (☎ *800/454–5768* ⊕ *www.elderhostel.org*).

CULINARY

"A Taste of Paradise: Hawaiian Style" to the Big Island (three nights each in Kīlauea and Kona) and Maui is another land-only Elderhostel tour. Travelers will wander the stalls of the Hilo Farmers Market where they'll find exotic fresh fruit like rambutan, soursop, jackfruit, and jaboticaba; vegetables such as hydroponic lettuce, organic spinach, eggplant, and baby ginger; anthuriums, protea, bonsai plants, herbs, and orchids; locally made crafts and gift items including Hawaiian hardwood bowls, clothing, and shell jewelry; and specialty food items such as dried fish, breads and pastries, jams, and jellies (including the incredibly delicious 'ōhi'a berry jam). There are visits to banana, papaya, coffee, cocoa, salad greens, vanilla, and anthurium farms, as well as the macadamia nut factory.

Contacts **Elderhostel** (☎ *800/454–5768* ⊕ *www.elderhostel.org*).

ECO TOURS

Hawai'i Forest & Trail's mission is to educate, inspire, and entertain visitors. For the past 15 years, the company has showcased the island's amazing diversity with adventures to waterfalls, rain forests, nature preserves, Mauna Kea and Hawai'i Volcanoes National Park. In 2006, Hawai'i Forest & Trail was awarded Ecotour Operator of the Year by the Hawai'i Ecotourism Association. The company can customize a multiday adventure tour for your group, including everything from caving in lava tubes and hiking to a secluded waterfall for a private picnic lunch to marveling at the nighttime lava flow of Kīlauea. Prices vary depending on activities chosen and size of group.

Want to hike and paddle on the Big Island? Since 1992, Betsy Morrigan has been guiding multisport adventure tours on the Big Island. The **Hawai'i Pack and**

Paddle camping trips showcase the entire island and are billed as "low-key and relaxing." All guides are lifeguards and certified in first aid and CPR. There is a guided four-day kayak/hiking trip suitable for beginners to advanced hikers that features three nights at B&Bs in Kona and in Hawai'i Volcanoes National Park. Included in the price ($300 per day per person, for four days; children ages six to 12 are half price) are kayak and group camping equipment, lightweight sleeping gear, food, tents, snorkel gear, and guide services. A seven-day adventure that includes two nights camping and four nights in a B&B is also available. Airfare is extra with both tours. Morrigan, a college professor of Hawaiian literature, also offers seven- to 10-day specialized educational tours for teachers to earn graduate credits. She can also custom design a tour program for your group.

"Under Hawaiian Skies: Big Island Adventure" is the theme of an eight-night trip sponsored by **Sierra Club Outings.** Highlights include swimming, snorkeling, and kayaking along the Kona coast; exploring Hawai'i Volcanoes National Park by hiking through crater trails, lava tubes, and rain forests, attending a "Star Party" at the Onizuka Center for International Astronomy located at the 9,300-foot level of Mauna Kea; touring 'Imiloa Astronomy Center in Hilo; and watching the 4th of July fireworks over Hilo Bay. Participants will also have opportunities to discover the uniqueness of Hawai'i's cultural heritage as they learn the hula and other ancient Hawaiian games; weave with coconut palm fronts; ride outrigger canoes; make a Hawaiian instrument; and taste traditional Hawaiian foods. Priced at around $1,600 per person, the tour includes accommodations, most meals, activities, and ground transportation.

Travelers must purchase their own airfare between the Big Island and their gateway city for all these tours.

Contacts **Hawai'i Forest & Trail**
(☎ 800/464–1993 ⊕ www.hawaii-forest.com).
Hawai'i Pack and Paddle (☎ 808/328–8911
⊕ www.hawaiipackandpaddle.com). **Sierra
Club Outings** (☎ 415/977–5522 ⊕ www.
sierraclub.org/outings).

HIKING

Sierra Club Outings offers a seven-night, hotel-based hiking tour, "Day Hikes & Creature Comforts." Off-the-beaten-path adventurers will explore many of the same trails once walked by ancient Hawaiians, beaches frequented by green sea turtles, rain forests, taro fields, extinct craters and vast lava fields. Participants will assist in a conservation activity and help prepare meals using fresh, local ingredients. The trip is designed for travelers who hike on a regular basis, as each day the group will log anywhere from four to eight miles. Priced at about $1,500 per person, the tour includes accommodations, most meals, ground transportation and activities.

"Hawai'i Three Island Hiker" is a seven-night hiking tour to the Big Island, Kaua'i, Maui. Included in the per person price of about $3,300 are accommodations, meals, interisland air between the islands, shuttle transportation, support vehicle, professional guides, a T-shirt, and water bottle. Hikers will spend two nights on the Big Island exploring Hawai'i Volcanoes National Park including hikes along the Crater Rim trail, which encircles Kīlauea's summit caldera; a coastline lava trail and into Kīlauea Iki crater. The trip is rated moderately easy to moderate. The World Outdoors has been organizing and leading adventure trips around the world for 20 years.

Timberline Adventures has a five-night hiking tour, "Hawai'i: Volcanoes & the Kailua-Kona Coast" designed to showcase the island's unique diversity. Highlights include hikes throughout Hawai'i Volcanoes National Park, Waipi'o Valley, Pu'uhonua O Hōnaunau, Captain Cook Trail, and along the coast from Miloli'i

to Aholi Holua, an ancient slide used by Hawaiians as a form of athletic competition. The trip costs about $2,200 per person and includes accommodations (three nights at Kilauea Lodge, and two nights at Outrigger Keauhou Beach Resort), meals, ground transportation, and activities.

Travelers must purchase their own airfare between the Big Island and their gateway city for all of these hiking tours.

Contact **Sierra Club Outings** (☎ 415/977–5522 ⊕ www.sierraclub.org/outings). **The World Outdoors** (☎ 800/488–8483 ⊕ www.theworldoutdoors.com). **Timberline Adventures** (☎ 800/417–2453 ⊕ www.timbertours.com).

WELLNESS

Licensed massage therapist Nancy Kahalewai leads retreats on the art of *lomi lomi* massage. This traditional Hawaiian massage uses kneading and gliding strokes to increase circulation, soothe nerves and loosen muscle tissue. And, because it is also designed to improve energy levels in the recipient by encouraging *pono* (righteous emotions and thoughts), it is considered a holistic treatment. The author of *Hawaiian Lomilomi, Big Island Massage,* and the former director of two massage, Kahalewai has been teaching massage therapy on the island since 1976.

Organic fitness trainer KeibaDawn Blacklidge owns and operates "BodyTemple Boot Camp: A Metamorphosis Program designed to Create and Manifest the Ultimate Ideal Live Body Life Force!" Designed to strengthen body, mind, and spirit, BodyTemple Boot Camp is a six-night customized program for one to three people priced at $1,000–$1,500 per week. Blacklidge has more than 20 years of fitness training experience and has competed and placed in several natural bodybuilding competitions. The program includes eco-cabin lodging; daily meals and snacks (participants choose either a raw vegan, raw non-vegan, or fruitarian meal plan); daily personal fitness sessions and outdoor adventures; three massages and yoga sessions; and airport shuttle transportation.

Yoga practioners might want to book one of the *"Nai'a"* (dolphin) retreats offered by The Lotus Way. Certified instructor Heather George has been teaching yoga for more than 15 years. Held at a private home alongside Kealakekua Bay, the retreats include six-night accommodations, daily yoga and meditation sessions, most meals, and free time for snorkeling, kayaking, and other activities. Rates are dependent on the size and needs of the group. George also can facilitate workshops in the healing art of Thai yoga therapy at Ramashala, a Balinese-inspired vacation retreat in the Puna district, across from the black-sand Kehena Beach.

Ramashala also can create customized group fitness and body tonics programs for families and groups. With its lush, tropical gardens and architecture that combines Asian and Eastern influences, Ramashala is ideal for vacationers seeking a luxurious, peaceful, and healthy getaway. There is an in-house vegetarian chef with more than 20 years experience as a personal chef, restaurant owner, and cookbook author.

Yoga Oasis, a solar-powered eco-retreat located in a rain forest five miles from the village of Pahoa on the Big Island's eastern tip, offers a number of yoga retreats. Prices vary depending on the retreats selected, but all include accommodations, meals, and yoga/workshop sessions.

Travelers must purchase their own airfare between the Big Island and their gateway city.

Contacts Big Island Massage (☎ *808/640–5755* ⊕ *www.bigislandmassage.com*). **Body-Temple Boot Camp** (☎ *808/965-9394* ⊕ *www.bodytemplebootcamp.com*). **The Lotus Way** (☎ *970/209-6723* ⊕ *www.thelotusway. org*). **Ramashala** (☎ *808/965-0068* ⊕ *www. ramashala.com*). **Yoga Oasis** (☎ *800/274-4446* ⊕ *www.yogaoasis.com*).

TRANSPORTATION

▌ BY AIR

Flying time to the Big Island is about 10 hours from New York, eight hours from Chicago, five hours from Los Angeles, and 15 hours from London, not including layovers. Some of the major airline carriers serving Hawai'i fly direct to the Big Island, allowing you to bypass connecting flights out of Honolulu. For the more spontaneous traveler, island-hopping is easy; flights depart every 20 to 30 minutes daily until mid-evening.

Although the Big Island's airports are smaller and more casual than Honolulu International, during peak times they can also be quite busy. Allot extra travel time to all airports during morning and afternoon rush-hour traffic periods. Plan to arrive at the airport 45 to 60 minutes before departure for interisland flights.

Plants and plant products are subject to regulation by the Department of Agriculture, both on entering and leaving Hawai'i. Upon leaving the Islands, you'll have to have your bags X-rayed and tagged at one of the airport's agricultural inspection stations before you proceed to check-in. Pineapples and coconuts with the packer's agricultural inspection stamp pass freely; papayas must be treated, inspected, and stamped. All other fruits are banned for export to the U.S. mainland. Flowers pass except for gardenia, rose leaves, jade vine, and mauna loa. Also banned are insects, snails, soil, cotton, cacti, sugarcane, and all berry plants.

You'll have to leave dogs and other pets at home. A 120-day quarantine is imposed to keep out rabies, which is non-existent in Hawai'i. If specific pre- and post-arrival requirements are met, animals may qualify for a 30-day or five-day-or-less quarantine.

Airlines & Airports **Airline and Airport Links.com** (⊕ *www.airlineandairportlinks.com*) has links to many of the world's airlines and airports.

Airline Security Issues **Transportation Security Administration** (⊕ *www.tsa.gov*) has answers for almost every question that might come up.

Air Travel Resources in Hawai'i **State of Hawai'i Airports Division Offices** (☎ *808/836–6417* ⊕ *www.hawaii. gov/dot/airports*).

AIRPORTS

Honolulu International Airport (HNL) is the main stopover for most domestic and international flights. From Honolulu, there are departing interisland flights to the Big Island departing regularly from early morning until evening. Some carriers now offer nonstop service directly from the Mainland to the Kona International Airport at Keāhole (KOA) and Hilo International Airport (ITO) on a limited basis. Like all of Hawai'i's airports, the two Big Island airports are "open-air," meaning you can enjoy those trade-wind breezes until the moment you step on the plane.

HONOLULU/O'AHU AIRPORT

Hawai'i's major airport is Honolulu International, on O'ahu, 20 minutes (9 mi) west of Waikīkī. To travel to the Big Island from Honolulu, you can depart from either the interisland terminal or the commuter-airline terminal, located in two separate structures adjacent to the main overseas terminal building. A free bus service, the Wiki Wiki Shuttle, operates between terminals.

Information **Honolulu International Airport (HNL)** (☎ *808/836–6413* ⊕ *www.hawaii. gov/dot/airports*).

BIG ISLAND AIRPORTS

Those flying to the Big Island of Hawai'i regularly land at one of two fields. Kona International Airport at Keāhole, on the west side, best serves Kailua-Kona, Keauhou, and the Kohala Coast. There are two Visitor Information Program (VIP) booths located at baggage claims A and B to assist travelers at the Kona International Airport. Additionally, there are news and lei stands, Maxwell's Landing restaurant and a gift shop.

Hilo International Airport is more appropriate for those going to the east side of the island. Here, visitors will find VIP booths across from the Centerplate Coffee Shop & Lounge near the departure lobby and in the arrival areas at each end of the terminal. In addition to the coffee shop, services include a Bank of Hawai'i automatic teller machine, gift shop, and news and lei stands. Waimea-Kohala Airport, called Kamuela Airport by residents, is used primarily for commuting among the Islands.

Information **Hilo International Airport (ITO)** (☎808/934–5838). **Kona International Airport at Keāhole (KOA)** (☎808/329–3423). **Waimea-Kohala Airport (MUE)** (☎808/887–8126).

GROUND TRANSPORTATION

Only Arnott's Lodge and the Hawai'i Naniloa Hotel provide airport shuttles to and from the Hilo International Airport. If you're not renting a car, you'll need to take a taxi. There are 13 taxi companies serving the Hilo Airport. The approximate taxi rate is $3 flip, plus $.30 every ⅛ mile, with surcharges for waiting time at $.30 per minute and $1 per bag. Cab fares to locations around the island are estimated as follows: Banyan Drive hotels $11, Hilo town $12, Hilo Pier $13, Volcano $75, Kea'au $22, Pahoa $50, Honoka'a $105, Kamuela/Waimea $148, Waikoloa $188, and Kailua town $240.

At the Kona International Airport, Speedi-Shuttle offers transportation between the airport and hotels, resorts, and condominium complexes from Waimea to Keauhou. There is an online reservation and fare quote system for information and bookings.

Contacts **SpeediShuttle** (☎877/242–5777 ⊕ www.speedishuttle.com).

FLIGHTS

Airline Contacts **America West/US Airways** (☎800/428–4322 ⊕ www.usairways.com). **American Airlines** (☎800/433–7300 ⊕ www.aa.com). **Continental Airlines** (☎800/523—3273 for U.S. and Mexico reservations, 800/231–0856 for international reservations ⊕ www.continental.com). **Delta Airlines** (☎800/221–1212 for U.S. reservations ⊕ www.delta.com). **Hawaiian Airlines** (☎800/367–5320 ⊕ www.hawaiianair.com). **Northwest Airlines** (☎800/225–2525 ⊕ www.nwa.com). **Southwest Airlines** (☎800/435–9792 ⊕ www.southwest.com). **United Airlines** (☎800/864–8331 for U.S. reservations, 800/538–2929 for international reservations ⊕ www.united.com).

Interisland Flights **go! Airlines** (☎888/434–5946 ⊕ www.iflygo.com). **Hawaiian Airlines** (☎800/367–5320 ⊕ www.hawaiianair.com). **Island Air** (☎800/652–6541 ⊕ www.islandair.com). **PW Express** (☎888/866–5022 ⊕ www.flypwx.com). **Pacific Wings** (☎888/575–4546 ⊕ www.pacific-wings.com). **Paragon Airlines** (☎800/428–1231 ⊕ www.paragon-air.com).

FOR INTERNATIONAL TRAVELERS

CURRENCY

The dollar is the basic unit of U.S. currency. It has 100 cents. Coins are the penny (1¢); the nickel (5¢), dime (10¢), quarter (25¢), half-dollar (50¢), and the very rare golden $1 coin and even rarer silver $1. Bills are denominated $1, $5, $10, $20, $50, and $100, all mostly green and identical in size; designs and background tints vary. You may come across a $2 bill, but the chances are slim.

CUSTOMS

Information **U.S. Customs and Border Protection** (⊕ *www.cbp.gov*).

DRIVING

Gas costs range from $2.50 to $3.50 a gallon.

Driving in the United States is on the right. Speed limits are posted in miles per hour (usually 50–55 mph on major highways). Watch for lower limits in small towns and on back roads (usually 30–40 mph). Most states require front-seat passengers to wear seat belts; many states require children to sit in the backseat and to wear seat belts. In major cities rush hour is between 7 and 10 AM; afternoon rush hour is between 4 and 7 PM.

Highways are well paved.

Gas stations are fairly far apart and those in rural towns may close early, especially on Sundays. If your car breaks down on the highway, pull onto the shoulder and wait for help, or have your passengers wait while you walk to an emergency phone (available in most states). If you carry a cell phone, dial *55, noting your location on the small green roadside mileage marker.

ELECTRICITY

The U.S. standard is AC, 110 volts/60 cycles. Plugs have two flat pins set parallel to each other.

EMBASSIES

Contacts **Australia** (☎ *202/797-3000* ⊕ *www.austemb.org*). **Canada** (☎ *202/682–* *1740* ⊕ *www.canadianembassy.org*). **United Kingdom** (☎ *202/588-7800* ⊕ *www.britainusa.com*).

EMERGENCIES

For police, fire, or ambulance, dial 911 (0 in rural areas).

HOLIDAYS

New Year's Day (Jan. 1); Martin Luther King Day (3rd Mon. in Jan.); Presidents' Day (3rd Mon. in Feb.); Memorial Day (last Mon. in May); Independence Day (July 4); Labor Day (1st Mon. in Sept.); Columbus Day (2nd Mon. in Oct.); Thanksgiving Day (4th Thurs. in Nov.); Christmas Eve and Christmas Day (Dec. 24 and 25); and New Year's Eve (Dec. 31).

MAIL

You can buy stamps and aerograms and send letters and parcels in post offices. Stamp-dispensing machines can occasionally be found in airports, bus and train stations, office buildings, drugstores, and convenience stores. U.S. mailboxes are stout, dark blue steel bins; pickup schedules are posted inside the bin (pull down the handle to see them). Parcels weighing more than a pound must be mailed at a post office or at a private mailing center.

Within the United States a first-class letter weighing 1 ounce or less costs 41¢; each additional ounce costs 17¢ up to 3.5 ounces. Postcards cost 26¢. A 1-ounce airmail letter or postcard to most countries costs 90¢, a 1-ounce letter or postcard to Canada or Mexico costs 69¢.

To receive mail on the road, have it sent c/o General Delivery at your destination's main post office (use the correct five-digit ZIP code). You must pick up mail in person within 30 days, with a driver's license or passport for identification.

Contacts **DHL** (☎ *800/225-5345* ⊕ *www.dhl.com*). **Federal Express** (☎ *800/463–3339* ⊕ *www.fedex.com*). **Mail Boxes, Etc./The UPS Store** (☎ *800/789-4623* ⊕ *www.*

mbe.com). **United States Postal Service**
(⊕ *www.usps.com*).

PASSPORTS & VISAS

Visitor visas aren't necessary for citizens of
Australia, Canada, the United Kingdom, or
most citizens of European Union countries
coming for tourism and staying for fewer
than 90 days. If you require a visa, the cost
is $100, and waiting time can be substantial,
depending on where you live. Apply for a
visa at the U.S. consulate in your place of
residence; check the U.S. State Department's
special Visa Web site for further information.

Visa Information **Destination USA**
(⊕ *www.unitedstatesvisas.gov*).

PHONES

Numbers consist of a three-digit area code
and a seven-digit local number. The area
code for all calls within the state of Hawai'i
is 808. Within many local calling areas you
dial only the seven digits; in others you dial
"1" first and all 10 digits—just as you would
for calls between area-code regions. The
same is true for calls to numbers prefixed by
"800," "888," "866," and "877"—all toll free.
For calls to numbers prefixed by "900" you
must pay—usually dearly.

For international calls, dial "011" followed by
the country code and the local number. For
help, dial "0" and ask for an overseas operator. Most phone books list country codes and
U.S. area codes. The country code for Australia is 61, for New Zealand 64, for the United
Kingdom 44. Calling Canada is the same as
calling within the United States, whose country code, by the way, is 1.

For operator assistance, dial "0." For directory
assistance, call 555–1212 or occasionally
411 (free at many public phones). You can
reverse long-distance charges by calling
"collect"; dial "0" instead of "1" before the
10-digit number.

Instructions are generally posted on pay
phones. Usually you insert coins in a slot

(usually 25¢–50¢ for local calls) and wait
for a steady tone before dialing. On long-
distance calls the operator tells you how
much to insert; prepaid phone cards, widely
available in various denominations, can be
used from any phone. Follow the directions
to activate the card (there's usually an access
number, then an activation code), then dial
your number.

CELL PHONES

The United States has several GSM (Global
System for Mobile Communications) networks, so multiband mobiles from most
countries (except for Japan) work here.
Unfortunately, it's almost impossible to buy
a pay-as-you-go mobile SIM card in the
U.S.—which allows you to avoid roaming
charges—without also buying a phone. That
said, cell phones with pay-as-you-go plans
are available for well under $100. AT&T, T-
Mobile and Virgin Mobile offer affordable,
pay-as-you-go service.

Contacts **AT&T** (☎ *800/331–0500* ⊕ *www.
att.com*). **T Mobile** (☎ *800/937–8997*
⊕ *www.t-mobile.com*). **Virgin Mobile** (☎ *No
phone* ⊕ *www.virginmobileusa.com*).

▌ BY BOAT

Superferry, a high-speed ferry service, now connects Oʻahu (Honolulu) and Maui daily, and at this writing service to the Big Island is scheduled to begin in 2009. Due to environmental concerns, service to Kauaʻi has been suspended.

Information **Hawaii Superferry** (☎877/443–3779 ⊕ www.hawaiisuperferry.com).

▌ BY BUS

Travelers can take advantage of the Hawaiʻi County Mass Transit Agency's free Hele-On Bus, which travels several routes throughout the island. A one-way journey between Hilo and Kona will take about four hours. There's regular service in and around downtown Hilo, Kailua-Kona, Waimea, North and South Kohala, Honokaʻa, and Pāhoa. There is a charge of $1 per piece for bicycles, luggage, and large backpacks that can't fit under a seat. Visitors staying in Hilo can take advantage of the Transit Agency's Shared Ride Taxi program which provides door-to-door transportation in the area. A one-way fare is $2 and a book of 15 coupons can be purchased for $30.

Information **Hele-On Bus** (☎808/961–8744 ⊕ www.co.hawaii.hi.us/mass_transit/transit_main.htm).

▌ BY CAR

Technically, the Big Island of Hawaiʻi is the only island you can completely circle by car, and driving is the best way to enjoy the sightseeing opportunities afforded by the miles of scenic roadway.

Instead of using compass directions, remember that Hawaiʻi residents refer to places as being either *mauka* (toward the mountains) or *makai* (toward the ocean) from one another. Hawaiʻi has a strict seat belt law. Those riding in the front seat must wear a seat belt and children under the age of 17 in the back seats must be belted. The fine for not wearing a seat belt is $92. Jaywalking is also very common in the islands so please pay careful attention to the roads, especially while driving in downtown Hilo, Kailua-Kona, and the smaller towns around the island.

GASOLINE

You can count on having to pay more at the pump for gasoline on the Big Island than on the U.S. mainland.

PARKING

Parking can be a challenge in downtown Kona. If you're willing to walk several blocks, you should be able to find free parking off Aliʻi Drive on some of the residential streets. Otherwise, there are municipal lots just off Aliʻi Drive with an honor system. You will be ticketed if you don't pay. In Hilo, there is a good availability of free parking.

ROAD CONDITIONS

It's difficult to get lost in most of Hawaiʻi. Roads and streets, although they may challenge the visitor's tongue, are well marked. Free publications containing good-quality road maps can be found on all Islands.

Roads on the Big Island are generally well-maintained and can be easily negotiated. Most of the roads are two-lane highways with limited shoulders—and yes, even in paradise, there is traffic, especially during the morning and afternoon rush hour. Unless you have a four-wheel drive vehicle, do not attempt Saddle Road between Hilo and Waimea; it's narrow, windy, and poor in many areas. Most rental car agencies do not allow driving on Saddle Road, and several companies make you sign a statement that you won't, even if you rent a four-wheel-drive vehicle.

Gas stations are fairly far apart and in rural areas it's not unusual for the stations to close early. If you see that your tank is getting low, don't take any chances; fill up when you see a station. In Hawaiʻi, turning right on a red light is legal, except where noted. Use caution during heavy downpours, especially if you see signs warning of falling rocks. The road to Ka Lae, the southernmost tip of the U.S., provides gorgeous views, but is narrow: if you're enjoying the views, pull over to the side.

ROADSIDE EMERGENCIES

If you find yourself in an emergency or accident while driving on the Big Island, pull over if you can. If you have a cell phone with you, call the roadside assistance number on your rental car contract or AAA Help. If you find that your car has been broken into or stolen, report it immediately to your rental car company and they can assist you. If it's an emergency and someone is hurt, call 911 immediately and stay there until medical personnel arrive.

Emergency Services **AAA Help** (☎ *800/222–4357*).

ON THE GROUND

▮ COMMUNICATIONS

INTERNET

If you've brought your laptop with you to the Big Island, you should have no problem checking e-mail or connecting to the Internet. Most of the major hotels and resorts offer high-speed access in rooms and/or lobbies. You should check with your hotel in advance to confirm that access is wireless; if not, ask whether in-room cables are provided. In some cases there will be an hourly or daily charge posted to your room. If you're staying at a small inn or B&B without Internet access, ask the proprietor for the nearest café or coffee shop with wireless access.

Contacts **Cybercafes** (⊕ www.cybercafes. com) lists over 4,000 Internet cafés worldwide. **JiWire** (⊕ www.jiwire.com) features a directory of Wi-Fi hotspots around the world.

CELLULAR PHONES

If you're taking your cell phone on vacation with you, make sure roaming is included; otherwise your minutes and bill will quickly add up. Prepaid phone cards are convenient and cost-effective.

▮ HEALTH

Hawai'i is known as the Health State. The life expectancy here is 79 years, the longest in the nation. Balmy weather makes it easy to remain active year-round, and the low-stress aloha attitude certainly contributes to general well-being. When visiting the Islands, however, there are a few health issues to keep in mind.

The Hawai'i State Department of Health recommends that you drink 16 ounces of water per hour to avoid dehydration when hiking or spending time in the sun. Use sunblock, wear UV-reflective sunglasses, and protect your head with a visor or hat for shade. If you're not acclimated to warm, humid weather you should allow plenty of time for rest stops and refreshments. When visiting freshwater streams, be aware of the tropical disease leptospirosis, which is spread by animal urine and carried into streams and mud. Symptoms include fever, headache, nausea, and red eyes. If left untreated it can cause liver and kidney damage, respiratory failure, internal bleeding, and even death. To avoid this, don't swim or wade in freshwater streams or ponds if you have open sores and don't drink from any freshwater streams or ponds.

On the Islands, fog is a rare occurrence, but there can often be "vog," an airborne haze of gases released from volcanic vents at Kīlauea. During certain weather conditions such as "Kona Winds," the vog can settle over the Islands and wreak havoc with respiratory and other health conditions, especially asthma or emphysema. If susceptible, stay indoors and get emergency assistance if needed.

The Islands have their share of bugs and insects that enjoy the tropical climate as much as visitors do. Most are harmless but annoying. When planning to spend time outdoors in hiking areas, wear long-sleeve clothing and pants and use mosquito repellent containing DEET. In very damp places you may encounter the dreaded local centipede. On the Islands they usually come in two colors, brown and blue, and they range from the size of a worm to an 8-inch cigar. Their sting is very painful, and the reaction is similar to bee- and wasp-sting reactions. When camping, shake out your sleeping bag before climbing in, and check your shoes in the morning, as the centipedes like cozy places. If planning on hiking or traveling in remote areas, always carry a first-aid kit and appropriate medications for sting reactions.

LOCAL DO'S & TABOOS

GREETINGS

Hawai'i is a very friendly place and this is reflected in the day-to-day encounters with friends, family, and even business associates. Women will often hug and kiss one another on the cheek and men will shake hands and sometimes combine that with a friendly hug. When a man and woman are greeting each other and are good friends, it is not unusual for them to hug and kiss on the cheek. Children are taught to call any elders "auntie" or "uncle," even if they aren't related. It's a way to show respect and can result in a local Hawai'i child having dozens of aunties or uncles. It's also reflective of the strong sense of family that exists in the Islands.

When you walk off a long flight, perhaps a bit groggy and stiff, nothing quite compares with a Hawaiian lei greeting. The casual ceremony ranks as one of the fastest ways to make the transition from the worries of home to the joys of your vacation. Though the tradition has created an expectation that everyone receives this floral garland when they step off the plane, the state of Hawai'i cannot greet each of its nearly seven million annual visitors.

If you've booked a vacation with a wholesaler or tour company, a lei greeting might be included in your package, so check before you leave. If not, it's easy to arrange a lei greeting for yourself or for your companions before you arrive. Contact Kama'āina Leis, Flowers & Greeters if you're arriving into Kona International Airport. To be really wowed by the experience, request a lei of plumeria, some of the most divine-smelling blossoms on the planet. A plumeria or dendrobium orchid lei are considered standard and cost $20/person. Hilo International Airport does not allow companies to provide lei greeting services, but there are lei vendors at the airport should you wish to purchase lei upon arrival.

Information Kama'āina Leis, Flowers & Greeters (☎800/367–5183 or 808/836–3246 ⊕www.alohaleigreetings.com).

LANGUAGE

Hawai'i was admitted to the Union in 1959, so residents can be sensitive when visitors refer to their own hometowns as "back in the States." Remember, when in Hawai'i, refer to the contiguous 48 states as "the Mainland" and not as the United States. When you do, you won't appear to be such a *malahini* (newcomer).

English is the primary language on the Islands. Making the effort to learn some Hawaiian words can be rewarding, however. Despite the length of many Hawaiian words, the Hawaiian alphabet is actually one of the world's shortest, with only 12 letters: the five vowels, *a, e, i, o, u,* and seven consonants, *h, k, l, m, n, p, w.* Hawaiian words you're most likely to encounter during your visit to the Islands are *aloha, mahalo* (thank you), *keiki* (child), *haole* (Caucasian or foreigner), *mauka* (toward the mountains), *makai* (toward the ocean), and *pau* (finished, all done). To learn even more Hawaiian words, visit ⊕*www. geocities.com/~olelo,* the Hawaiian language Web site.

Hawaiian history includes waves of immigrants, each bringing their own languages. To communicate with each other, they developed a sort of slang known as "pidgin." If you listen closely, you'll know what is being said by the inflections and by the extensive use of body language. For example, when you know what you want to say but don't know how to say it, just say "you know, da kine." For an informative and somewhat-hilarious view of things Hawaiian, check out Jerry Hopkins's series of books titled *Pidgin to the Max* and *Fax to the Max,* available at most local bookstores in the Hawaiiana sections.

■ HOURS OF OPERATION

Even people in paradise have to work. Generally local business hours are weekdays 8–5. Banks are usually open Monday–Thursday 8:30–3 and until 6 on Friday. Some banks have Saturday-morning hours.

Many self-serve gas stations stay open around-the-clock, with full-service stations usually open from around 7 AM until 9 PM. U.S. post offices are open weekdays 8:30 AM–4:30 PM and Saturday 8:30–noon.

Most museums generally open their doors between 9 AM and 10 AM and stay open until 5 PM Tuesday–Saturday. Many museums operate with afternoon hours only on Sunday and close on Monday. Visitor-attraction hours vary throughout the state, but most sights are open daily with the exception of major holidays such as Christmas. Check local newspapers upon arrival for attraction hours and schedules if visiting over holiday periods. The local dailies carry a listing of "What's Open/What's Not" for those time periods.

Stores in resort areas sometimes open as early as 8, with shopping-center opening hours varying from 9:30 to 10 on weekdays and Saturday, a bit later on Sunday. Bigger malls stay open until 9 weekdays and Saturday and close at 5 on Sunday. Boutiques in resort areas may stay open as late as 11.

ATMS & BANKS

Automatic teller machines for easy access to cash are everywhere on the Islands. ATMs can be found in shopping centers, small convenience and grocery stores, inside hotels and resorts, as well as outside most bank branches. For a directory of locations, call 800/424–7787 for the MasterCard/Cirrus/Maestro network or 800/843–7587 for the Visa/Plus network.

CREDIT CARDS

Throughout this guide, the following abbreviations are used: **AE**, American Express; **D**, Discover; **DC**, Diners Club; **MC**, MasterCard; and **V**, Visa.

It's a good idea to inform your credit-card company before you travel, especially if you're going abroad and don't travel internationally very often. Otherwise, the credit-card company might put a hold on your card owing to unusual activity—not a good thing halfway through your trip. Record all your credit-card numbers—as well as the phone numbers to call if your cards are lost or stolen—in a safe place, so you're prepared should something go wrong. Both MasterCard and Visa have general numbers you can call (collect if you're abroad) if your card is lost, but you're better off calling the number of your issuing bank, since MasterCard and Visa usually just transfer you to your bank; your bank's number is usually printed on your card.

Reporting Lost Cards American Express (☏ 800/528–4800 in the U.S., 336/393–1111 collect from abroad ⊕ www.american express.com). **Diners Club** (☏ 800/234–6377 in the U.S., 303/799–1504 collect from abroad ⊕ www.dinersclub.com). **Discover** (☏ 800/347–2683 in the U.S., 801/902–3100 collect from abroad ⊕ www.discovercard.com). **MasterCard** (☏ 800/622–7747 in the U.S., 636/722–7111 collect from abroad ⊕ www.mastercard.com). **Visa** (☏ 800/847–2911 in the U.S., 410/581–9994 collect from abroad ⊕ www.visa.com).

TRAVELER'S CHECKS

Some consider this the currency of the caveman, and it's true that fewer establishments accept traveler's checks these days. Nevertheless, they're a cheap and secure way to carry extra money, particularly on trips to urban areas. Both Citibank (under the Visa brand) and American Express issue traveler's checks in the United States, but Amex is better known and more widely accepted; you can also avoid hefty surcharges by cashing Amex checks at Amex offices. Whatever you do, keep track of all the serial numbers in case the checks are lost or stolen.

Contacts American Express (☎ 888/412–6945 in the U.S., 801/945–9450 collect outside of the U.S. to speak to customer service ⊕ www.americanexpress.com).

▌ SAFETY

Hawai'i is generally a safe tourist destination, but it's still wise to follow the same common sense safety precautions you would normally follow in your own hometown. Hotel and visitor-center staff can provide information should you decide to head out on your own to more remote areas. Rental cars are magnets for break-ins, so don't leave any valuables in the car, not even in a locked trunk. Avoid poorly lighted areas, beach parks, and isolated areas after dark as a precaution. When hiking, stay on marked trails, no matter how alluring the temptation might be to stray. Weather conditions can cause landscapes to become muddy, slippery, and tenuous, so staying on marked trails will lessen the possibility of a fall or getting lost.

Ocean safety is of the utmost importance when visiting an island destination. Don't swim alone, and follow the international signage posted at beaches that alerts swimmers to strong currents, man-of-war jellyfish, sharp coral, high surf, sharks, and dangerous shore breaks. At coastal lookouts along cliff tops, heed the signs indicating that waves can climb over the ledges. Check with lifeguards at each beach for current conditions, and if the red flags are up, indicating swimming and surfing are not allowed, don't go in. Waters that look calm on the surface can harbor strong currents and undertows, and not a few people who were just wading have been dragged out to sea.

Women traveling alone are generally safe on the Islands, but always follow the safety precautions you would use in any major destination. When booking hotels, request rooms closest to the elevator, and always keep your hotel-room door and balcony doors locked. Stay away from isolated areas after dark; camping and hiking solo are not advised. If you stay out late visiting nightclubs and bars, use caution when exiting night spots and returning to your lodging.

▌ TAXES

There's a 4.16% state sales tax on all purchases, including food. A hotel room tax of 7.25%, combined with the sales tax of 4%, equals an 11.41% rate added onto your hotel bill. A $3-per-day road tax is also assessed on each rental vehicle.

▌ TIME

Hawai'i is on Hawaiian Standard Time, five hours behind New York, two hours behind Los Angeles, and 10 hours behind London.

When the U.S. mainland is on daylight saving time, Hawai'i is not, so add an extra hour of time difference between the Islands and U.S. mainland destinations.

▌ TIPPING

Hawai'i is a major vacation destination and many of the people who work at the hotels and resorts rely on tips to supplement their wages, so tipping is common. Tip cabdrivers 15% of the fare. Standard tips at restaurants and spas run from 15% to 20% of the bill, depending on the quality of service; bartenders expect about $1 per drink. Bellhops at hotels usually received $1 per bag, more if you have bulky items like bicycles or surfboards. Tip the hotel maid $1 per night, paid daily. Tip doormen $1 to $5 for assistance with taxis, bags, or golf clubs; tips for concierges vary depending on the service.

INDEX

A

Aaah, The Views! ⊤, 237
Adriana's ✕, 214–215
Adventure study tours, 273
Aerial tours, 134, 136
Ahalanui Park, 73, 108
Ahu'ena Heiau, 47
Ahu Pohaku Ho'omaluhia
   Hawaii Island Eco Retreat
   ⊤, 235–236
'Ai'opio, 99
Air travel, 278–279
booking your trip, 268–269
carriers, 279
charter flights, 269
Airports, 12, 278–279
'Akaka Falls State Park, 83
Alan Wong's Hualalai Grille
   at the Four Seasons Resort
   Hualalai ✕, 195
Aloha Angel Cafe ✕, 213
Aloha Dive Company, 121–122
Aloha Guesthouse ⊤, 247
Aloha Vacation Cottages ⊤,
   237
'Alula, 100
Amy B. H. Greenwell Ethnobo-
   tanical Garden, 53
'Anaeho'omalu Beach (A-Bay),
   96
Antiques and Orchids, 164
Art galleries and museums
Hilo, 80
Volcano, 67
Waimea, 42
Art tours, 273
Astronomical facilities, 89
Atlantis VII Submarine, 129
ATMs, 286
ATV tours, 136–137

B

Ba-Le ✕, 209
Bamboo Restaurant ✕, 197
Bangkok House Thai Restau-
   rant ✕, 213
Banks, 286
Banyan Drive, 77, 78
Bars and lounges, 187–188
Bay House ⊤, 254
Beaches, 92
children's activities, 22, 108
Hāmākua Coast, 85–86
Hilo, 105, 107–108
Kailua-Kona, 99–102
Ka'u, 57, 64, 102–105

Kohala Coast, 92, 95–97, 99
safety concerns, 98, 100
South Kona, 102–105
Bears' Coffee ✕, 218
Bed & Breakfast Mountain
   View ⊤, 252
Bed and breakfasts, 222, 224
Hilo, 254–256
Kailua-Kona, 245–246
Kohala District, 235–236
South Kona, 247–248
Volcano, 250–251
Waimea, 237–238
Big Island Candies, 168
Big Island Country Club, 141
Big Island Grill ✕, 209
Big Island Pizza ✕, 219
Big Island Visitors Bureau, 77
Biking, 137–139, 273–274
Bird-watching, 274
Black Sand Beach, 64, 104–105
Blane's Drive-In ✕, 218
Boat and ferry travel, 282
Body Glove Cruises, 124
Bodysurfing, 112
Boogie boarding, 112
Booking your trip, 266–277
Boston Basil's ✕, 210
Brown's Beach House at the
   Fairmont Orchid Hawai'i
   ✕, 195
Bubba Gump Shrimp
   Company ✕, 205–206
Buddhist temples, 64
Burial mounds, 47
Bus travel, 282
Business hours, 286–287

C

Cabin rentals, 251
Café 100 ✕, 218
Café Pesto ✕, 193, 219
CanoeHouse at the Mauna
   Lani Bay Hotel & Bungalows
   ✕, 197
Cape Kumukahi Lighthouse,
   72–73
Captain Beans' Polynesian Din-
   ner Cruise, 178
Captain Cook Monument,
   49–50
Captain Dan McSweeney's
   Whale Watch, 131
Car rentals, 12, 269–271
Car travel, 280, 282–283
Carnival Cruises, 24

Casa de Emdeko ⊤, 242
Celebrity Cruises, 24
Cell phones, 281, 284
Chalet Kīlauea Collection ⊤,
   250
Chef Daniel's Seafood Café
   ✕, 205
Children and travel, 22–23
dining, 190, 218
lodging, 22, 225, 227, 230,
   239, 242, 251, 253
shopping, 166
Children's attractions
beaches, 95, 101–102, 107, 108
Hāmākua Coast, 85, 87
Hilo, 79
submarine tours, 129
Churches
Hilo, 78
Kailua-Kona, 47, 48
Puna, 74
South Kona, 53
Waimea, 42
Circle Island tours, 52
Climate, 16
Coast Grille at Hāpuna Beach
   Prince Hotel ✕, 195
Coconut Island, 78
Coffee cherries, 50
Coffee mills
Hilo, 78
South Kona, 54
Coffee Shack ✕, 50, 213
Colony One at Sea Mountain
   ⊤, 247
Condos and vacation rentals,
   235, 243, 245
Kailua-Kona, 242, 244–245
Kohala District, 233–235
South Kona, 247
Waimea, 237
Conservation concerns, 46
Cook, Capt. James, 49–50
Credit cards, 6, 286
Cruising, 24–25
Cuisine, 210
Culinary tours, 275
Culture tours, 274–275
Currency, 280
Customs, 280

D

Deep-sea fishing, 112–115
Dining
with children, 190, 218
dress, 190

Farm tours, 206
Fodor's choice, 191
Hāmākua Coast, 84–85
Hawai'i Volcanoes National
    Park, 63
Hilo, 78, 217–220
hours, 190
Kailua-Kona, 44, 47–48,
    205–206, 208–213
Ka'u, 64
Kohala District, 35, 39,
    193–198
lū'au, 178–179, 180, 199–200
meals and mealtimes, 201,
    203, 210
plate lunches, 219
price categories, 190
Puna, 217–220
reservations, 190
smoking, 190
South Kona, 50, 213–215
strategy, 190
symbols related to, 6
tipping, 287
Volcano, 67, 215, 217
Waimea, 42–43, 198, 205
Dinner cruises and shows, 178
Disappearing Sands Beach,
    102
Dive Makai, 122
Dolphin Bay Hotel ☷, 253
Dolphins, 119
Don the Beachcomber at
    the Royal Kona Resort ✕,
    211–212
Donatoni's at the Hilton Waiko-
    loa Village ✕, 193
Dragonfly Ranch ☷, 247–248

E

Eco tours, 275–276
Edelweiss ✕, 198
Electricity, 280
Embassies, 280
Emergencies, 280
roadside emergencies, 283
Energy labs, 45
Etiquette and behavior, 285

F

Fair Wind Cruises, 124
Fairmont Orchid Hawai'i ☷,
    225
Farm visits, 206
South Kona, 53, 54
Waimea, 41–42
Farmers' markets, 75, 168,
    169, 170
Festivals, 179–181

Film, 181
Firehouse Gallery, 42
Fish Hopper Restaurant ✕, 212
Fishing, deep-sea, 112–115
Fodor's choice
dining, 191
lodging, 223
Four Seasons Resort Hualālai
    ☷, 225, 227
Fujimamas ✕, 212

G

Gardens
Hāmākua Coast, 84, 87
Hilo, 77, 79
South Kona, 53
Volcano, 67
Gasoline, 282
Gear, 264
Getting oriented, 10–11
Golf, 67–68, 140–145
Graffiti, 39
Grand Palace Chinese Restau-
    rant ✕, 193
Green Sand Beach, 57, 104
Greenwell Farms, 54
Greenwell Store, 53
Grill at the Fairmont Orchid
    Hawai'i ✕, 197
Guided tours, 83, 88, 90,
    272–277

H

Haili Church, 78
Hakone Steakhouse & Sushi
    Bar at the Hāpuna Beach
    Prince Hotel ✕, 193–194
Hale Ho'ōla Spa in Volcano,
    171
Hale Ho'onanea ☷, 236
Hale Hualalai ☷, 245–246
Hale Kai ☷, 254
Hale Ohia Cottages ☷, 250
Hale-o-Keawe Heiau, 50
Hale Samoa at Kona Village
    Resort ✕, 195
Hāmākua Coast
beaches, 85–86
dining, 84–85
exploring, 80–87
lodging, 256, 258
shopping, 169
Happy Valley Seafood Restau-
    rant ✕, 217
Hāpuna Beach Prince Hotel
    ☷, 227
Hāpuna Beach State Recreation
    Area, 96
Harbor House ✕, 206

Harrington's ✕, 217
Hawai'i Nautical, 25
Hawai'i Tropical Botanical
    Garden, 84
Hawai'i Volcanoes National
    Park, 59–63
Hawaiian islands, 26–0
Hawaiian Sunset Pūpū Cruise
    and Dolphin Adventure, 178
Hāwī, 35
Healing rituals, 171
Health concerns, 284
Hikiau Heiau, 53
Hiking, 145–146, 150–151, 276
Hilo
beaches, 105, 107–108
dining, 78, 217–220
exploring, 74–80
lodging, 253–256
nightlife and entertainment,
    181, 188
shopping, 167–169
Hilo Bay Café ✕, 217
Hilo Coffee Mill, 78
Hilo Farmers' Market, 75, 168
Hilo Hattie, 165, 168
Hilo Hawaiian Hotel ☷,
    253–254
Hilo Honu Inn ☷, 254
Hilton Waikoloa Village ☷,
    227, 230
Holidays, 280
Holland America, 24
Hōluakoa Cafe ✕, 44
Hōlualoa, 43–44
Hōlualoa Inn ☷, 246
Hōlualoa-Kona Coffee Com-
    pany, 54
Home exchanges, 255
Honeymoons, 20–21
Honoka'a, 84
Honokōhau Beach, 99–100
Honoli'i Beach Park, 107
Honomū, 84
Ho'okena Beach Park, 103–104
Horseback riding, 151–152
Hostels, 255
Hotel Honoka'a Club ☷, 256
Hours of operation, 286–287
Hualālai Resort, 141
Huggo's ✕, 212
Hula, 182–184
Hula Bean ✕, 43
Hula Kai, 128
Huli Sue's BBQ and Grill ✕,
    205
Hulihe'e Palace, 45
Humpback whales, 132

I

'Imiloa Astronomy Center, 75, 77
'Imiola Congregational Church, 42
Inn at Kulaniapia Falls ☂, 254–255
Insurance
for car rentals, 271
trip insurance, 264–265
Internet access, 284
Ironman competitions, 138
Island Lava Java ✕, 47–48
Itineraries, 18–19
circle island tour, 52

J

Jacaranda Inn ☂, 237–238
Jacke Rey's Ohana Grill ✕, 211
Jack's Diving Locker, 122–123

K

Ka Lae (South Point), 57
Kahalu'u Beach Park, 102
Kahilu Theatre, 181, 186
Kahuna, 83
Kai at the Sheraton Keauhou Bay ✕, 212
Kailua Bay, 101–102
Kailua-Kona
beaches, 99–102
dining, 44, 47–48, 205–206, 208–213
exploring, 43–45, 47–48
lodging, 238–239, 242, 244–246
nightlife and entertainment, 179, 187–188
shopping, 44, 160, 164–167
Kailua Pier, 45, 47
Kainaliu, 53
Kalaekilohana ☂, 248
Kalākaua Park, 78
Kaloko-Honokōhau National Historical Park, 99–101
Kalōpā State Park, 85
Kamakahonu, 47
Kamakahonu Beach, 101–102
Kamuela Museum, 42
Kamuela Provision Company at the Hilton Waikoloa Village ✕, 196
Kanaka Kava ✕, 209
Kapa'au, 35
Kapoho Tide Pools, 73, 108
Ka'u
beaches, 57, 64, 102–105

dining, 64
exploring, 53, 57, 64
lodging, 246–248
Kauna'oa Beach, 95–96
Kawaihae Harbor, 39
Kawaihae Harbor Grill & Seafood Bar ✕, 197
Kayaking, 115, 118–119
Kealakekua Bay, 48–50, 53, 123
Keauhou Kona Surf & Racquet Club ☂, 242
Ke'ei Café ✕, 214
Kekaha Kai State Park, 99
Kekala Farm Tour, 41
Kenichi Pacific ✕, 210
Ken's House of Pancakes ✕, 218
Kiawe Kitchen ✕, 215
Kīholo Bay, 96–97
Kīlauea, 59, 60
Kīlauea Caverns of Fire, 66–67
Kīlauea Lodge ✕ ☂, 215, 248, 250
Kimura's Lauhala Shop, 165
King Kamehameha's Kona Beach Hotel ☂, 47
King Kamehameha Statue, 39
Kohala District
beaches, 92, 95–97, 99
dining, 35, 39, 193–198
exploring, 34–35, 39–40
lodging, 225, 227, 230, 232–236
nightlife and entertainment, 178–179, 187
shopping, 156, 158–159
Kohala Coffee Mill & Tropical Dreams ✕, 35
Kohala Mountain Road Lookout, 41
Kohala Rainbow Cafe ✕, 39
Kohala Sports Club & Spa at the Hilton Waikoloa Village, 172
Kolekole Beach Park, 85–86, 105
Kona Brewing Company & Brewpub ✕, 206, 208
Kona coffee, 54
Kona Coffee Living History Farm, 53, 54
Kona Country Club, 142–143
Kona Historical Society, 43
Kona Inn Restaurant ✕, 44, 208
Kona Inn Shopping Village, 44
Kona Magic Sands ☂, 244
Kona Mix Plate ✕, 209

Kona Nalu ☂, 244
Kona Pacific ☂, 244
Kona Tiki Hotel ☂, 238–239
Kona Village Resort ☂, 179, 230, 232
Kua Bay, 97
Kuamo'o Battlefield, 47
Kūhiō Grille ✕, 218
Kulani Trails, 137–138

L

La Bourgogne ✕, 208
Language, 285
Lapakahi State Historical Park, 41
Laupāhoehoe Point Park, 86
Laupāhoehoe Train Museum, 86
Lava flows, 13, 61
Lava Rock Café ✕, 67
Lava Tree State Park, 73–74
Leis, 161–163, 285
Lekeleke Burial Grounds, 47
Leleiwi Beach Park, 107–108
Lighthouses, 72–73
Lili'uokalani Gardens, 77
Lodging
alternatives, 255
with children, 22, 225, 227, 230, 239, 242, 251, 253
Fodor's choice, 223
Hāmākua Coast, 256, 258
Hilo, 253–256
Kailua-Kona, 238–239, 242, 244–246
Ka'u, 246–248
Kohala Coast, 225, 227, 230, 232–236
price categories, 222
Puna, 251–253
reservations, 222
South Kona, 246–248
symbols related to, 6
tipping, 287
Volcano, 248, 250–251
Waimea, 236–238
Los Habaneros ✕, 211
Lū'au, 178–179, 180, 199–200
Luquin's Mexican Restaurant ✕, 219–220
Lyman Museum & Mission House, 79

M

Macadamia factories, 79
MacKenzie State Recreation Area, 73
Made on the Big Island, 164

Magic Sands Beach, *102*
Mahina Pizza ✕, *210*
Māhukona Beach Park, *95*
Mail, *280–281*
Mailekini Heiau, *35, 39*
Makalawena, *97, 99*
Mamalahoa Hot Tubs and Massage, *172–173*
Mana Ranch ☲, *238*
Manago Hotel ✕ ☲, *213–214, 246–247*
Mandara Spa at the Waikoloa Beach Marriott Resort, *173–174*
Manta rays, *121*
Manuka State Wayside, *64*
Marine life, *103, 127*
Massage, *173*
Mauna Kea, *87–90*
Mauna Kea Beach, *95–96*
Mauna Lani Bay Hotel & Bungalows ☲, *232*
Mauna Lani Point Villas and the Islands of Mauna Lani Condominiums ☲, *233–234*
Mauna Lani Resort, *144*
Mauna Lani Spa, *174*
Mauna Loa Macadamia Factory, *79*
Merrie Monarch Festival, *180–181*
Merriman's ✕, *205*
Merriman's Farm Visits and Dinner, *41–42*
Merriman's Market Café ✕, *194*
Mi's Italian Bistro ✕, *214*
Mixx Bistro ✕, *208*
Moku'aikaua Church, *47*
Mo'okini Heiau, *35*
Museums. ⇨ *Also Art galleries and museums*
 astronomy, 75, 78
 coffee, 54
 in Hāmākua Coast, 86
 Hawaiian history, 42
 in Hilo, 75, 77, 79
 natural history, 79
 Parker family, 42
 in South Kona, 54
 trains, 86
 tsunamis, 79
 volcanoes, 60
 in Waimea, 42
Music, *186*
My Best Friend's Closet, *165*
My Island Bed & Breakfast Inn ☲, *251*

N

Naha stone, *79*
Nāmakani Paio Cabins ☲, *251*
Nancy's Hideaway ☲, *246*
Nani Mau Gardens, *79*
Nāpō'opo'o Beach Park, *102–103*
Native Hawaiian sites
 Kailua-Kona, 47
 Kohala District, 35–36
 South Kona, 50, 53
Natural Energy Lab of Hawai'i, *45*
Naung Mai ✕, *220*
Night Marchers, *85*
Nightlife, *187–188*
Norio's Sushi Bar & Restaurant ✕, *194*
Norwegian Cruise Lines, *25*

O

O'Keefe & Sons Bread Bakers ✕, *78*
Old Kona Airport State Recreation Area, *101*
Onekahakaha Beach Park, *107*
Onizuka Center for International Astronomy Visitor Information Station, *89*
Online travel tools, *263, 266, 267*
Orientation, *10–11*
O's Bistro ✕, *212*
Outrigger Fairway Villas at Waikoloa ☲, *234*
Outrigger Kanaloa at Kona ☲, *244*
Outrigger Keauhou Beach Resort ☲, *239*
Outrigger Kolea at Waikoloa ☲, *234*

P

Pacific Tsunami Museum, *79*
Package deals, *271–272*
Packing, *264*
Pahala, *64*
Pāhoa, *73*
Pahui'a at the Four Seasons Resort Hualālai ✕, *196*
Palaces, *45*
Palms Cliff House Inn ☲, *256, 258*
Panaewa Hawaiian Homestead Farmers' Market, *169*
Pana'ewa Rain Forest Zoo, *79*
Pancho & Lefty's ✕, *211*
Papakōlea Beach, *57, 104*

Parasailing, *119*
Parker Ranch Visitor Center & Museum, *42*
Parking, *282*
Parks
 Hāmākua Coast, 83, 85–86
 Hawai'i Volcanoes National Park, 59–63
 Hilo, 78, 105, 107–108
 Kailua-Kona, 99–101, 102
 Kohala District, 40, 92, 95, 96
 Puna, 73–74
 South Kona, 102–104, 105
Passports, *281*
Peaberry & Galette ✕, *208–209*
Pe'epe'e Falls, *77*
Pele, The volcano goddess, *85*
Pescatore ✕, *219*
Phones, *281*
Pinao stone, *79*
Pine Tree Café ✕, *209*
Planning the trip, *12–13*
Plants of Hawai'i, *147–149*
Plumeria Hill Bed & Breakfast ☲, *252*
Pololū Valley, *35*
Pololū Valley Beach, *92, 95*
Polynesian revues, *178–179*
Price categories
 dining, 190
 lodging, 222
Princess Cruises, *24–25*
Puna
 dining, 217–220
 exploring, 68, 73–74
 lodging, 251–253
Punalu'u Bakeshop & Visitor Center ✕, *64*
Punalu'u Beach Park, *64, 104–105*
Pu'uhonua O Hōnaunau, *50*
Pu'ukoholā Heiau National Historic Site, *35, 39*

Q

Quinn's Almost By the Sea ✕, *208*

R

Rainbow Falls, *77*
Reeds Bay Beach Park, *107*
ResortQuest Kona by the Sea ☲, *245*
ResortQuest Shores at Waikoloa ☲, *234–235*
Restaurant Hayama ✕, *210*
Reuben's Mexican Restaurant ✕, *220*

Richardson Ocean Park,
107–108
Road conditions, 282–283
Roadside emergencies, 283
Royal Caribbean, 25
Royal Kona Coffee Museum &
Coffee Mill, 54
Royal Kona Resort ⬚, 239
Royal Siam ✕, 220
Roy's Waikoloa Bar & Grill
✕, 196
Ruth's Chris Steakhouse ✕,
197–198

S

S. Hata Building, 80
Safety, 287
beach safety, 98
kayaking, 118
sun safety, 100
Sailing, 120
St. Benedict's Painted Church,
53
St. Michael's Church, 47
St. Peter's of Kahalu'u, 48
Scuba diving, 120–123
Sea turtles, 106, 127
Seaside Restaurant and Aqua
Farm, The ✕, 220
Sheraton Keauhou Bay Resort
& Spa ⬚, 239, 242
Shipman House Bed & Break-
fast Inn ⬚, 255–256
Shopping, 156
Hāmākua Coast, 169
Hilo, 75, 167–169
Kailua-Kona, 44, 160, 164–167
Kohala, 156, 158–159
Waimea, 159–160
Sig Zane Designs, 168
Silver Oaks Guest Ranch ⬚,
245
Skiing, 152, 154
Snorkeling, 123–128
with children, 23
Snuba, 129
Solimene's ✕, 198
Sombat's Fresh Thai Cuisine
✕, 220
South Kona
beaches, 102–105
dining, 50, 213–215
exploring, 48–50, 53
lodging, 246–248
South Point, 53, 57, 64
South Point Banyan Tree House
⬚, 247
Spa Without Walls at the Fair-
mont Orchid Hawai'i, 176

Spas, 169, 171–176
Spencer Beach Park, 95
Star of the Sea Painted Church,
74
Steam Vent Inn and Retreat
⬚, 252
Submarine tours, 129
Sun safety, 100
Surfing, 129–130
with children, 22–23
Sushi Rock ✕, 194
Symbols, 6

T

Tacos El Unico ✕, 211
Tako Taco ✕, 198, 205
Tante's Bar & Grill ✕, 198
Taxes, 287
Tennis, 154
Teshima's ✕, 214
Tex Drive-In ✕, 84–85
Thai Rin Restaurant ✕, 213
Thai Thai Restaurant ✕, 217
Theater, 181, 186
Time, 287
Timing the visit, 12
Tide pools, 73, 103, 108
Tipping, 287
Tommy Bahama's Tropical Café
✕, 196
Torpedo Tours, 123
Travel agencies, 266, 268
Travelers' checks, 286–287
Tres Hombres Beach Grill ✕,
194
Trip insurance, 264–265

U

Umauma Falls, 87
Uncle Billy's ✕, 218
U-Top-It ✕, 208

V

Vacation packages, 271–272
Vacation rentals. ⇨See Condos
and vacation rentals
Visas, 281
Visitor information, 263–264
Vista Waikoloa ⬚, 235
Vog (volcanic smog), 63
Volcano
dining, 67, 215, 217
exploring, 64, 66–68
lodging, 248, 250–251
Volcano Art Center, 186
Volcanoes
birth of the islands, 70–73

Hawai'i Volcanoes National
Park, 59–63
Volcano Farmer's Market, 67
Volcano Garden Arts, 67
Volcano Golf and Country
Club, 67–68
restaurant, 215
Volcano Places ⬚, 251
Volcano Teapot Cottage ⬚,
251
Volcano Winery, 68

W

Waianuhea ⬚, 258
Waikoloa, 178–179
Waikoloa Beach Grill ✕, 193
Waikoloa Beach Marriott ⬚,
232–233
Waikoloa Beach Resort,
144–145
Wailoa Center, 80
Waimea
dining, 42–43, 198, 205
exploring, 41–43
lodging, 236–238
shopping, 159–160
Waimea Coffee & Company
✕, 42–43
Waimea Country Lodge ⬚,
236–237
Waimea Gardens Cottage ⬚,
237
Waipi'o Valley, 83
Waipi'o Wayside ⬚, 258
Wasabi's ✕, 210–211
Waterfalls
Hāmākua Coast, 83, 87
Hilo, 77
Waterfalls Inn Bed & Breakfast
⬚, 256
Weather, 16, 62
Weddings and honeymoons,
20–21
Wellness tours, 276–277
Whale-watching, 130–132
When to go, 16
White Sands Beach, 102
Windsurfing, 132
Wineries, 68
Wood Valley Temple, 64
World Botanical Gardens, 87

Y

Yoga Oasis ⬚, 252–253

Z

Zoos, 79

PHOTO CREDITS

and 2, *Douglas Peebles/eStock Photo*. 5, *Pacific Stock/SuperStock*. **Chapter 1: Experience the Big Island:** 8-9, *Pacific Stock/SuperStock*. 10 (top and bottom), *Big Island Visitors Bureau*. 11 (top left), *Photodisc*. 11 (top right and bottom), *Big Island Visitors Bureau*. 14 (top left), *Photo Resource Hawaii/Alamy*. 14 (bottom left), *Cornforth Images/Alamy*. 14 (top center), *Photo Resource Hawaii/Alamy*. 14 (bottom center), *Waterframe/Alamy*. 14 (right), *Douglas Peebles Photography/Alamy*. 15 (left), *Big Island Visitors Bureau*. 15 (top center), *Andre Seale/age fotostock*. 15 (bottom center), *Hemis/Alamy*. 15 (top right), *Photo Resource Hawaii/Alamy*. 15 (bottom right), *Stephen Frink Collection/Alamy*. 17, *Douglas Peebles/eStock Photo*. 19 (left), *Douglas Peebles/age fotostock*. 19 (right), *Castle Resorts & Hotels*. 21-22, *Hilton Hawaii*. 23 (left), *Photo Resource Hawaii/Alamy*. 23 (right), *Michael S. Nolan/age fotostock*. 24, *Bryan Lowry/Alamy*. 27, *Douglas Peebles/eStock Photo*. 29 (left), *SuperStock/age fotostock*. 29 (right), *Photo Resource Hawaii/Alamy*. **Chapter 2: Exploring the Big Island:** 31, *Douglas Peebles/eStock Photo*. 33, *Big Island Visitors Bureau*. 40, *Photo Resource Hawaii/Alamy*. 49, *Big Island Visitors Bureau*. 55-56, *Pacific Stock/SuperStock*. 58, *Big Island Visitors Bureau*. 59, *Russ Bishop/age fotostock*. 61, *Photo Resource Hawaii/Alamy*. 62, *Cornforth Images/Alamy*. 63 (top), *Pacific Stock/SuperStock*. 63 (bottom), *Linda Robshaw/Alamy*. 65, *Pacific Stock/SuperStock*. 66, *Interfoto Pressebildagentur/Alamy*. 69, *Greg Vaughn/Alamy*. 70, *Pacific Stock/SuperStock*. 81, *Russ Bishop/Alamy*. 82, *Cornforth Images/Alamy*. 86, *SuperStock/age fotostock*. **Chapter 3: Beaches:** 91, *Preferred Hotels & Resorts Worldwide*. 93, *Pacific Stock/SuperStock*. 97, *Cornforth Images/Alamy*. 101, *Luis Castañeda/age fotostock*. 106, *Douglas Peebles/eStock Photo*. **Chapter 4: Water Activities & Tours:** 109, *WaterFrame/Alamy*. 111, *Russ Bishop/Alamy*. 113, *Blaine Harrington III/Alamy*. 122, *Andre Seale/Alamy*. 125, *Ron Dahlquist/HVCB*. 126, *SuperStock/age fotostock*. 127 (all illustrations), *William Wu*. 128, *David Fleetham/Alamy*. 131, *Stephen Frink Collection/Alamy*. **Chapter 5: Golf, Hiking & Outdoor Activities:** 133, *HTJ*. 135, *Douglas Peebles/eStock Photo*. 143, *Pacific Stock/SuperStock*. 147, *Luca Tettoni/viestiphoto.com*. 148, *Kaua'I Visitors Bureau*. 149 (top illustrations), *William Wu*. 149 (bottom), *Jack Jeffrey*. 150, *Pacific Stock/SuperStock*. 153, *Photo Resource Hawaii/Alamy*. **Chapter 6: Shops & Spas:** 155, *Hilton Hawaii*. 157, *Sri Maiava Rusden/HVCB*. 161 (top), *Linda Ching/HVCB*. 161 (bottom), *Sri Maiava Rusden/HVCB*. 162, *Michael Soo/Alamy*. 163 (top), *leisofhawaii.com*. 163 (2nd from top), *kellyalexanderphotography.com*. 163 (3rd, 4th, and 5th from top), *leisofhawaii.com*. 163 (bottom), *kellyalexanderphotography.com*. 175 (all), *Mauna Lani Spa*. **Chapter 7: Entertainment & Nightlife:** 177, *Hilton Hawaii*. 182, *Hawaii Visitors & Convention Bureau*. 183, *Thinkstock LLC*. 185, *Hawaii Visitors & Convention Bureau*. **Chapter 8: Where to Eat:** 189, *Four Seasons Hotels & Resorts*. 199, *Polynesian Cultural Center*. 200 (top), *Douglas Peebles Photography*. 200 (top center), *Douglas Peebles Photography/Alamy*. 200 (center), *Dana Edmunds/Polynesian Cultural Center*. 200 (bottom center), *Douglas Peebles Photography/Alamy*. 200 (bottom), *Purcell Team/Alamy*. 201 (top, top center, and bottom center), *HTJ/HVCB*. 202 (top), *Danita Delimont/Alamy*. 202 (bottom), *Douglas Peebles/Alamy*. **Chapter 9: Where to Stay:** 221, *Waianuhea*. 226 (all), *Kyle Rothenborg/Four Seasons Hualalai*. 231 (top), *Kona Village Resort*. 231 (bottom), *Ahu Pohaku Ho'omaluhia, hawaii-island-retreat.com*. 257 (all) *Waianuhea*.

NOTES

NOTES

ABOUT OUR WRITERS

Cathy Sharpe, who handled Big Island Essentials, was born and reared on Oʻahu. For 13 years, she worked at a Honolulu public relations agency representing major travel industry clients. Now living in Maryland, she is a marketing consultant. Cathy returns home once a year to visit family and friends, relax at her favorite beaches, and enjoy island cuisine.

Amy Westervelt was lucky enough to spend summers growing up on the Big Island, and she now divides her time between Kona and San Francisco. She writes about travel and the environment for publications including *Allure, Sustainable Industries, Travel + Leisure, Modern Bride*, and the *San Francisco Chronicle*. Amy updated the Experience the Big Island, Exploring the Big Island, Beaches, Water Activities & Tours, Golf, Hiking & Outdoor Activities, Shops & Spas, Entertainment & Nightlife, Where to Eat, and Where to Stay chapters of this book.